MODERN TRENDS IN MANUFACTURING TECHNOLOGY

THE EDITORS

Prof. N.K. Tewari and **Prof. P.V. Rao** are Senior Faculty Members in the Mechanical Engineering Department at the Indian Institute of Technology, Delhi. **Prof. G.S. Yadav** is the Senior Faculty Member at ITTMEC at the Indian Institute of Technology Delhi. **Mr. Pradeep Chaturvedi** is a Member of the Mechanical Engineering Board of The Institution of Engineers (India).

THE INSTITUTION OF ENGINEERS (INDIA)

The Institution of Engineers (India), IEI is the first professional body of engineers founded in India in 1920 and incorporated by Royal Charter in 1935, to promote and advance the art and science of myriad fields of engineering and technology.

IEI represents India in several international bodies such as, the World Energy Council, World Mining Congress, World Federation of Engineering Organisations, Commonwealth Engineers Council, International Council of Aeronautical Studies and Several others.

As the Indian Member Committee of the World Energy Council since inception, The Institution of Engineers (India) was privileged to host this International Conference on Energy-Asia Energy Vision 2020—particularly when several countries including India, have made political decisions, towards a free market economy and globalisation of Industry and commerce.

MODERN TRENDS IN MANUFACTURING TECHNOLOGY

Proceedings of the 13th National Convention of Mechanical Engineers, organised by The Institution of Engineers (India) Delhi State Centre, during November 6-8, 1997 at New Delhi

Editors

PRADEEP CHATURVEDI

N.K. TEWARI

G.S. YADAV

P.V. RAO

Published by

CONCEPT PUBLISHING COMPANY, NEW DELHI-110059

for

THE INSTITUTION OF ENGINEERS (INDIA)
DELHI STATE CENTRE

ISBN 81-7022-645-7

First Published 1998

Published and Printed by

Ashok Kumar Mittal
Concept Publishing Company
A/15-16, Commercial Block, Mohan Garden,
New Delhi - 110059 (India)

Phones: 5554042, 5504042
Fax No. 091-11-5598898

PREFACE

Quality, cost and timely delivery of products are the key factors in the present day manufacturing. Meeting the needs indigenously is another important factor, particularly for defence requirements. For quite some time for security reasons only the defence establishments had been manufacturing the products needed by the services. However, seen the trend all over the globe it has been realised that the civilian sector can play a vital role in meeting the needs of manufacture of sophisticated devices through its knowhow and infrastructure in time and in a cost effective manner. For this, increasing opportunities of dialogue need to be created to understand each others capabilities and requirements.

This Seminar has been organised by The Institution of Engineers (India) with the aim of understanding with the requirement of the defence services in the R&D capabilities of the civilian sector. It is obvious that all aspects of manufacturing cannot be covered in a short period of this convention. In view of the same, the organisers have identified seven important sub-sectors for discussion viz., matter forming technologies, manufacturing requirements for defence application, automation in manufacturing, flexible manufacturing systems and the factories of the future, artificial intelligence and robotics in production, micro-machining processes and environmental concern in manufacturing. The presentations will bring out points of common interest and thereby usefully serve the national interest.

The Technical Committee would like to thank the authors who have contributed papers for this Seminar, the referees for sparing their valuable time for evaluation and the Organising Committee for organising the Convention.

PRADEEP CHATRUVEDI
Co-Chairman
Organising Committee
November 6, 1997

PROF. N.K. TEWARI
Chairman
Technical Committee

CONTENTS

III. AUTOMATION IN MANUFACTURING

IV. FLEXIBLE MANUFACTURING SYSTEMS AND THE FACTORIES OF THE FUTURE

V. ARTIFICIAL INTELLIGENCE AND ROBOTICS IN PRODUCTION

I

METAL FORMING TECHNOLOGY

INFLUENCE OF CASTING PROCESSES ON UPSETTING OF COPPER - TIN ALLOYS

1

A.N. Prakash[1], Dr. B.K. Muralidhara[1], Dr. V.K. Basalalli[1] and Dr. C.R.R. Char[2]

Department of Mechanical Engineering,[1]
University Visvesvaraya College of Engineering, K.R. Circle, Bangalore.
Rapsri Engineering Industries Ltd.,[2]
Gowdanapalya, Bangalore.

ABSTRACT

Copper-Tin alloy slugs (conforming to ASTMB-139 specifications) produced from shell moulding process and continuous casting process have been subjected to different % reduction of heights in a commercial press. Formability of these castings was assessed by study of variation of hardness with variation of L/D ratios and by visual examination. The results indicate that within the scope of this investigation, the castings produced by shell moulding process are formable upto 70% reduction in height where as the castings produced by continuous casting process are formable only upto 60% reduction in height, indicating that the shell moulded slugs can be subjected to upsetting process to a greater extent as compared to slugs produced from continuous casting process.

1. INTRODUCTION

Forming or the use of pressure on unconfined metal shaping operations, involves deformation of the crystalites of which the metal is composed. Such operations comprise stamping, cupping, flanging, spinning, drawing, forming, bending, upsetting etc.

Cold working produces an improved surface finish, scale-free and bright surface and closer dimensional tolerance. Cold working processes are generally used in making end-use products because of their economy in producing the desired shapes. It is also used to produce residual stress into certain metals in order to have improved fatigue life.

Copper and copperbase alloys are used for a wide variety of electrical and thermal conductivity applications. Among these alloys, ASTMB-139 is a copper-tin alloy which is used for fittings, cable connectors, cable dead ends, spacers, inductor heads, switch parts and automobile spare parts etc. These components can be produced by different cold forming methods successfully and conveniently because of its inherent advantages.

Before subjecting any alloy for forming operation, slugs of the given alloy have to be produced. For producing the slugs normally casting process is employed. The mechanical properties of slugs is dependent upon the type of casting process that is adopted for producing the slugs. Further, the formability of slugs is in turn dependent on the mechanical properties of the slug. Thus, the type of casting process adopted for producing the slug is having some influence on the formability of the material.

From the survey of published information, it appears that very little systematic work has been carried out in the area of influence of casting process on the forming parameters of non ferrous alloys, especially ASTMB-139 (cu-sn) alloy.[1-6]

Therefore in this investigatioN,[7] experiments have been systematically planned to :

(a) Produce copper-tin alloy slugs of different L/D ratio confirming to ASTMB-139 specifications by two different casting processes, namely shell moulding process and continuous casting process, and machine them.
(b) Subject these different L/D ratio slugs to different extents of upsetting (different % reduction of heights) using a commercial press.
(c) Assess the formability by way of visual examination and hardness measurement.

2. EXPERIMENTAL DETAILS

In this short-term investigation, Copper-Tin alloys conforming to ASTMB-139 specifications (i.e. Copper - 96%, Tin - 3.5%, Lead - 0.8%, Phosphorous 0.03%, Zinc - 0.3%, Iron - 0.1%, max.) having 20 mm diameter and different heights (20mm, 25mm, 30mm, 35mm and 40 mm) were produced by shell moulding process and continuous casting process. The production of slugs has been done at M/s. Rapsri Engineering Industries Ltd., Bangalore, Karnataka. These different L/D ratio slugs were subjected to different % reduction of heights (10%, 20%, 30%, 40%, 50%, 60%, 70%, 75%) at M/s. Polyhdron (P) Ltd., Belgaum, Karnataka.

Formability of castings produced by both the processes was assessed by: (a) Study of variation of hardness with variation of % of reduction in height of the slugs (L/D ratio), and (b) Visual examination of castings which were subjected to upsetting operation. The comparison of formability of castings produced from shell moulding process has been made with the formability of castings produced by continuous casting process.

In Figure - 1 the details of the experimental work carried out has been shown schematically.

3. RESULTS AND DISCUSSION

Typical visual examination results and hardness of slugs (having L/D ratio = 1.5) which are produced by shell moulding process and by continuous casting process when subjected to different % reduction in height at a press speed of 15mm per second have been presented in Table - 1.

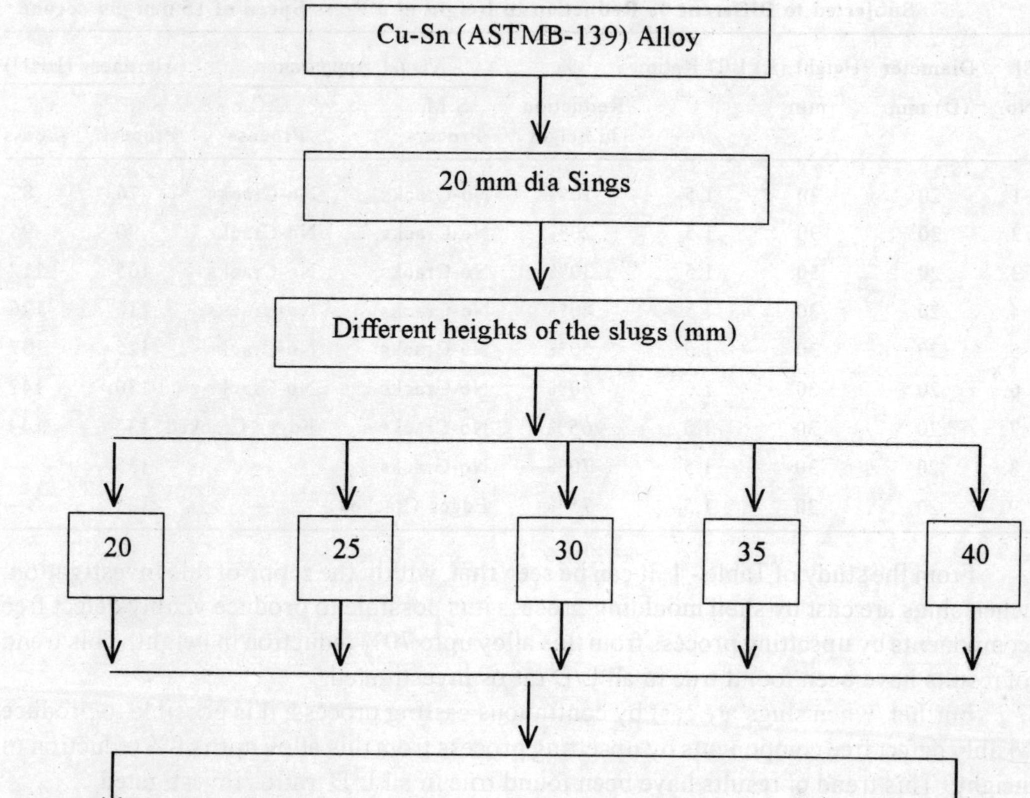

Figure 1: The details of the experimental work.

TABLE 1: **Typical Visual Examination Results and Hardness of Slugs (having L/D ratio = 1.5) which are Produced by Shell Moulding Process and Continuous Casting Process when Subjected to Different % Reduction in Height at a Press Speed of 15 mm per second**

Sl. No.	Diameter (D) mm	Height (L) mm	L/D Ratio	% Reduction in height	Visual Appearance S.M. Process	Visual Appearance C.C. Process	Hardness (BHN) S.M. Process	Hardness (BHN) C.C. Process
1.	20	30	1.5	10%	No-Cracks	No-Cracks	76	82
2.	20	30	1.5	20%	No-Cracks	No-Cracks	90	96
3.	20	30	1.5	30%	No-Cracks	No-Cracks	105	112
4.	20	30	1.5	40%	No-Cracks	No-Cracks	116	126
5.	20	30	1.5	50%	No-Cracks	No-Cracks	125	137
6.	20	30	1.5	60%	No-Cracks	No-Cracks	130	142
7.	20	30	1.5	65%	No-Cracks	Edges Cracked	135	142
8.	20	30	1.5	70%	No-Cracks	—	135	—
9.	20	30	1.5	75%	Edges Cracked	—	135	—

From the study of Table - 1, it can be seen that, within the scope of this investigation, when slugs are cast by shell moulding process it is possible to produce visibly defect free components by upsetting process from this alloy upto 70% reduction in height. This trend of results have been found true in all L/D ratios investigated.

Further, when slugs are cast by continuous casting process, it is possible to produce visibly defect free components by upsetting process from this alloy upto 60% reduction in height. This trend of results have been found true in all L/D ratios investigated.

In other words, the shell moulded slugs can be subjected to upsetting process to a greater extent as compared to slugs produced form continuous casting proces.

Further, from the study of the Table - 1, it can observed that for each L/D ratio of slugs, the hardness of shell moulded cast slug is lesser by approximately 6-12 BIIN as compared to that of slugs produced from continuous casting process for the same percentage reduction of height. This trend of results has been found true for all the L/D ratios investigated. (i.e. 1.0, 1.25, 1.5, 1.75 & 2.0).

For illustrating the above findings, in Figure 2 (a), photograph of typical slugs having L/D ratio of 1.5 which are: (i) As-cast, (ii) subjected to 50% reduction in height, and (iii) subjected to 75% reduction in height produced from shell moulding processes have been presented. Further, in Figure 2(b). Photograph of typical slugs having L/D ratio of 1.5 which are: (i) As-cast, (ii) Subjected to 50% reduction in height, and (iii) Subjected to 65% reduction in height produced from continuous casting process have been presented.

In Figure 3(a), the variation of hardness versus per cent reduction in height of slugs produced from shell moulding process for typical L/D ratio of 1.5 has been presented. Further in Figure 3(b), the variation of hardness reduction in height of slugs produced

Figure 2 (a) Photograph of Visual Examination of Slugs for (i) As Cast, (ii) 50% reduction in height, (iii) 75% reduction in height produced from Shell Moulding Process for typical L/D ratio = 1.5

Figure 2 (b) Photograph of Visual Examination of Slugs for (i) As Cast, (ii) 50% reduction in height, (iii) 65% reduction in height produced from Continuous Casting Process for typical L/D ratio = 1.5

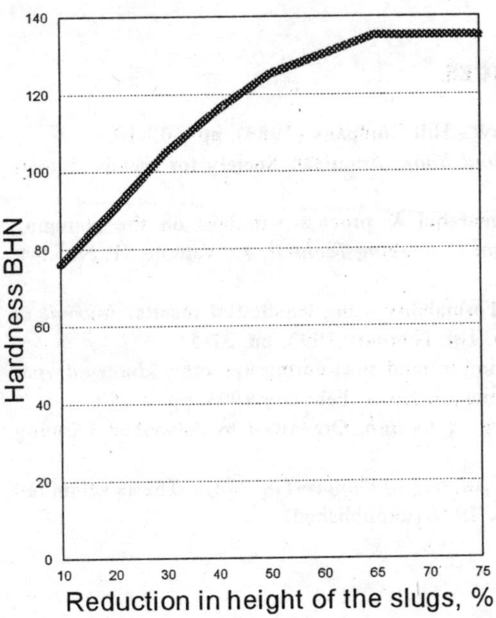

Figure 3 (a) Variation of hardness versus % of reduction in height of slugs produced from shell moulding process for L/D ratio = 1.5

Alloy	:	ASTMB - 139
As cast hardness	:	50-60 BHN
Press Speed	:	15 mm / sec.

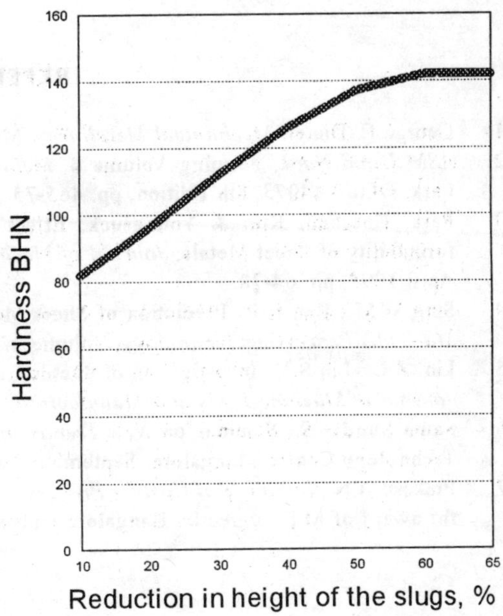

Figure 3 (b) Variation of hardness versus % of reduction in height of slugs produced from continuous casting process for L/D ratio = 1.5

Alloy	:	ASTMB - 139
As cast hardness	:	80-90 BHN
Press Speed	:	15 mm / sec.

from continuous casting process has been presented.

From these figures it can be observed that when slugs are cast by shell moulding process, there is an increase in the hardness upto nearly 65% reduction in height. However, with further reduction in height, there has been no increase in the hardness of the slugs. On the other hand, when slugs are produced from continuous casting process, there is an increase in the hardness upto nearly 60% reduction in height and with further reduction in height there has been no increase in the hardness of the slugs.

4. CONCLUSIONS

The results suggest that it is possible to produce visibly defect free components from shell moulded Copper-Tin alloy (conforming to ASTMB - 139) slugs by upsetting process upto 70% reduction in height. Where as, the same objective can be achieved from continuously cast slugs only upto 60% reduction in height. This has been found true in all different L/D ratios investigated indicating that the shell moulded slugs can be subjected to upsetting process to a greater extent as compared to slugs produced from continuous casting process.

REFERENCES

1. George E. Dieter, *Mechanical Metallurgy*, McGraw - Hill Company (1988), pp. 503-10.
2. *ASM Hand Book*, Forming Volume 4, *Metals hand book*, American Society for metals. Metals Park, Ohio - 44073, 8th Edition, pp. 465-75.
3. Park, Kaecheo, Kim & Youngsuck, Effect of material & process variables on the stamping formability of Sheet Metals, *Journal of Mechanical Processing Technology*, Volume 51, No. 1-4, April 1995, pp. 64-78.
4. Sing W.M ; Rao K.P., Prediction of Sheet Metal Formability using tensile test results. *Journal of Materials Processing Technology*, Volume 37, No. 1-4, February 1993, pp. 37-51.
5. Lin, Z.C.; Lin S.Y., Investigation of ductile fracturing in mild steel during upsetting. *International Journal of Machine Tools and Manufacture*, Volume 33, No. 1, February 1993, pp. 31-50.
6. Sama Sunder S., Seminar on *New Trends in Forging Design*, Organised by Advanced Forming Technology Centre, Bangalore, September 1996.
7. Prakash A.N., *Influence of Casting Processes on Upsetting of Copper-Tin Alloys*, Thesis submitted for award of M.E., dgree by Bangalore University, 1997 (unpublished).

RECENT DEVELOPMENTS IN ANNEALING FURNACES FOR MANUFACTURING OF QUALITY STEEL STRIPS

2

K.N. Pandey,[1] B.C. Roy[1] and N.K. Kakkar[1]

Research & Development Centre for Iron & Steel,[1]
Steel Authority of India Ltd., Ranchi

ABSTRACT

Quest for ever increasing quality standards at competitive prices, over supplied market place and decreasing trade barriers have caused intense competition as well as many developments in every facets of steel industry and annealing furnaces are no exception to it. Annealing furnaces which condition and prepare strips for cold rolling by relieving stresses caused by previous operations, have undergone many changes in recent years. Some of these important developments like introduction of hydrogen as protective gas, and numerous detail improvements such as high capacity base fans, better design diffusers, use of lighter but effective furnace insulation, fuel efficient burners, advanced cooling covers and above all incorporation of state of art instrumentation and control system has lead to significant improvement in product quality and furnace productivity. These are some of the important aspects of development which have been highlighted in this paper.

INTRODUCTION

Heat treatment is an important operation in the manufacturing process of steel. Only by heat treatment, it is possible to impart the high mechanical properties to steel required for the normal operation during its usage.

Annealing is one of the most important widely used operation in the heat treatment of steel. The purpose of annealing is to obtain softness, improve machinability, increase or restore ductility and toughness, relieve internal stresses, reduce or eliminate structural inhomogeneity, refine grain size, and to prepare steel for subsequent treatment.

During cold rolling of strips, to obtain strips of the desired thickness, work-hardening takes place within the strip. Before further processing, this adverse effect needs to be eliminated. This is performed by annealing of the strip. In the recent years, the market demand for sheet products of superior metallurgical uniformity and mechanical properties has led to the development of safer and efficient annealing furnaces.

TYPES OF ANNEALING

There are several types of annealing.

1. Full Annealing,
2. Incomplete annealing,
3. Isothermal annealing,
4. Annealing to obtain granular cementite (spheroidising), and
5. Diffusion annealing (homogenising).

It can also be classified as the "batch type", as exemplified by box annealing and open coil annealing, and the "continuous type", such as continuous annealing and stand annealing and normalising. In the former, stationary, light wound or open wound coils are subjected to a long heat treating cycle by varying temperature of the furnace that surrounds them, whereas in the latter, a single thickness or a few thicknesses of the cold reduced strip are passed through a furnace in a relatively short time and are subjected to a heat treating cycle determined largely by the temperature distribution in the furnace and the dimensions and rate of travel of the strip. Thus, 'batch type' has got flexibility of annealing variable quantity and sizes of strips and is not capital intensive where as 'continuous type' provides higher throughput and investment is high.

In the continuous process since the effective recrystallization time and temperature, is relatively short, the grains have no time to grow to each other and hardly any grain absorption takes place. Batch annealed steel has uniform grain size which is slightly larger than the continuously annealed product. The yield strength to ultimate strength ratio of continuous annealed strip is slightly lower than that of box annealed material, meaning that continuous annealed material will be some what stiffer than the box annealed material, annealed at the same temperature. The drawability of the strip of continuous annealed material is better than box annealed material for the higher temperature ranges.

In this paper, hood annealing furnace, continuous annealing followed by latest trends in batch annealing will be dealt with.

HOOD ANNEALING FURNACE

It consists of base, base fan, convector plate, diffuser, protective gas cooler/cooling covers, inner cover and the furnaces. A schematic diagram showing different components, and the flow pattern of the gases is presented in Fig. 1.

The coils to be annealed are delivered to the annealing department, transferred by overhead cranes and transfer cars. These coils are placed on the bases and covered with chrome-nickel steel covers and are maintained air tight. These covers fit into a groove in the annealing base and this trough is filled with screened silica sand. In some cases, this requirement is met with heat resistant rubber seals. Thermo couples are provided to

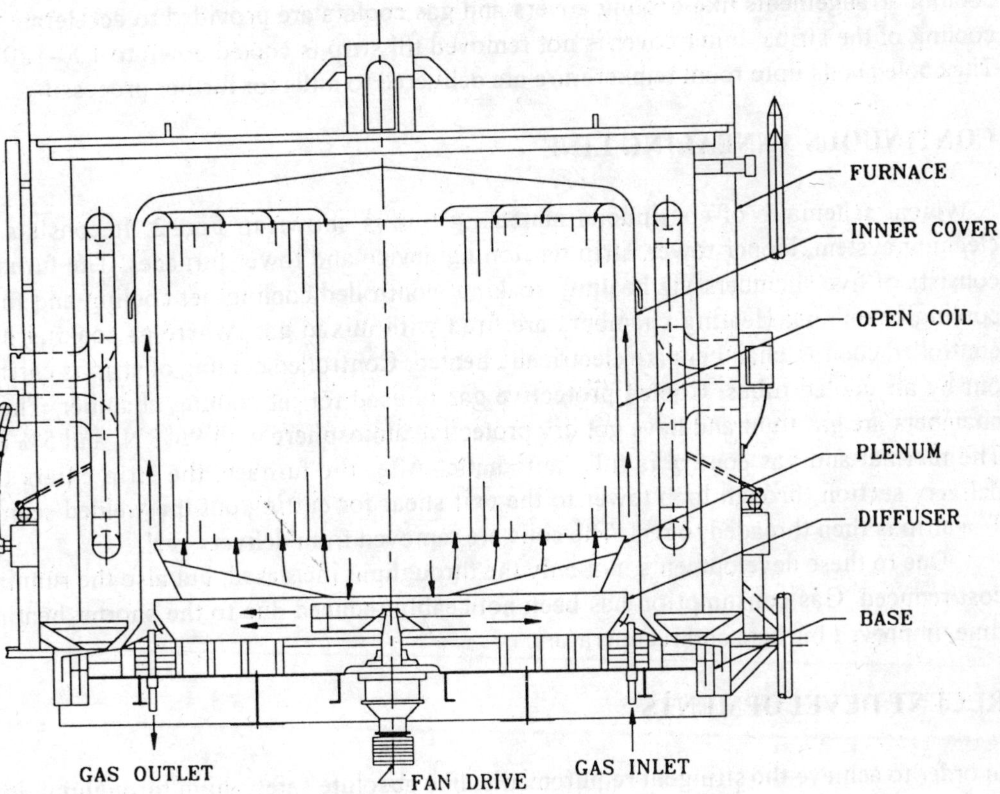

Fig. 1: Furnace for Open-Coil Annealing

measure the temperature of coils being annealed underneath the cover. A gas inlet is also provided under these covers for connection to a supply of protective gas, while the coils are being annealed as well as during cooling operation. Coils are heated upto 680°-720°C and are soaked at this temperature. An inert atmosphere is provided inside the inner covers to prevent oxidation of the coils, that is why care is taken to maintain perfect sealing and no oxygen even few ppm is not desirable in nitrogen.

Same grades of the steel are charged to each individual batch as different temperature and period are used for various charges. The governing factors in each case being softness and ductility that is required for each particular lot, depends on the end usage and customer specification. The charges are made ready on a stationary base, inner covers are kept over the base to cover the charge. Proper sealing is provided and the furnace is lowered on the base by means of overhead cranes. Protective gas usually nitrogen and hydrogen mixture (N_2-95%, H_2-5%) is passed to purge out the air from inner cover to create inert atmosphere. The furnace is moved from base to base as the number of bases is more than the number of covers.. After the completion of heating and soaking cycle, the gas is turned off and the furnace is removed from the base. Various types of cooling arrangements like cooling covers and gas coolers are provided to accelerate the cooling of the strips. Inner cover is not removed till strip is cooled down to 100-120°C. The cooled coils upto room temperature are delivered to mills for further processing.

CONTINUOUS ANNEALING LINE

A typical schematic of continuous annealing line is shown in Fig. 2. It consists of cleaning system, looper tower, strip tensioning device and tower furnaces. The furnace consists of five chambers viz heating, soaking, controlled cooling, jet cooling and final cooling chambers. Heating chambers are fired with mixed gas, where as soaking and controlled cooling chambers are electrically heated. Controlled cooling of strip is carried out by air cooled tubes. Cooled protective gas is used for jet cooling chamber. These chambers are gas tight and have got dry protective atmosphere with 95% N_2 and 5% H_2. The thermal and gas control is fully automatic. After the furnace, the strip enters the delivery section through loop tower to the exit shear for cutting out the welded seams. The strip is then threaded to reel. The coils are removed from delivery reel.

Due to these developments, not only the throughput increased, but also the running cost reduced. Gas consumption has been noticeably reduced due to the shorter heating time, improved burners and recuperators.

RECENT DEVELOPMENTS

In order to achieve the stringent requirements, like absolute safety, high throughput, low capital investment, running and maintenance cost, best as annealed mechanical properties, best surface cleanliness without decarburization and without grain boundary oxidation, many developments have taken place, some of which are discussed as follows:

Hydrogen as Protective Gas

In a batch annealing furnace heat is transferred by radiation from the furnace to the inner cover. The heat is transferred to the charge by radiation from the inner cover and by convection heat transfer by the recirculating atmosphere gas. The atmosphere gas, which is a hydrogen—nitrogen mixture, scrubs heat of the inner cover. The gas then transfers the heat to the coils as it passes through the convector plates. The main barrier to transferring heat to the charge is the low radial thermal conductivity of the coils. A coil obviously contains thousands of wraps of steel, each wrap representing resistance to heat conduction.

In order to obtain fast heating and cooling rates and good coil temperature uniformity, convection heat transfer to the charge must be optimised. The overall heat transfer rate is given by equation -1 and the equation -2 shows the important factors that

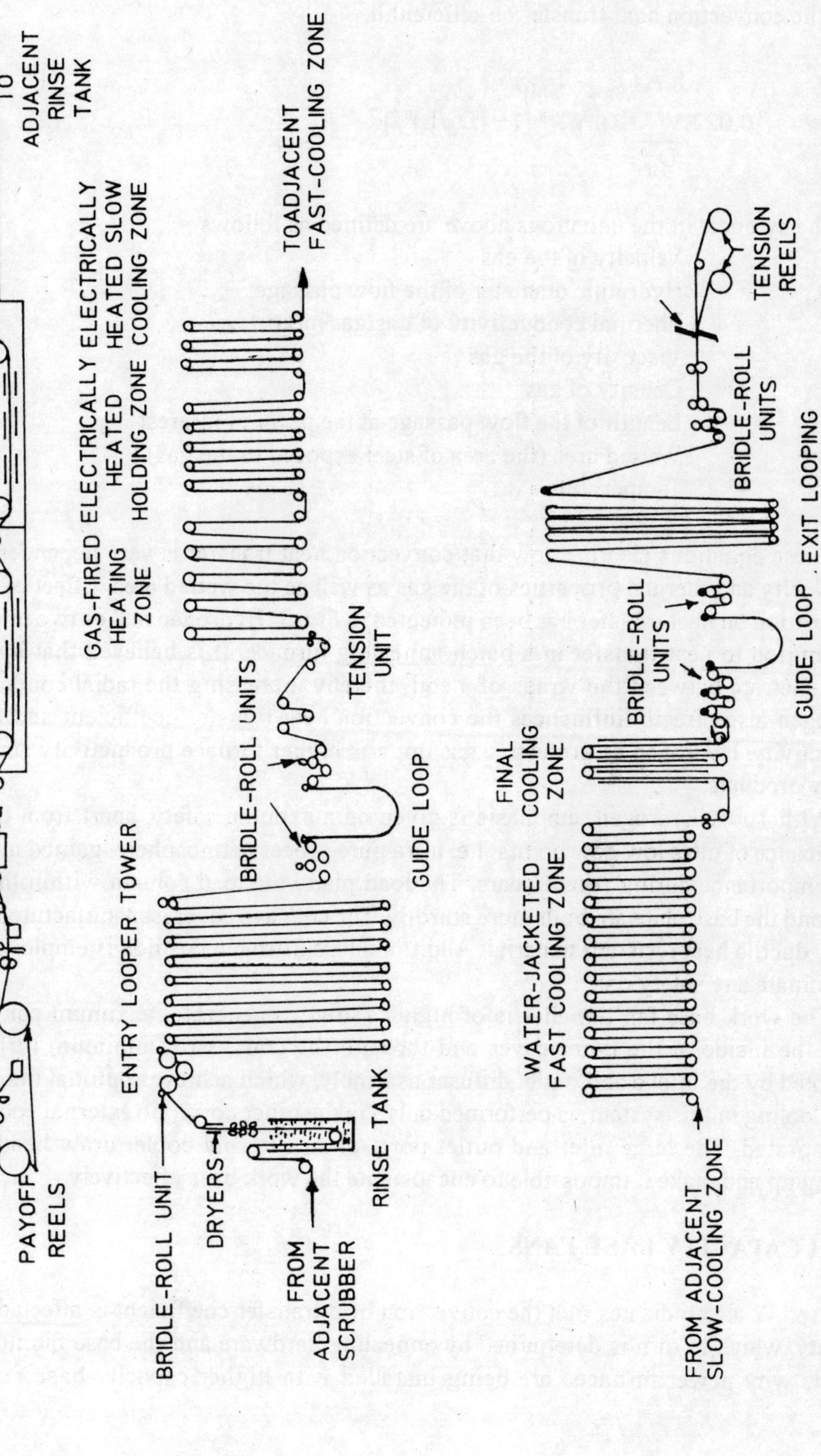

Fig. 2: Schematic of continuous-annealing line designed to operate at a strip speed of 1,500 feet per minute

affect the convection heat transfer co-efficient h.

$$Q = h.A\,(T_{gas} - T_{steel}) \qquad .... \qquad (1)$$

$$h = \frac{0.023\, V^{0.8} K(\mu/\rho)^{0.8} [1 + (D_H/L)^{0.7}]}{D_H^{0.2}} \qquad .... \qquad (2)$$

The symbols in the equations above are defined as follows :

V = Velocity of the gas
D_H = Hydraulic diameter of the flow passage
K = Thermal conductivity of gas/gas mixture
μ = Viscosity of the gas
ρ = Density of gas
L = Length of the flow passage at the point of interest
A = Wetted area (the area of steel exposed to the gas)
T = Temperature

These equations clearly show that convection heat transfer is very dependent upon the velocity and thermal properties of the gas as well as the wetted area. Effect of the gas composition on heat transfer has been indicated in Fig. 3. Hydrogen makes two important contribution to heat transfer in a batch annealing furnace. It is believed that hydrogen may penetrate between the wraps of a coil, thereby increasing the radial conductivity. Hydrogen also directly influences the convection heat transfer coefficient and furnace productivity. Hydrogen as protective gas imparts higher furnace productivity and better quality products.

With 100% hydrogen, emphasis is given on maximum safety, apart from this, the significance of ultra low dew points, i.e. ultra pure process atmosphere, gained more and more importance during recent years. The load plate, the load column within the work base, and the base plate are built more sturdily. The concave cover is manufactured from a highly ductile heat resistant material. Additionally, a nitrogen cushion is employed so as to eliminate any safety risk.

The work base fan impeller is of higher rating to generate maximum convection along the inside of the inner cover and through the coils, with minimum turbulence promoted by the intake and outlet diffuser assembly, which achieves optimal fluid flow.

Cooling in this system, is performed only via the inner cover, no external coolers are incorporated. The large inlet and outlet ports of an external cooler draw heat during heating up and make it impossible to encapsulate the work base effectively.

HIGH CAPACITY BASE FANS

Equation -2 also indicates that the convection heat transfer coefficient is affected by gas velocity, which in turn is determined by annealing hardware and the base fan flow rate. That is why newer furnaces are being installed with higher capacity base fans. The

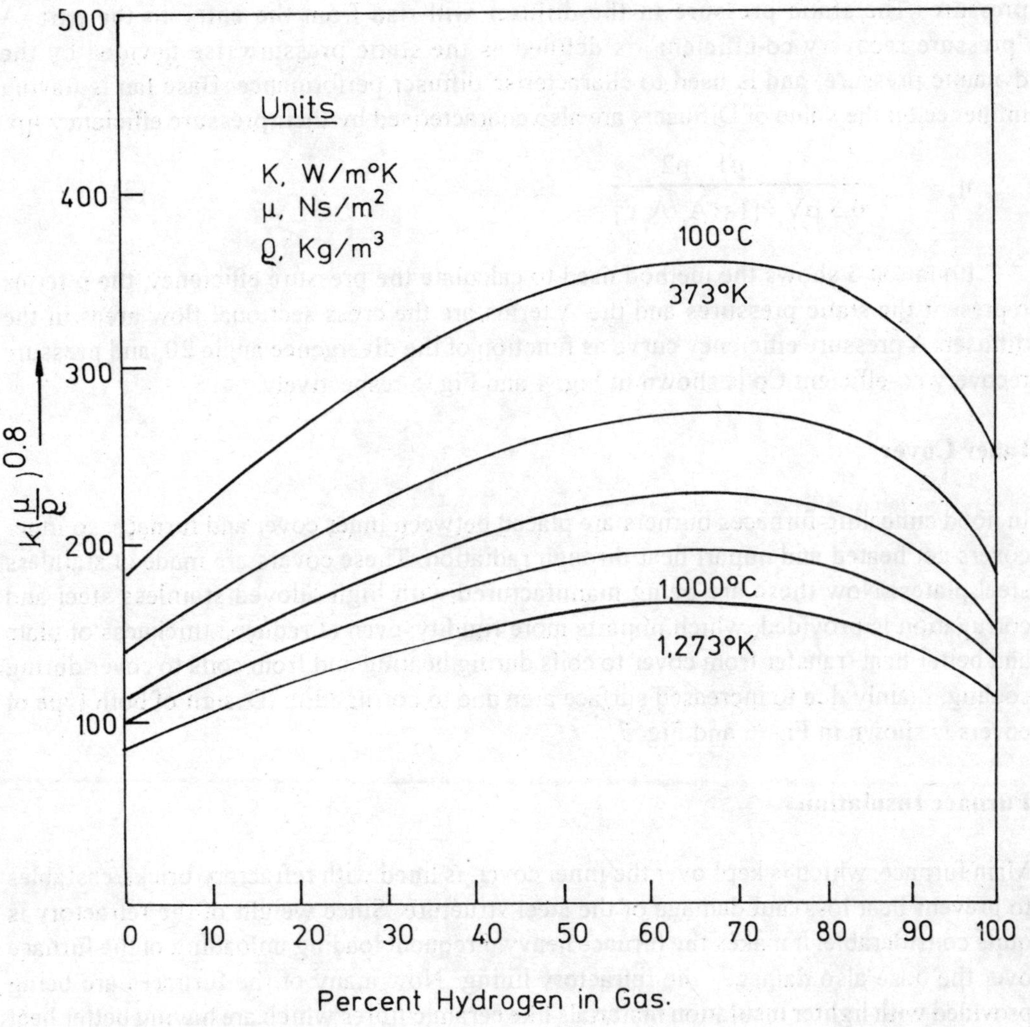

Fig. 3: The effect of the gas composition on the convection heat transfer coefficient

protective gas scrubs of the heat from inner cover so higher the base fan capacity, higher is the heat scrubbing rate. It is worth mentioning that for almost same size furnaces installed in seventies, for the furnaces installed in eighties and nineties is 14kw, 22kw and 40kw respectively. In earlier design, impeller of the base fan were water cooled, which used to cause maintenance problem due to the deposition of the muck, now air cooling of the impeller is a design improvements over old one..

Better Design Diffusers

The general purpose of a diffuser is to convert a high velocity gas flow profile into static pressure. The static pressure in the diffuser will rise from the entry to the exit. A "pressure recovery co-efficient" is defined as the static pressure rise devided by the dynamic pressure, and is used to characterise diffuser performance. Base fan is having influence on the value of Diffusers are also characterised by their pressure efficiency ηρ.

$$\eta_p = \frac{p1 - p2}{0.5\, \rho V_1^2\, [1 - (A_1/A_2)^2]} \quad \text{.... (3)}$$

Equation 3 shows the method used to calculate the pressure efficiency, the p terms represent the static pressures and the A terms are the cross sectional flow areas in the diffuser. A pressure efficiency curve as function of the divergence angle 20, and pressure recovery co-efficient Cp is shown in Fig. 4 and Fig. 5 respectively.

Inner Cover

In hood annealing furnaces burners are placed between inner cover and furnace, so inner covers get heated and impart heat through radiation. These covers are made of stainless steel plates. Now these are being manufactured with high alloyed stainless steel and corrugation is provided, which imparts more rigidity, even at reduced thickness of plate and better heat transfer from cover to coils during heating and from coils to cover during cooling, mainly due to increased surface area due to corrugation. Design of both type of covers is shown in Fig. 6 and Fig. 7.

Furnace Insulation

Main furnace, which is kept over the inner cover, is lined with refractory bricks/castables to prevent heat loss and damage of the steel structure. Since weight of the refractory is quite considerable, it makes the furnace heavy. Frequent loading unloading of the furnace over the base also damages the refractory lining. Now many of the furnaces are being provided with lighter insulation materials like ceramic fibres which are having better heat insulation properties. These insulations make the furnace lighter, prevent heat loss and prolong furnace life.

Change in Burner Design

Comparatively old furnaces were provided with injection type of burners in which combustion air is sucked from atmosphere at ambient temperature whereas latter design uses forced convection burners. In these burners combustion air is supplied to burners from separate blowers mounted on the furnace itself. In such furnaces product of combustion recuperate heat with combustion air and raise the temperature upto 150-200°C.

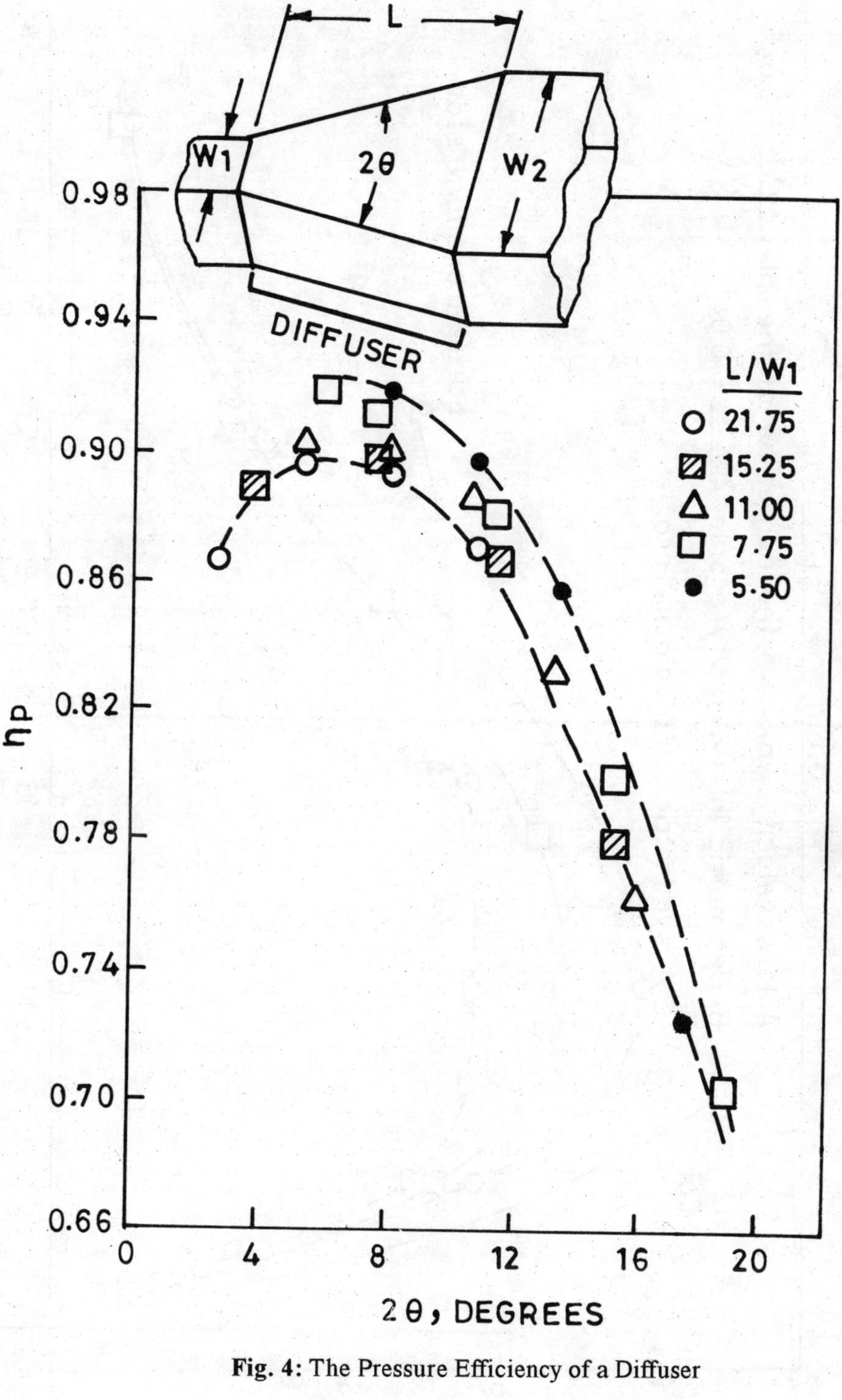

Fig. 4: The Pressure Efficiency of a Diffuser

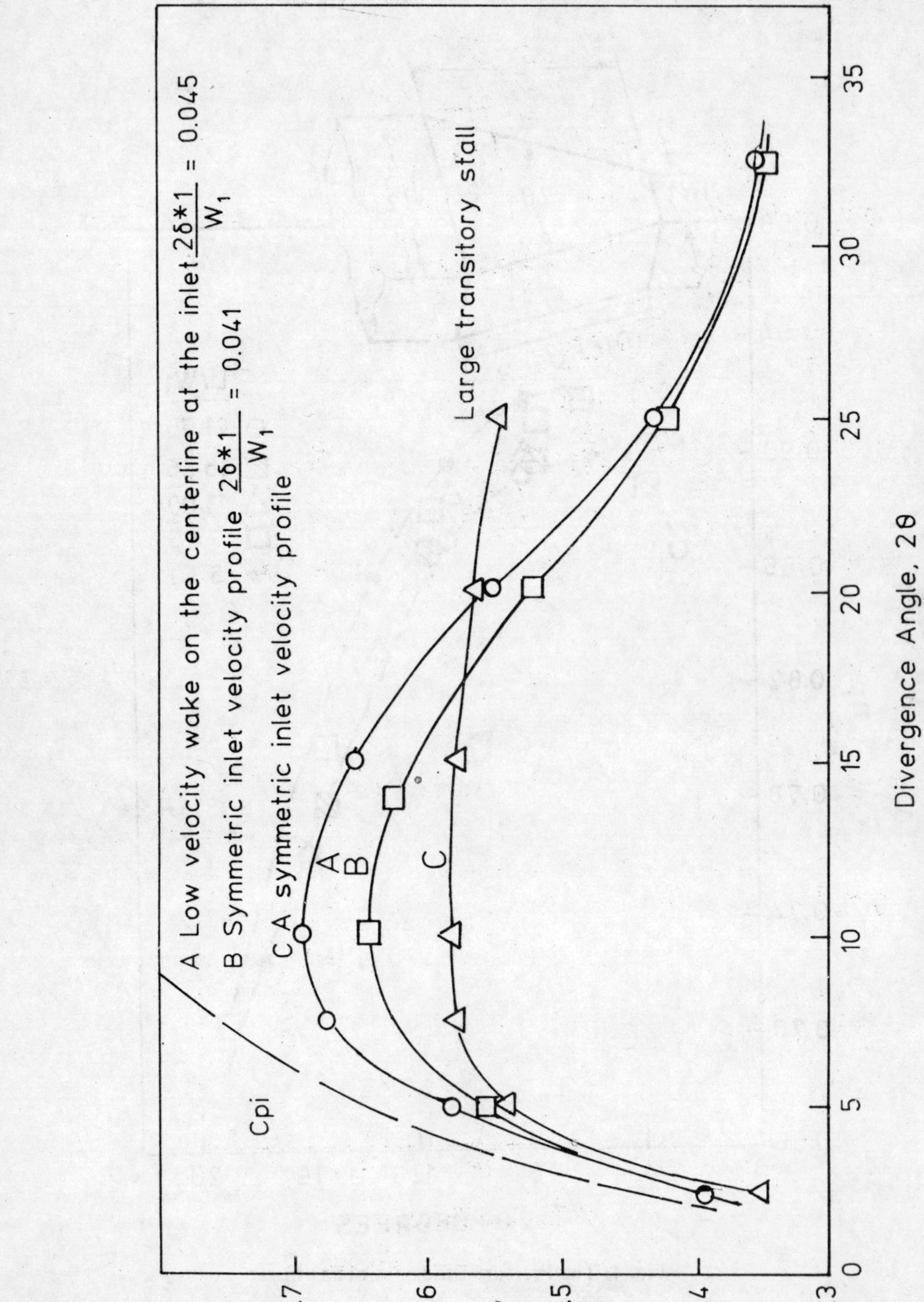

Fig. 5: The effect of diffuser inlet flow conditions on the pressure recovery coefficient

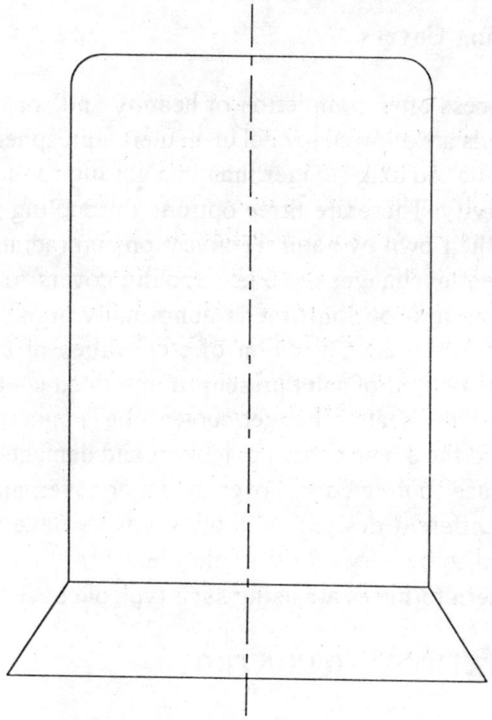

Fig. 6: Inner Cover Conventional Type

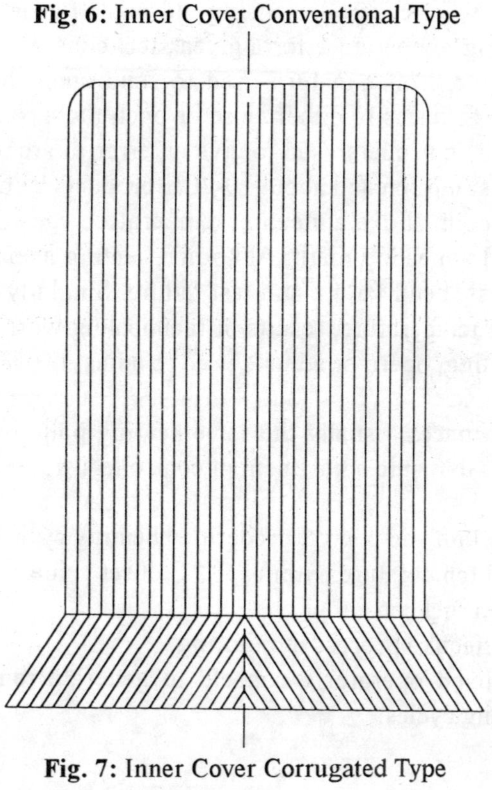

Fig. 7: Inner Cover Corrugated Type

Advanced Cooling Covers

In annealing process after completion of heating and soaking cycle furnace is removed from the base, coils are allowed to cool in an inert atmosphere. It is preferable that cooling cycle should not be too long (longer than one getting for desired cooling rate) for higher furnace productivity. There are three options for cooling i.e. allow the coils and inner cover to cool of their own by natural convection and radiation, recirculate the protective gas through a heat exchanger or to use cooling covers for faster cooling due to forced convection. In the first option time is abnormally high, in the second option though cooling time is shortened, corrosion of steel tubes of cooler, clogging due to scale formation and deposition of salts present in untreated cooling water cause maintenance problems. If any of the heat exchanger/cooler tube is punctured water gets mixed up with protective gas and the steam causes oxidation and damage of strip surface quality. Third alternative is to use cooling covers over the inner cover and create forced convection for faster cooling. Different designs of cooling covers have been shown in Fig. 8. These coolers are found to be very efficient and impart trouble free operation of the furnace. Most of the modern furnaces are using such type of covers.

INSTRUMENTATION AND CONTROL

Earlier furnaces were controlled, using old analog type single loop controllers. The required annealing temperature for a given steel charge was set by the operator on the controllers. The controller in turn used to send open/close signals to the motorised actuation on the furnaces to either close or open the air/gas valves. However, the poor accuracy of these controllers used to give an error of around $\pm$ 25°C, which resulted in more energy consumption and about 10-20% products being below desired quality level. Overheating of coils above annealing temperature causes several surface defects like sticker mark and annealing mark. Abnormal heating also results in mechanical defects like high hardness, bend failure and test failure. Similarly due to under heating of coils below annealing temperature, results in reannealing wasting more energy and time. At the end of annealing, operator adjusts/used to adjust the set temperature to zero to shut-off the furnace.

In earlier furnaces, usually the same heating patterns were used for all types and grades of coils as dynamic adjustment of controllers was not possible.

— To maintain and control predecided heating cycle more accurately.
— Control temperature within $\pm$ 10°C of set value.
— Reduced fuel consumption.
— More effective process monitoring.
— Centralised operator's console to generate remote set points for different annealing cycles.

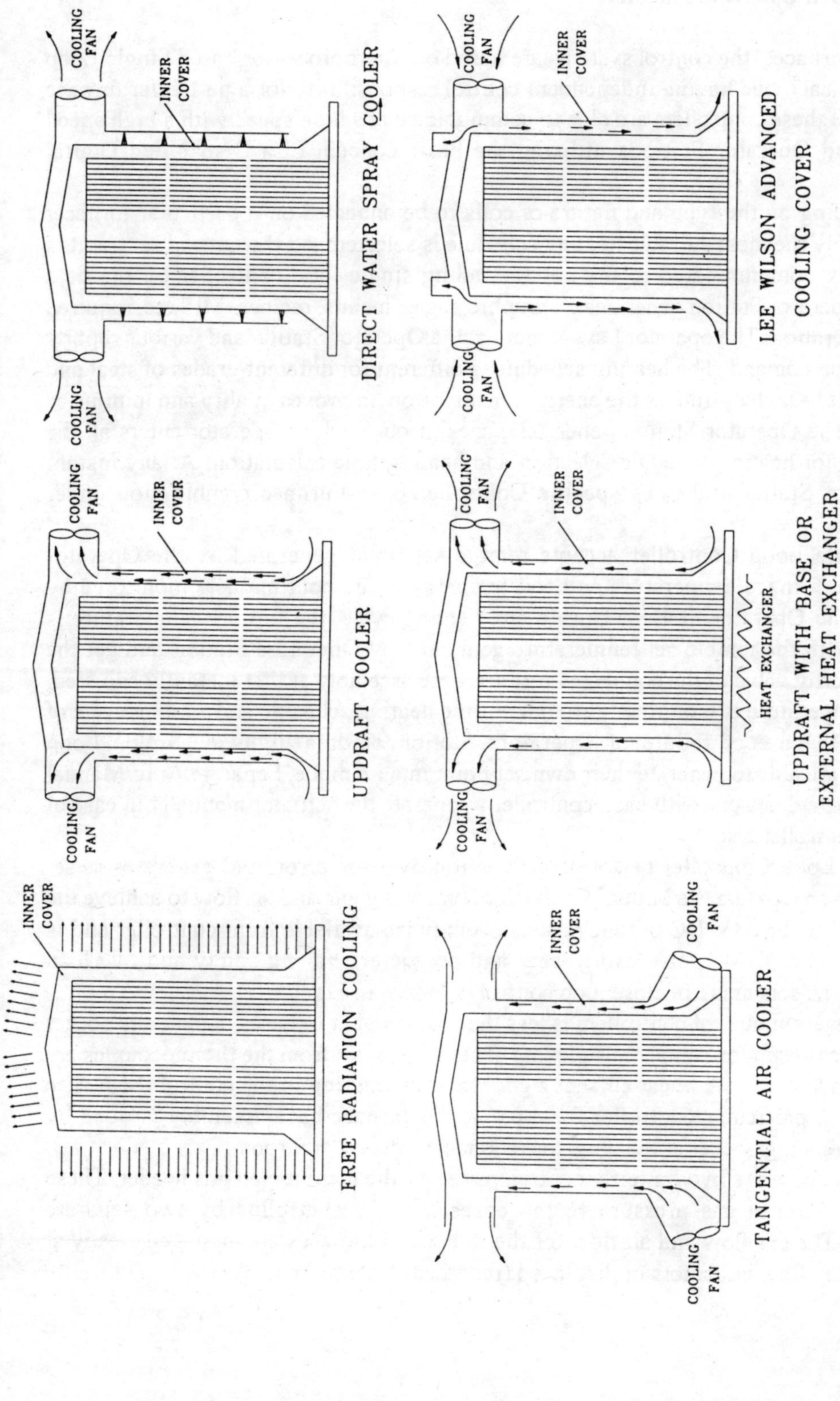

Fig. 8: Batch Annealing Cooling Systems

Control Scheme in New Furnaces

In modern furnaces, the control systems are based on Microprocessor based Single Loop Controllers, each one having independent control responsibility for a particular furnace at a time. All these controllers are able to communicate at a high speed with a high speed data bus and Operator Stations utilising the basic concept of a Distributed Digital Control.

Depending on the type and nature of coils to be annealed on a particular furnace/ base assembly the most suitable heating schedule is selected and the desired set point is continuously communicated to the corresponding single loop controller by the data highway. Operator Station generates all graphic pages, menus, recipes, MIS etc. required for plant operation. The operator keys-in data at the Operator Station and various reports are printed on demand. The heating schedule is different for different grades of steel and types of coils, which optimises the energy consumption, improves quality and minimises rejections. The Operator Station generates pages through which operator enters all the related data for heating schedule selection and heating/time calculation. At any instant the Operator Station indicates specific Controller-Base-Furnace combination under operation.

A Single Loop Controller accepts remote set point generated by the Operator Station. The furnace temperature and coil temperature are continuously monitored by controller and Operator Station. During any heating cycle, the furnace temperature is compared with the remote set temperature generated by Operators Station and get the gas/air butterfly valve of the connected furnace/base assembly at that instantly adjusted. The coil temperature is monitored through out the heating schedule and cooling cycle of annealing. In case of failure of Operators Station or data highway, Single Loop Controllers are able to generate their own set point in auto mode. Separate Auto/Manual Station is provided alongwith each controller to operate the actuator manually in case of failure of controller also.

Single Loop Controller performs PID action over the error, and generates raise/ lower pulses to regulate the butterfly valve for controlling gas and air flow to achieve the desired result. The 24V DC output raises/lowers pulse available from controller and is converted in 220V AC pulse using relay and contactors having safety and overload interlocks. The schematic of close loop control is shown in Fig. 9.

Whenever number of controllers is less than the number of bases, a plug and socket arrangement is used for signal multiplexing. The mV signals from the thermocouples are converted to 4 to 20 mA linear current signal for transmission in the control room. The selection of a particular controller for a particular furnace/base assembly is done by interchanging plug/socket at the plug/socket panel in the control room.

Usually there are two butterfly control valves on the main mixed gas header. These are used to control gas pressure to the bases and are controlled by two separate controllers. The gas flow and air flow for the individual furnaces are indicated locally at the furnace by flow indicators or displayed (recorded in control room).

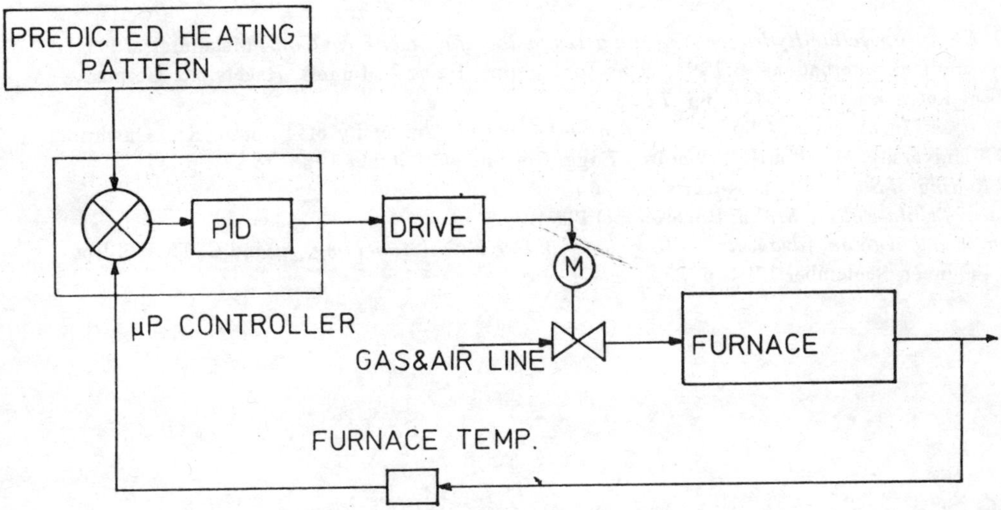

Fig. 9: Schematic of Close Loop Control

The mV signal outputs coming from the thermocouples (for coil temperatures) are connected directly to field control unit. After soaking is over, furnace is lifted and cooling hood is placed. The coil temperature is monitored on Operator Station unless it is below 100°C.

CONCLUSION

It is evident from the foregoing discussions that technology is now available which has facilitated the design, installation and operation of of annealing furnaces with almost double the productivity of conventional equipment. Most of the productivity improvement may be attributed to high convection heat transfer within inner cover. Hundred percent hydrogen provides uniform heating and mechanical properties. The increased capacity of base fan and cooling system virtually eliminate overheating of outer wraps of coils thereby resulting in improved final product quality.

The coil temperature is monitored through out the heating schedule and cooling cycle of annealing. In case of failure of Operators Station or data highway, Single Loop Controllers are able to generate their own set point in auto mode. Separate Auto/Manual Station is provided alongwith each controller to operate the actuator manually in case of failure of controller also.

ACKNOWLEDGEMENT

The authors are grateful to the Management of Research and Development Centre for Iron and Steel, Steel Authority of India Limited, Ranchi for their permission for presenting this paper.

REFERENCES

1. *Latest High Convection Hydrogen Annealing Technology for Steel Strip Coil*—Metallurgical Plant and Technology International 5/1994, Hans-Toni Junius, Heinz Hafingoff, Hagets etc. Germany, Heribent Lochnerditinz, Austria, pp. 72-78.
2. *The Process Technology of Batch Annealing*—AR Perrin, University of Toronto; RIL Gutshrie McGill University; BC Stonehill, Wardrop Engg. Consultant; October 1988, I&SM, p. 28.
3. *Cold Rolling of Steel* by W.L. Roberts, p. 726.
4. *Manual of Cold Rolling Mill* at Bokaro Steel Plant.
5. *Improvements with an Advanced Cooling Cover in Batch Coil Annealing,* Arvind C. Thekdi, Iron Steel Engineer, September 1994, p. 27.

DESIGN AND DEVELOPMENT OF STEEL ARCH SETTING DEVICE

An Important Phenomenon for Underground Mines

3

Dr. S.N. Maity

Scientist, Central Mining Research Institute, Dhanbad.

1. INTRODUCTION

In underground mines, supporting is an important phenomena. Due to fall of roof or side walls around 80% of the casualties occur in Indian mines. In underground mines where there is a requirement of high support density in the galleries, particularly for working under greater depths or under bad roof conditions, steel arches are being used for providing better support to the roof. However, the present practice of the erection of these arches in Indian mines is not very efficient. This method not only involves a lot of man power but is also quite arduous and unsafe. To eliminate these problems and to make the practice more efficient, the author in this paper tries to put forward the design of an hydro-mechanically operated Arch Setting Device, which he thinks is not only economically viable but will also smoothen the operation of arch setting.

2. PRESENT PRACTICE AND ITS LIMITATIONS

In India the yielding type arches are used in mines of BCCL and IISCO. Here the arch supports are generally set in a single piece or in a set of three pieces of U-section steel in arch shape being clamped together by steel fasteners and are tightened with the walls by inserting sleepers or others means between the arches and the tunnel walls. By this method of wedging between the arch and the wall considerable setting load is not achieved. To provide a minimum setting load is always a better criterion for better supporting and this prevents further deterioration of roof by limiting extension of fracture due to convergence. Proper load transfer from the walls is only possible if the contact of the arch with the roof is better. This process is very cumbersome too, because for installation of arch, each time one needs to erect chocks of wooden sleepers on either side of the roadway as resting platform of the arch. The central and the main part of the steel arch is the heaviest and to lift that up and to keep in position is very difficult. After lifting all the three pieces these are then clamped together. Generally a group of 13-15 persons can install a maximum of three arches in a shift of 8 hours, which seems to be a very poor performance. Thus this particular method of erection is very unsafe as well inefficient and therefore, it calls for some improvement in this method.

In developed countries like Europe or USA, the driving of mine galleries are generally followed by arching and concreting subsequently. The arches are set with the help of monorail and partially by manual labour. The monorail is fixed with the roof, and is continuously laid with the advancement of working face by the utilisation of lifting machine and thus provides advantages of suport, but with this method also considerable setting load can not be given to arches.

3. NEW DEVELOPMENT

Considering the acute problem of setting steel Arches in underground mines, CMRI, Dhanbad has very recently developed an equipment which is really a suitable device for setting arches in mine tunnels.

3.1 Design

Fig. 1 shows the schematic diagram of the Arch Setting Device from its side and Fig. 2 shows the schematic view of the device from its front along with the arch in operating condition.

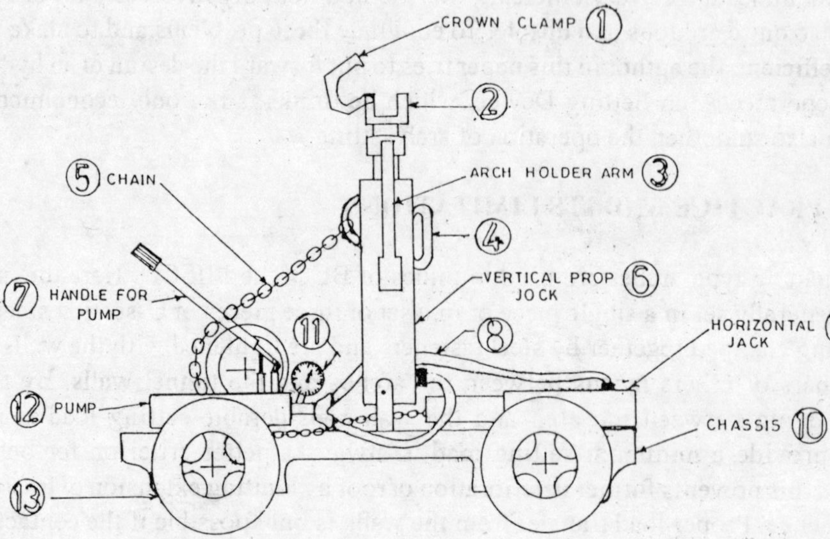

Figure 1: Arch Setting Device

The present design of the device useful for installing arches in underground tunnels, comprises of a base frame (10) mounted on wheels (13). The base frame has a main

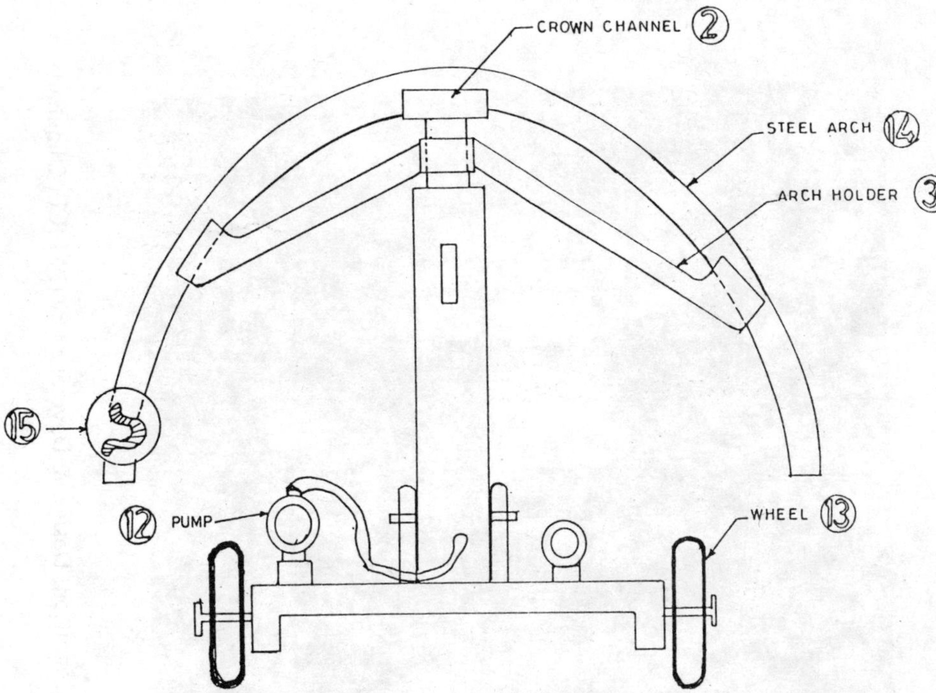

Figure 2a: Arch Setting Device with Steel Arch

hydraulic jack (6) hinged on to it in such a manner as to allow horizontal and vertical movement. The main Hydraulic jack is provided with a chain (5) and pulley (7) arrangement connected to an auxiliary jack (9) for lifting the main jack from horizontal to vertical position. The main jack and auxiliary jack are connected by means (8) to a pump (12) having a pressure gauge (11). The said main jack is provided with a handle (4) and means (1, 2 & 3) for holding an arch section (14, 15) in position.

3.2 Operation

The device of the present design is an equipment easily manuervable and can be moved in underground by manual pulling, but can be motorised also. To drive galleries or roadways where quick supporting is required, this equipment could be taken to the suporting position and the the main jack (6) is lowered in horizontal position with the chain pulley arrangement. The big curved piece of the three piece arch or a single piece arch is then clamped on to the gripping system (1, 2 & 3) provided at the top of the main jack. By pumping the auxiliary jack the main jack is lifted to vertical position by the chain pulley arrangement. The main jack is pumped, so that the arch is tightened with the roof with a load of 5-10t. After the required setting load is achieved, the top piece of the arch is fixed with the other two legs at the bottom side by means of steel clamps, or if it is a single arch,

Figure 2b: Steel Arch Setting Device in Operating Condition, Design & Developed by C.M.R.I., Dhanbad.

it is set by putting wooden logs or other means at the bottom of the legs of the arch. The jack is then unlocked and brought down and the equipment is shifted for fresh operations at the face. After withdrawl of the jack the yielding type three piece arch can hold about 60 to 80% of the setting load given by the pump.

3.3 Qualities

The main object of the present design is to provide a device useful for installing arches in underground tunnels which obviates the drawbacks of the conventional system and to provide a smoothly operating, economically viable instrument which can be used for easy installation of steel arches in underground mines with high setting load and thus would significantly free the system from manual components, there by increasing its efficiency, effectiveness and will provide much safer working at the same time.

3.4 Main Advantages of the Present Machine Design are

1. It can set arches easily with a little manual effort.
2. It improves the speed of the gallery drivage process.
3. Increases safety of the workers.
4. It gives the arches a better contact with the roof and a higher setting load.
5. It is portable and easily manuervable in mines.
6. Easy to operate and requires least cost for maintenance.
7. Running cost is nill for this machine.
8. A gang of 3 persons can easily set atleast 15 arches in a shift.

4. CONCLUSION

With the increase in the demand of various minerals in the market whether it is Coal, Gold, Copper or Uranium, the underground mines are going deeper and deeper. For higher safety at greater depth steel arches will be preferred for roadway supporting in the near future. Therefore, this new device will play an extensive role in world mining scenario. The introduction of the Arch Setting Device in mines will certainly be a boon to the day to day supporting operations of the mine and will smoothen the whole arching operation with maximum safety.

II

MANUFACTURING REQUIREMENTS FOR DEFENCE APPLICATIONS

TECHNOLOGY SUBSTITUTION BY INDIGENOUS EFFORTS

4

Lt. Col. T.V. Sadasivan, ME, FIE

Offg. CQCE, HQ TG EME, Delhi Cantt., New Delhi

INTRODUCTION

1. Today technology itself is a moving target. What is latest or what is the state of the art is claimed by the one who maintains the know how of the future position. The gap he creates from those who are at the present position or those who are even left behind is the key to success. It gives him adequate control in that particular field. This control is not only on technology but indirectly even on economy. The economic control and consequently the economic strength that the gap generates is the most serious implication meriting our attention. Some attempts are made here to suggest methods that must be capable of encountering the situation based on technology substitution by indigenous efforts.

2. Before the subject is discussed, an analysis is carried out on what is conceived by technology substitution and indigenous efforts. A logical follow up is to suggest some methods for technology substitution by indigenous efforts. In doing so, discussions on the relevance of technology substitution, meaning of indigenous efforts and approaches to achieve technology substitution by indigenous efforts are treated as the most important part.

3. While studying the relevance of technology the difference in the concepts between "closing the technology gap" and "Creating the technology gap" is brought out. The urgent need to abandon the stagnant approach of closing the existing gap by adopting more aggressive approach of creating the gap for others to close is proposed. Justification in this direction are also attempted.

4. Technology substitution by indigenous efforts, it is proposed, should concentrate on strategic selection of thrust areas in well defined terms strictly based on the economic policy of the nation. The existing infrastructure as well as the probable potential of the infrastructure in the near future should also be considered. All these can be a success only if we have a technology vision to focus on to the technology objective. Other factors which are thought of to influence the policy on the indigenous efforts also include concurrency between market requirements, devoloping activities and manufacturing capabilities.

TECHNOLOGY SUBSTITUTION

5. When we say technology substitution we mean any of the following.

(a) Alternative Indian design to achieve same performance level as the imported design to ensure.

(i) Reduction of investment cost.
(ii) Improve efficiency

(b) New designs to ensure enhanced capabilities.

6. Alternative methods to ensure same performance level may be employed either to achieve cost effectiveness or to improve efficiency. Cost effectiveness is achieved in several ways. One of the methods is by using material and man power available in the country instead of using high cost raw meterials and more costly transferred technology Improving efficiency may be by using the same basic design as that of imported model but giving certain modifications to ensure that the system performs more effciently.

7. New methods to ensure new and advanced capability may be based on thinking what is required ahead. We must be convinced that the present system is always imperfect. For every design there is a future design. If some one else is competent in deriving that design we must be confident that we will design it before some one.

CREATING GAP

8. For those professionals watching the technology race, it will be interesting to note the upgradation measures in weapon systems, unending and unlimited till entry in battle field. Those who disagree with me may be surprised with the experiences quoted in war which demonstrated that while there are many measures of combat potential improvements which are deemed necessary there are still others which although known are never implemented until the system encounters its enemy. It is this "Created gap" that promises surprise and so promises success which means that before it is too late we must realise that at least in defence technology crying need of the day is the "the created gap" and not the "closed gap". It is now made amply clear that closing the gap makes you march in same level of technology where as created gap takes your technology ahead of others.

EVOLUTION AS REVOLUTION

9. The strategic selection of thrust areas for technology substitution by indigenous efforts should also be based on economic policy of the nation. The world leaders in planning military budgets today pause to wonder themselves on the modernisation,

upgradation or retrofitment as it is the most cost effective route to convert the more than 30 years old war machine to the present day miracle capable of doing its job more effectively, in terms of speed and operational efficiency to multiply your force. The impact of such a trend is the vast retrofit market, flooding and flourishing with huge profit potential while expanding globally presenting challenges of stiff competition.

TECHNOLOGY VISION

10. It is not the figures or statistics of the past that are significant here. It is the concept and the confidence in the concept that should deliver the goods. We must make ourselves free from all such obsessions and be prepared to evolve a technology vision that permits unlimited urge for creativity. The technology objective of such a vision is the willingness to accept that for every present design there is a future design that will be claimed by an ordinary mortal like you or me—any one. But the one who believes in it is the only one who can perceive it and the only one who is capable of achieving it. There are many instances. Let us look at one case illustrated in the following paragraphs.

INGENUITY IN ACTION

11. When ingenuity is in action, innovations will focus on solutions not only to survive the competitors but also to challenge the competitors to kick up the profit graphs exponentially. Take the case of "Simula", a company making armour schemes.

12. Simula supplied more than two thirds of the worlds crashworthy Helicopter seats. Now the company has drawn on its engineering expertise to establish a growing presence in add on armour programmes for land and sea and their applications. How did they achieve this? The company originally teamed with an armour supplier when their seat systems required special materials. As the company determined to conquer the field of armour market it began to develop its own armour system to remain competitive and control the quality of the product. The success signal of this achievement is the family of armour schemes identified as LICAR (Light Weight Composite Armour).

13. The uniqueness of Simula is that they are not material manufacturer. Some companies may have expertise in fabrication of a certain ceramic or other type of material. But at Simula, the experts analyse, review, and consider all materials which have potential for developing armour schemes. Selection of a material like kevlar, fibre glass, or ceramic carbide will depend on customer application and manufacturing process. Here it is seen that there is no better example to illustrate concurrence between market requirements, development activities and manufacturing capabilities.

CONCLUSION

14. Having given a brief introduction to the subject, the concept of technology substitution is is dealt in brief. The meaningful aspects of creating gap instead of closing

the gap is discussed. It is brought out as to how strategic selection of the thrust areas for technology substitution can convert evolution into revolution justifying the need for a technology vision. A case study is presented to illustrate how ingenuity when put into action can kick up profit graphs.

15. It can thus be seen that technology substitution by indigenous efforts can only be realised if there is a vigorous dedicated approach springing from a combination of original thinking, creativity and purpose driven tenacity.

REFERENCES

1. M.J. Gething, "Technology's Growing Impact", *Jane's Defence System Modernisation*, August 1996
2. R.M. Ogorkiewicz, "Combat Vehicle Armour Progress", *IDR*, June 1995.
3. S.R. Gourley, *et al.*, "Upgrade Programme Guide: Special Focus on US Modernisation", *Jane's Defence System Modernisation*, August 1995.
4. S.R. Gourley, "Simula Adds Armour", *Jane's Defence Systems Modernisation*, August 1995.

MANUFACTURING A DIMAOND ANVIL CELL (DAC)

5

N. Gunasegaran,[1] N. Easwaran[1] and K. Balachander[1]

Central Workshop, TEAM Group, Indira Gandhi Centre for Atomic Research[1]
Kalpakkam - 603 102

ABSTRACT

Diamond Anvil Cell (DAC) is used for studying the behaviour of materials at very high pressure of upto 500 GPa and temperatures. Such conditions exist in the interior core of the earth for instance and are also generated when materials are subjected to explosive stresses. The DAC was indigenously designed and manufactured for different experiments in condensed matter physics.

This paper deals with selection of materials and diamond, precision machining and assembling of Mao-Bell Type DAC. In Mao-Bell type DAC, a Piston-Cylinder Assembly is employed to contain the diamond anvils. Different precision machining processes such as milling, turning, grinding and EDM were used to machine the hardened maraging steel. Critical reqirements are: (1) the axes of the piston and the cylinder must be exactly concentric, and (2) the cell axis must be perpendicular to the diamond anvil culets and pass through the centre of the anvils. In order to transmit the load on to the diamond anvils, a Type-II lever design is used and a drive screw is used to transmit the load in a controlled way.

1. INTRODUCTION

Diamond Anvil Cell (DAC) has revolutionized high pressure research, both in terms of the range of static pressure that can be reached and variety of techniques that can be employed to study the behaviour of matter at high pressure. It has made it possible to synthesize, process and fundamentally study materials at high ultra pressure of the megabar range. Such pressure are significant for atleast two basic reasons. Profound changes are expected in the chemical properties at ultra high pressures. The second reason is that the strength of materials are far smaller than the stresses achieved in ultra high-pressure experiments.

The deformation (plastic flow) associated with slightly non-uniform pressures typical at ultra-high pressure conditions, results in full density, super hard poly crystalline aggregated of even the strongest and most brittle materials. A significant motivation for research at ultra high pressure has been "applied" reason that such conditions exist deep inside planets, the pressure at the Earth's Centre being 365 GPa, for example and metallic hydrogen is located deep with in stellar and giant planetary interiors.

A very significant step in the Pressure Cell design was the development of the DAC by Mao and Bell. It employs a longer Piston and Cylinder Assembly to ensure proper alignment of diamond anvils even at the highest pressure and a generously proportioned body and lever arm system. For alignment two tungsten carbide half cylinders, whose axes are perpendicular to each other, are provided and these can be translated and tilted. This cell is capable of a few hundred GPa (Mbar) pressures when the anvil diamonds are properly shaped.

2. MATERIALS CONSIDERATION

DAC has the following main components: (1) Piston Cylinder Assembly, (2) Pressure Cell Holder, (3) Half Cylindrical Rockers, (4) Diamond Anvils, (5) X-ray Collimator, and (6) Belle Ville Spring.

Fig. (1) depicts a DAC Assembly. Since the DAC has to sustain a load in the range of 10^4N, high strength steel is used as the material of construction for the Piston Cylinder Assembly and Pressure Cell Holder. Maraging steel with hardness of 60RC was used by us for the component (1) and (2)

2.1 Half Cylindrical Rockers

Half Cylindrical Rockers are made of tungsten carbide. As diamond has a very high compressive strength of approx. 35 GPa and the hardened maraging steel 2.5 GPa, it is desired that there should be a material of intermediate strength. Tungsten Carbide is best suited for this requirement and hence chosen for rockers.

2.2 Diamond Anvils

Selection of diamonds and the size depends upon the type of DAC and nature of investigation. Diamonds with low luminescence are chosen for light scattering studies and Type-II diamonds for Infrared Absorption Methods. Type-I diamonds are generally satisfactory. The size varies from 1/8 carat to 1/2 carat. The anvil flats range from 0.2 to 0.7 mm. A Culet of 16- sided polygon gives good performance. Incorporation of a bevel increased the pressure sustaining capability by a factor of 4 to 8. Another paramount imorpance is the near total parallelism of the culet and the table of the diamond anvil and flatness. For the diamond anvil to sustain a pressure of approx. 100 GPa safely, the accepted values of flatness and parallelism are 2.5 nm, and 3-20 minute of an arc respectively. Type-I Diamond was chosen for our DAC.

2.3 Gasket

Metal Gaskets such as Inconel X750, tempered T301 stainless steel (45RC) and

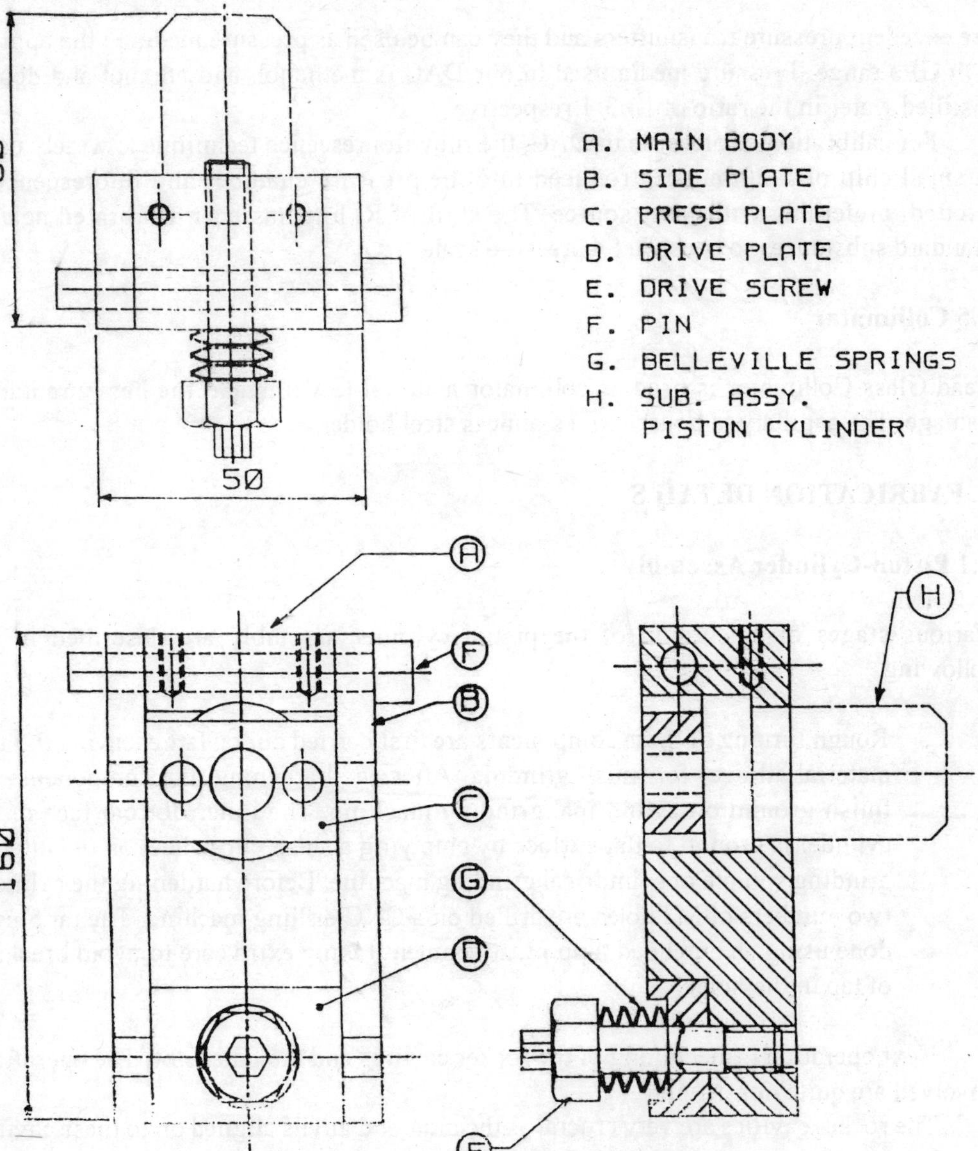

Fig. 1: Diamond Anvil Cell Assembly

waspalloy are used for containment of sample and pressure medium. The Gasket extrudes around the diamonds and acts as a supporting ring for the anvil faces. The metal gasket is first compressed and provided with a hole of approx. 200 mic. dia. at the center. The gasket used in our DAC is of AISI 304 stainless hardened to 65 RC by cold rolling.

2.4 Pressure Media

A mixture of four parts of methanol to one part of ethanol is a very convenient pressure medium for hydrostatic experiments upto 10 GPa at room temperature. Xe, Ar, He and H_2

are excellent pressure transmitters and they can be used as pressure media in the approx. 100 GPa range. Pressure media used in our DAC is methanol, and ethanol and double distilled water in the ratio of 16:3:1 respectively.

For calibration of pressure in DAC, the ruby flourescence technique is widely used. A small chip of 5-20um is introduced into the pressure chamber and fluorescence is excited, preferably with laser source. The shift of Rl line has been calibrated against standard substances to construct a pressure scale.

2.5 Collimator

Lead Glass Collimator is used as collimator material to withstand the heavy radiation damage. The capillary is housed in a stainless steel holder.

3. FABRICATION DETAILS

3.1 Piston-Cylinder Assembly

Various stages of machining of the piston cylinder assembly are described in the following:

> Rough turning of these components are first carried out on lathe leaving 0.5 mm material all over for finish grinding. After age hardening, the components are finish ground on cylindrical grinding machine. The inner bottom face of the cylinder is ground to flat surface by emplying a small cup-wheel on the internal grinding spindle of cylindrical grinding machine. Before hardening the cylinder, two numbers of M3 holes are drilled on a CNC drilling machine. The tapping is done using an extended tapping attachment taking extra care to avoid breakage of tap in the hole.

Next operation is machining of the rocker cavities and the taper slot. The operations involved are quite non-trivial.

The rocker cavities are very crucial as the diamond anvils aligned on to these cavities decide the pressure attaining capability of the DAC and the life of the diamonds. Because of the typical half cylinder shapes, the scooping out of the material to form cavity can not be done using any conventional machine and this requires the use of an Electrical Discharge machine (EDM).

Accuracy achieved in any EDM operation depends upon the accuracy of the electrode used. In this case, both the cavities are machined using similar electrodes. The tapered slot on the cylinder upper face is completed using a double taper electrode. Commercial grade copper has been used as electrode material in our case. Rocker electrodes are machined on lathe and taper cavity electrode is machined on a milling machine. The rocker cavity in both cylinder and piston has two side holes for adjusting the rockers axially so that the alignment of the diamond anvils can be achieved perfectly. The piston-cylinder assembly is shown in Fig. 2.

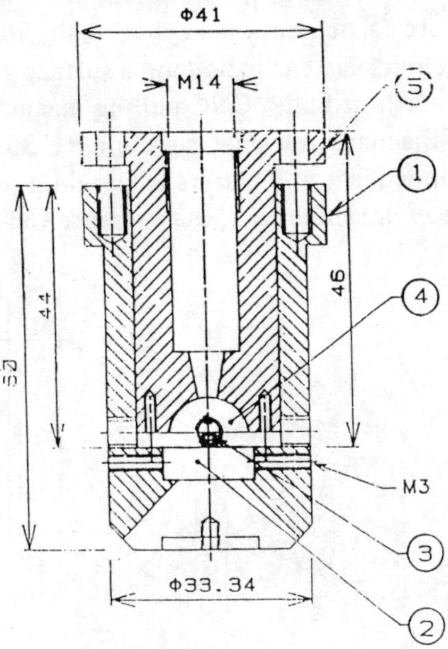

Fig. 2: Sub Assembly Piston-Cylinder

Sl. No.	Qty	Description	Materials
1	1	Cylinder	Maraging Steel
2	1	Cylinder Rocker	Tungsten Carbide
3	2	Diamond Anvils	Diamond
4	1	Piston Rocker	Tungsten Carbide
5	1	Piston	Maraging Steel

3.2 Pressure Cell Holder

This assembly consists of six parts namely, main body, levers, drive plate, press plate, drive screw and connecting pin. The main parts are machined out of rectangular shape raw materials on a milling machine. Machining in annealed condition is carried our leaving adequate allowance for finish grinding after heat treatment. The parallelism of opposite faces with perfect squarness between the adjacent faces is very important in these components for the proper assembly to transfer the pressure coaxially to the piston-cylinder assembly. Extra care is to be taken while machining the press plate and the drive plate to have the side pins in one line without any shift in the axis. A shift in the axis may lead to unequal loading on the piston which may lead to breakage of diamond anvils.

The major portion of this assembly is machined on a milling machine. The press and drive plates are first machined on a milling machine and then taken on a lathe for side pin machining. Rough machining is carried out leaving 0.5 mm material all over for final grinding after heat treatment. Final grinding operation of main body cylinder hole and press & drive plate pins are carried out on a cylindrical grinding machine. Flat grinding operation on other components are carried out on a surface grinding machine. The radius portion of main body is machined on a CNC milling machine in the annealed condition itself. As the hardness of the maraging steel is around RC 35, it does not pose any special problem in machining. Tipped face mill cutters are used for the milling operations and for finishing operations. The exploded view of the Pressure Cell Holder is shown in Fig. 3.

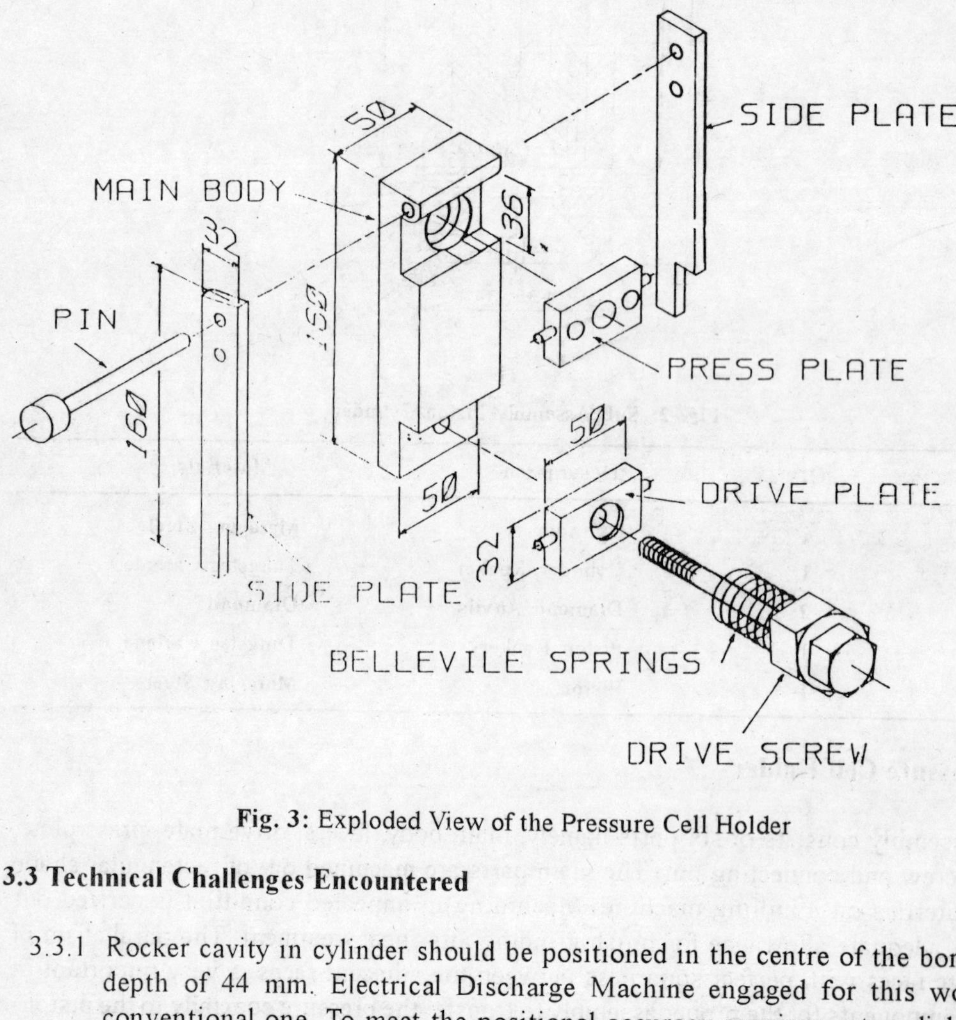

Fig. 3: Exploded View of the Pressure Cell Holder

3.3 Technical Challenges Encountered

3.3.1 Rocker cavity in cylinder should be positioned in the centre of the bore at a depth of 44 mm. Electrical Discharge Machine engaged for this work is conventional one. To meet the positional accuracy requirement, a disk with collar was used for mock up operation. Overall thickness of the disk was 12 mm and diameter of the disk was maintained to have sliding fit with the bore of the cylinder. The electrode for machining rocker cavity was positioned with reference to the bore of the cylinder.

After fixing the mock up disk at the top of the cylinder bore, cavity was made upon a depth of 3 mm. Then the cavity position in the disk was checked with reference to the diameter in UMM Machine. Correction of the position of the electrode was made by using dial gauges and once again trial cut was made on the mock up disk, keeping the cylinder fixed on the table. Thus by trial cuts and inspection followed by adjustment of the electrode position, correct position of the cavity was achieved.

3.3.2. Drilling of the two M3 holes in the cylinder bore at a depth of 44 mm was carried out in CNC drilling mahine. Long drills were procured and drilling was carried out with care. For tapping at 44mm depth, shank length ot the tap was increased by welding suitable rod and grinding the same with reference to the threaded portion. Care was taken to avoid breakage of the tap while tapping.

3.3.3. Maraging steel with hardness RC35 was supplied in the form of rectangular blocks which involved heavy material removal to make cylinder and piston. With normal P30 and P40 grade tips, frequent changes of the tips had to be made while machining. Hence inserts coated with TiN (ISO DNMG) were used and material removal was made easy comparatively.

3.4 Rockers

The starting material for the rocker is a precision tungsten carbide cylinder with the diameter variation within 1.5 micrometer over a length of about 25mm. Fortunately, such high quality cylinders are available in India. A segment from the cylinder, with overall dimensions given in Fig. 4, is cut using a precision diamond saw. (For example, a precision crystal cutting machine equipped with a diamond saw is admirably suitable for this task). The flatness of the surface and its parallelism with the axis achieved are 10 micrometer and 7 minutes of an arc respectively. By subsequent lapping, these numbers are improved by a factor of 3-4. The cylindrical segments are loaded on an EDM and with the tungsten-copper electrodes having the required shapes, conical hole and the double tapper slot on the piston-rocker and the cylinder-rocker respectively are made.

3.5 X-ray Collimator

For carrying out the X-ray experiments, it is necessary that a fine collimated beam derived from the X-ray source be incident on to the sample inside the diamond anvil cell. The Collimator head should be as close as possible to the sample so that any increase in the beam size can be avoided. X-ray collimator of the dimensions as depicted in Fig. 5 has been fabricated. The important aspect of this collimator is that the X-ray passes through a lead glass capillary of about 80 micrometer diameter and 18mm length. This avoids any X-ray diffraction from the gasket material used to contain the sample in the DAC. When

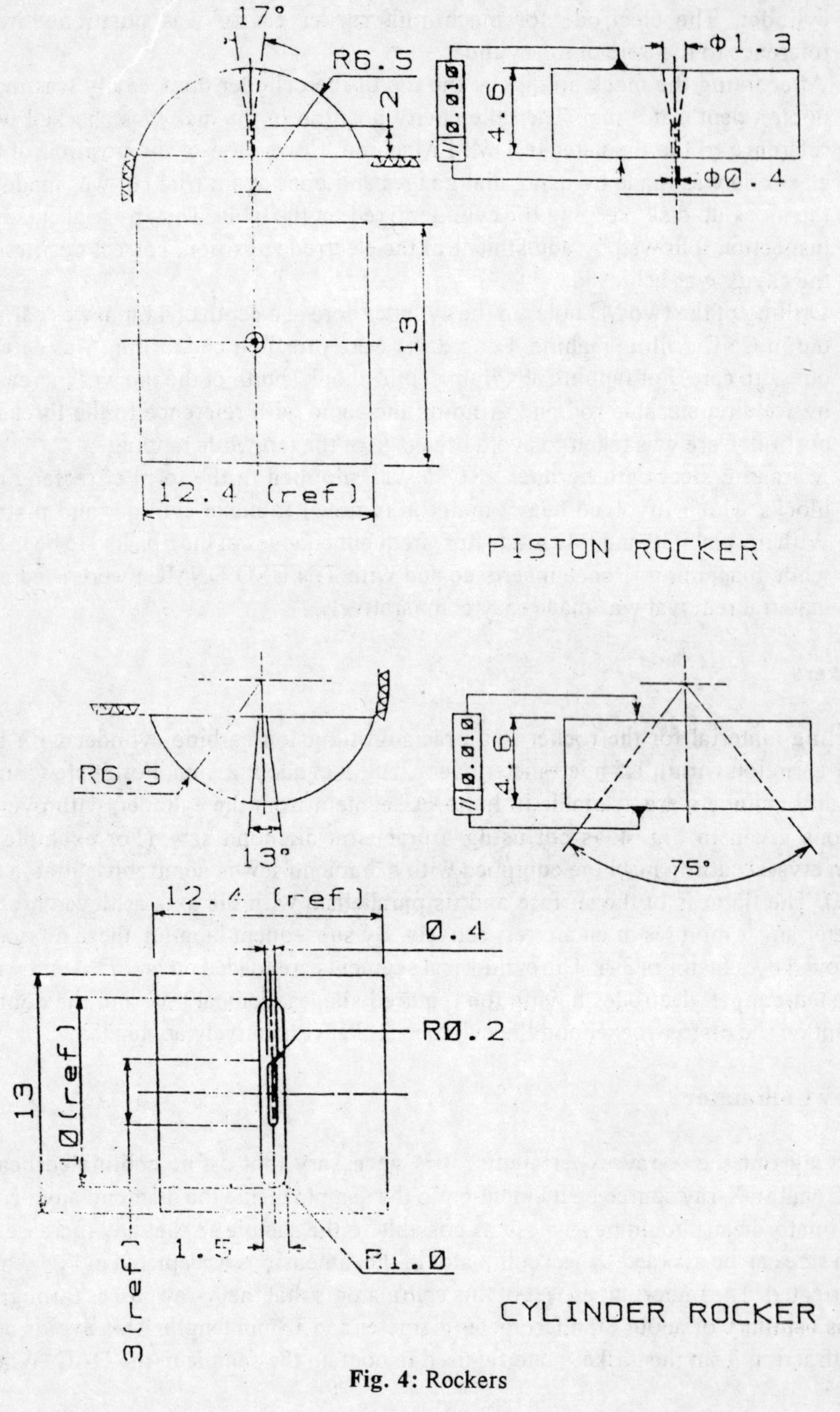

Fig. 4: Rockers

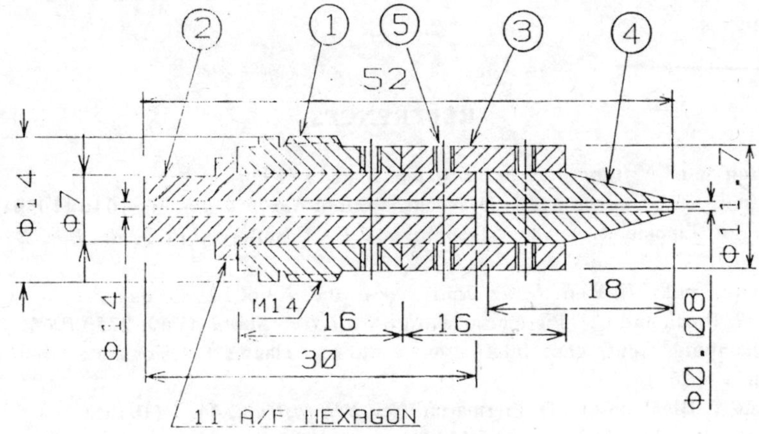

Fig. 5: Sub Assembly Collimator

Sl. No.	Qty	Description	Matl.
1	1	Guide Tube Holder	SS
2	1	Guide Tube	SS
3	1	Collimator Holder	SS
4	1	Collimator	Glass
5	12	M2 Grub Screws	HSS

the collimator is inserted into the piston, the gap between the diamond anvil and the lead glass capillary is less than 1 mm.

4. INSPECTION AND PERFORMANCE OF THE DAC

All the components machined are subjected to standard inspection procedure and metrology for geometrical accuracies. The parts of the DAC are imspected in sophisticated inspection equipments like a Universal Measuring Machine and found that they meet the drawing specifications.

All the components of the DAC are assembled and the diamond anvils are aligned following the procedure described by Jephcoat *et al.*[15] The well known ruby fluorescence line shift procedure[7] was used to test the performance of the DAC. It is observed that the Cell is sustaining a pressure of about 25 GPa. Testing of this Cell for higher pressure capability is in progress.

ACKNOWLEDGMENTS

Authors are thankful to Shri M.K. Ramamurthy, Director, TEAM Group, IGCAR for encouragement and continued support. They thank Shri S. Manohar for his neat and efficient typing.

REFERENCES

1. A.W. Lawson and T.Y. Tang, *Rev. Sci. Instrum.* 21, 815 (1950).
2. J.C. Jamieson, A.W. Lawson and N.D. Nachtrieb, *Rev. Sci. instrum.* 30, 1016 (1959).
3. C.E. Weir, E.R. Lippincott, A. Van Valkenburg and E. N. Burting, *J.Res. Nati. Bur. Stand.* A 63, 55 (1959).
4. G.J. Piermarini and C.E. Weir, *J. Res. Natl. Bur. Stand.* A 66, 325 (1962).
5. C.E. Weir, S. Block and G.J. Piermarini, *J. Res. Natl. Bur. Stand.* C 69, 275 (1965).
6. A. VanValkenburg, Conference Internationale Sur-les- Hautes Pressions, Le Creusot, Saone-et-Loire, France (1965).
7. J.D. Barnett, S. Block and G. D. Piermarini, *Rev. Sci. Instrum*, 44, 1 (1973).
8. A. Jayaraman, *Rev. Mod. Phys.* 55, 65 (1983).
9. G.J. Piermarini, S. Block, J.D. Barnett and R.A. Forman, *J. Appl. Phys.* 46, 2774 (1975).
10. H.K. Mao and P.M. Bell, *Carnegie Institution of Washington Year Book*, 77, 904 (1978).
11. H.K. Mao and P.M. Bell, *Science 200*, 1145 (1978).
12. P.M. Bell, H.K. Mao and K. Goettel, *Science* 226, 542 (1984); W.C. Moss, J.O. Hallguist, R. Reichlin, K.A. Goettel and S. Martin, *Appl. Phys.* Lett. 48, 1258 (1986).
13. J. Xu, H.K. Mao and P.M. Bell, *Science* 232, 1401 (1986).
14. A.L. Ruoff, H. Xia and C. Xia, *Rev. Sci. Instrum.* 63, 4342 (1992).
15. A.P. Jephcoat, H.K. Mao and P.M. Bell, 1987 *Hydrothermal Experimental Techniques*, G. C. Ulmer and H.L. Barnes (eds.) (New York, John Wiley), p. 469.

PLANNING OF GRINDING OPERATIONS USING EXPERT SYSTEM

6

Dr. Rupinder Gupta

Head, Workshop, Central Road Research Institute,
New Delhi - 110 020

ABSTRACT

This paper describes the use of expert system in planning of grinding operations. A knowledge based computer programme to suggest grinding parameters for surface, cylindrical and internal grinding has been developed using Turbo Prolog language. Optimal grinding condition can be obtained by repeated analysis.

Key Words: Expert system, Grinding, Optimal condition

1. INTRODUCTION

Expert systems are concerned with study and creation of computer programmes that exhibit some form of intelligence or thinking ability. These are designed to help solve problems in a way that could be considered intelligent if tackled by a human being.[1] The expert system incorporate judgment, experience, rules of thumb and intuition and provide knowledgeable advice about how best to solve a problem in a narrow domain. A typical expert system consists of a knowledge base (database) and a tool for understanding questions and finding right answers to them. The power of an expert system lies in its knowledge base therefore, the term 'knowledge based' system. The domain of knowledge embedded in the system determines the field of application of the system. Such systems would be of great help of planning as well as shop floor engineers.

Development of expert systems started about three decades back. The expert systems have been developed and applied in the field of medicine, mineral exploration, fault diagnostics etc.[2,3] The use of expert systems for planning and decision making functions in manufacturing has attracted a lot of potential users.[4-7]

The process of building an expert system involves inter-action between an expert system designer, that is, a knowledge engineer and one or more human experts of the problem domain. The building blocks of a typical expert system are given in Fig. 1. The task of a knowledge engineer is to collect knowledge from the domain experts and assemble them into a usable database. Another component of the expert system known as the inference engine searches the database and solves the problem by deductive reasoning, emulating a human expert solving a similar problem. The user interface provides interactive communication with the computer.

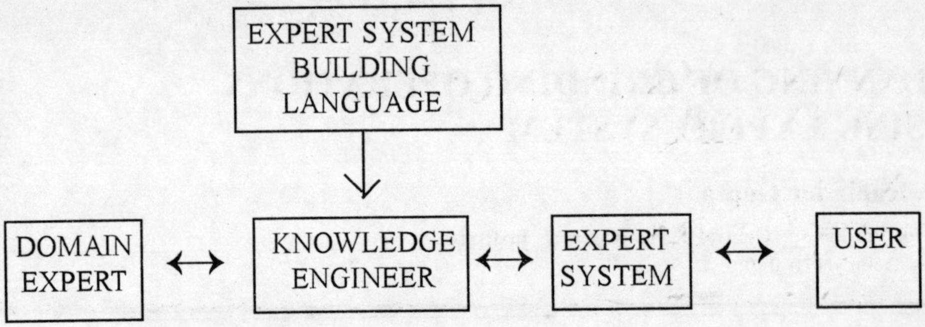

Fig. 1: Building Blocks of an Expert System

2. STRUCTURE OF AN EXPERT SYSTEM

The essential components of an expert system are a knowledge base, an inference engine and a user interface. All these components interact with each other roughly in the manner shown in Fig. 2. The commonly used methods of representing knowledge in the knowledge base are rule and frame based.[3] The generic structure of a rule is:

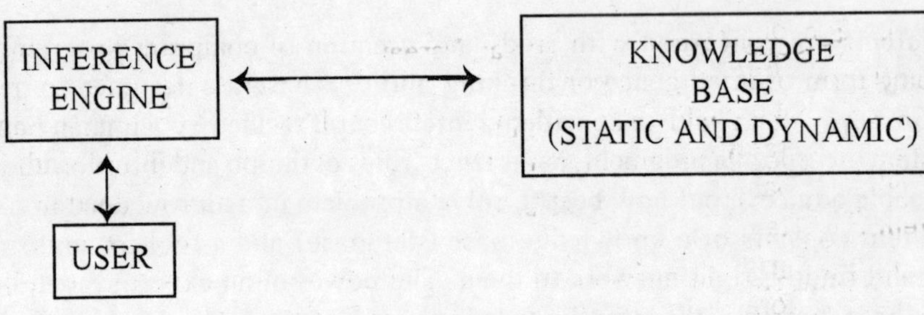

Fig. 2: Basic Structure of an Expert System

IF (Action) THEN (Conclusion). Heuristic knowledge, facts, and data can be represented using rules. The second type of knowledge representation uses a hierarchy of frames where each single frame is a 'template' that holds unit of data, facts, rules, hypothesis or knowledge.[8]

Two strategies called the forward chaining and backward chaining are commonly used for searching the data for a solution. In forward chaining, the system starts with known facts and searches the data to determine which rules are satisfied by the facts. The rules which are true lead to conclusion. The search is continued till a solution or a set of solution is found. During backward chaining, search proceeds backwards to support a goal or a hypothesis. Some systems use a combination of the above two strategies.[9]

The inference engine, also called the inference mechanism, performs two important tasks: first is reasoning or inferencing and the second controlling.[1] The inference process uses "IF-THEN" rules to manipulate facts and interpret rules. The control part determines the order in which rules are selected and "fired". The control mechanism has built-in means for limiting search.[10]

3. PROGRAMMING LANGUAGES

The early expert systems were written in special language interfaces derived from Fortran and LISP. Then languages such as ROSIE, KEE, OPS and PROLOG were developed. LISP and PROLOG are commonly used as these have been specially developed to handle symbolic computing. Of the two, PROLOG has come to be used more widely.

3.1 Prolog as a Programming Language

PROLOG is a declarative computer language as compared to procedural languages like FORTRAN and C. The programmer can locate a solution by inferences drawn from the facts and the rules. The execution of such a program does not follow a rigid algorithm, but depends upon the responses of the user and the database. The PROLOG language is based on predicate logic. It utilizes pattern matching, tail recursion and backward chaining to search the database. The inference of the rules is made from left to right and searched in a sequential order using depth-first strategy.[10] (For further study of the language reader may see references 10 and 11).

4. EXPERT SYSTEMS IN MANUFACTURING

The expert system approach has been successfully used in the fields of manufacturing[12-21] to select cutting tools, machining sequences, speeds, feeds etc. The expert system aproach has been used in selecting grinding parameters by various authors.[13, 14 & 19-21]

5. PLANNING OF GRINDING OPERATIONS

In general the selection of grinding parameters starts with the part or a data file that contains information on the work-piece. The workpiece data is processed to choose appropriate ginding machine, grinding wheel and inspection gauges etc. from available equipment. The grinding cycle parameters are selected so as to produce parts that meet the finished part specifications.

The grinding operation generates high temperatures in the work-piece with the gradient from the surface into the work-piece. The high temperature gives rise to thermal damage of the work-piece causing unfavourable residual stress. This condition can be avoided by monitoring the process for actual rate of power consumption. A sudden increase in input power would indicate the start of work-piece thermal damage.[22]

A computer programme to plan grinding parameters for surface, cylindrical and internal grinding developed by the author has been discussed elsewhere.[23] This programme in addition to suggesting grinding parameters also helps in selecting a machine and computes grinding cost. The programme also determines the condition at which there is likelyhood of thermal damage of the work-piece. Important features of the programme are discussed in the following paragraphs.

6. SELECTION OF GRINDING PARAMETERS

The programme built in Turbo Prolog version 2 language is supported by 'Tool Box' files to create menu functions automatically for questions with several alternative answers. The programme saves information gathered from the user and results of partial solutions obtained during the execution of the programme and builds a dynamic database. The dynamic database grows as the execution of the pgoramme proceeds. At the end of the consultation the dynamic database is deleted automatically.[11]

The databases have been built using information from research literature, catalogs of grinding wheel manufacturers and experts in the field. The database on grinding machines has been built using brochures of leading grinding machine manufactures. The present research work has been developed for ferrous materials as these are used extensively for producing ground components. Databases on cutting data, grinding wheels and material properties have been prepared.[24-26] The information has been stored in the form of rules and facts. The database on machines has been built using frames.

The programme consists of one main module and seven sub-modules as shown in Table 1. Three 'Tool Box' files have also been 'included' to create menu functions automatically. Each module performs the assigned task and saves the partial solution in the dynamic database.

7. AN EXAMPLE OF THE SYSTEM APPLICATION

The programme starts with an introduction followed by a query on the surface to be produced. The user enters the type of grinding required to produce the surface. Next the overall dimensions of the work-piece are queried. Then another module is automatically invoked to select machines capable of physically accommodating the work-piece. The user next selects one material from the displayed menu on materials. The material selection leads to automatic capturing of relevant properties of the work material from the database. The user is then asked to specify the hardness of the work material and the desired surface finish on the work-piece.

The programme then captures the values of cutting parameters, namely, infeed, work-speed, abrasive material, grain size and dress lead from the data-base. As an alternative the user may give his own values to these parameters.

TABLE 1: **Different Files in the System**

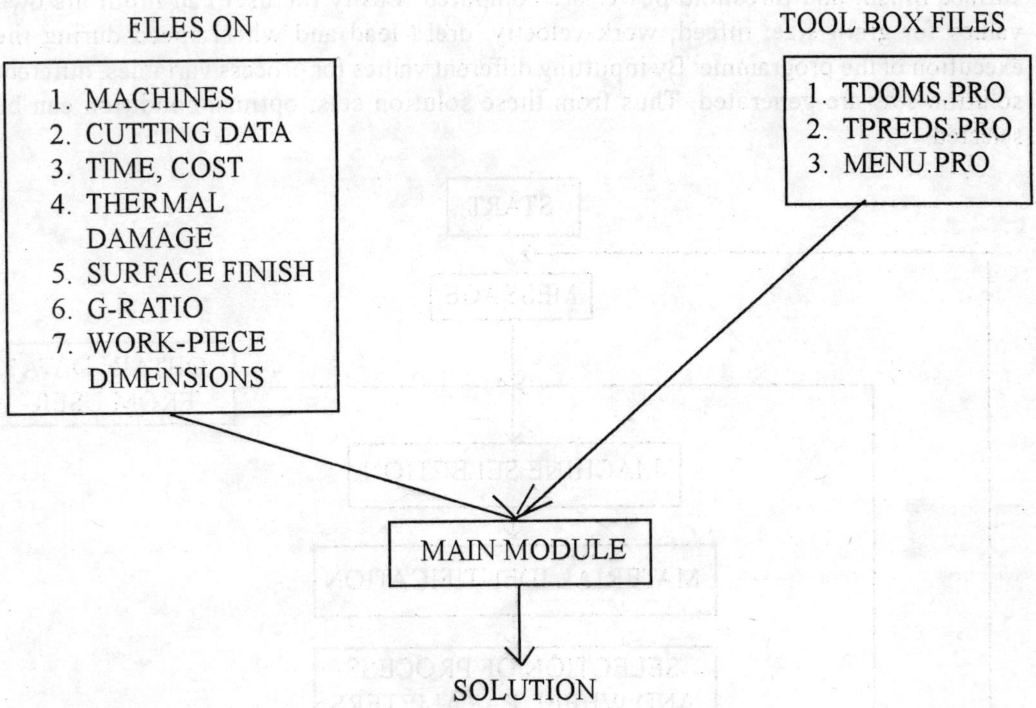

Then the user is asked to make a selection of a grinding machine from the list displayed by the programme. The dimensions of the grinding wheel are based on the size of the selected machine or the user can give wheel dimensions other than those recommended. Now the programme computes certain output variables, namely, the surface finish, g-ratio, grinding time, grinding cost per piece and the so called 'threshold power'. The g-ratio and threshold power are defined as the volume of material removed per unit volume of wheel wear and power beyond which there is a likely-hood of work-piece burn. The user is next given a choice to select an alternative machine for evaluation. When the code for a new machine is entered, a part of the dynamic databases saved subsequent to the selection of earlier machine is purged. The programme recomputes the output parameters. When the user finds a satisfactory solution, the consultation ends. The user can go in for another run of the programme if so desired. The flow diagram of the program is shown in Fig. 3.

8. OPTIMIZATION

The optimization strategy is to get high 'g-ratio' subject to production constraints. Firstly, if the system recommends more than one machine, iteration on machines will generate different solution sets. Secondly, the infeed suggested by the expert system is varied in small steps. For each infeed value grinding time, grinding cost per piece, g-ratio, surface finish, and threshold power are computed. Lastly the user can input his own values for grain size, infeed, work-velocity, dress lead and wheel speed during the execution of the programme. By inputting different values for process variables, different solution sets are generated. Thus from these solution sets, optimal condition can be selected.

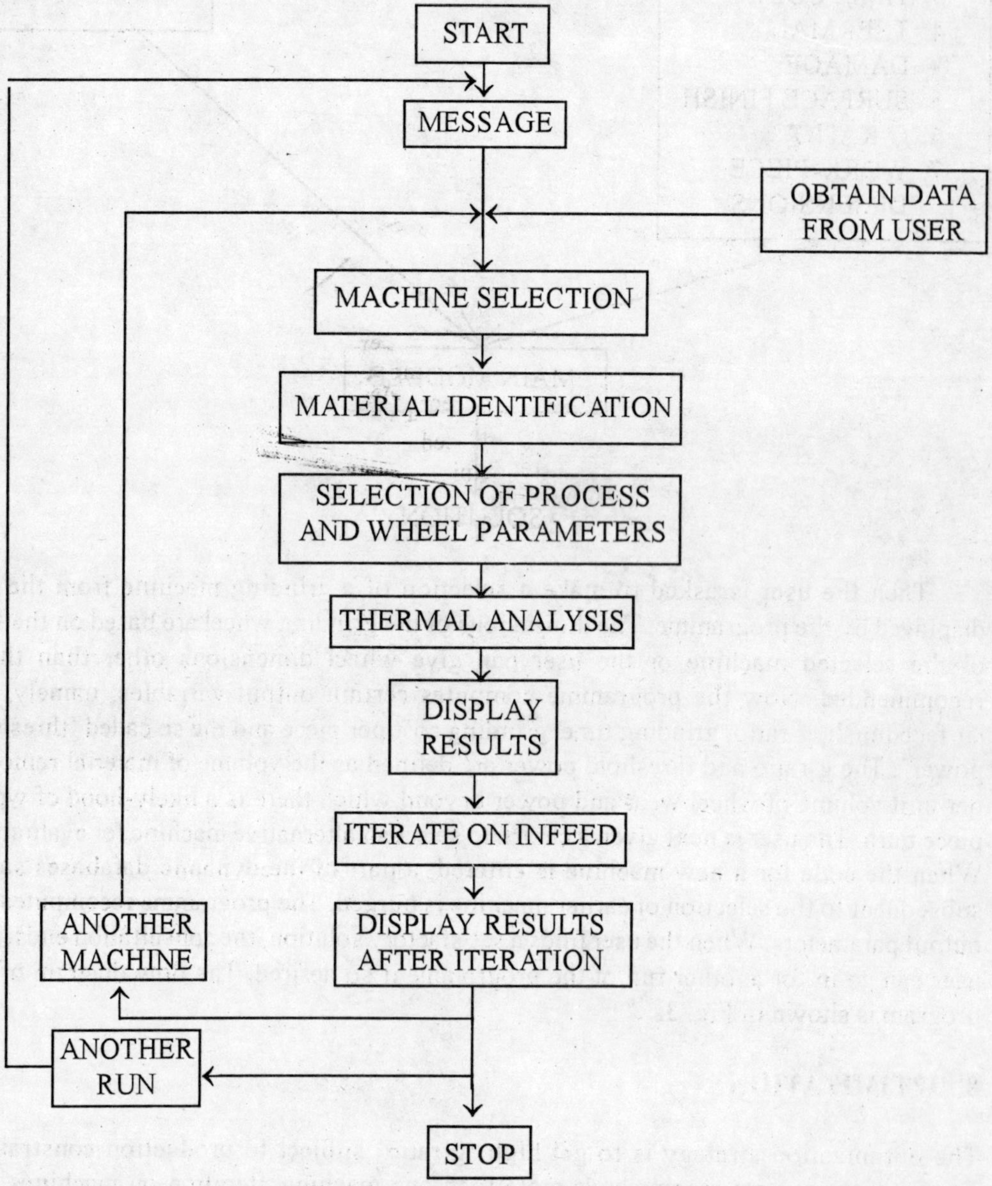

Figure 3: Flow Diagram of the System

9. SYSTEM VALIDATION

Table 2 shows the out-put of the system for a sample example.[27] The input parameters to the system were modified as per the data available in the example (column ii). The output parameters from the system and the results given in the example are in agreement.

TABLE 2: **System Validation for Cylindrical Grinding Work-piece**

WORK-PIECE SPECIFICATIONS

Diameter	38 mm
Final diameter	37.82 mm
Length	70 mm
Material	En 8
Material hardness	40 HRC (assumed)

	Parameters			
Column	i	ii	iii	iv
	Suggested by the system	Inputs to the system (from the user)	Final output of the system	Available results from the example
Abrasive			A1, wheel	A1, wheel
Grain size	60	60	—	60
Grade	—	—	i	k
Structure			5	5
Bond			V	V
Infeed mm	0.0125	0.0148	—	0.0148
Surface finish µm		0.4	0.353	—
Dressing lead mm/rev.	0.01	0.01	—	—
Wheel diameter mm	300	400		400
Workspeed m/min	25	14	—	14
Power safety Factor %	80	80	—	—
G-ratio			80	—
Threshold	—	—	40	42
Grinding energy				
Coolant			Dry or water soluble oil	water soluble oil

To get optimal grinding condition, the infeed is iterated in small steps by the programme itself. These values and other data are given in Table 3. The iterated values of the infeed give a number of solution sets. The user can then select a condition which meets his requirements.

TABLE 3: **Output Parametrs for Different Infeed Values**

PROCESS: CYLINDRICAL GRINDING

INPUT

Workpiece diameter	50 mm
Workpiece final diameter	49.85 mm
Workpiece length	200 mm
Material	En 14
Material hardness	55 HRC
Surface finish	0.5 μm
Grain size	60
Infeed	0.0125 mm
Dress lead	0.05 mm
Wheel diameter	250 mm
Wheel thickness	25 mm
Workspeed	28 m/min

OUTPUT (PREDICTED)

INFEED mm	G-RATIO	SURFACE FINISH μm	GRINDING TIME Sec.
0.01	67.5	0.30	39
0.0125	54	0.34	31
0.015	45	0.37	26
0.0175	38.5	0.40	22
0.0075	90	0.29	52

10. CONCLUSION

Grinding operations can be successfully planned using expert system. A computer programme written in Turbo Prolog has been developed which selects various grinding parameters and computes the condition at which thermal damage of the work-piece is likely to occur. Optimal condition can by achieved by iteration on the grinding machines and the input parameters.

11. ACKNOWLEDGEMENT

Thanks are due to Prof. G.S. Sekhon and Prof. K.S. Shishodia, IIT, Delhi for their guidance in the preparation of this paper and the Director, Central Road Research Institute, Delhi for granting permission to publish this paper.

REFERENCES

1. Waterman, D.A., *A Guide to Expert Systems*, Reading MA, Addison Wesley Publishing Co., 1985.
2. Shortliffe, E., *Computer Based Medical Consultation: MYCIN*, Elsevier, New York, 1976
3. Hayes-Roth, F., (1976), *The Knowledge Based Expert System: A Tutorial*, Computer, Vol. 98, pp. 11-28.
4. Sohlenius, G. and Kjellberg, T., (1986), Artificial Intelligence and its Potential Use in the Manufacturing System, *Annals of the CIRP* 35/2, pp. 425-32.
5. Chryssolouris, G., Wright, K., (1986), Knowledge Based Systems in Manuf., *Annals of CIRP*, Vol. 35/2, pp. 437-39.
6. Merchant, M.E., (1994), Manufacturing in the 21st Century, *J. Mater. Process Technol.*, 44 (1994), pp. 145-55.
7. Rowe, B., *et al.* (1994), Applications of Artificial Intelligence in Grinding, *CIRP Annals*, 43/2, pp. 521-31.
8. Mockler, R. Jr., *Knowledge Based System for Management Decisions*, (1987), Prentice Hall, New Jersy.
9. Kinnucan, P., (1984), *Computers that Think Like Experts, High Technology*, Vol. 1, Jan. 1984), pp. 30-42.
10. Clocksin, W.F. and Mellish, C.S., (1989), *Programming in Prolog*, Narosa Publishing House, New Delhi.
11. Rich, K.M. and Robinson, P.R., *Using Turbo Prolog*, Berkeley, CAL., Borland Osborne/McGraw Hill, 1988.
12. Barkocy, B.E. and Zdeblic, W.J., (1984), *A Knowledge Based System for Machining Operation Planning*, Conf. Pr. Autofact, October 1-4, 1984, Anahein, Cal., pp. 2-11 to 2-25.
13. Gupta, R., *et al.* (1996), CAP-GO: Computer Aided Planning of Grinding Operations for Ferrous Components, *J. of Mater Proc. Tech.*, 65 (1997), pp. 34-40.
14. Gopalakrishnan, B., (1989), "Computer Integrated Machining Parameter Selection in a Job Shop Using Expert Systems, *J. of Mech. Working Technology*, 20, pp. 163-70.
15. Zhu, C.B. et al. (1993), A Dynamic Modelling Approach to Computer Aided Optimum Selection of Grinding Parameters, *J. of Mater. Proc. Tech.*, Vol. 38, pp. 227-46.
16. Gordon, S. (1988), Surfex: An Expert System for 3-D Surface Machining Data, Advances in Manufacturing Technology, III, Proc. of Fourth National Conf. on Production Research, Sheffield City Polytechnic, Sheffield, 1988.
17. Press, K. and Kaplansky, E. (1984), *Automated CNC Milling by Artificial Intelligence Methods*, Conf. Pr. Autofact 6, Oct. 1-4, 1984, Anaheim, Cal. pp. 2-40 to 2-59.
18. Alder, G.M., *et al.* (1986), Selection of Machining Processes by Intelligent Knowledge Based Systems, International Conf., *Computer Aided Production Engineering*, Ed. J.A. Mc Geough Edinburg-April 1986, pp. 61-66.
19. Venk, S. and Govind, R. (1990), An Expert System Approach to Optimization of the Centreless Grinding Process, *Annals of the CIRP*, Vol. 30/1, pp. 489-92.

20. Midha, P.S., et al. (1991), Optimum selection of grinding parameters using process modelling and knowledge based system approach, *J. of Mater. Proc. Tech.*, 28, pp. 189-98.
21. Wen, X.M. et al. (1992), "Micro-Computer based optimization of the surface grinding process", *J. of Material Processing Technology*, Vol. 29, pp. 75-89.
22. Malkin, S., *Grinding Technology, Theory and Applications of Machining with Abrasives*, Ellis Horwood, 1989.
23. Gupta, R., *Computer Aided Planning of Grinding Operations for Ferrous Components*, (1995), Ph.D. Thesis, I.I.T. Delhi.
24. Central Machine Tool Institute (1987), Bangalore, *Machine Design Hand Book*, Tata McGraw Hill, New Delhi.
25. *Machining Data Handbook*, 3rd edition, Vol. 2, Machinability Data Center, Metcut Research Associates, Inc., Cincinnati, Ohio, 1980.
26. Smithells, C.J., *Metals Hand Book*, Vol. II, Butterworth Scientific Publications, London, 1955.
27. Row, W.B., et al. (1988), Avoidance of thermal damage in grinding and prediction of the damage threshold, *Annals of the CIRP*, Vol. 37/1, pp. 327-30.

MANUFACTURING REQUIREMENTS FOR DEFENCE APPLICATIONS WITH SPECIAL EMPHASIS ON REPAIR OF IN SHIPS

7

A.V. Ramesh[1] and Ramesh K. Pillai[2]

Manager (Engineering),[1]
Naval Ship Repair Ward, Kochi.

Deputy Manager (Engineering)[2]
Naval Ship Repair Ward, Cochi.

1. INTRODUCTION

The Indian Navy has a high profile presence in the Asian region and is highly regarded around the world. The Naval dock yards are vital to make this possible. India has been traditionally a maritime nation and handles considerable amount of sea trade. The commercial ship yards are vital to maintain it so. Both types of yards have to invest in emerging new technology to keep pace with modern times. This paper looks at a few areas of emerging technology and presents the importance of making a begining in investing in them.

Those, in the industry, who are not already dealing with the Indian Navy may be unaware of the way the Naval Dockyards operate. Hence the salient aspects of the methods of operation are presented briefly. Though there is considerable interaction between the Navy and the industry already, there is of scope for further improvement. These areas and the problems encountered are discussed from the Navy's perspective. It is hoped that this paper kindles the interest of the corporate world and leads to more synergetic cooperation between the Navy and the industry.

2. FUNCTION OF NAVAL YARDS

The Indian Navy has dockyards at Mumbai and Visakhapatnam and Repair Yards at Kochi and Port Blair. The function of these is to keep the Indian Naval ships operational and fighting fit. These yards are predominantly staffed by civilian personnel with naval officers in the managerial cadre. The success of these yards is evident from the high operational availability of Indian Naval Ships.

3. CONCEPT

The Indian Navy follows the concept of planned preventive maintenance due to which ships follow cycles consisting of operational phases followed by maintenance phases. The periodicity of the cycles depend upon the type of the ship. The various maintenance periods are called Self-Maintenance Periods, Assisted Maintenance Periods, Short Refits, Normal Refits, Medium Refits and Long Refit/Modernization Refit/D2 Refit.

4. REFITS

Refits are periods when major maintenance and repair work are undertaken. The work package in a refit consists of :

(a) Planned Preventive Work,
(b) Defects observed during the operational phase, and
(c) Additions and Alterations which enhance the operational efficiency of the ship.

5. SHIPS ARE DRY DOCKED DURING REFITS TO CARRY OUT MAINTENANCE/REPAIR WORK IN THE UNDERTAKEN AREAS

6. OPERATIONAL DEFECTS

In contrast to refits which are planned in advance, the dockyards have to undertake rectification of defects which occur during the operational phase of ships. This work is unplanned and unpredictable in nature. Maintenance units are positioned in dockyards exclusively to deal with such work. The work beyond the capacity of these units has to be undertaken by the dockyards. This places a strain on dockyards particularly if the number and nature of defects is large at a time when yards are operating near their capacity with scheduled work.

7. ORGANIZATION

The dockyards are broadly organized into:

(a) Planning group which plans the flow of work and issues necessary work orders.
(b) Production group which undertakes the actual repair work.
(c) Technical group which looks after dockyard maintenance, augmentation projects, yard utility etc.
(d) Quality assurance group.
(e) Personnel and administration group.
(f) Material procurement group.

In addition to these the dockyards also have:

(a) A division looking after provision of boats, ferries and movement of ships in harbour.
(b) Medical division.
(c) Security division.

8. METHOD OF OPERATION

The refits of ships consist of complex work packages which require enormous amount of planning, scheduling and monitoring. The complexity is further increased due to the fact that more than one ship is normally under refit at any given time and all these vie for the same work facilities. The dockyards follow the Refit Planning Programme which defines the steps to be followed so that various activities like processing and consolidating defect list, estimating and demanding spares, planning and issuing of work instructions etc. can be done in an organized manner.

9. CIVILIAN PERSONNEL

The dockyards employ a very large number of civilian personnel. These form the permanent part of work force with the service personnel posted to the dockyards being rotated after relatively shorter periods. All the industrial rules applicable in civilian industries are applicable in Naval Dockyards. Recognized trade unions are allowed to operate. Shop committees, work committees and joint consultative machinery are existent. It can be stated that by and large excellent relationship exists between the labour and management.

10. CONTRAST WITH CIVIL SHIP YARDS

The differences between Civil and Naval ship yards are:

(a) Expertise for repair of Weapon systems and submarines exist in Naval dockyards only,
(b) The number of unscheduled jobs of operational nature are very large as compared to a civil dockyard which tends to strain existing facilities and disrupt carefully planned refits.
(c) Naval dockyards handle sensitive work and are privy to information that can be classed as highly sensitive to national security.
(d) Operational availability of ships takes precedence over everything else for Naval Dockyards.
(e) Naval Officers constitute almost the entire management setup of dockyards. However there is frequent turnover of officers manning the dockyards with average tenures of around 3 years.

11. COMMERCIAL SHIP YARDS

The long 5900 km coast line of India contains 11 major ports and about 140 minor ports. Our country has the largest merchant shipping fleet among the developing countries and ranks fifteenth in the world in shipping tonnage. To cater for the repair and maintenance of our considerable merchant fleet we have four major and three medium size ship yards in the public sector and about thirty-five small ship yards in the private sector. Thirteen dry docks are available for commercial ship repair activities out of which the dry dock at Cochin ship yard is the largest being capable of accommodating about 1,00,000 DWT ships.

12. EMERGING TECHNOLOGY

A global survey reveals the emergence of new technologies and the refinement of existing technologies at a pace faster than the pace at which it can be absorbed and utilised in ship yards. Awareness of such technology is the first step towards absorbing and utilising it. The importance of modernising and using new technology needs no emphasis if our ship repair industry is to stay in the fore front and be globally competitive. Though it is impossible to record all such emerging technology in a paper like this, a few areas of current research are mentioned below.

(a) Metal Work

Rapid strides are being made in areas of hull work such as:

(i) In order to reduce handling of smaller plates and associated welding related problems the trend is towards profile cutting of very large sections of plate i.e., "one piece manufacturing" using laser portal system as against the conventional thermal cutting using oxy acetylene or plasma. The problems related to handling such large sections requires use of special systems like the Dual Walking Beam developed by Total Transportation System (TTS), Norway.

(ii) Welding speeds are on the increase with the use of high speed welding by the Rapid Arc/Rapid Melt welding process. This results in an increase of production upto three times from the current rate.

(iii) Improvements are also taking place in cutting of curved blocks like the line cutting system being used by Odense Lindo Ship Yard in Denmark.

(iv) Non-infinitely rotating plasma heads for bevel cuts required for weld edge preparation are the latest in plating work field.

(b) Corrosion and Coatings

The emergence of new and stricter legislations is spurring the development of technology to combat corrosion. The traditional sand or grit blasting constitutes a health hazard for the workers particularly if it is to be used in confined spaces. The new Ultra High Pressure Hydroblasting (UHP) system is making inroads in surface preparation. Slurry blasting is also a technology that is being tried out. With modern passenger ships having large glass covered areas, new techniques in glass surface protection are being used. New barnacle protection fluids are also being tried out against the conventional underwater painting schemes.

(c) New Materials

Research has always been directed towards development of new materials to replace steel in ship building. Some of the materials to make inroads in the areas where steel has been used are Nomex and Kevlar independently or in combination, glass—Kevlar combination GRP and FRP. GRP has been extensively used in minesweepers and boats. The recent use of GRP is to make composite drive shafts which offers advantages of higher specific strength and elastic flexibility leading to reduction in number of flexible couplings, plummer bearings and ability to follow hull deformation truthfully. There are a lot research projects currently going on in the use of new materials. The outcome of three of these by TNO (Netherland's Organisation for Applied Scientific Research) CMC (Centre for Mechanical Research) mentioned below are eagerly awaited by shipping industry. These are

(a) DYCOSS (Dynamic Behavior of Composite Ship Structures)
(b) EUCLTD (European Cooperation for Long Term in Defence)
(c) MATSTRUSS (Materials and Structures for Surface Effect Ships)

(d) Automation

The use of robotics to undertake complex metal work and other jobs is on the increase. The latest use is for machining of propeller profiles by Multicraft, Oslo. The Korean and Danish Ship yards are increasingly switching over to robotics due to an anticipated shortfall of skilled welders in future. This also results in reduction of manufacturing costs and also frees workers of unhealthy work.

(e) Software

Software development applicable to ship repair management has always been in the forefront of emerging technologies. Complete packages are available which deal with tendering, costing, work estimating, project scheduling and monitoring and the whole gamut of managerial work from start to finish of ship building. Also the software TRIBON by Kockum Computer Systems, Sener's FORAN software and developments by IBM and Dassault are noteworthy.

(f) Surface Engineering

The concept of surface engineering, i.e., the production of surfaces to meet particular application requirements, from hull to galley hot plates, is also being addressed to currently.

(g) Information Technology and Electronics

The explosion of information technology and its effective integration with ships is a topic of current development. Electronics has always been in the fore front of development world wide and latest developments are finding their way into shipping industry also. The use of latest engine monitoring systems, platform management and control system are example these. All the major navies of the world are also developing and perfecting their weapon systems and sensors.

(h) Propulsion Systems

New machinery configurations are finding increasing applications. Use of electric drive in either geared or direct mode and pod/thruster propulsion are being experimented with against the conventional shaft line drives. Developments in the field diesel engines like sequential turbo charging, intercooling, exhaust pulsing and gas turbines like improved combustor and recuperator design, variable area nozzles are mention worthy. Research is also on in the areas of closed cycle diesel and gas turbines and fuel cells.

13. APPLICATION OF NEW TECHNOLOGY IN INDIAN SHIP REPAIR INDUSTRY

In India, we have always been lagging behind the industrial nations in both development and application of new technology in many fields. The ship repair industry is no exception. The clear lead enjoyed by Korean, Japanese, Danish and British shipping industry is due to the use of such cutting edge technology besides better management skills. These nations invest heavily is research and enjoy the fruits of the return. They keep an open mind and are always looking for means of improving quality of production and productivity.

Ship building is not a profit making business in India and the ship building yards are using their assets for ship repair. Even in this we are hot technologically competitive. Unless we can find the ways and means for effective use of new technology, we will not be able to improve productivity and bring down costs.

As new technology is costly, a beginning can be made in adoption of those which do not require a major change in the infrastructural setup. Such technology is bound to pay for itself in the medium term. Technology which requires high investment and major infrastructural changes should be looked at judicially and should be invested in depending upon the returns expected in the long term. In any case, the ship repair business is on an upswing currently and any investment in new technology can easily be recuperated as profits within a reasonable time frame.

14. INTERACTION BETWEEN NAVY AND CIVIL INDUSTRY

There has always been a healthy and positive interaction between the Navy and civil industry. With the collapse of the Soviet Union and the consequent problems in the supply of spares to the Indian Navy, the avenues of interaction have been considerably increased. This is the time for Indian industry to step in and fill the vacuum created. If the industry can take on the job of providing spares manufactured as per the Navy's specification, a vast market can be tapped. A few examples of items of interest to the Navy are:

(a) Diesel, steam and gas turbine components.
(b) H.P and L.P air compressors and components.
(c) Pumps for firemain, ballast and other application and their components.
(d) Oil and water centrifuges and components.
(e) Components for air conditioning and refrigerating systems.
(f) Piping, valves, cocks, etc., for a variety of systems like sea water, fresh water, fuel, lub oil, air etc.
(g) All types of electrical and electronic components.
(h) Materials such as castiron, steel, aluminium, brass etc., in sheet, bar, ingot forms.
(i) A variety of rubber products.

The list is only indicative and by no means exhaustive. The Navy already has a considerable supply network for the items required by it. But there is room for many more from the Industry to join in and augment the supply base.

15. PROBLEM AREAS

There have been certain problem areas whenever the Navy has interacted with civil trade and which new entrants must be aware of. They are:

(a) Quality

The Navy places a very high emphasis on quality. Quality could make the difference between life and death for personnel on board and between victory and defeat in war. Till a few years ago, this stringent requirement for quality used to present problems when accepting service/spares from the civil trade. With other navies of the world converting to the use of equipment available "off the shelf", the Indian Navy has also modified quality requirements so that industrial products can be readily used. Simultaneously, the quality of industrial products has also steadily gone up and the difference between the naval requirement and general industrial standard has reduced considerably.

(b) Inflated Cost

The costs quoted by the civil trade are sometimes very exorbitant and unjustified. This happens particularly in the case of the small time contractors who hope to make easy money at the Navy's expense. It is seen that they donot analyse the scope of work properly leading to either overquoting and losing the contract or underquoting and acquiring loss. In the case of the latter, the tendency is to overquote on the next contract to make good the loss and losing credibility altogether.

(c) Middlemen or Agents

It is seen that middlemen or agents operate between the actual supplier and the Navy. Many of the established firms are not willing to deal with the Navy in cases where order quantity is small. There is a general perception that the Navy's payment system is slow and complicated. This leaves room for the agents to operate. Navy is aware of this problem and is making efforts to eliminate it. If more established firms are willing to deal with the Navy directly agents can be avoided and costs reduced there by benefiting both the Navy and the industry.

(d) Red Tape

The Navy like any other government organisation, has to operate within a set of rules and regulations, most of which are necessary. These tend to make the process of dealing with the Industry slow and cumbersome and give rise, in part, to situations amenable for the operation of agents and inflated costs. The government and the Navy have been steadily making efforts the reduce the red tape. Financial powers and decision-making powers have been considerably decentralised leading to a more comfortable operating environment. Navy is fighting hand to make the new management strategy work and if the results are satisfactory, greater decentralisation can be expected.

16. CONCLUSION

The Navy and the commercial shipyards in India are at a point in time when big winds of change are sweeping across the whole nation. Deregulation, privatisation and economic reforms are transforming the way traditional business was transacted in India. These changes cannot be ignored. Modernisation and adopting new technology is one of the ways to stay ahead.

Indian Navy is in a position where an interaction with the industry can be beneficial to both. The spectrum of opportunities for industrial interaction is very large—from participating in warship building to supply of nuts and bolts. If the industry and the Navy sit together and discuss all these areas could be analysed and the bottlenecks towards better participation can be eliminated. Those industrial players who have not considered dealing with the Navy will be surprised at the market available for them. The degree of interaction can be increased from what it is at present to much high level. In that position the Navy, commercial ship yards and supporting industry can step into a more confident twenty-first century.

MANUFACTURING REQUIREMENTS FOR DEFENCE APPLICATIONS

8

Major C.P. Venkatesalu

DADEME, HQS, Northern Command, C/O 56 APO.

GENERAL

1. The weapon systems and equipment in the Armed Forces cover a wide spectrum of technology. They are generally multi-disciplinary in nature. The level of technology and degree of sophistication of the military hardware depends mainly on the vintage and country of origin. The major activity in the Army Base Workshop is to overhaul these weapon systems and equipment which include efficient management of various inputs, the major one being the adequate supply of correct spare parts/components, besides a large number of other complex aspects of overhaul. Non-availability of spare parts, particularly in the case of imported weapon systems and equipment and the inventory carrying cost have been a cause of serious concern at all levels of maintenance management in the Army demanding a meaningful, immediate and cost-effective solution.

AIM

2. Aim of this paper will be to discuss the reclamation technology specific to Defence applications.

A CASE FOR RECLAMATION

3. There has been an on-going debate on restoring system reliability after overhaul through out-right replacement of worn out components or through reclamation-repair. Smart decisions have been arrived at in the light of situational facts listed above in favour of reclamation repair for reasons listed below:

(a) Reclamation technology provides for not only restoring of functional characteristics of mechanical spare parts/components, be it metallic or no metallic, but also enhancement of performance (Life Prolonging Factor (LPF) in large number of cases, thus faithfully meeting the qualitative requirements of system reliability at normal process cost.

(b) Reclamation helps in reducing the cost of inventory of spare parts and carrying of the same, thus bringing in cost-effectiveness in maintenance management.

(c) Reclamation helps in conservation of natural resources by allowing recycling of worn-out/scrapped spare parts which otherwise would have been consigned to scarp yard, thus slowing down depletion of resources.

(d) Reclamation helps in improving availability of spare parts/components, thus salvaging a situation of scarcity, particularly in the case of imported weapon systems and equipment where the problem has been compounded because of uncertainty in global political conditions.

STATE-OF-THE-ART: RECLAMATION TECHNOLOGY

4. There have been great advancements in the reclamation technology over the last two decades or so. Peculiar qualitative requirements of military hardware have brought in variety of materials i.e. metals, alloys and non-metals like iron, aluminium cobalt, chromium, nickel, plastics etc. Reclamation of spare parts/components has been successfully done employing state-of-the-art techniques such as Thermal Spray Technology, Electrodeposition. No Heat Molecular Welding etc. The pace of development in this fields has been encouraging the world over including indigenous developments. As regards the availability of technical know-how, associated equipment and consumables, a large number of firms in the country in collaboration with their principals abroad, like M/S Larsen & Turbo Ltd., Advani-Oerlikon Ltd., ESAB India Ltd., Garrard Plasma Systems Ltd. and many others in the field are serving the consumers in industry and defence against a reasonable degree of competitions.

RECLAMATION USING WELDING PROCESS

5. During the last two centuries or so, welding technology has evolved into a sophisticated science not only to join metal parts together but also to re-inforce them with strength that could withstand tremendous operational stresses for applications in industry, defence and space. Today, the state-of-the-are techniques can be employed to join any metal parts of any shape, size, thickness, composition etc. The technology has been effectively adopted for repair/reclamation of critical and expensive metal parts, components and tools. The process could be used with equal success for rotating/non-rotating parts. The basic steps in the process include rebuilding of worn-out portion of the component and appropriate machining to required specifications using approved application procedures (APP) and consumables. The techniques have been developed to perfection to overcome the traditional limitations of welding process. Some of the important techniques have been discussed as representative cases. Thermal spray processes like wire metallising, metal power spraying or plasma spraying are widely accepted techniques to rebuild worn-out machinery parts and to salvage mis-machined

components. METCO (USA), DEGUSSA (Germany), FONTAGEN (Switzerland), Eutectic-Castolin Institute with its R&D centres located throughout the world are some of the leaders in development and practice of these techniques. These organisations have revolutionalised the concepts of maintenance management and are adequately represented within this country for production/marketing of their products and providing training. The techniques are compatible for jobs on almost all kinds of metals and their alloys under various trade marks and patents.

NO HEAT-MOLECULAR WELDING

6. Special repair and reclamation techniques are available using epoxymetal-ceramic materials for recycling of worn-out metallic/non-metallic spare parts. The techniques do not require any heating of the job and could be successfully employed at room temperatures. However, the process maturing could be accelerated by using recommended temperatures. The process usually consists of two components, one being the hardening compound and the other could be suitably selected to meet a particular application. The components are mixed and then applied over the worn-out or corroded surface. The surface so obtained has required mechanical properties and could be machined suitable for appropriate shape/size. The technique is universal and could be used for rotating/non-rotating parts. A variety of such products are freely available ex-trade under different patents and trade marks. MECATEC (L&T), BELZONE (UK/US) are a few examples of this cold repair and reclamation system. Process of electro-plating is also used for reclamation by providing metal depositions of fine metallic layer like hard-chrome plating. Reclamation of rubber components is done using techniques like BELZONA ELASTOMERS (UK/US) or any equivalent system.

MAJOR AREAS OF APPLICATION

7. Major areas of application of reclamation techniques in the Army Base Workshop are 'B' vehicles. 'A' vehicles (including tracked vehicles of Ad Weapon Systems), engineer equipment, instruments etc. Choice of appropriate technique could work wonders to overcome the serious problem of non-availability of spare parts. Specific areas which have been identified and tackled successfully in many areas which have been identified and tackled successfully in many Army Base Workshops are mainly pertaining to engine, transmission system, brakes, body etc. of vehicles, armaments and other weapon systems. The actuals could run into thousands, the will to work could be the only constraint. The issue of reclamation of mechanical components of Schilka and Kavdrat AD Weapon Systems has been closely examined in 510 Army Base Workshop over the years and specific applications have been successfully identified and tackled using EUTALLOY and Rototec Techniques of M/s Larson & Toubro Ltd.

CONCLUSION

8. Spare parts are a major input for overhaul of weapon systems and equipment of the Army at the Army Base Workshops. These are costly and in short supply, particularly in the case of imported systems. Reclamation technology provides an answer to these problems which not only caters for requirements of system reliability but also results in appreciable savings, besides adding to conservation of resources by recycling process. In the Army Base Workshops reasonable work has already been done in this area using indigenous or imported techniques. Certainly much more could be done in this field by suitably harnessing the technological advancements in this specialised area.

RECLAMATION AND REBUILDING OF COMPONENTS THROUGH COLD PROCESSING

9

Major C.P. Venkatesalu

DADEME, HQS, Northern Command, C/O 56 APO.

INTRODUCTION

1. In any kind of industry using different kinds of plant and machinery wear & tear is inevitable. If this wear & tear is not arested/prevented, it may lead to replacement of expensive machinery/components or parts. It is not economical to go for the replacement so frequently in developing like ours.

2. Apart from the cost of investments, any replacement involves expensive down time of the machinery thus leading to loss of production. It is, therefore, necessary to rebuild/condition the machinery/components and thereby prolong the life of the equipment.

3. Recently cold curing/reactive resins have been used to rebuild/reclaim these worn out parts/damaged parts as an alternative to conventional methods of maintenance.

WEAR-CAUSES AND EFFECTS

4. There are different forms of common wear and tear these are:

(a) Mechanical wear,
(b) Errosion/Corrosion,
(c) Impingent Attack, and
(d) Cavitation.

5. While the later three occur primarily in fluid handling situations due to a combination of electrochemical & hydrodynamic factors, the first type occurs in any type of machinery either due to continuous operation due to imbalance & accident.

6. The result of all these types of wear is the same i.e. *Eating away of the substrate*. To maintain this it is necessiates.

(a) The deposit of the substrate,
(b) Further protection to prevent/delay the reccurence of wear.

Re-deposition of Substrate

7. In conventional method this is achieved by welding techniques, which results in development of thermal stresses in the component & requires post application operation.

8. In cold/reactive resin technology, there are no thermal stresses as it is a normal cold process & even the post application operations are minimised.

Cold Repair Technique

9. Chemical reactions occur when reactive moleciles are brought together. In some cases reaction starts spontaneously but an amount of energy known as 'energy of activation' is require to initiate the reaction which is sgenerally provide by external heating. This is not desireable from repair/maintenance point of view. Certain chemical reactive resins have been developed to react at O C. Thus resulting in cold repair technique. These resins are mixed with hardners in various proportion to give optimum performance for various type of job.

10. In conventional welding the redeposition of worn out substrate takes place by the process of interlayer fusion. In the cold repair technique this occur by mechanical & electrical adhesion between the resin & the original substrate. The bonding is critical.

11. The cold repair is carried out in following three stages :

(a) Pre application,
(b) Application,
(c) Post application.

Pre Application

12. As adhesion/bonding is the most crucial, hence in this type of repair preparation of surface is of utmost importance. This is done in following manner :

(a) Clean and degrease the general area.
(b) Abrade and roughten the abration area.
(c) Degrease the repair area immediately prior to applica tion. Cleaning & degreasing process to be carried out as per direction of the product being used.
(d) Roughening/abrading could be done by any of the following method :

(i) Abbrasive blasting using various blasting material like steel slag, steel grit, silicon carbide,
(ii) Needle Gunning,
(iii) Grinding,
(iv) Filing,
(v) Rought machining,

(vi) Wire brushing,
(vii) Hand abrading.

Application

13. These resins normally consist of two components i.e base and hardner. Following points to be observed in application stage:

(i) Mixing of base and hardner in the correct proportion as per specification for all types of job.
(ii) Thorough uniform mixing.
(iii) Use of mixure weithin the time limits specified.

Post Application

14. To restore the correct profile the component will be required to be :

(a) Machined,
(b) Moulded weith formers.

In case of moulding care to be taken to complete the operation weithin the working life of the compound & also release agents to be applied to the formers used to present their bonding to the resin.

Typical Application

15. (a) Fractured/damaged sumps.
(b) Cracked engine blockss and gear boxes.
(c) Worn bush housing, corroded alternator housing.
(d) Repairing cracked/holed bodies.
(e) Re-seating sealing rings.
(f) Re-building fractured sections.

CONCLUSION

16. The cold reactive resins can be used to rebuild/reclaim/recondition the worn/fracture part/machinery. This method is much more effective & simple than the conventional reclamation method (Re welding) as there is no thermal stress involved. The compound can also be formed and machined and hence any kind of job/component can be reconditioned at minimal cost.

INDIGENISATION OF HIGH PRESSURE RUBBER SEALS/PACKING RINGS

10

Capt. Hans Raj Chandel

Workshop Officer, Station Workshop,
EME, Type 'D', Post Box No. 43, Allahabad-311 001, U.P.

INTRODUCTION

The post independence scenario of our country has seen the induction of a large variety of equipment into our defence forces. Bulk of the imports have been from East European countries. Due to financial constraints the equipment imported is used far beyond its life expectancy. This leads to a shortfall of spares imported which had catered for a specified period. Subsequent endeavours to procure more spares is time consuming and is dependent on diplomatic relations with the country at that time. This has had more relevance since the breakup of the Soviet Union and formation of independent nations of CIS. Perforce we have to develop self-reliance by indigenising these spares.

Sustenance of these imported equipment during their service life depends to a large extent on the regular supply of Engineering Support Materials (ESM). It has been observed that the country of origin neither parts with the technical knowhow nor drawings. In addition requirements projected to them are not fully met. To cope with the situation there is a need to appreciate the problem, identify options and initiate immediate action so as to ensure that a regular flow of ESM is maintained.

DGQA has been indigenising most of the spare parts of import origin equipment. However, it is extremely difficult for DGQA to indigenise all the items required for both overhaul and field maintenance requirements in range and depth. Majority of the imported equipment comprise of hydraulic and preumatic systems where rubber seals/ packing rings are used; and these are subjected to high pressures. Often these seals give way under pressure and have to be replaced. They are also changed at regular periodicity to ensure serviceability of the equipment.

AIM

To examine the existing system of indigenisation of high pressure rubber seals/packing rings and suggest measures taken by the Corps of EME.

GENERAL

The process of indigenisation by Army Base Workshops can be reviewed under the following heads :

(a) DGQA's definition of indigenisation.
(b) Present system of indigenisation.
(c) Limitation of present system.
(d) Proposed system.

DGQA'S DEFINITION OF INDIGENISATION

A product is deemed to have been indigenised if and when at least two manufactures haver started its free flow production using material available in the country.

EXISTING SYSTEM OF INDIGENISATION BY DGQA

The requirement of spares for various foreign origin equipment is worked out by the Ordnance Depot based on the provision review and a Draft Depot List (DDL) is made. These lists are made equipment and country-wise on a yearly basis.

The DDLs are then subjected to vetting by the concerned AHSP for correctness of Part No. nomenclature and applicability. After vetting the list, it is forwarded to the Technical Sub Committee (TC). The Committee is headed by DHGQA rep and attended by EME and Ordnance rep as members. The details of the composition of TCs is given below:

(a)	Chairman	—		Controller Quality Assurance
(b)	Members	—	(i)	Dy. Controller concerned discipline
			(ii)	MAG
			(iii)	Rep of concerned depot
			(iv)	ACDA

The TC reviews the list and earmarks the non free flow items for import or indigenisation, either through trade or manufacture by EME/Depot. The criteria adopted for selection of times to be indigenised are as under:

(a) Availability of samples/drawings.
(b) Availability of raw materials.
(c) Manufacturing process.
(d) Criticality of the times.
(e) Status of the items.

Depending upon the capacity and ability of the Army Base Workshops, EME selects the items for manufacture in the Base Workshops. Headquarters, Technical Group EME nominates the workshop for undertaking the manufacture and same is communicated to the concerned Ordnance Depots. On receipt of immitation regarding nomination of the Army Base Workshops, the depot places the workorder at the periodicity decided mutually; in monthly/fortnightly/weekly batches.

The DDL is forwarded to the Technical Committee for their approval. The approval proforma for various courses of procurement recommended by the sub-committee is cleared by the Technical Committee. Final Depot List (FDL) is then prepared for times planned to be indigenised through trade and forwarded to CQA. The CQAs then call for the available samples from the depot for preparation of drawings. After preparation of drawings, tender enquiries are floated on the propective suppliers. Items whose source is well established through PSUs are off loaded to them on single window concept for indigenisation.

LIMITATIONS OF THE PRESENT SYSTEM

(a) Indigenisation Capacity of IC/AHSP-The Technical Committee has a limited capacity of indigenisation of stores. For instance TCV can indigenise to the extent of 1200 items per year. AHSP has a capacity of making drawings of 1200 items covering 2500 sheets in a year. Although they claim an optimum capacity of 3000 drawing sheets annually this target has not been achieved so far. The items selected for indigenisation is much higher than their optimum capacity.

(b) Factors contributing to delay in Indigenisation—The factors contributing to delay in indigenisation of imported spares, through trade are as under:

(i) *Non-availability of Samples*—The first requirement of indigenisation of an item is availability of a sample. The availability of sample alone determines whether the preparation of drawing can be undertaken and specification of item determined.

(ii) *Preparation of Drawings*—Procurement of drawings is required to be made at the time of induction of equipment. In case drawings are not provided alongwith the main equipment due to contractual constraints them at least for critical and fast moving items drawings must be prepared in the normal usage time.

(iii) *Indigenisation capacity of TC/AHSP*—The capacity of TC/AHSP—The capacity of TC/AHSP for indigenisation of items is limited as explained earlier.

(iv) *Publicity*—Procurement of defence oriented spares are confined to few manufacturing units in the country. Non-participation of industries are mainly due to lack of awareness of defence requirements, primarily due to lack of publicity.

(v) *Meagre Requirements*—The requirement of spares projected by EME in some cases is very meagre and doesn't form the economic order quantity; hence not lucrative enough to attract the business community. Besides, most of the items are peculiar to defence only having no civil end-use. In view of the prohibitive development cost vis-a-vis the marketability factor, the civil industries stay away from defence orders.

(vi) *Fluctuations of Requirements*—One of the major factors which discourage firms from entering into defence deals, has been the fluctuations in the demands. While a spurt in requirements puts a supplier out of gear, a steep fall in the requirements puts a supplier to disadvantage due to blocked capital.

INDIGENISATION BY ARMY BASE WORKSHOPS

Army Base Workshops are the biggest consumers of spare parts of various military hardwares held by Indian Army. The overhaul scales are made by these workshops for the requirement of spares during overhaul of the equipment. Further some of the spares are required for the field maintenance of the equipment.

It is seen from experience that the complete range and depth of spares required for field maintenance and overhaul are not met. Ordnance depots do take timely action to procure the same from ex-import or through trade. But due to various constraints, ordnance depots are not able to meet the workshop requirements. As enumerated the indigenisation capacity of TC/AHSP is limited. With these limitations the indigenisation of spares for imported equipment is drastically reduced. Further ban on import of technology imposed by the Government has reduced the availability of spares.

In view of the above, it is proposed to indigenise the spares required by Army Base Workshop by supplementing the DGQA effort on indigenisation. The task of indigenisation of spares by Army Base Workshops are already being carried out wherever it is required. The indigenisation of spares in Army Base Workshops should encompass the following:

(a) Procurement of components/spare parts off the shelf whether indigenous or imported.
(b) Procurement of standard items.
(c) Manufacture of civil end-use-like items by established manufacturers.
(d) Manufacture of specific to military equipment items.
(e) Manufacture by EME.
(f) Design of unit/higher assys. where feasible.
(g) Reclamation/rebuilding of worn out parts.

PROPOSED SYSTEM OF INDIGENISATION

A detailed flow process chart for the proposed system of indigenisation is attached at Sketch 'Q'.

The initial stocking guide (ISG) is prepared as soon as a new equipment is

Proposed System of Indigenisation

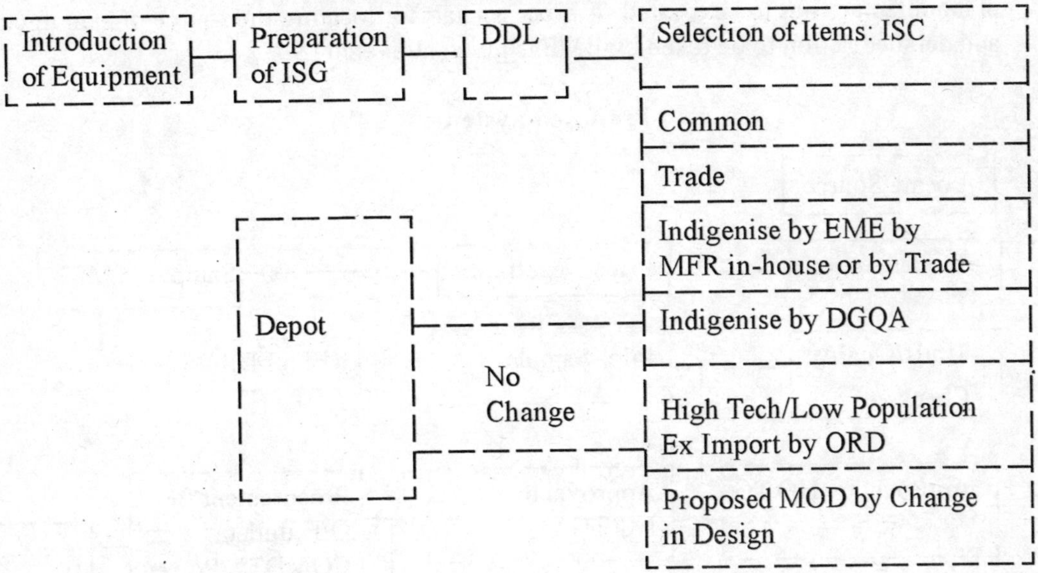

Sketch 'Q'

introduced into service. The ordnance depot should prepare the DDL based on the ISG. The items that require indigenisation should be presented before the ISG. EME should be given the maximum opportunity to select the items to be indigenised in Army Base Workshops.

The final depot list is prepared by the ordnance depot for items related by EME for manufacture. The HQ TG EME nominates the base workshop to undertake the manufacturing job or by trade under EME. The flow process chart is attached at sketch 'R'.

Proposed System

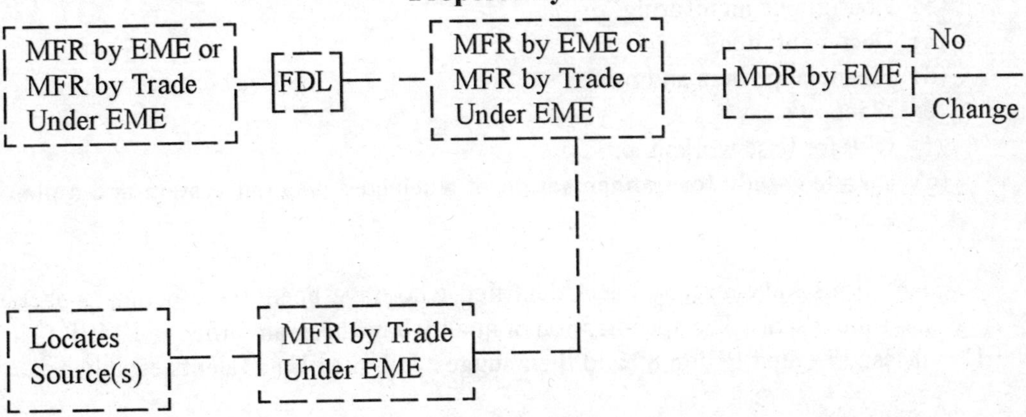

Sketch 'R'

The items that are identified to be manufactured by trade under EME, proper source of manufacture has to be located. A process chart for locating the source of manufacture and detailed action to be taken by EME is given at Sketch 'S'.

Proposed System

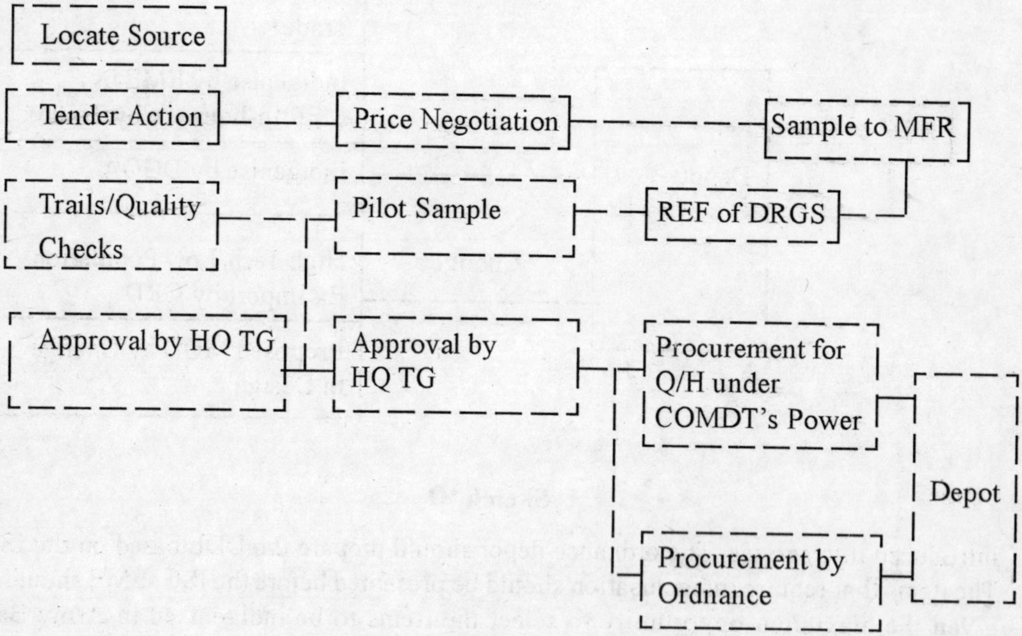

Sketch 'S'

For effective participation of Army Base Workshop in indigenisation activity the following issues should be considered:

(a) Composition of TSC.
(b) Continuous monitoring.
(c) Documentation.
(d) Financial powers and funds.
(e) Manpower.
(f) UPP for base workshops.
(g) Detailed study for indigenisation of a selected weapon system and a plan of action.

Some firms have already been identified who have been manufacturing packing rings and rubber seals. The specification of quality have been amplified in EMER GN/W 01No. 1 issue 1 dated 19 Jun 89 and their suggested Indian Equivalents established.

CONCLUSION

Army Base Workshops are well equipped with men and machines to undertake the indigenisation of spares. The base workshops can accept work orders for manufacture of high tech and sophisticated components of military hardware.

There are local industries who are prepared to undertake the development work for indigenisation of spares/assys/sub assys. In all these cases the development cost will be high because the industry has to design and develop the system from the first principle.

TECHNOLOGY SUBSTITUTION THROUGH INDIGENOUS EFFORT

11

Maj. Rajiv Khosla

297, IRW (7001 CMA WKSP)

INTRODUCTION

1. India has made tremendous progress in the past 50 years since Independence. We have also come a long way in the field of technology and engineering but we still have miles to go before we become self reliant and a force to reckon with ; to stand shoulder to shoulder with the developed countries. While we rejoice in our achievements, it is also time to take stock of our strengths and weaknesses.

2. With progress and socio economic changes on one hand and LIC (Low Intensity Conflict in J&K and North-East) sponsored by our neighbouring countries on the other hand, India can ill afford to be complacent with its defence needs. There is thus a constant requirement of keeping the forces equation balanced which translates into periodic purchase of hi-tech weapons, equipments, aircrafts and a host of armaments. Needless to say that all this is at the cost of precious foreign exchange being siphoned off.

3. Should it therefore, not be prudent to design and manufacture each and every eqpt for the defence forces in our own country but then would it not be fool-hardy to start from inventing the wheel all over again. The solution therefore lies in technology substitution through indigenous effort; the efforts being directed towards areas where we have an inherent potential and the infrastructure to support.

REQUIREMENT FOR TECHNOLOGY SUBSTITUTION

4. We have already identified the need for defence preparedness. Let us list the requirements for technology substitution .

(a) It is an important step in the direction of self-reliance and progress for a country.
(b) To maintain equipment without dependence on the country of origin of eqpt.
(c) To prolong and enhance the life of equipment beyond the contractual period of engineering support with the country whose equipment has been purchased.
(d) To save the foreign exchange resource getting depleted.

(e) For integration with other equipment and technology .
(f) To have a equipment which is most suitable for Indian environment and usage.

IDENTIFICATION OF AREAS OF STRENGTH AND WEAKNESS

5. Over the years India has seen the exodus of some of the best brains to the Western Countries particularly the USA in search of better opportunities. These very persons are sitting at the helm of affairs at most of the important places ; one among them being NASA. It underlines a fundamental observation that there is no dearth of talent and brains in the country. Some of the areas where our strength lies and is acknowledged is given below:

(a) Software development : Indians have been particularly good and at par with the best in the field of computers and software development.
(b) Information technology : India is already credited with the launch of its own satellites and communication network. A elaborate infrastructure exists in the country where state of the art communication equipment is being manufactured.
(c) Missile technology : This is another field where a lot of effort has been directed, culminating in the design and manufacture of Prithvi, Agni, Trishul and Nag missiles.

6. While we may have made good progress in the field of missile technology, computers and software development, the same can not be said for other branches of engineering such as Tank technology, Armament, small arms and Aeronautics to name a few. Despite years of efforts, India's MBT Arjun still leaves much to be desired and we are no where near producing our own Guns & other armament. The shortcomings in our engineering set up is enumerated below :

(a) Lack of precision and quality control in our manufacturing techniques : The weapons be it a Small arm or a 130mm Gun is a lethal bit of machinery with a specific purpose. It calls for highest levels of quality control and precision in manufacture; right from the design stage.
(b) Acceptance of below standard eqpt : Indians have a attitude to accept some thing less than 100% for we are willing to be content with less than the best. In the case of weapon system this attitude is myopic.
(c) Lack of R&D effort : The resource crunch affects the allocation of funds for R&D too. Unless the product can qualitatively compete and sell in the international market there is no taker except own defence forces. It seldom is a profit making undertaking.

EMERGING TRENDS IN MODERN WARFARE

7. The art of warfare has undergone sea change from the times when battles were fought

with swords and spears to the present day when there may not be much physical contact between enemies till at a later stage in war when physical occupation of enemy territory is to be accomplished. The Gulf war has changed the perspective on modern warfare. We are now in the era of computer guided intelligent missiles with deadly accuracy and which can travel considerable distances. We are also talking about Satellite aided communication and Navigation systems which can connect one from any part of the world. In short it is a electronic warfare. The conventional weapons though not redundant, come into the scene much later. This then leads us to conclude that modern warfare depends heavily on technology that deals with communication, missiles, and computers the three areas where we have considerable potential as brought out above.

INDIGENISATION OF ELECTRONICS BASED TECHNOLOGY

8. Electronics has made inroads into practically everything, be it a common household gadget or a sophisticated weapon system. Having identified our strengths in the field of technology, it would be most desirable to concentrate our efforts and resources to further develop in these directions. The aim should be to design and develop communication equipment, missiles and computers which are totally indigenous and for which we do not have to depend on the international market. Obviously maintenance of such equipment would be much simple and economical. It would, therefore, be prudent to invest substantially in the R&D effort related to IT, missiles, computers & software related projects. We already have big organisations such as DRDL, LRDE, ISRO etc. which are doing a pioneering work in their field of chosen technology. They must be given clear cut goals for achievement with adequate funds. The efforts of the engineers and the scientist must be recognised and awarded to encourage our young engineers to accept the challenges at home rather than look towards the Western countries.

TECHNOLOGY SUBSTITUTION IN OTHER AREAS

9. It is suggested that indigenisation in the areas where the country has identifiable weaknesses should only be done to a limited extent. What is implied is that while we may opt for purchase of equipment such as Guns, Tanks and other armament from international markets but indigenous support for maintenance of the same must be catered. It would be worth considering to open up our own industry to back up the requirement of spares. It has often been seen that for want of a small spare a sophisticated equipment lies in disuse. Why not throw the challenge to the private industries to cater for the particular requirement rather than confining it to the PSU dealing only with defence requirement. Therefore, in so far as spares requirement and maintenance of equipment is concerned we must capitalise on the existing infrastructure in the country as long as it does not jeopardise the security aspect. Towards this end our efforts to indigenise would be achievable at a reasonable cost.

CONCLUSION

10. The indigenous efforts for technology substitution should be concentrated in the field of IT, missiles and computers/simulators with the aim to become totally self-reliant, while efforts in the field of technology related to Tanks, Guns, armament etc. should be limited to development of infrastructure for spare support to provide self-reliance as far as maintenance of that equipment is concerned.

TECH PAPER ON TECHNOLOGY SUBSTITUTION BY INDIGENOUS EFFORT

12

MAJOR M.S. PAL

Station Workshop, EME, Lucknow

INTRODUCTION

1. While India as a whole thrives on the imported technology in the field of various engg streams, Armed Forces in particular proves this rule to a very large extent. While this ensures ready-to-use equipments at the hands of the troops it also creates a stumbling block to the effective engg support during the exploitation phase of the equipments. The reason is attributed to the scarce or nonavailability of spares. There is an inherent long lead time for procurement of spares for imported equipments which is further exacerbated by the high cost, erratic supply sources and cumbersome procedures. All these lead to a high down time and hence low utilisation rate of equipments.

2. Efforts are afoot to indigenise the equipments by resorting to following methods:

(a) Technology transfer.
(b) Reverse Engg.
(c) Technology Substitution.

3. While the technology transfer demands its own cost and reverse engg helps building up data bank without any involved R&D effort, technology substitution specifically deals with the indigenous R&D.

AIM

4. Aim of this technical paper is to discuss various aspects regarding indigenous efforts for technology substitution.

WHAT IS TECHNOLOGY SUBSTITUTION

5. Any equipment is designed and developed following a defined process logic. All hardware and firmware related to that equipments strictly conform to that logic. As part of the indigenisation of the equipments an effort can be made to develop a substitute not for

the spares but for the inherent process logic itself. This will give rise to new techniques which will not only replace the out dated imported ones but also will open up new vistas for developing new applications. For example our missile programme has supplemented the space research to a very large extent. Thus technology substitution is a process to find an updated alternative for the outdated technologies used in imported equipments.

SCOPE

6. The technology substitution if undertaken will give a tremendous fillip to the indigenous R&D effort which has been persistently neglected in this country. A strong R&D has always been the bedrock of success a la developed countries which a country with borrowed technology can never aspire to become. As for the Armed Forces it will work as a technology multiplier as far as DRDO is concerned and also drastically improve the utilisation rate of equipments.

PRESENT SCENARIO

7. In post independence era the country as a whole has shown utter callousness in R&D effort. As far as Govt is concerned a meagre 1% (average) of GDP has been spent for R&D in various govt sponsored institutes.

8. Different universities, IITs in particular were supposed to provide the basic input of merit. Instead they have become the conduit for brain drain.

9. The private sector has been largely apathetic to in house development and thrived on borrowed technology. This was also fuelled to a large extent by faulty Government policies.

SUGGESTIONS

10. Given the malaises affecting the R&D in the country a number of steps can be taken to improve the situation.

(a) R&D should be accorded its due priority in the overall strategy of development.
(b) More financial allocation for Government R&D organisations who despite having excellent infrastructure are throttled to pursue the projects due to want of funds.
(c) Policies should be formulated to reduce the trend of importing technology. Private sector organisations should be rather forced to allocate more funds in this regard.
(d) Universities including IITs should be encouraged to take up projects. The industries in all sectors should come forward to sponsor them. If the scope is available in house it will curb the brain drain also to a large extent.

ADVANTAGES

11. The technology substitution once taken up with right earnestness will result in the

following advantages:

(a) In house R&D will get a fillip.
(b) The technology developed will be cheaper, readily available and will have a stable market interface.
(c) Dependency on foreign sources for spares will drastically reduce.
(d) Savings in terms of foreign exchange.
(e) Any technology developed always opens new vistas leading to other new applications. Info sharing between various stream of research always benefits mutually.
(f) Avenues open up for new industries to come up. This is also supplemented by ancillary industries.
(g) Ready availability of technology and spares improves the utilisation rate of equipments.

CORPS OF EME AND TECHNOLOGY SUBSTITUTION

13. Though the Corps of EME is essentially a repair organisation a good amount of effort is being made in Simulator Development Division (SDD) in terms of R&D. The simulators which are being developed are excellent examples of technology substitution which are state-of-the-art as well as easy to fabricate and maintain subsequently and also cheap. The functional scope of SDD can be further expanded to explore the feasibility of technology substitution in imported equiptments and then develop a prototype which can be fabricated through the base workshops. HQ Tech Gp EME, MAGs and AsHSP should maintain a close liaison in this regard to reach the logical conclusion of each project.

CONCLUSION

14. Technology substitution in the process of indigenisation of imported equipments also boosts the R&D effort in the country. It should be recognised as a Key Result Area without any further delay by our policy planners. However, following points should be borne in mind while carrying it out:

(a) The technology developed should have a technical cutting edge over the existing one.
(b) The developed technology should also have a smooth market interface in terms of availability of spares and other infrastructural requirements.
(c) It should be cost effective.
(d) It should be upgradable with changing time and demand.

INDIGENISATION OF SPARES FROM REVERSE ENGINEERING

13

Gurmit Singh Malhi and Sukumar Sahu

HQ 612, EME Battalion C/o 56, APO.

INTRODUCTION

1. Innovation and self reliance have been the hall mark of Indian Army's rich traditions and history. Capabilities of our service to adopt new ways to overcome the critical financial challenges and harness indigenisation of new technologies for our professional competence and effectiveness has always been an area of our strength and excellence.

2. The Indian Army today is made to handle a large inventory of war like eqpt and majority of them are of imported origin. State of operational fitness of such eqpt and their sustainability is largely dictated by the back up of spares/assys and their availability. In case of imported eqpt, more often than not we have (not surprisingly) stock outs and non-availability of such spares have been a major cause of concern particularly due to long lead time coupled with uncertainty of availability and exhorbitant price.

3. The import of war like eqpt is likely to continue and hence the need for indigenisation is persistent.

REVERSE ENGINEERING

4. Reverse Engineering is normally adopted under two conditions:

(a) When an eqpt/sub assys is desired to be copied exacting the parameters of the original eqpt/subassys without any compromise.

(b) When an eqpt/subassys are available without the technical documents/ specifications and the details of the eqpt/subassys are required to be known.

INDIGENISATION OF SPARES

5. Indigenisation of spares for imported eqpt was started during early 1960s. The necessity of indigenisation arise under the following circumstances :

(a) An effort to reduce import with an aim to achieve self-sufficiency.

(b) The supplier fails to supply spares due to:

(i) Eqpt not currently in production.

(ii) Requirement and offer may not be compatible.

(iii) Requirement status does not coincide with the production cycle of the Original Eqpt Manufacturer (OEM).

(c) Unplanned extension of eqpt life cycle.

ORGANISATIONAL STRUCTURE AND FUNCTION OF TECHNICAL COMMITTEE

6. The overall responsibility for coordinating the indigenisation efforts rests with a Central Technical Committee. This committee is chaired by Secretary Defence Production & Supply (DP&S) and has seven technical committees for various disciplines, functioning under the chairmanship of the technical director of the concerned discipline. The technical committees assist the department of Defence Supplies in locating indigenious sources of supply of defence stores being imported. The broad functions of the technical committees are :

(a) Selection of item for indigenisation/substitution.

(b) Developmentand registration of vendors for defence supply.

(c) Selection of vendors and negotiation with firms for supply and its progress.

(d) Governs quality assurance services.

(e) Guidance to procurement and production agencies on all technical matters.

SAMPLE ROOMS

7. To attract the manufacturers and to involve them in indigenisation activities, sample rooms have been establised in the four metropolis and these are being operated under the aegies of Director General of Quality Assurance.

CRITERIA FOR INDIGENISATION PROCESS

8. Criteria for indigenisation process is linked with the requirement pattern of spares during the service life of an eqpt. The requirement of spares for an eqpt during its life cycle can be broadly classified as under:

(a) User's maint spares—low tech, fast moving expendable items.

(b) Field maint spares—major functional components exhibiting random failure rate.

(c) Overhaul spares.

9. A multi discipline weapon system, such as a tank, is made up of thousands of components and it is not possible to undertake indigenisation of all the items as a one time measure. Therefore, indigenisation of spares may be phased over during the first service life. Major factors deciding indigenisation of spares of imported eqpt are :

(a) Population of equipment in the service.
(b) Policy on retention.
(c) Repair policy.
(d) Lead time required for the development and manufacture of items.

SELECTION OF ITEMS FOR INDIGENISATION

11. On completion of Annual Provision Review, ODs project their requirement in the forms of Draft Depot List (DDLs). These include items for which there is no known source of supply. After due vetting by concerned technical committees, the requirements are projected as Final Depot List by Ordnance and are met through the following :

(a) Import of essential requirements.
(b) Indigenisation through trade.
(c) Indigenisation/manufacture through EME workshops.
(d) Local procurement/manufacture by ordnance depots.

12. A tech sub-committee having member reps from Ordnance, EME, AHSP and technical committees select the items out of the DDLs for indigenisation. The items selected for indigenisation during the next financial year are listed in the forms of Final Depot List (FDL).

PROCESS OF INDIGENISATION THROUGH REVERSE ENGINEERING

13. Such processes are extremly complex and need expertise in all aspect of engineering productions. The broad outline of requirements for an indigenisation process through reverse engineering, is as follows:

(a) Availability of upto date functional samples.
(b) Time frame stipulation for the indigenisation process.
(c) Availability of personnel, having total expertise on critical technical analysis with knowledge on various manufactring processes.
(d) Availability of high precision mechine tools, measurements, testing eqpts.
(e) Resources, within the country and from import, regarding availability of materials for indigenisation.
(f) Acceptable tolarance limits, depending upon factors such as cost, quality and requirement.

14. Items may be ascribed to EME for manufacture by Army Base Workshops only. Such items are normally of the following types :

(a) Items for which the projected requirement is meagre for attracting response from the trade.

(b) Items for which samples are not available with Ordnance.

15. Indigenisation through reverse engineering is carried out in stages. At the first step, the main assys are dismantled and properly documented. Thereafter the sub assys are disassembled and documented. The most important out come of the reverse engineering is the drawing which includes all required specifications concerning meterial, surface parameters, technical parameters, tolarance, measurements, testing etc. Other parameters, that are also assessed, are environment, load, life expectancy etc.

TIME FRAME FOR INDIGENISATION

16. As a policy spares for new eqpt are procured from the country of origin, initially to meet the maint requirements for two years based on Manufacturers Recommeded List of Spares (MRLS), duly vetted by the maint agency and overhaul requirement by another 25% of the total buy. This gives the necessary lead time for execution of the indigenisation programme. Keeping in view the requirements of spares during the life cycle of an eqpt, endeavour should be made to complete the indigenisation by the time the eqpt reaches its mid life or the stage of first overhaul. This will permit a lead time of 3 to 5 years for completing the indigenisation of spares/sub-assys and 8 to 10 years for completing the indigenisation of a new eqpt. The suggested time frame is as follows :

(a) N = The year eqpt inducted into service.

(b) N+3 yrs = Indigenisation of spares required under phase I should be completed.

(c) N+5 yrs = Indigenisation of spares required under phase II should be completed.

(d) N+8 yrs = Indigenisation of the equipment, if required, should be completed.

GENERAL RESPONSE FROM TRADE

17. Response from trade may be lacking due to any of the following reasons :

(a) Peculiarity of requirements projected by the Army.
(b) Cost of devolopment is high.
(c) The items does not fit in the production line of the firm.
(d) The quantities projected may not be attractive.
(e) Repetition of orders not assured.

(f) Raw meterials, as per specifications, may not be available in the country.

(g) Rigidity of specifications and inspection criterias.

CONCLUSION

18. A large population of eqpt of different disciplines and origin, having specification of varying standards are held on the Army's inventory. The present requirement of spares both for maint and overhaul is heavy and the range of spares is extremely diverse. Some of these eqpt are in the last phase of life.

19. Besides, indigenisation of spares through reverse engineering is a difficult task and requires ultimate expertise in all aspects of engineering process. Time and cost are also major aspects to be taken into account for such an endeavour. The process of indigenisation through reverse engineering can only take shape provided active participation and co-operation of our R & D, trade and industrial infrastructures are duly co-ordinated, integrated and taken advantage of at all levels.

III

AUTOMATION IN MANUFACTURING

RETROFITTING
A Case Study

14

K. Rama Bhupal Reddy[1], K.V.F. Maharaja[2] and V.S. Murali[2]
Mechanical Engg. Dept.,[1]
Indian Institute of Technology, Delhi.
Machine Tool Division,[2]
Hindustan Machine Tools Ltd., Kalamassery.

ABSTRACT

The changing needs of the user industries throw up an unprecedented challenge to the Indian Machine Tool Industry. While computer technology has made wide-spread automation (theore-tically feasible), yet for more than a decade, barriers of size and cost had blocked the economical application of computer capabilities, in most work-settings. This paper presents some aspects of retrofitting, for machine tools in general and that of a point-to-point control system in particular, which is a low cost alternative towards automation without discarding old machines.

1. INTRODUCTION

The production technology of machining is developing in a faster way to answer the incessant demand from their manufacturing sector. Machining cycle time for any component consists of two parts, namely, metal cutting time and machine idle time. Productivity can be increased either by reducing metal cutting time which is a function of machine tool or by reducing any or all elements of machine idle time like setting, positioning or measuring time. Research on maximum obtainable reduction in machining time and the maximum achievable accuracy and surface finish in machining, is going on all over the industrialised countries. But emphasis at present is on the possible reduction that can be obtained in operation time, preparation time and in various non-machining times. This resulted in the evolution of newer and better techniques of manufacture and brought about thorough change(s) in the design of machine tools. Many new technologies covering the fields of machine rigidity, drives and controls have now helped considerable to reduce the non-cutting time and also to slash down the preparation time especially with the development of new electronic controls and positioning devices. Technology upgradation is now a priority in the industry, to enable manufacturers to meet the growing, changing and challenging needs of user industries, both in India and abroad.

This paper outlines the design of a numerically controlled co-ordinate table attachment on to a radial drilling machine for accurate positioning requirements, to enhance production capabilities of the firm. The co-ordinated table movements are generated by servo driven recirculated ball screw assemblies along with each axis, controlled by SINUMERIK 805 system. A closed loop control system is designed for accurate positioning requirements. Comparison of machine-hour rate for conventional machine and retrofitted system was carried. The integration would ultimately lead to not only reduction of through-put times and costs, but also provide a great degree of flexibility.

2. NEED OF RETROFITTING

The updating of production technology in shop floors has become mandatory, for tracking towards higher productivity. Very high under utilisation of machine tool capacity in conventional manufacturing results in high costs, and also unpredictable delivery schedules. The production time increases almost exponentially with the degree of work piece complexity and closeness of dimensional tolerances. Also special work holding and tool guiding devices are used to position the work piece, as well as to guide the cutting tool during the operation. It is the operator who is responsible for many of the inputs to the machine.[5] To cope with these problems several improvements have been made in manually operated machines. Such an improvement can be characterised by the improved quality, accuracy and cost of production. The introduction of computer technology has given boost to entrepreneurs, both big and small, to enhance their production capacity. Thus the industries are presently taking technological upgradation issue on priority basis, in order to meet ever changing requirements, by shifting from Conventional machines to Computer Numerical Control (CNC) machines. There are still many small entrepreneurs (back bone of the country's economy) who cannot afford to buy full fledged CNC machines. The prohibitive prices of full-fledged CNC machines (varying from Rs.15 lacs to Rs.80 lacs) has slowed down the process of modernising the shopfloors and has kept small entrepreneurs at a distance. In such circumstances the capabilities of existing machines can be substantially enhanced by retrofitting servo drives and control system on to them, without discarding old machines. These systems offer a low cost alternative to employing more expensive capital machinery, and the same time such technology bring in the latest culture into manufacturing operations, that of CNC.

2.1 What is CNC Retrofitting?

Retro-Fit means to add accessories onto a given object, in this case a machine tool. The concept of CNC Retrofit has been applied to machine tools and refined over the last fifteen years. Depending on the type of systems available in the market many varieties of retrofits have been offered. The end user today is in a totally confused state and finds it very difficult to understand what he can expect out of a CNC retrofitted machine. It is prudent then to analyse in a down-to-earth manner what a retrofit should be. It depends on the type of components or jobs that are presently being manufactured and probably will have to be improved upon.[7]

Before one starts laying down guidelines for selection of retrofit systems, it is important to realise that different levels of retrofitting are possible as also different types of systems are available.[6] One has to be very careful while deciding on a retrofit. The initial euphoria on CNC retrofit possibilities have led to all type of machines being retrofitted and expected results not achieved. Even though initial investments on retrofit system is high, a given part can be produced at lesser prices in the long run. Improved accuracy and repeatability results into the ability to produce better jobs with lower cost, inturn will result in increased profits.[4] If the retrofitted system has the facility of providing a switch over to original operation of the machine, it will be an added advantage as the machine need not be down due to system failures.

Advantages of Retrofitting

The advantages of CNC machines over conventional machines are a common knowledge. Use of CNC machine has lot of tangible and intangible benefits. What one must remember is that to have the full benefits of CNC machines, the workshop discipline will also have to change. This point is usually overlooked and a direct comparison of machining time is done. Following is a brief list of advantages of going in for CNC Retrofits.[7]

- Utilisation of the existing plant resulting in reduced capital outlay.
- Retrofits are an introduction for further CNC investments.
- CNC Retrofits result in improved workshop discipline.
- Retrofits represent the fastest and the cheapest way of modernising conventional machining.
- Retrofits provide very quick returns and short payback periods.
- CNC machines result in reduction in work-in-process/progress set up times, very expensive reworks and scrap.
- Eliminates the need for most machine tool accessories, special sized tools and form tools.
- De-skilling of the operations result in reduction of overdependence on skilled labour.
- Since the jobs produced depend on the CNC control, it results in less operator fatigue.
- Increased competitiveness because of the ability to produce better jobs and with lower cost. This is turn will result in increased profits.
- Improved accuracy and repeatability results in improved quality.

3. THE EXISTING MACHINE

It is a Radial Drilling Machine (RM 62), manufactured by M/s HMT Ltd., is used for applications such as drilling, reaming, tapping, counter boring etc. The drill head is mounted on radial arm, which can be swivelled about the vertical column, further the drilling head can be moved on rails along the radial arm. The base plate is a rigid structure on which the column and sleeve assembly is fixed, also contains coolant chamber of capacity 44 litres. The worm drive assures uniform drill thrust at the drilling spindle. A spring loaded safety clutch is situated between the feed drive and the worm drive to protect any adverse overloads. The feed mechanism offers three types of feeds, viz., automatic feed, fine feed by hand and coarse feed by hand with different mechanisms. Two safety limit switches are provided at the top and bottom to stop further movement of arm up and down beyond the safe working limits. The lubrication is effected by a plunger pump mounted on the top of drill head. The oil is sucked through filter situated at the bottom of the drill head. Further particulars are given in manual.[2]

3.1 Features of the Attachment

The co-ordinate drilling table attachment is designed to provide accurate positioning to perform the operations, any position on the XY plane in the work envelope of the table. The movement of the workpiece mounted on the table with respect to the cutting tool until it arrives, is a numerically defined position and then the motion is get slowed down, and stopped automatically. The cutting tool performs the required task either manually or automatically, with the axis stationary and the drill moves out in a rapid traverse feed upon the completion of the task the workpiece can be moved to next point for the next operation. The data for each desired position is given by its co-ordinate values, through control system. The control unit operates the drives coupled to the ball screws and receive the feedback signals of the actual position and velocity of the each of the axis from the encoders. After checking for the life, allowable axial loads, allowable rotational speed, rigidity, etc., ballscrews were selected for each axis. Each ballscrew is equipped with a separate servomotor, rotary encoder, etc., which are connected to the system into forming a closed loop. The micro switch and dog assemblies are provided on each axis to stop the movement of the table beyond the safe working limits. The Figures 1 and 2 gives the details of the accessories of X and Y drives respectively, incorporated in to the system. For the convenience of manufacturing, as far as possible same type of elements were designed for both the x and y axes. As the ballscrews and guideways require adequate protection from the dirt or any foreign matter such as chips, coolant etc., hence same is covered by telescopic covers designed specially for this application. Telescopic covers are made of 2mm thick steel, in number of sheets which will run on another with the supporting of sliding shoe. Five sheets on y-axis and four sheets on x-axis, of different lengths are tightened to the table and saddle respectively, to protect the guideways and ball screws from the falling of chips and dirt.

4. ECONOMIC CONSIDERATIONS

Despite the high productivity and accuracy achieved with NC machine tools, NC is not always a cost-effective solution in the manufacturing of parts. However, even the

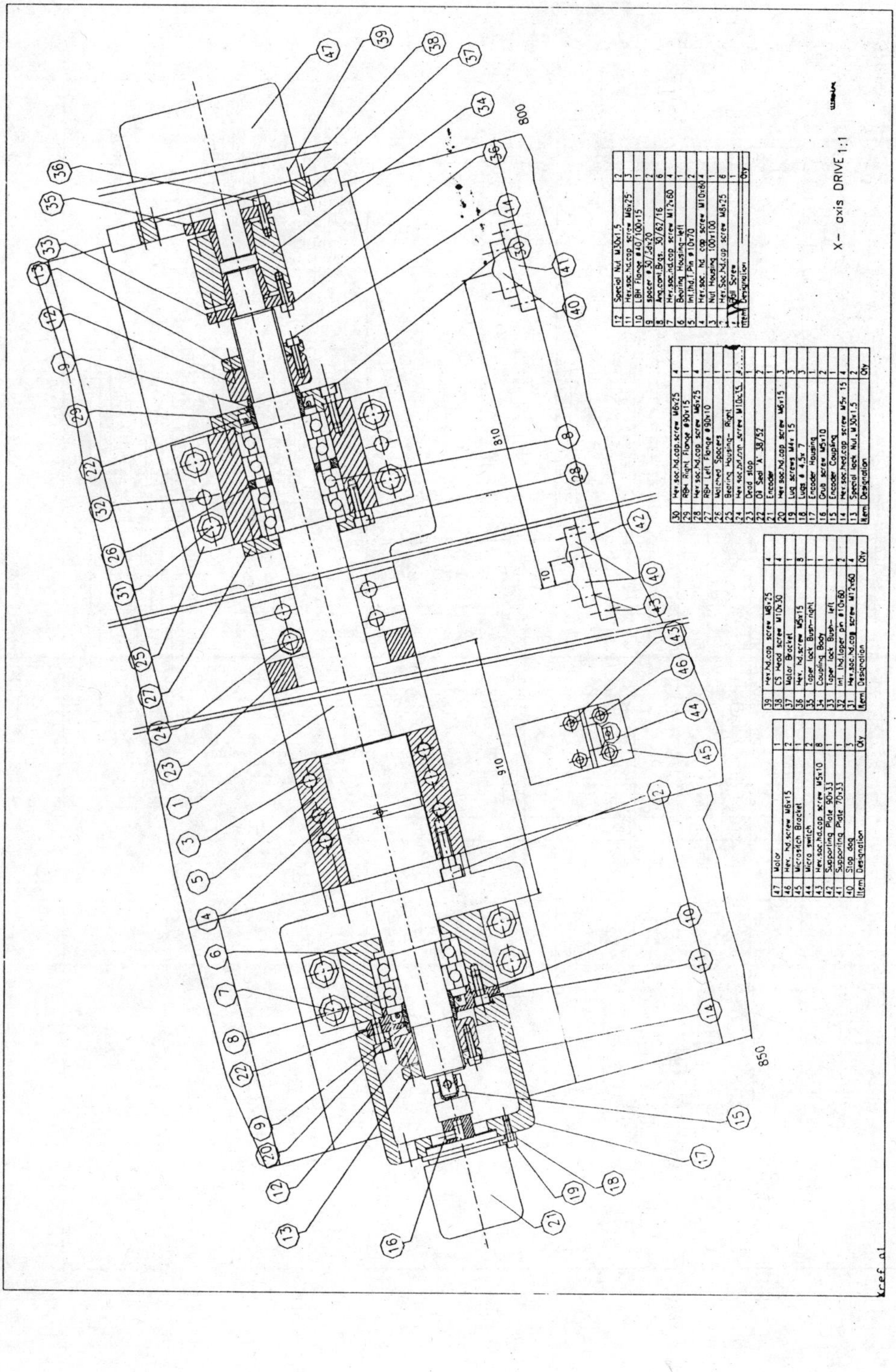

Item	Designation	Qty
12	Special Nut M30x1.5	2
11	Hex.soc.hd.cap screw M6x25	3
10	LBH Flange ø40/100x15	1
9	spacer ø30/3dx20	2
8	Ang.cont.Brgs. 30/62/16	6
7	Hex.soc.hd.cap screw M12x60	4
6	Bearing Housing-left	1
5	Int.thd.T.Pin ø10x70	2
4	Hex.soc. hd cap screw M10x80	4
3	Nut Housing 100x100	1
2	Hex.Soc.hd.cap screw M8x25	6
1	Ball Screw	1

Item	Designation	Qty
30	Hex soc.hd.cap.screw M6x25	4
29	RBH Right Flange ø90x15	1
28	Hex soc.hd.cap screw M6x25	4
27	RBH Left Flange ø90x10	1
26	Matched Spacers	1
25	Bearing Housing- Right	1
24	Hex soc.hd.cap screw M10x35	4
23	Dead stop	1
22	Oil Seal 'A' 38/52	2
21	Encoder	1
20	Hex soc.hd.cap screw M6x15	3
19	Lug screws M4x 15	3
18	Lugs ø 4.5x 7	3
17	Encoder Housing	1
16	Grub screw M5x10	2
15	Encoder Coupling	1
14	Hex soc.hed.cap screw M5x 15	4
13	Special lock Nut, M30x1.5	2

Item	Designation	Qty
39	Hex.hd.cap screw M8x25	4
38	CS Head screw M10x30	4
37	Motor Bracket	1
36	Hex. hd.screw M5x15	8
35	Taper lock Bush-right	1
34	Coupling Body	1
33	Taper lock Bush- left	1
32	Int. thd.taper pin ø10x60	2
31	Hex.soc.hd.cap screw M12x60	4

Item	Designation	Qty
47	Motor	1
46	Hex. hd.screw M6x15	2
45	Microswitch Bracket	1
44	Micro switch	2
43	Hex.soc.hd.cap screw M5x10	8
42	Supporting Plate 90x33	1
41	Supporting Plate 70x33	1
40	Stop dog	3

Fig.1 X–axis drive

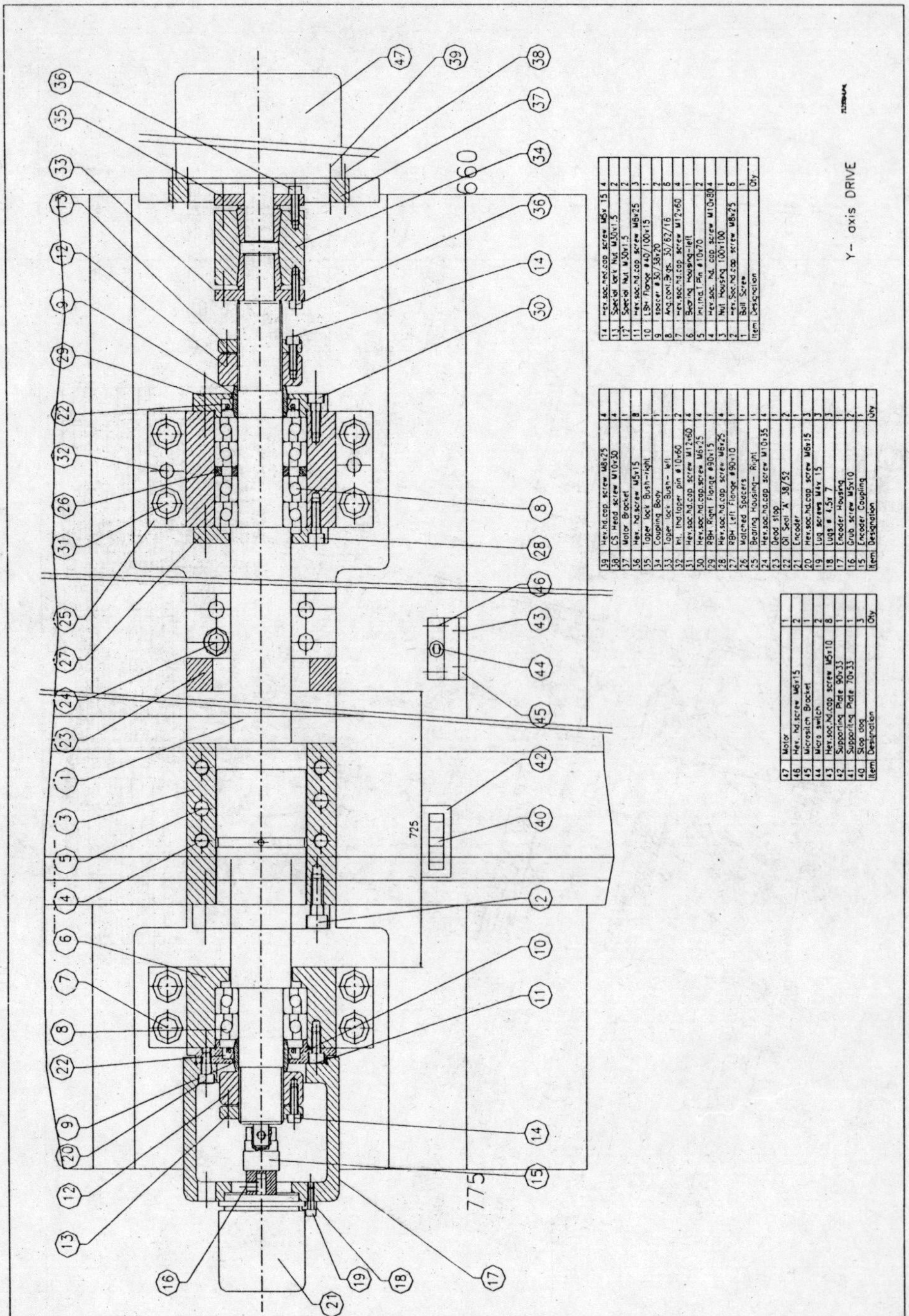

Item	Designation	Qty
14	Hex.soc.hed.cap screw M5x 15	4
13	Special lock Nut M30x1.5	2
12*	Special Nut M30x1.5	2
11	Hex.soc.hd.cap screw M6x25	3
10	LBH Flange ø40/100x15	1
9	spacer ø30/38x20	2
8	Ang.cont.Brgs. 30/62/16	6
7	Hex.soc.hd.cap screw M12x60	4
6	Bearing Housing-left	1
5	Int.thd.T.Pin ø10x70	2
4	Hex.soc. hd. cap screw M10x80	4
3	Nut Housing 100x100	1
2	Hex.Soc.hd.cap screw M8x25	6
1	Ball Screw	1

Item	Designation	Qty
39	Hex.hd.cap screw M8x25	4
38	CS Head screw M10x30	4
37	Motor Bracket	1
36	Hex. hd.screw M5x15	8
35	Taper lock Bush-right	1
34	Coupling Body	1
33	Taper lock Bush- left	1
32	Int. thd.taper pin ø10x60	2
31	Hex.soc.hd.cap screw M12x60	4
30	Hex.soc.hd.cap.screw M6x25	4
29	RBH Right Flange ø90x15	1
28	Hex.soc.hd.cap screw M6x25	4
27	RBH Left Flange ø90x10	1
26	Matched Spacers	1
25	Bearing Housing- Right	1
24	Hex.soc.hd.cap screw M10x35	4
23	Dead stop	1
22	Oil Seal 'A' 38/52	2
21	Encoder	1
20	Hex.soc.hd.cap screw M6x15	3
19	Lug screws M4x 15	3
18	Lugs ø 4.5x 7	3
17	Encoder Housing	1
16	Grub screw M5x10	2
15	Encoder Coupling	1

Item	Designation	Qty
47	Motor	1
46	Hex. hd.screw M6x15	2
45	Micrositch Bracket	1
44	Micro switch	2
43	Hex.soc.hd.cap screw M5x10	8
42	Supporting Plate 90x33	1
41	Supporting Plate 70x33	1
40	Stop dog	3

Fig.2 Y—axis drive

production of a single part on an NC machine can be economically justified if the part contains complicated surfaces which make it extremely difficult to be produced on conventional machine tools. An attempt is made to show the cost benefit of retrofitting system, by comparing the machine-hour rate for conventional machine with retrofitted system. Even though, machine-hour cost is more for retrofitted system, it completes the operations on the work-piece in less time and cost with high accuracy, when compared to the conventional machine.

Machine-hour Rate Analysis

The existing machine is going to be retrofitted after 11 years. Comparison was made by taking three components, presently the operations are performed by the existing Radial Drilling machine (RM 62).

	Initial Cost (Rs.)	Annual cost		Hourly cost	
		maintenance (Rs.)	others (Rs.)	Labour (Rs.)	Over-heads (%)
RM 62	3,00,000.00	5,000.00	15,000.00	10.00	200
NC System +Accessories	5,50,000.00	10,000.00	6,000.00	10.00	200

(i) For Conventional Machine

No. of working hours/annum (2 shifts a day) $= 16 \times 6 \times 52 = 4992$ hrs.

Depreciation $= (C—S)/Y$
$=$ Rs.14,250.00

{Where, C - Initial Cost, Y - Expected life (20 yrs.), S - Scrap value (5% of initial cost)}

Interest/annum (I = 18%) $= \{(C—S)/2+S\} \times I$
$=$ Rs.28,350.00

Total Annual cost = Depreciation + Interest + Maintenance + Others
= Rs.62,600.00

Hourly cost = Labour + Overheads
= Rs.30.00

Machine-Hour Rate = { Annual cost/(Working hrs × m/c utility)} + Hrly. cost

(m/c utility is assumed to be 60%) = Rs.51

(ii) After Retrofitting

To be retrofitted after 11 years, the depreciated amount will be equal to Rs.1,43,250.00 Further investment of Rs.5,50,000.00 for retrofitting.

Total value of m/c = Rs.6,93,250.00
Assuming further usage of 20 years.
Depreciation/annum = Rs.33,912.50
Interest/annum = Rs.63,742.50
Total annual cost = Rs.1,13,655.00
Hourly cost = Rs.30.00
Machine-hour rate = Rs.68.00

(iii) Comparison

	Conventional Machine	Retrofitted Machine
M/c-hr rate	Rs.51.00	Rs.68.00
Component #1		
Time for machining	21 min.	11 min.
Machine rate	Rs.17.85	Rs.12.50
Component #2		
Time for machining	29 min.	14 min.
Machine rate	Rs.24.65	Rs.15.90
Component #3		
Time for machining	48 min.	21 min.
Machine rate	Rs.40.80	Rs.23.80

Amount of saving per component #1 = Rs. 5.35
Amount of saving per component #2 = Rs. 8.75
Amount of saving per component #3 = Rs.17.00

This comparison gives the machine-hour cost for conventional machine and retrofitted system. The retrofitted system produces that the components at less cost and time, compared with conventional machine. Depending on the number of components of manufactured a day, pay back period can be estimated.

5. CONCLUSIONS

CNC retrofit has infinite possibilities, if and only if it is rightly done. A system can only be as good as the machine to which it is retrofitted, it cannot and will not overcome the inherent geometrical inaccuracies of the machine. Retrofitting is a stepping stone for any end user to go in for full-fledged CNC machines. For the convenience of manufacturing, as far as possible same type of elements were designed for both the x and y axes. Automatic tool changing mechanism and control of drill spindle are not provided here to avoid the excess cost. These are to expected to be done manually, is due to fact that the structure of existing machine is not to be disturbed, as switch over to the old machine will be an added advantage. The machine-hour rate analysis shows the cost benefit of the Retrofitting system and ability of producing the job in less time and cost.

REFERENCES

1. Harold A.Rothbart : *Mechanical Design and Systems Hand Book*, McGraw-Hill Book Co., 1964.
2. *HMT: Operation and Maintenance Manual* - HMT Radial Drilling Machine (RM62).
3. Khan, M.Y., and Jain, P.K. : *Financial Management Text Problems*, Tata McGraw-Hill Pub. Co. Ltd., 1992.
4. Koren, Y : *Computer Control of Manufacturing Systems*, McGraw-Hill Book Co., 1983.
5. Roger S. Pressman and John E. Williams : *Numerical Control and Computer Aided Manufacturing*, John Wiley & Sons, 1977.
6. Thyagarajan, S : *Guidelines on Selection of Retrofit - Key note paper*, 14th AIMTDR Conference, Bombay, 1990.
7. Vibhute,V.B., and Vishwakumar, R: Retrofitting with CNC Controls and Servodrives, MT&M, pp. 3-9, Feb. 1990.

COMPUTER AIDED GEAR CUTTING ATTACHMENT FOR MILLING MACHINE

15

V.J. Kakhandki[1] and P.S. Dabeer[1]

Assistant Professors, Mechanical Engineering Dept.,[1]
College of Engineering, Kopargaon - 423 603 Dist. Ahmednagar (M.S).

ABSTRACT

Gear cutting is a special operation and generally carried out on milling machine, or on hobbing machine. On milling machine only a tailor made gears are cut and is generally not preferred for mass production. Hence here is an attempt made to develop an attachment which is run through a PC. Number of teeth, feed rate are to be given and a layman can enter these data to the computer. A program written in C language runs the computer and controls the ON/OFF of cutter, table traverse, indexing. The operator has to just load the gear blank and run the computer. Rest all is done through computer. It is a low cost automation, and an attempt made is successful.

Key Words : Indexing, CNC, Interfacing

NOTATION

dN : Number of steps indexed
dθ : Angle indexed
E : Accumulated error in indexing
l : Linear travel in mm
t : Number of teeth
θ : Total angle indexed

1. INTRODUCTION

Computer aided control of machines are generally called as Computer Numerical Control (CNC) machines. CNC machine tools may be defined[1] as method of automation in which various functions of machine tools are controlled by letters and symbols.

1.1 Need of Computer Aided Machining System

The need of CNC machines was felt for machining complex shaped small batch components as those belonging to an air craft. In 1948, John.T.Parsons demonstrated the concept of numerical control to US air force, which subsequently led to the development of a prototype NC milling machine, at the Massachusetts Institute of Technology. The first demonstration of this prototype was held in 1952.

2. BASIC COMPONENTS OF COMPUTER AIDED MACHINING SYSTEM

2.1 Program of Instructions

The program of instructions is the detailed step by step set of directions which tell the machine tool what to do. It is coded through program in numerical or symbolic form on some type of input medium that can be interpreted by the control unit. In our case we used C language as instruction media and a program was written and compiled. This compiled program stored on a floppy disk was used to run the 8086 computer and control units.

2.2 Controller Unit

The controller unit consists of the electronics and hardware that read and interprets the program of instructions and convert it in to mechanical actions of the machine tool. It should be noted that all modern CNC systems today are sold with a micro computer as control units and we also used a 8086 based computer as control unit along with ADDON card.

2.3 The Machine Tool

It is the part of the CNC system which performs useful work. In our case it is Milling Machine. It is basically consists (Refer fig. 1) of a spindle driven by an AC motor through gear box (for varying the speed of spindle), table to mount work piece and an indexing attachment to index the job. There are hand wheels to move the table up/down, to and fro. We have used two independent stepper motors, one for indexing and another for table traversing.

3. GEAR GEOMETRY AND ITS PRODUCTION

3.1 The Gear Geometry

The spur and helical gears are generally have involute curves as the tooth profile. The involute may be defined[2] as the locus of a point on a straight line which rolls without slipping on the circumference of a circle. The advantages of using involute curve is, it provides constant pressure angle, flexibility in shifting centers of gears a little and acts as a conjugate profile, ease of adopting it for manufacturing purpose, as the involute of a rack is a straight line and is used to build hob cutters.

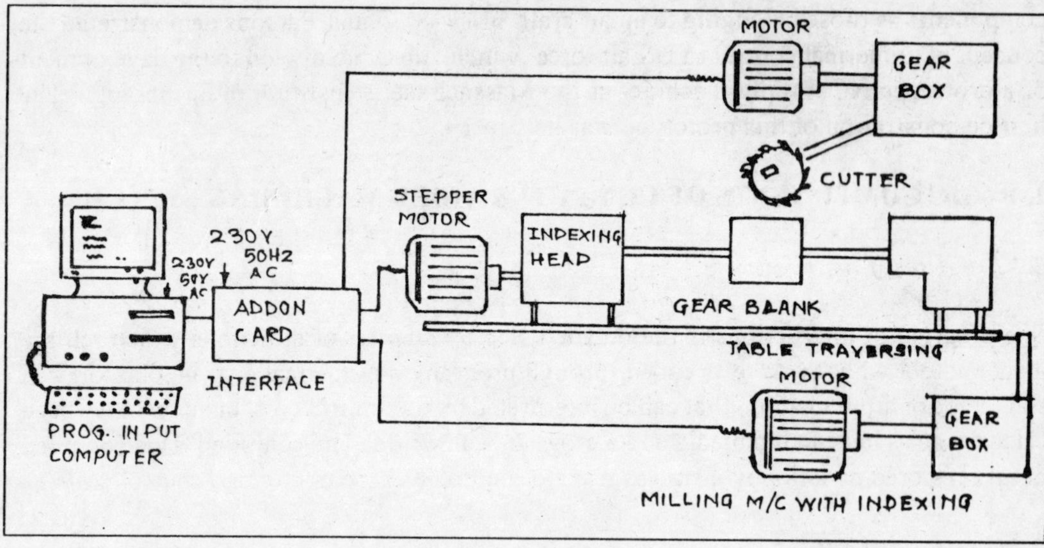

Figure 1: Arrangement of CNC Milling Machine for Gear Cutting

3.2 The Production

The production of gears on milling machine generally carried out manually. The gear cutter is mounted on the spindle and rotates while the work piece is mounted on the table and reciprocated under the cutter. Once the cutter finishes tooth profile, the work piece is indexed to the next position, and again tooth profile is cut. If this machine is adopted with automatic indexing and table traverse, then, the gear production can almost be made automatic, except loading/unloading of gear blanks. Small workshops can adopt this technology to manufacture gears at cheaper rates.

3.3 Experimentation

Here is an attempt made to produce gears on milling machine, with the help of computer. The overall arrangement (Refer fig. 2) consists of:

(i) Adaptation of stepper motor for indexing head,
(ii) Adaptation of another stepper motor for table traversing,
(iii) Controlling of these two (i & ii) with the help of computer,
(iv) Interfacing card, and
(v) Programming.

These topics are explained in the following sections.

Figure 2: Photograph Showing Overall Arrangement on Milling M/C

4. INDEXING

The operation of rotating the job through a required angle between two successive cuts is the basic requirement of gear cutting operation on milling machine. This is accomplished with the help of a milling attachment known as dividing head (Indexing head). In plain indexing it is possible to obtain almost any number of divisions desired except prime numbers and certain odd numbers greater than 50.

4.1 Reduction Gear

An indexing head of reduction 1:40 was selected and a stepper motor (2 N-m) was connected through a reduction gear (reduction ratio 2.5) to achieve a total reduction of 1:100 (Refer fig 3.). As the stepper motor rotates 1.8 degree per pulse and with this 1:100 reduction per pulse the work piece rotates 0.018 degrees . As we proceed to next tooth the error gets accumulated. Here the soft ware takes care and when the accumulated error becomes greater than the least error permissible, one extra step is given while indexing. The accumulated error is always—ve and the extra step introduces +ve error, thus the total error gets eliminated.

4.2 Logic of Indexing

It is seen in previous article that per step the rotation will be 1.8 degree. We will see the

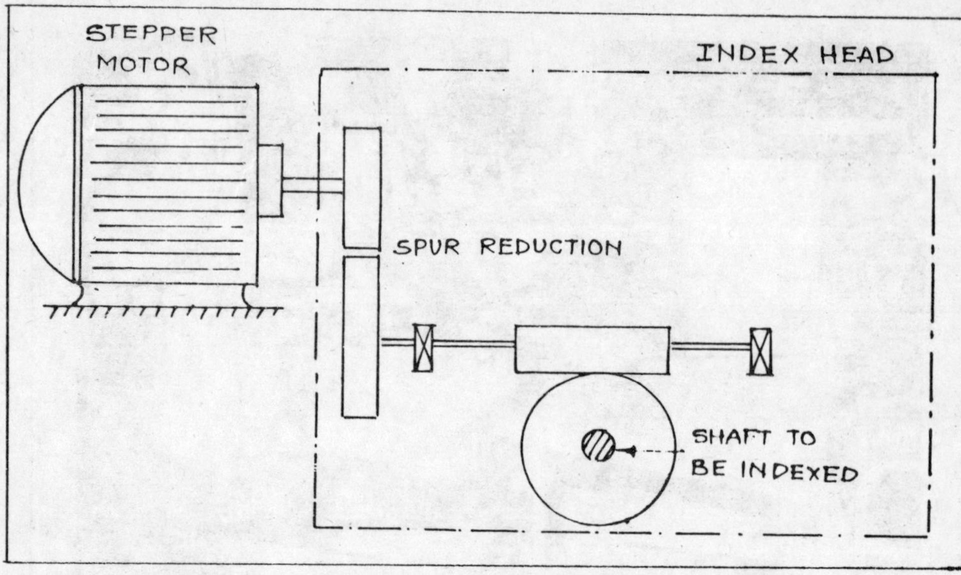

Figure 3: Indexing Head and Stepper Motor Arrangement

error calculation with an example. Suppose, we want to cut 18 teeth on a gear blank, then indexing angle required per tooth is dθ.

$$d\theta = \frac{360}{T} \frac{360}{18} = 20 \text{ degrees.}$$

Now, number of steps required

$$dN = \frac{d\theta}{0.018} = \frac{20}{0.018} = 1111.1111$$

It is possible to give 1111 steps or 1112 steps, so it induces an error of either—0.1111 step or +0.8888 steps i.e in degrees either—0.001998 or 0.016 degree. First of all 1111 steps are introduced and it accumulates the—ve error, when it becomes greater than or equal to half of the +ve error i.e. 0.016/2 = 0.008 degree, one extra step is introduced i.e. 1112 steps,which now introduces a +ve error, the next effect is to eliminate the—ve error, so the process repeats, till the entire gear is cut. The same logic is used in developing program in C language.

5. TABLE TRAVERSING

The milling machine differs from other machines in the movements of tool. Here work piece is moved (feed) and tool rotates on fixed axes. The table is given to and fro motion with the help of nut and screw mechanism. Here, screw shaft is extended to connect hand wheel, the same is used to connect the stepper motor (2 N-m). There is a reduction of 1:100 (1:2 from simple gear reduction and 1:50 from worm and worm wheel reduction, refer fig. No 4 & 5). The purpose of reduction is to increase the torque, required for table traversing and not to slower the traversing speed, as the stepper motor does not develop that much torque even at low speeds.

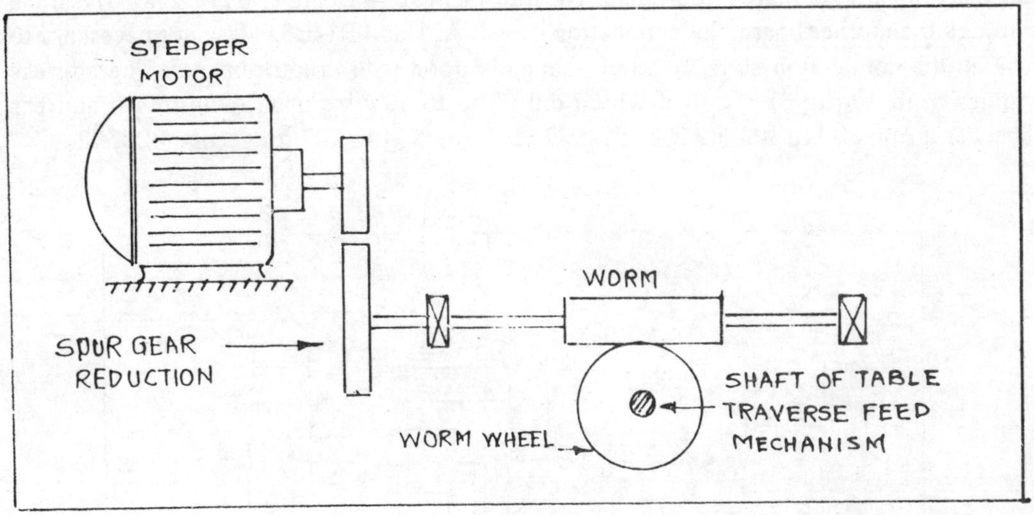

Figure 4: Table Traversing Feed Mechanism with Stepper Motor

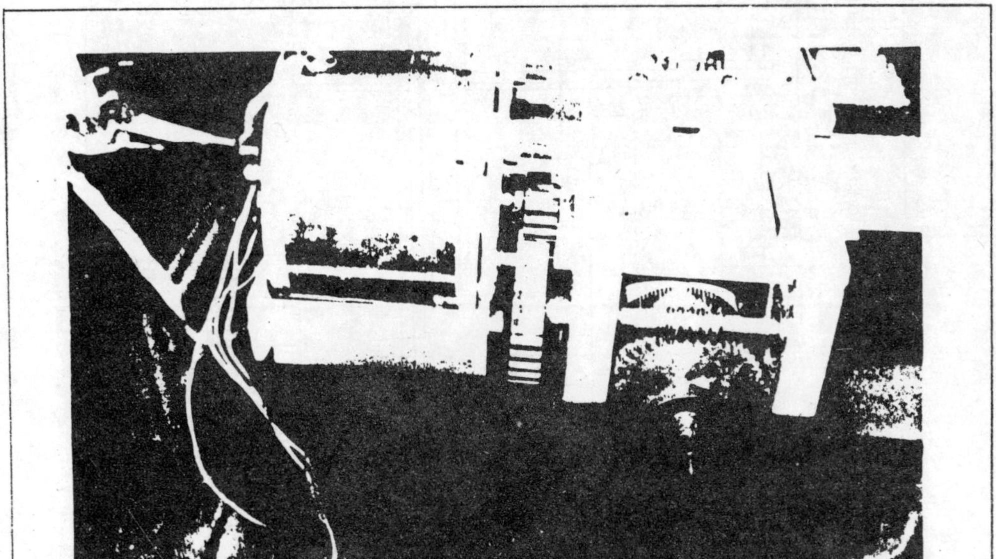

Figure 5: Photograph Showing Table Traversing Feed Mechanism

6. INTERFACING DEVICES

6.1 The Cards

Interfacing card interfaces the computer to the machine (here the milling machine) through ON/OFF switches and drives stepper motors. Interfacing of the computer with the machine has got more importance. The interfacing of the card (Refer fig no. 6) is done through the mother board slot connection i.e A1-A31 and B1-B31. It is not necessary to use all the connection slots, it totally depends upon users requirements. The address ranges from 300 to 3FF, out of which only 300 to 307 are used, along with address decoder. From 300 to 303 are used first 8255#1 and 304 to 307 for second 8255#2 .

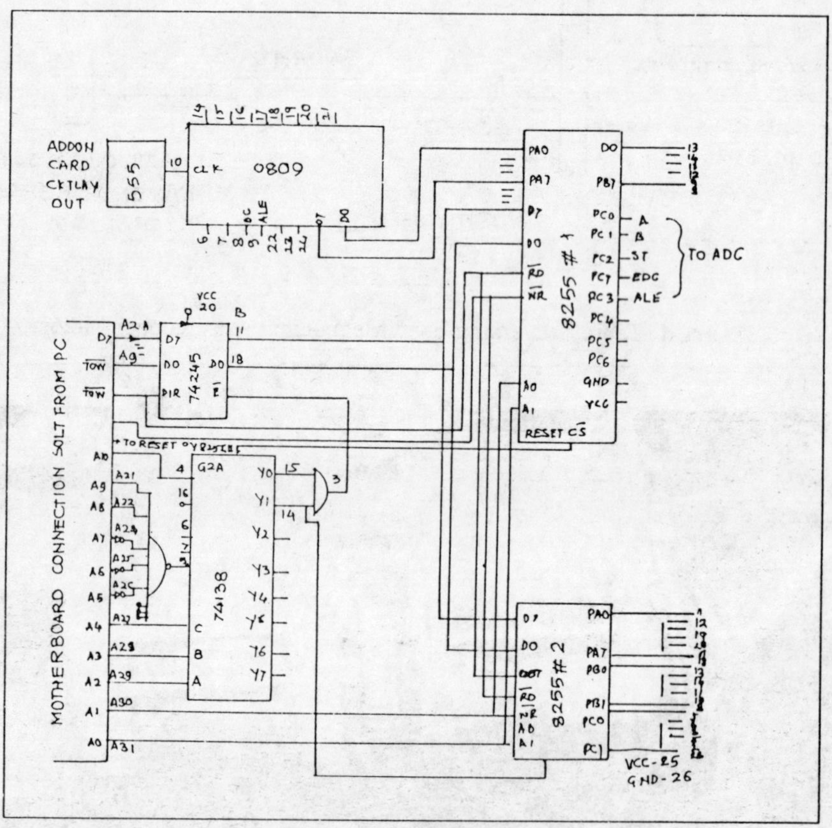

Figure 6: Circuit Diagram of Interfacing Card

6.2 The IC

The programmable peripheral interface (8255) is the main unit which interfaces the computer with the external circuit. Rather using one PPI there are two PPI used for fuhrer application and it is quite conventional concept. Each PPI has got its own IC select (CS) signals from the decoding logic, which consists of IC (74138), and can be enabled by 8 input NAND gate IC (7430) and address enable pin from mother board slot. It is necessary to use (74245) bi-directional buffer latch, for data transfer. The direction of data transfer takes place from A to B if IOR=0 and from B to A if IOR=1 . This IC is enable by the output of the AND gate whose input is two of eight output of 3:8 decoder IC (74138). The trans-receiver is enabled when one of the input of 7408 is becoming 0.

6.3 The Connections and Control Signals

Referring fig.no. 6, the address line A1,A0 are used to select the port of 8255. Line A4, A3, A2 are given to the 3:8 decoder, A2 to LSB of 74138 and A4 to MSB . A5, A6 and A7 are the inputs of the 8 input NAND gate sent through the NOT gate. The first three inputs are inverted and then applied to the 8 input NAND gate and kept low . The inputs A9 and A8 are high, so they are directly given to the 8 input NAND gate (74130) . The remaining three input of the NAND gate are tied to Vcc. Decoding IC 74138 are enabled by the output of 7430 . When A4, A3, A2 are at 0, 0, 0 and then Y0 out put (74138) is selected to enable the peripheral IC 8255#1 and when it is at 001 then it is selected Y1 which enables the 8255#2 . The ADC IC 0809 can be used to convert input analog data in to its equivalent digital data. This IC has got control signals from peripheral IC i.e. A, B, C START, ALE etc. output enable (OE) of this IC is tied to Vcc. The channel of this IC is selected by the A, B, C input from the port C of peripheral IC . Each analog data are converted in to its digital equivalent and sent on the line D7-D0 to the PA7 - PA0 of 8255#1 .

The pin of 8255#1 corresponding to indicated port is connected to the pin of 0809 as indicated in front of the pin. The pins D0-D7 of 0809 are connected to the PA0-PA7 of 8255#1 accordingly. The PA0-PA4 and PB0-PB4 of 8255#2 are connected as switching signals to the driver card. The output from the driver card is given to the two stepper motors.

6.4 The Driver Circuit

Electronic switching is the latest one and used to drive the stepper motor (Refer fig. no. 7). The stepper motor which draws approximately 3.3 amperes for each winding when it is ON. To increase the current rating, two transistors 2N3055 and CL100S are used in Darling ton mode. 2N3055 acts as switching transistor and CL100S is used to provide increased current gain, when transistors switched OFF, a large voltage due to the collapsing field is generated in the motor winding. This voltage forward biases the diode and breakdown is avoided. R1 and R2 act as voltage divider to protect CL100S . The current carrying capacity of 2N3055 is 15 amperes and our requirement is to connect 6.6 amperes load. Hence it is much safer.

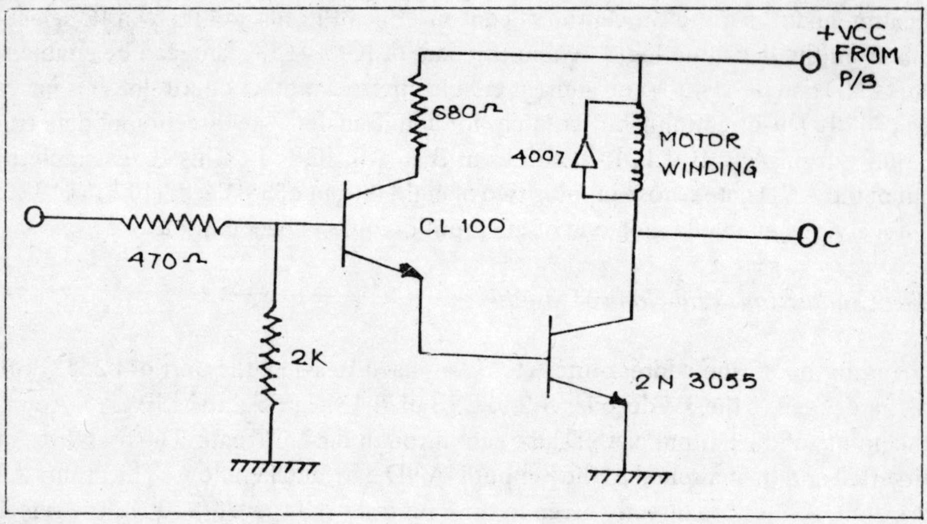

Figure 7: Circuit Diagram of Stepper Motor Driver Card

6.5 Power Supply

One stepper motor requires 3.3 amperes at 6 volts. Here two motors are connected in parallel, because each motor has got its own driving circuit in series with itself. To meet the needs of the power supply a step down transformer (220 V to 6 V) was designed and built. A capacitor (2200 μF, 63 V) is connected across the DC output of the rectifier to filter the DC supply.

7. THE FLOW CHART AND COMPUTER PROGRAMMING

The flow chart (Refer fig.no. 8) reads number teeth and linear travel of table and calculates the number of steps required for indexing and number of steps required for linear travel. It also calculates the parameters required for calculating the error. The soft ware written in C language itself checks the error time to time and gives proper number of steps to the motor which is driving the indexing head. After indexing it gives the required number of steps to the motor driving the table to feed it against the cutter. After one complete cut the table is given reverse motion to come back to its initial position.

Now the blank is to be indexed again and forward cut starts. When all teeth are cut, the control comes out of the loop and stops the entire process.

8. GEAR CUTTING

Experimentations were carried out, on milling machine with and without CNC attachment and it is observed about 10% of reduction in total machining time. A little

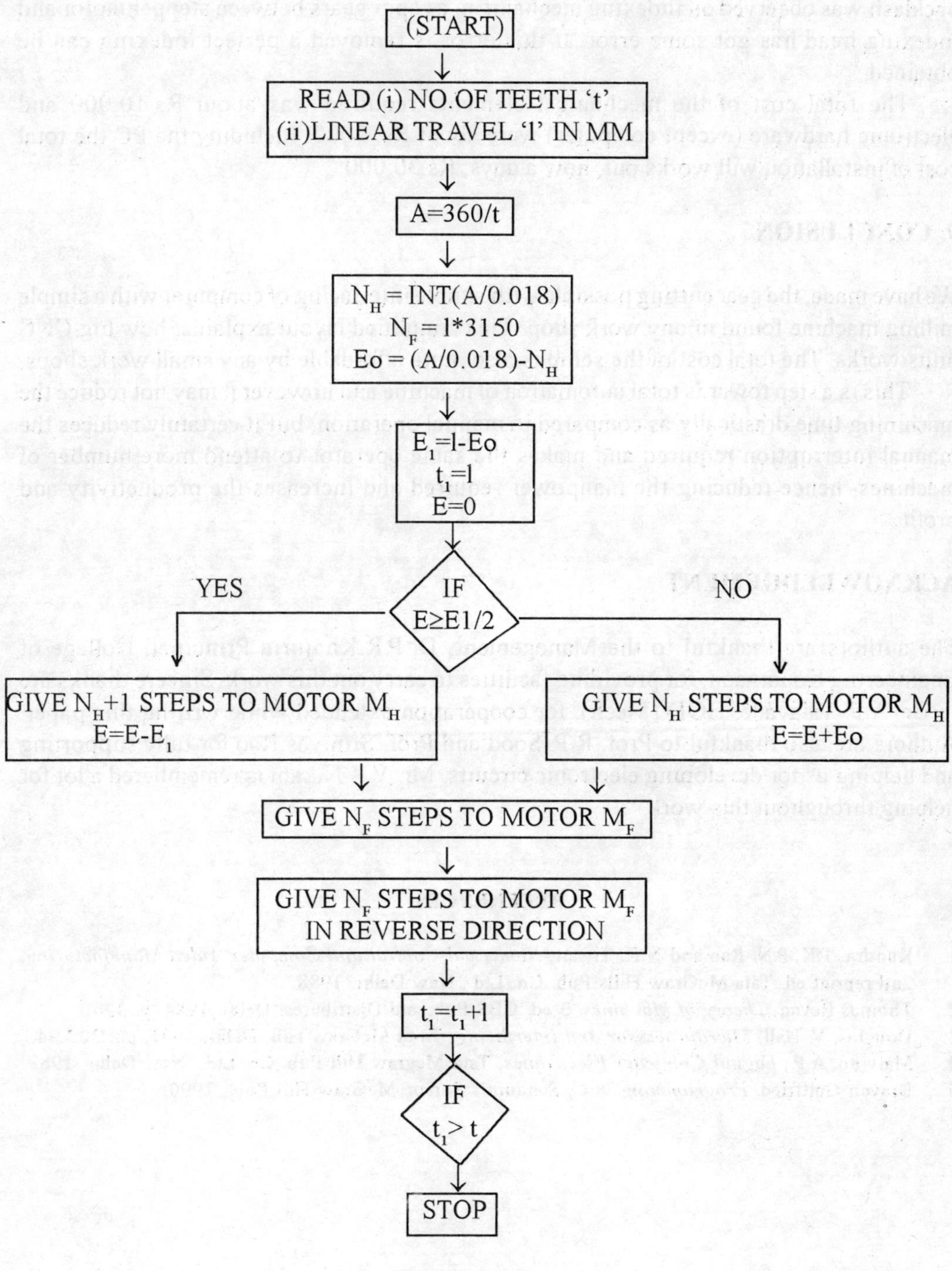

Figure 8: The Flow Chart

backlash was observed on indexing mechanism, as spur gears between stepper motor and indexing head has got some error. If this error is removed a perfect indexing can be obtained.

The total cost of the mechanical elements required was about Rs.10,000 and electronic hardware (except computer) were about Rs. 2000. Including the PC the total cost of installation will works out, now a days, Rs.30,000.

9. CONCLUSION

We have made, the gear cutting possible with simple interfacing of computer with a simple milling machine found in any work shop. This simplified layout explains, how big CNC units works. The total cost of the setup is also quite affordable by any small work shops.

This is a step towards total automation of machine and however it may not reduce the machining time drastically as compared to manual operation, but it certainly reduces the manual interruption required and makes the same operator to attend more number of machines, hence reducing the manpower required and increases the productivity and profit.

ACKNOWLEDGEMENT

The authors are thankful to the Management, Dr.P.R.Khajuria Principal, College of Engineering Kopargaon, for providing facilities to carry out this work. Sincere thanks are to Dr. A.P. Valavade, HOD (Mech), for cooperation extended while writing this paper. Authors are also thankful to Prof. R.P. Sood and Prof. Srinivas Rao for fully supporting and helping us for developing electronic circuits. Mr. V.P. Nikam is remembered a lot for helping throughout this work.

REFERENCES

1. Kundra. T.K, P.N. Rao and N.K. Tiwari, *Numerical Control and Computer Aided Manufacturing*, 2nd reprint ed. Tata McGraw Hills Pub. Co. Ltd., New Delhi. 1988.
2. Thomas Bevan, *Theory of Machines*, 3 ed. CBS Pub. and Distributes, Delhi, 1984, p. 326.
3. Douglas, V. Hall, *Microprocessor and Interfacing*, Ta-ta McGraw Hill, Delhi, 1991, pp. 302-04.
4. Malvino, A.P., *Digital Computer Electronics*, Tata Mcgraw Hill Pub. Co. Ltd., New Delhi, 1983.
5. Brayon Gottfried, *Programming in C*, Schaum's Series, McGraw Hill Pub., 1990.

A CIM APPROACH FOR SCHEDULING IN NAVAL DOCKYARD

16

Lt. P. Jayakumar

Naval Headquarter, New Delhi.

1. INTRODUCTION

This paper deals with Computer Integrated Manufacturing approach using Artificial intelligence techniques for scheduling of ship repairs in Naval Dockyard. The Naval Dockyards at Bombay and Visakhapatnam are the main stay of the Indian Navy with regard to ship repairs. These yards undertake routine maintenance and repair works of Naval Ships. The extensive work being undertaken by the dockyards call for an integrated approach of Macro and Micro level planning of refits and shop floor activities. This, however, is a very deep subject matter and may a require a vast and comprehensive research to establish all aspects, an attempt is made here to give a brief overview of the problem. This paper is not intended to be extensive and comprehensive but of an introductory nature.

2. SCHEDULING

The productivity and efficiency of any organisation is directly affected by the scheduling and manufacturing processes adopted by the organisation. The strategic goals of the organisation translate into long term plans and further evolve into macro and micro level plans progressively.

The strategic objective of the Naval Dockyard is to keep the Naval fleet in a healthy state of readiness to protect the Nation's maritime interests. This further translates into Annual refit schedules, quarterly schedules, monthly schedules, dry-docking plans, shop floor loading charts, manpower and material planning.

3. MANUFACTURING/PRODUCTION ENVIRONMENT

In scheduling it is important to effectively reflect the manufacturing and production environment including internal and external constraints. Unlike conventional manufacturing and production activities, ship repair has many uncertainties and interdependencies built into it. In Naval Dockyards the repairs are carried out by various work centres geographically and functionally separated over vast distances and specialising in specific tasks. The repair work may necessitate the assembling of various centres on the ship at a particular time or sequential action of various centres or the job being routed through the geographical locations of various shop floors to complete the repair work. In either case the repair activities would involve multicentres and multi activities and hence would call for careful co-ordination and monitoring.

3.1 Definition of Task Boundaries

Accurate description of the type and quantum of job forms an important aspect of definition of task boundaries. Where as some activities have specific task boundaries, some are nebulous. For instance, it is possible to a large extent to define task boundaries in respect of motor overhaul or hull painting or crop and renewal of specified areas of ship structure or replacement of equipment. While in the case of repairs to a grounded ship structure, survey and repair of ship structure, repair works involving trouble shooting, such as malfunctioning of weapon equipment or propulsion machinery and systems, it is difficult to a priori route or schedule the job are to lack of complete knowledge of the nature of repair and the consequent activities, centres and their interdependence involved. There have been cases where the yard accepts a work package for a certain number of man days and involving a certain number of centres and the work has expanded to many times these numbers. These are uncertainties involved in ship repair and this is further compounded by the compartmentalised functional structure of the dockyards with respect to flow of information and rigidity in re-scheduling due to various other factors which dictate the functioning of the individual work centres.

3.2 Other Constrants

The repair work of the dockyard require a broad and effective logistic support base. Machinery spare parts and yard materials flow into the dockyard from various sources which including foreign manufacturing enterprises. This logistic support is given by the Materials Organisation of the Navy. However, this logistic dependence brings in additional uncertainties into the working environment. The ideal schedule would cuter for the characteristics of the logistic support base and provide for flexibility in case of logistic irregularities.

4. PLANING AND CONTROL

Planning is the scheduling activity prior to the execution of the task and the objective of production control is the implementation of a predetermined plan or policy and the control of all aspects of production according to this plan. The activities of production planning and control are linked through data dependencies and the fact that the decisions made during planning often determine the nature and degree of control necessary at shop floor. Data gathered from shop floor will influence future plans.

The functions occurring during the production planning and control have dependencies which impact the initial scheduling activity and any re-scheduling that might become necessary. Scheduling occurs prior to shop floor activity as does planning. The requirement for real time control and the need for re-scheduling are governed by accuracy and amount of flexibility in the original schedule and in the environment. Scheduling accuracy is then dependent upon the accuracy and efficiency of the plan for production.

4.1 Scheduling for Production Control: (Monitoring and Re-scheduling)

Any solution to the scheduling problem must include methods for identifying deviant behaviour in the shop floor and methods for removal or reduction of the problem behaviour. Data collection and monitoring provides feed back for both short and long term scheduling tasks and support for management decisions. As an extension to planning and scheduling the monitoring and control of work can result in changes in the current plans and schedules in reaction to changing environments. However, the effects of an unpredicted event can be difficult to forecast and difficult to respond to in an optimal manner. For example a machine break down may require rescheduling of affected jobs only whereas a revision of production priority may require rescheduling of entire shop activities.

Another example is material non-availability which is often the case for delays. This would be a major aspect of scheduling, namely, logistic monitoring and feed back system, in the dockyard environment.

Presently monitoring and re-scheduling is done on a dynamic day to day basis referent on the feed back obtained from shops and ships under repair periodically. All deviant behaviour is addressed in review meetings. This procedure is effective but tedious and sometimes time consuming and cumbersome. The knowledge base if properly built and structure to incorporate all the aforesaid details then the CIM scheduling can greatly reduce the frequencies, length and necessity of such meetings.

Progressive standardisation of schedules for specific refit operations would be a great help in such on endeavour. Attempts are in hand for standardisation of various refit operation at Naval Dockyard one such existing standardised schedule is place at Table (1).

Development of such standard activity charts and establishing area of uncertainties and interdependencies would be an important aspect of the knowledge base that would be required for the CIM project.

4.2 Preventive Maintenance

When creating detail schedules, preventive maintenance of installed assets of the dockyard must also be included in it as it requires the same allocation of manufacturing

TABLE 1: **List of Items to be Degutted for Lifting of STBD, Main Engine-Ship 'A'**

S.No.	Description	Dept.	ETC.
I.	Engine Room (on Top of the Engine)		
(A)	Removal of Firemain System Pipes Pipes and Domestic FW System	SAX	D+1 Week
(B)	Removal of M/E Expansion Tank and its Pipes	FAB/SAX	D+1 Week
(C)	Removal of LO System Pipes	SAX	D+1 Week
(D)	Removal of Air Trunkings	FAB	D+1 Week
(E)	Removal of Electrical and Light Fittings	ELE	D+1 Week
	STBD. Fan Compartment		
(A)	Removal of Degausing Bed	FAB	D+2 Week
(B)	Removal of Hydrophore Tank	FAB	D+2 Week
(C)	Removal of SW and FW System Pipes	SAX	D+2 Week
(D)	Removal of Air System Pipes	SAX	D+2 Week
(E)	Removal of Electrical Starter with Cables	SAX	D+2 Week
(F)	Removal of FW Filter and its Pipes	FAB/SAX	D+2 Week
(G)	Removal of Halon Pipe Lines	SAX	D+2 Week
(H)	Removal of SW Hydrophore Tank (400 ltrs.) and Pipes	FAB/SAX	D+3 Week
(J) (I)	Removal of A/C Trunkings	FAB	D+3 Week
(II)	Disconnect/Decouple Shaft and System Pipes	GS	D+3 Week
(K) (I)	Removal of Electrical DB Boxes	ELE	D+3 Week
(II)	Disconnect and Removal of Slippings and Connections	ELE	D+3 Week
(I)	Removal of Air Trunkings	FAB	D+3 Week
(M) (I)	Removal of Electrical Light Fittings and Cables	ELE	D+3 Week
(II)	Removal of M/E EXHT, Fuel, LO, SW and FW Systems	PGS	D+3 Week
	STBD. Side "X" Gun Deck		
	The Following Items are to be Disconnected for Lifting of the Funnel:-		
(A)	Remove AFU Units and Trunkings	FAB	D+3 Week

(Contd.)

TABLE 1 *(Contd.)*

S.No.	Description	Dept.	ETC.
(B)	Remove Harbour DA Exhaust Trunkings	PGS	D+3 week
(C)	Remove Air Trunkings	FAB	D+3 week
(D)	Remove Electrical Connections and Fittings	ELE	D+3 week
(E)	Cut and Remove "X" Gun Deck (Extension of Soft Pathc)	FAB	D+4 week
(F)	Lifting of Funnel and Further Gas Cutting Assitance on X-Gun Deck as Required by C-123	PGS	D+4 week
(G)	Removal of Foundation Bolts and Lifting of Main Engine	PGS	D+4
II			
(A)	Engine of Foundations Bedding and QC Clearance	PGS/QC	D+5
(B)	Deformation Checks on SV Mountings, Grouping of Mountings and Blue Impression Checks on Foundation Frame	CDL/PGS/QC	D+5 week
(C)	Engine Lowering, Jerk Bolt Alignment, Manufacturing of New Shims, Alignment on Foundation Frame.	PGS/QC	D+8
(D)	Engine Exhaust, Fuel, LO, SW, Starting Air and FW System Pipes Fitment.	PGS	D+10 week
(E)	Assistance for Cutting, Jigging, Modification in-situ and Clamping.	FAB/SAX	D+10 weekl
(F)	Regutting of All Systems as Per Sl.No.1	ALL CONCERNED DEPTS.	D+14 week

Glossary:

ETC — Estimated time for completion.
D — Starting date.
SAX — System Auxiliaries Department.
FAB — Fabrication Department.
ELE — Electrical Department.
GS — Gearing and shafting Department.
PGS — Propulsion Gearing and Shafting Department.
QC — Quality Control Department.
CDL — Central Dockyard Laboratory.

resources as a refit job, viz. Material, labour, tools etc.

5. *SCHEDULE EVALUATION

Schedule evaluation is useful for determining both the efficiency of the schedule and for input to subsequent planning and scheduling activities. The information used to determine the efficient use of materials and resources is derived from data gathered through the monitoring function of shop floor control. The information indicates the effectiveness of a given schedule based on cost and time performance criteria. Percent utilisation of labour and machine time, set up time, inventory levels and total work content are also indicative of schedule effectiveness.

6. *SCHEDULE AND AI IN THE CIM ENVIRONMENT

The complexity and uncertainty of the manufacturing environment result in two issues that make scheduling solutions difficult and identify the problem as appropriate for the application of AI techniques. The first difficulty is due to the size of the search space and the process of finding a sequence of actions that will achieve a goal state. As the environment becomes more complex, the number of possible combinations increases exponentially with the addition of each new operator. When large numbers of sequences are possible and a large problem space must be searched for the appropriate sequence of problem-solving operations, the result is combinatorial explosion and a loss of scheduler efficiency. The second difficulty issues from relationships among interacting subproblems and the resulting additional complexity and uncertainty for the search function to handle.

The factory scheduling problems is typically associated with a poor ability to predict shop behaviour. One goal of the research in scheduling has been to improve this predictive capability. Attempts have been made to produce a scheduler capable of generating production schedules that accurately reflect both the full complexity of the factory environment and the stated objectives of the organisation.

There is another aspect to the scheduling problem, however. This other aspect concerns the ability to react intelligently to changing circumstances, i.e. flexibility. Even though the schedule reflects the complexity of the environment and the objectives of the organisation, the shop floor is a dynamic environment where unexpected events continually occur. The occurrence of events such as machine breakdown, failure of in process orders to pass intermediate quality control inspections, lack of operators, and so on, quickly results in the need to revise previously scheduled activities. A complete solution to the scheduling problem must include the function of predictive planning coupled with an ability to alter schedules in response to changing factory conditions.

7. *A SOLUTION TO THE SCHEDULING PROBLEM: KNOWLEDGE BASED SYSTEM

When discussing scheduling solutions and AI it is important to understand the knowledge requirements for the scheduling activities. The knowledge required for accomplishing the task of scheduling must be complete, well-define and carefully structured. Methods for representing and using this knowledge must result in schedules that are efficient yet flexible.

An approach to scheduling that will produce a usable schedule that is both robust and efficient is to build real-time knowledge-based process schedules using AI techniques combined with some aspect of current simulation. A knowledge-based approach allows the effective handling of system dynamics and incomplete information, which characterise this class of problem (Ford and Floyd, 1986). A carefully arranged combination of data structure and interpretative procedures that define the knowledge system can be used to produce a scheduler which behaves intelligently.

The expert system approach is applicable to scheduling because it facilitates the co-ordination of general purpose knowledge with dedicated information provided by the shop floor manager, data from the shop monitor and any other relevant information provided by CIM structure. Schedulers using this approach are real-time and knowledge based in the sense that the production of an efficient schedule for a task required detailed knowledge and understanding of the process domain. The domain description can be contained in a knowledge base that is used in conjunction with current task data for the timely development of a schedule that is not only flexible but also efficient.

CONCLUSION

The key to achieving success is better utilisation of resources. Effective scheduling in dockyards can lead to reduction of inventory, docking time, refit durations and manpower consumption. Scheduling will also be useful to route refits in an optimal manner. Expert systems can be used for both inventory and production scheduling for decision support. The Naval Dockyard is an appropriate environment for such an attempt. With modern manufacturing techniques catching up all over the world, the Navy is also moving towards computer integrated approaches in manufacturing. CIM based scheduling would play an important role in such an environment.

*Excerpted from Ref. [6]

REFERENCES

1. Barrankin, E.W., 1952. The scheduling problem as an algebraic generalisation of ordinary linear programming. *Industrial Logistics Research Project, Discussion Paper No.18.*, University of California, Los Angeles, California.
2. Borwne, J., Boon, J.E. and Davies, B.J., 1981. Job Shop Control. *International Journal of Production Research*, 19(6): 633-643.
3. Ford, D. and Floyd, S. 1986. *An Expert System for Dynamic Scheduling.* In, Porc. SIGART Int.. Symp. On Methodologies for Intelligent Systems, pp.56-63.
4. Graves, S.C. 1981. *A Review of Production Scheduling.* Operations Research, 29(4):646-675.
5. Harrington, J. 1984. *Understanding the Manufacturing Process.* Marcel Dekker, New York.

6. Kusiak, A. *Artificial Intelligence: Implications for CIM*, Springier, Verlong.
7. Melnyk, S.A. *et al.*, 1985. *Shop Floor Control*. Dow Jones Irwin, Homewood, Illinois.
8. Salvador, M.S., 1978. *Scheduling and Sequencing*. In, Moder, J. and Elmagharby, S.E. (Eds.), *Handbook of Operations Research : Models and Applications*, Vol. 2, pp. 268-300. Van Nostrand, Florence, Kentuchky.
9. Wlaker, T.C. and Miller, R.K. 1986. *Expert System 1986—An Assessment of Technology and Application*, pp. 121-128. SEAI Technical Publications, Madison, Georgia.
10. Wild, R. 1971. *The Techniques of Production Management*. Holt, Rinehart and Winston, New York.

RAPID PROTOTYPING—AN OVERVIEW OF THE PRESENT STATE-OF-THE-ART

17

M. Sreenivasa Kumar

Asst. Professor, Dept. of Mechanical Engineering,
K.I.T.S. Ramtek - 441106, Nagpur (Dt.).

ABSTRACT

Due to the world-wide competitive situation, interest in new methods,business practices and technologies to improve and accelerated product development have increased continuously over the last few years. Production benefits in industry have been obtained with such techniques as simultaneous engineering and total quality management and CAD, CAM, CAE and NC technologies. In product development, Rapid Prototyping (RP) and Rapid Product Development (RPD) have turned out to be the instruments to save time and money and develop innovative products.

Beginning in the late 1970's new technologies have been developed aimed at improving and hastening the manufacturing time of prototypes, contrary to other automated fabrication technologies in use, the basic principle of these new technologies is an additive process, where a conventional automated prototyping normally uses subtractive processes such as NC milling or grinding. In a period of only few years Rapid Prototyping has changed from a number of inaccurate technologies widely met with a pitying smile, to a mighty significant tool. Now it is hard not to imagine that it is not used in the automotive industry and related branches. Nowadays, R&D activities on Rapid prototyping are located at a large number of Universities and research centers and the number of additive fabrications is still increasing, even if most processes have still not been commercialize. The object of this paper is to give an over view of the present state-of-the art, commercial technologies, R&D activities and trends in Rapid prototyping. This paper also discuss about system selection of Rapid Prototyping.

1. INTRODUCTION

Prototyping involves producing a component in small numbers before commencing large scale production. The need creating prototypes arieses due to several reasons which includes: (1) Verification of physical objects, (2) Testing for fit, form and assembly, (3) Feedback from different people, (4) Review of the product. The first commercial apparatus was presented at the AUTOPACT show in Detroit (USA) and was based on selectively curing a surface layer of photo polymer using a laser and building three dimensional objects with successive layers. Up to 1990, about 150 commercial machines based on Sterolithography were sold before the first the new additive fabricators such as fused deposition modelling, laminated object manufacturing, solid ground curing and selective laser sintering came on the market. At that time, the systems were relatively inaccurate and the choice of materials limited but it was possible to manufacture prototypes in days instead of months. Therefore, first applications and benefits were possible in rapidly manufacturing prototypes of low quality, which were used for design tests and as acquisition and communication tools. According to these abilities, the additive processes were given the term rapid prototyping.

2. WORKING PRINCIPLE

Present commercial Additive Fabricators allow the building of prototypes in a limited choice of materials. Most materials used are photosensitive polymers, nylon, polycarbonate, a wood-like material and some other plastics. Recent developments allow direct production in a metallic alloy. To obtain prototyping in other materials, post-processing such as surface finishing or sintering or subsequent processes such as moulding or casting are necessary. Nevertheless, the number and quality of materials is increasing rapidly. The size of the process chambers of all systems is still below one meter in each direction. Larger objects have to be built as separate small parts and glued together afterwards.

3-D CAD data of an object is the common information source for AF's because all AF's build the objects layerwise, which means that material is added layer by layer, all machines need information on a number of parallel cross sections of the objects at a given distance. Fig. 1 shows the most commonly used procedure preparing 3-d CAD data for AF's. In most cases the CAD data are converted into neutral data format. In Rapid prototyping the STL format became a defacto standard for the representation of the 3-D geometry description of objects.The objects are represented by facets building an approximated closed description of the surface objects. Basic elements of the STL format are triangles with a normal vector. Most 3-D CAD systems include an STL interface.The

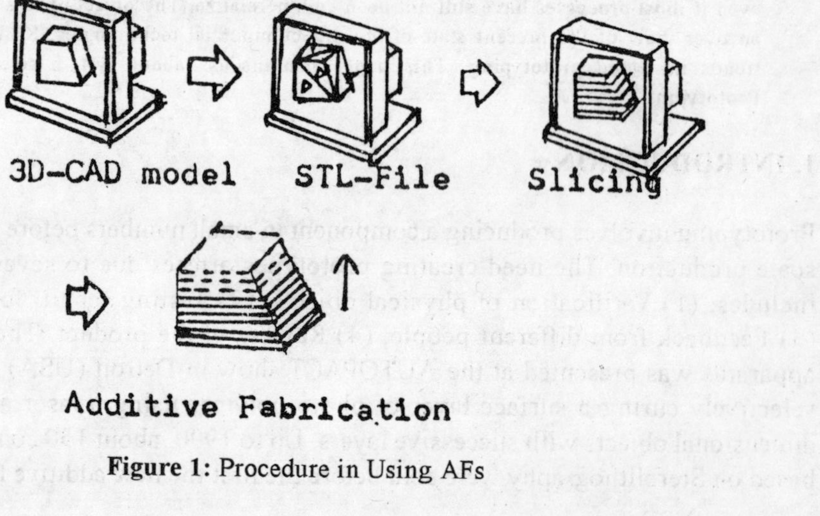

Figure 1: Procedure in Using AFs

STL file of an object is the input for a slice computer. The result is a number of parallel cross sections. Each cross section involves information where material has to be added. The distance to the following cross-section fixes the height of the single layer. Hence AFs could be seen as 3-D plotters The slices serve to control the fabricator depend ent on the actual principle.

The different systems may be categorized by the different basic working principles as:

1. Selective hardening of photo sensitive material by radiation
2. Selective fusing or sintering powder by a laser beam.
3. Selective freeform deposition of material.
4. Contour cutting and adhering of sheets.

Most of the systems need some degree of post processing to in fluence the quality of the finished model.

2.1. Selective Hardening of Photosensitive Material by Radiation

Basic to all systems is a photo initiated radical polymerization process. "Polymerization is the process of linking small molecules (monomers) into larger molecules (Polymers comprised of many monomer units". A loose bonding exists between small organic molecules (carbo compounds) based on Vander waals interactions. Therefore, these molecules tend to exist in a liquid phase. If the molecules have a carbon double bonding, it can be forcibly broken by a catalyst. Such catalysts are commonly free radicals which initiate a chain reaction. Large carbo chains arise from monomers in micro regions near the site of the catalysts. The vander waals interaction between the molecules increases with the length of the molecules and therefore, the material cures in regions of polymerization. The key to an AF is to control the locations where the polymerization happens. The material is selectively exposed by radiation (mostly Ultra Violet light). The catalysts (free radicals) are formed from a photo initiator in the resin by a photo chemical process. The photo-initiator is trimmed to absorb photons with a special frequency. In consequence, if the resin is exposed to radiation with the right frequency, the fluid is immediately hardened by low energy absorption, because of the initiation of chain reactions.

2.1.1 Stereolithography

Fig. 2 described the principle and construction of an SLA 250 made by 3D systems INC. The light source is an HeCd laser. The Laser beam is focused by lenses and deflected to the surface of a Vat by two rotating mirrors. A computer uses the slice information to control the mirror (scanner). If one layer is ready, the platform is moved one layer thickness downwards. The level of the resin surface is measured by a HeNe laser using a

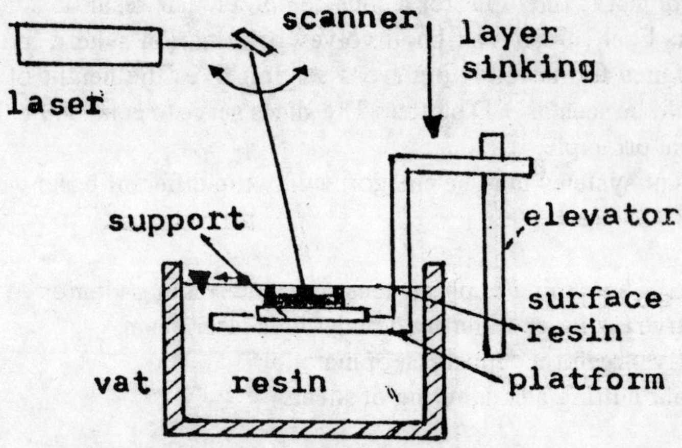

Figure 2: Stereolithography

triangulation method and adjusted accordingly. A recoating system wipes over the resin and ensures a flat surface. The laser beam scans the contours of the next slice .Then the, interior of the contours is scanned line by line, like a hatch pattern.The speed of the laser beam and therefore, the intensity over an area is adjusted, so the exposed area cures in a depth a little over the thickness to ensure good bonding to the last layer. The whole object is to built by repeating this process cycle up to the last layer.At the end the platform is raised and the object removed from the platform. Because the material is not completely hardened the object is usually cured in a UV oven.

Based on this process, there are several systems by different vendors on the market. Some of these are 3D system (valencia, CA, USA) offers three AF's (SLA 190, SLA 250, SLA 500) based on the stereolithography process, which cost from $ 110,000 to $ 450,000 each.

2.1.2. Simultaneous Layer Curing

Two commercial systems do not use layers to expose the resin. A strong UV lamp or liquid crystal display (LCD) is used to produce the necessary light.

A thin layer of liquid is spread: (a) and exposed to a UV light source through a mask, (b) each layer is thus fully cured at the intended locations by on flash. Each excess liquid, which is not polymerized, is removed, (c) by vacuum section and replaced by wax, (d) to support the model during construction. Following this the layer is milled smoothly to the controlled Z value. The process cycle is repeated until the parts are finished.

2.2 Selective Fusing or Sintering Powder by a Laser Beam

The process of the following systems resembles stereolithography, although the main differences are that the material is not a fluid photo polymer but a thermoplastic powder, and is the laser heat, not the light, that causes the hardening. Therefore high-power infrared lasers are used. The parts are produced by selective melting or sintering of powder caused by a laser beam controlled by CAD data.

2.2.1 Selective Laser Sintering

As the selective laser sintering process begins, a very thin layer of heat fusible powder is deposited onto the part-building cylinder within the process chamber. A laser is then used to sinter only the powder that is inside a cross-section of the part. The intersection of the laser beam with the powder elevates the temperature to the point of melting, fusing the powder particles and forming a solid mass. The intensity of the laser beam is modulated to melt the powder only in areas defined by the objects design geometry. Once the layer has scanned the entire cross section, another layer of powder is laid on top and the whole process is repeated. DTM Corporation (Austin, USA) brought the first commercially system onto the market. The sinteration 2000 uses a CO_2 laser as heat source.

2.3 Selective Freedom Deposition of Material

The main principle of the following technologies is the selective trapping of the material. It should be considered that this is one of the main principles of how things originate in nature and technique. It could be realized by many physical and chemical effects. Rapid Prototyping realizes the selective freeform extrusion of material. It is a principle used in an increasing number of AF systems with a lot of technical variants. All of the following technologies use a moving nozzle or jet through which material is extruded. The developments began with fused deposition modeling (FDM), 3D-printing and ballistic particle manufacturing.

2.3.1 Fused Deposition Model

FDM was invented by scott crump in 1988 and is sold by stratasys INC. The parts are built layer by layer. Liquid thermoplastic material is extruded and then deposited into thin layers. The main feature of the system is an X-Y controlled heat head. The liquid material solidifies very quickly after it is effected from nozzle. After this the platform is lowered one width layer and the deposition continues. In brief the process could be termed as an inverse NC milling process. This FDM is shown in Fig. 3.

2.3.2 3-D Printing

3-D printing is a process developed at the Massachusetts Institute of Technology (MIT) in Boston, USA. Whereas most AF's first focussed on plactic parts, 3-D printing is a process developed to directly produce metallic and ceramic parts. Similar to selective laser sintering of coated powder, first a green part of powder binder mixture is built during the

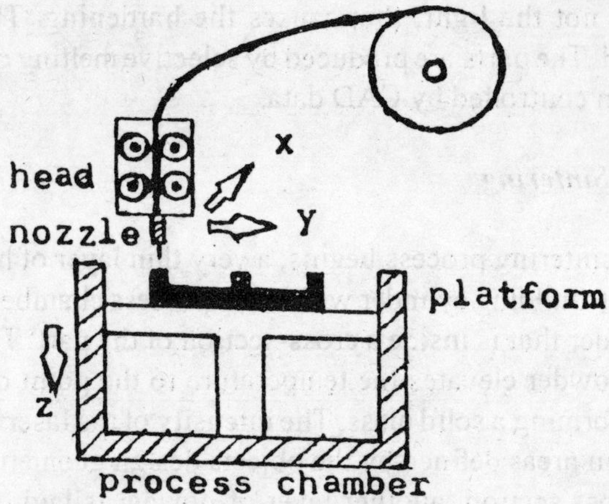

Figure 3: Fused Deposition

process. The powder is selectively joined together by deposition of a liquid binder using a process similar to inkjet printing. After lowering the platform the cycle is complete. A license to commercialize the process for metal casting was granted to soligen, USA. They call the process direct shell production casting (DSPC). The DSPC parts are somewhat less accurate than those produced by stereolithography.

2.4 Contour Cutting and Adhering of Sheets

Gluing flat pieces together to create 3-D models is a method long used in art, architecture and other applications. The computer aided automation of this process started in the early 1990's. The basic principle of such machines involves two main steps. One is to glue planar slices together, the second is to cut the shapes out a planer piece. The methods under this process are laminated object manufacturing. Rapid Prototyping system. Selective adhere and hot press process, Sparx AB (Sweden).

2.4.1 Laminated Object Manufacturing

Helisys Inc (Torrance, CA, USA) which was formerly hydronetics, developed and commercialized the laminated object manufacturing process (LOM) Fig. 4. The parent material is Polyethelene coated paper, which is available on a paper drum. Using CAD data a focused layer beam above a table covered with a sheet of heat-activated adhesive coated paper. The beam cuts a two-dimensional cross-section of the object to be built by incising the slices out line in the paper. A second layer of paper is then bonded to the top of the first, and the next cross-section is cut. The result is a part that looks like laminated wood. The machine is available in two sizes.

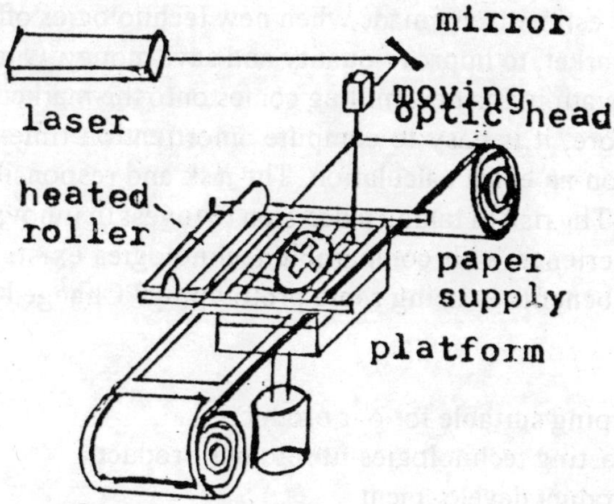

Figure 4: Laminated Object Manufacturing

3. SYSTEM SELECTION

Methods and tools to help the staff in the product development department to select the process will come on the market soon. The basis of these methods is to find a relationship between the process and properties of prototypes. A modified version of the "House of Quality" is one method to select prototype manufacturing process on the basis of product features.

The Basic Steps in this procedure are:

1. First of all the relevent product features are recorded. The preferred direction of measurable features is entered as a symbol. Limit values for measurable features are also entered.
2. The importance of the feature in the prototype required at the current stage of development is defined and entered in the form of weighting.
3. The possible prototype manufacturing processes are selected. Then the evaluation matrix is filled in.
4. The evaluation in the matrix are multiplied by the feature-weighting and individual values for each process are added.
5. As further refinement the limiting conditions are entered. These include anticipated costs and time until the prototype is available.
6. The product features are examined in pairs to determine their influence on each other.

4. CONCLUSIONS

The accuracy and surface roughness of Rapid Prototyping differ from process to process.

The primary aim of introducing Rapid Prototyping technologies is to improve product development. Investments are made when new technologies offer possibilities to reduce the lead time to market, to improve quality and save money. One problem of AF's is their high level of innovation. If a new milling comes onto the market which is twice as fast as the one used before, it is easy to compute amortization time. The decision for investment can be done on an exact calculation. The risk and responsibility of decision-maker is completely low. The risk in taking a decision to invest in innovative technologies is higher when less experience with comparable technologies exists. The often heard question "Are there real benefits in using rapid prototyping? Changed to questions such as:

1. Is rapid prototyping suitable for our products.
2. What AF and casting technologies fit into our product.
3. Line and our product development.
4. What is the fastest way to produce tools?
5. What should be considered if want to use Rapid Prototyping.

Nevertheless the use is no guarantee for a successful product development. The situation is well described with the following formula. Rapid Prototyping can deliver tremendous benefits for a lot of products, but only if the overall business plan is good. More and more companies understand the benefits and limits of rapid prototyping. About 80% of the sales have been made by USA system Manufacturers. Japan follows and then Europe.

Acknowledgements

The author is very much thankful to the Management and Principal Dr. G. Thimma Reddy, K.I.T.S. Ramtek for their encouragement, kind permission to present this paper.

REFERENCES

1. Roon Lewald, *New Approach in Rapid Prototyping*, American Ma chinist, Dec. 1991.
2. "Rapid Prototyping is Coming Age", *Mechanical Engineering*, July 1995, pp. 63-65.
3. "Rapid Prototyping Systems", *Mechanical Engineering*, April 1991, pp. 34-43.
4. Alan S. Brown, "Rapid Prototyping—Parts Without Tools", *Aerospace America*, Aug. 1991, pp. 18-23.
5. Jacobs, Paul F., "Rapid Prototyping and Manufacturing", *Society of Manufacturing Engineers*, Dearborn, 1992.

RECLAMATION TECHNIQUES IN ARMY BASE WORKSHOPS

18

Lt. Col. P.C. Jagia

512, Sena Base Workshops, Kirkee, Pune

INTRODUCTION

Reclamation literally implies recall. In technological terms it would relate to bringing back worn components to their original specifications. The process of reclamation is a boon for such organisations where the requirement of spares does not match the availability. This is very much relevant in the Army Base Workshops or Factories dealing with overhaul of equipment involving complete strip and rebuild.

BENEFITS OF RECLAMATION

Reclamation has a wide variety of benefits. In a production oriented industry, like an Army Base Workshops, actual requirement of spares and components cannot be expected to match with what will be available at any point of time to meet scheduled targets. Hence reclaiming old components becomes a very handy tool.

With regards to imported equipment, it may so happen that the spares are not available from the country of origin. Further, there may be no equivalents available within the country. Under such circumstances, the only viable option available is reclamation.

At times, the cost of replacement items may be exhorbitant. Reclamation offers us an alternate solution at a fraction of the cost.

In case of obsolence equipment, the only avenue offering a solution is reclamation.

While undertaking reclamation, it is imperative, that, to ensure reliability, quality of reclamation has to be of the highest standard. The factors that may be taken into consideration are physical and chemical properties, resistance to corrision, types of stresses, hardness of machined surface, degree of accuracy and extent of wear etc.

SCOPE OF RECLAMATION

With the advancement of welding techniques such as metal spraying and introduction of epoxy resins and sophisticated rubber compounds, it is possible to reclaim almost all spares pertaining to veh and equipment, provided proper machining facilities exist.

ECONOMICS OF RECLAMATION

It is rather difficult to access accurately the economics of reclamation in a Base Workshop, due to non-availability of vocab rates, both for the spares and the raw material.

Sometimes, though technically possible, it becomes uneconomical to reclaim a few items, whereas a larger number becomes an economical proposition. Again sometimes it may not be adviseable to reclaim certain components, for a proper cost analysis may reveal that it would be cheaper to buy new parts. Reclamation should therefore, be attempted only after the economics have been studied, unless shop floor bottlenecks dictates immediate requirement. In case of warlike spares, especially of imported origin, the question of economic assumes secondary importance.

RECLAMATION OF ASSEMBLIES AND COMPONENTS

Reclamation and regeneration of components is a major activity undertaken today in 512 Army Base Workshop. Approximately 80% of the tank components are reused after regeneration. It is thus this very important factor which keeps the cost of overhaul to about 30 to 40% of the cost of a new tank. A T-55 tank after overhaul is supposed to get a new lease of life of about 10000 km/12 years. Thus a regenerated component should be able to give 80% (if not more) life obtained from a newly manufactured component. Techno economics of the regenerated components have to be carefully examined so as to ensure that the cost of regeneration does not exceed 30 to 40% of.

A large variety of components of the Armoured Vehicles are being subjected to reclamation. These can broadly be classified as follows:

(a) Mechanical components
(b) Electronic components
(c) Instruments
(d) Armaments

Mechanical Components—These form the major chunk of the reclamation process, by virtue of their high cost and low availability. Moreover, these components are also readily amneable to reclamation process in vogue. The components that are being subjected to reclamation are as follows:

Electronic Components—The number of electronic/electrical components that are being reclaimed are relatively few as compared to mechanical components. The process being undertaken in this field relate to reclamation of plugs and sockets which are approximately of 100 different types.

INSTRUMENTS

In the Army, instruments cover a wide field ranging from compasses, binoculars, telex machines to IR equipment and thermal imaging equipment.

ARMAMENT

Gun and its components being of a sensitive nature, from safety point of view, stringent checks are maintained. Hence very few armament components are being subjected to reclamation. The only assy being reclaimed is the Cradle Assy.

PLANT AND MACHINERY

In order to carry out reclamation in a Army Base Workshop, the following plant and machinery would be very essential:

(a) Magnetic crack detector,
(b) Ultrasonic Flaw detector,
(c) Electronic microscope,
(d) Crank & cam shaft grinding machines,
(e) Profile grinding machine,
(f) Gear teeth grinding machine,
(g) Broaching machine,
(h) Gear milling machine,
(i) Various types of welding like Submerged arc welding, Tig/Mig welding, electron beam welding, plasma welding, thermit welding, laser welding etc.,
(j) Heat treatment plant, and
(k) Electroplating plant etc.

RECLAMATION TECHNIQUES

With the advancement in technology, the variety of techniques available for reclamation has also taken a quantum jump. Reclamation has become more of an art, the techniques available may be enumerated as follows:

(a) Maintenance Welding,
(b) Metal Spraying,
(c) Hard chrome plating,
(d) Electro vibration,
(e) Electro deposition,
(f) Rubber bonding,
(g) Epoxy bonding, and
(h) Rototec process.

MAINTENANCE WELDING

This is the simplest form of reclamation where the metallic component is joined together, if cracked/broken, with the use of suitable electrode using arc welding. It may also be by gas welding. However, during this process, there is possibility of very high localised temperatures, which could result in distortion of the components, thus the process requires great care while being performed.

RECLAMATION BY METAL SPRAYING

Metallising or metal spraying is a process whereby any metal in wire form, is fed through a special gun to a nozzle, where it is melted in an oxygen gas flame and atomised by a blast of compressed air, which carries metal particles to a previously prepared surface. The process involves the following:

(a) Cleaning the surface thoroughly to remove all traces of oil and grease.
(b) Undercutting of the job is done to provide space for the sprayed end for effective bonding. The thickness of coating should be .010" for 1" dia or less, and .005" for every addl. inch of dia upto a max of .040".
(c) The undercut surface is roughened for proper bonding by threading or knurling.
(d) There are various wires which are used as spray steel.
(e) The ends of the undercut sec are first sprayed. The metal may be deposited in either single or multi-passes.
(f) Coating thickness not to exceed .005" to .010" per pass.
(g) The work should be heated to a temp at 80 C to 100 C.
(h) Finishing is then done by machining or grinding.

ELECTRO DEPOSITION PROCESS

Hard chrome deposit by this process has higher wear resistance, good corrosion resistance properties. The process involves the following:

(a) Procedure

(i) Degrease by vapour degreasing.
(ii) Mask surfaces not required to be plated by dipping component in molten wax.
(iii) Suspend job in hard chrome vat.
(iv) Apply reverse current for 15 sec to 60 sec as per job.
(v) Normalise current.
(vi) Remove job after obtaining required deposition.
(vii) Rinse in running water.
(viii) Grind article to size.

This process can be used for cylinder liners, crank and cam shafts, rocker arm shafts etc.

RECLAMATION BY RUBBER BONDING

There has been development of many rubber bonded components, ranging from engine and radiator foundations to mounting of vehicle steel cabs and steel bodies. The stages of reclamation are as follows:

(a) Perished rubber is removed.
(b) Base metal is cleaned.
(c) Adhesive solution is applied.
(d) The metal component is placed in a moulding die which is packed with pieces of untreated synthetic rubber.
(e) Untreated rubber is baked for the laid down period.
(f) Excess material is cut off and the rubberised surface is finished by buffing.

RECLAMATION BY EPOXY RESINS

Epoxy resins are plastics made by the reaction of bisphenol and epichloro hydrin, and include a number of types of resins, all of which are tough, flexible, adhesive and chemically resistant. They exhibit low shrinkage, and excellent electrical insulation properties, leading to their application in air craft and auto industries.

M-seal is an epoxy resin which has a resin and hardener. So also Araldite. Before application, the surface has to be prepared, to eliminate dirt, grease, oil and moisture. Surface is roughened by sand blasting. Epoxy compound is then applied and allowed to cure for specified time. It can then be machined for finishing.

RECLAMATION BY ROTOTEC

This is low heat input process which has been made possible by the development of special exothermic bonding power, which enables the basic metal to retain its original properties without distortion or warping.

The reclamation procedure involves the following:

(a) The work piece is thoroughly degreased.
(b) The work is set up truly between centres on a lathe.
(c) Masking of areas around the worn out area is done by Eutectic solution IO3 as well as holes slots, keyways etc.
(d) The worn area is undercut to provide greater strength to the coating. The min depth should be 0.75 mm. Shoulders are bevelled at 45°.
(e) The undercut is then roughened by threading.
(f) Preheat the work piece to 150°C.
(g) Keep the tip of gun 12mm from the workpiece and 25 mm beyond the end of the undercut.

(h) Slide the powder feed valve back and start traversing over the worn area, covering it completely. A layer of .05" should be adequate.

(i) Final coat should be of sufficient thickness to rebuild to original dimension, with excess to allow for finishing.

(j) Machine the excess metal and finish off by grinding.

CONCLUSION

During the existing environment of resource crunch all around, reclamation can prove to be the saviour for the industry. There are reclamation processes available for every type of job. It is essential that before carrying out reclamation, the correct process, most suited to a specific job, is ascertained. For this purpose, the availability of adequate testing facilities is imperative.

Reclamation can provide us saving in terms of cost and equipment down time. In case of equipment of import origin, through reclamation we are able to overcome the problem of obsolecence and reuse components which are otherwise not available from the country of origin. Thus reclamation is one of the most versatile tool in the hands of the technician.

RECLAMATION AND REBUILDING TECHNIQUE

19

Maj. M. Ravi

6016 INDEP Armed Wksp EME

INTRODUCTION

From the beginning of technological era to medevial period not much of attention was paid to repair failed/worn-out parts, probably due to the availability of raw materials and also due to the proper know how to repair the failed parts was not available. A great deal of research work has gone into this particular aspect of repair to save money and reduce equipment down time and which has revolutionised day to day applications.

AIM

The aim of this paper is to discuss the reclamation and rebuilding techniques, steps involved and the economics involved.

LAYOUT

The layout of the paper is as under :

(a) Definition.
(b) Necessity
(c) Types of reclamation.
(d) Factors affecting reclamation.
(e) Methodology of reclamation & rebuilding.
(f) Economics of reclamation & rebuilding.
(g) Conclusion.

DEFINITION

A process by which worn out parts/components are restored to their original condition, i.e. original shape, size, metallurgical properties and useful life, compatible with the expenditure incurred. Components reclaimed by employing a proper technique can last as long as the original, and may some times out last the life of the original component even.

NECESSITY

There are many aspects that favour reclamation in present day context. When an equipment goes out of action, the down time i.e. the time when the equipment goes out of action till the time it is repaired, costs heavily to an industrial set up. Economy is the prime aim. The down time affects this parameter adversely. Reclamation ensures reducing the down time, and also reduced cost of the component. The following are the salient features of reclamation :

(a) To reduce the lead time between demánd and provisioning.
(b) To ensure quick availability of equipment in fd army.
(c) To reduce burden on local purchase of components thus some percentage of saving in funds.
(d) To reduce the equipment down time.

TYPES OF RECLAMATION

Repair Welding: By this method a groove is cut wherever the damage has taken place, metal deposited by simple welding and machined for finish. Even worn-out bearing surfaces can be built up by this process. This process is adopted mainly for the following:

(a) All reasonably thick sections, fairly large parts and broad surfaces.
(b) Parts which require multi pass machining or sometimes with single thick pass process.
(c) Where ever rapid deposition is required.
(d) Weld protective coating requiring the best combination of hardness and toughness.

Rototec Process: This is a type of metal spraying technique which facilitates to restoration of the bearing surfaces on mechanical parts like shaft journals etc. back to original/designed dimensions, with the unique exothermic reaction of the bond coat powder. Temp of process never exceeds 250 C. The coating can withstand metal to metal frictional wear conditions very well. Some times the parts reclaimed by this process outlast the original part. In this process, rototec torch is mounted on the tool post of lathe or is hand held. Spray pack modules (metal powder container) are locked on the torch and the powder is gravity fed in to the torch flame and propelled to the core piece through the flame. The process is carried out when the job is mounted on lathe. The operation is completed in two stages i.e. a bond coat followed by final coat. The steps involved are :

(a) The job is cleaned.
(b) The part is mounted on the lathe.
(c) Under-cut the work piece.

(d) The under-cut portion is threaded for better bonding.
(e) On the adjoining portion masking solution is applied to protect the area from spray.
(f) The job is preheated.
(g) First a bond coat is applied and is then followed by a final coat.
(h) The job is finished by further machining if required.

Eutalloy Process: A metal joining process which combines the advantages of the heat input of brazing with greater strength and homogeneous joints obtained by fusion welding of parent metal. The base metal is not brought to the fusion temparature and the heat input is diminished considerably when compared with that of fusion welding. Eutalloy process utilises a specially designed oxy acetylene torch to \aspirate and propel powder alloy on to a base metal surface. It is a one step process whereby spraying and fusion occur simultaneously. The process provides the capability for depositing a wide range of alloys with high precision (as high as 0.075m) and ability to control the shape of the build up with unmatched accuracy. Powders like molibdenum, nickel, cobalt, tungsten can be used. The advantages are:

(a) Low heat input thereby causing minimum disturbance to base metal.
(b) Simple and easy to apply.
(c) Less time for build up and joining.

Terometac Process: This is a type of maintenance and repair welding which employs flux core, self shielded continous electrodes and can be automated. The advantages are :

(a) High rate of deposition.
(b) The infrastructure developed for this type of process is light & can be moved to any place for carrying out the job.
(c) Since the process is self-shielded i.e. shielding is provided by the flux additives, no shielding is required. This makes it suitable for outdoor applications.
(d) The process is automated and with one adjustment the job can be finished.
(e) Consumes less power and can use both AC & DC.
(f) For large scale applications the process can be automated.
(g) Wide range of electrodes can be used.

FACTORS AFFECTING RECLAMATION AND REBUILDING

Following factors affect the reclamation and rebuilding of a part:

(a) Design of the component. Simpler the design simpler is the reclamation .
(b) Material of the component.
(c) Physical characteristics i.e. shape, size etc.

(d) Machinability.
(e) Resources for reclamation i.e. type of process etc.
(f) Volume of work.
(g) Intended function of the component. This governs surface finish, type of heat treatment to be subjected to, accuracy of the affected surface etc.

METHODOLOGY OF RECLAMATION AND REBUILDING

The methodology of reclamation and rebuilding is discussed in subsequent paras.

Base Metal: It is very essential to know the base metal of the spare part for selection of electrode or powder and type of process to be adopted for repair. By knowing the base metal the correct type of electrode or powder can be selected.

Diagnosis/Analysis of Wear: For this sophisticated instruments/test equipment are required but by experience the cause of wear/failure can be detected by visual inspection. This is essential for adopting the type of process.

Preparation: It is essential to prepare the component to achieve high standard of repair. It can be divided into the following :

(a) *Cleaning*: The part should be cleaned of dirt, rust, grease etc. for better bonding or else the deposit will be fragile and will fail early. Following types of cleaning can be adopted :

(i) *Chemical Cleaning*

(aa) Vapour degreasing,
(bb) Emulsifiable solvent cleaning,
(cc) Alkaline cleaning,
(dd) Pickling, and
(ee) Electro cleaning.

(ii) *Mechanical Cleaning*

(aa) Brush/power brush,
(bb) Ultra sound cleaning,
(cc) Buffing,
(dd) Polishing, and
(ee) Tumbling.

(b) *Opening of Cracks:* Just depositing metal on the failed part will have only superficial bonding since the crack or the defect will exist in the inner portion of the part. Hence the part reclaimed in such a way will fail at the first instance when subjected to its intended function. Hence it is essential that the part is prepared properly. The following are examples:

(i) *V Grooves:* V grooves are cut where the part has failed due to cracks. The groove should be as deep as the crack to ensure that the penetration is complete to achieve a strong joint. Also on either side of the crack a hole has to be drilled to arrest further propagation of the crack.

(ii) *Turning and Fine Thread Cutting:* This is essential wherever pitting or chipping has occurred generally on rotating parts and bearing surfaces. The part is turned till the pitting or chipping is completely neutralised and finally fine thread is cut to give better bonding strength to the deposit.

(c) *Preheating*: This is essential to remove any stress that has been subjected to on the work piece while preparing the part. Also preheating is necessary for following reasons :

(i) To minimise the distortion of the blank/part.
(ii) To prevent cracking of the deposit .
(iii) To prevent cracking of part.
(iv) To prevent melting of base metals.
(v) To prevent differential expansion at the region adjacent to the operation carried out.
(vi) To avoid contamination of the parent metal.

Selection of Welding Alloys : Based on the diagnosis of the base metal and type of wear the electrode is selected. Also the machinability and mechanical properties of the welding alloys conditions which is essential to perform the intended function. This can be broadly classified in to :

(i) Compatible to that of parent material.
(ii) Functional aspect of the component.
(iii) Wear pattern.

Selection of Welding Technique: Though a wide range of welding processes are available, right welding technique has to be selected to get a good finished part. The broad guidelines are :

(a) Should not melt the base metal during the process.
(b) Minimised heat input so that the metallurgy of the components should not change.

Post Weld Treatment : This is required to give final shape to the part i.e. repaired, generally the following process is adopted so that the repaired part does not fail prematurely.

(a) Finishing operation like turning grinding etc.
(b) Electro plating nickel plating etc.
(c) Stress relieving operation to relieve stress induced during welding or machining.

ECONOMICS OF RECLAMATION

Economics is an important aspect of reclamation as the cost should be less than that of original part other wise the aim of reclamation is defeated. Only in extreme cases the reclamation is carried out when the cost is more than original item that is when the part is not available at market, when the lead time is more or heavy production loss is expected to incurr. The factors are :

(a) Reliability and cost effectiveness.
(b) Raw material available.
(c) Complexity of reclamation.

The mathematical relation for annual cost due to failure is :

$$\frac{D+C1}{L1}$$ if replaced by a new component.

$$\frac{D+C2}{L2}$$ if reclaimed

Where

C1 - Cost of original component.
C2 - Cost of reclaimed component.
D1 - Longevity of new component.
D2 - Estimated life of reclaimed part.
D - Equipment down time cost i.e the loss of production

$$\frac{D+C2}{.L2} < \frac{D+C1}{L1}$$

$$\frac{D2}{D1} < \frac{D+C2}{D+C1}$$ normally C2 is always less than C1.

CONCLUSION

As discussed above a wide range of techniques are available for reclaiming and rebuilding any component. With careful analysis and selection of right type of reclamation and rebuilding technique considerable expenditure can be saved. Some time the reclamation and rebuilding cost is fraction of percentage of total cost of the part. This technique comes in handy when the component is not available in the market. It is quite imperative due to above facts that the answer for quick repair of any equipment is reclamation and rebuilding.

RECLAMATION AND REBUILDING OF COMPONENTS

20

Maj. Sameer Garg

604, EME BN, Central Command, Lucknow

INTRODUCTION

The Armed Forces today hold a large inventory of war like and common usage equipment. Majority of war like equipment are of imported origin. Sustainability and state of operational fitness of such equipment is largely dictated by backing of spares/assemblies and their timely availability. In case of imported equipment, availability of spares has been a major cause of concern particularly due to long lead time for procurement, coupled with uncertainty of availability and exorbitant prices quoted. All this demands for a meaningful, immediate and cost-effective solution.

THE NECESSITY FOR RECLAMATION OF COMPONENTS

The necessity of reclamation arises under the following circumstances :

(a) Limited/non-availability of spare parts/components, particularly for imported weapon systems and equipment.
(b) High cost of spare parts and equally high cost of carrying the same.
(c) Increasing dumps of scrap (failed/worn-out spare parts) causing depletion of natural resources.
(d) Favourable advancements in science and technology in the field of recycling of wasted resources (reclamation).

THE ADVANTAGES OF RECLAMATION OF COMPONENTS

Wear is the single major cause of failure in context of mechanical components of weapon system and equipment. There has been an on going debate on restoring system reliability after overhaul through right replacement of worn out components or through reclamation-repair. The major advantages achived by going in for reclamation of components is as follows :

(a) Reclamation helps in reducing the cost of inventory of spare parts and carrying the same thus bringing in cost effectiveness in maint management.
(b) Overcoming continuous non-availability of assemblies and spares, particularly in case of imported weapon systems.
(c) Correcting of malfunctions and/or improvement in performance.
(d) Better engineering technique.
(e) Renewal of life of equipment which are obsolescent and for which no provisioning commitment of spares arise or for which any changes to sealed particulars are of no consequence.
(f) Reclamation helps in conservation of natural resources by allowing recycling of worn-out/scrapped spare parts which otherwise would have been consigned to scrap yard, thus slowing down depletion of resources.

RECLAMATION TECHNIQUES

These are standard engineering practices or processes performed on equipment with a view to restore them to their original specifications. The engineering processes are generally confined to metal depositing, metal spraying, machining, grinding, welding operations etc; where no special stores other than expendable and authorised spares are used. These are generally required to be carried out on service equipment which have shown signs of malfunctions, wear and fatigue. These result in giving a new lease of life to the equipment by rendering the components/assemblies serviceable. Reapir and reclamation techniques normally do not alter the sealed particulars of the equipment.

STATE OF THE ART: RECLAMATION TECHNOLOGY

There have been great advancements in the reclamation technology over the last two decades or so. Peculiar qualitative requirements of military hardware have brought in variety of materials i.e. metals alloys and non-metals like iron, aluminium, cobalt, chromium, nickel, plastics etc. Reclamation of spare parts/components has been successfully done employing State-of-the-Art techniques such as thermal spray technology, electrodeposition. No heat molecular welding etc. The pace of development in this field has been encouraging the world over including indigenous developments. As regards the availablity of technical know-how, associated equipment and consumables, a large numaber of firms in the country in collaboration with their principals abroad, like M/S Larsen & Tourbo Ltd., Advani—Overlikon, ESAB India Ltd, Garrad Plasme System Ltd. and many others in the field are serving the consumers in industry and defence against a resonable degree of competition.

RECLAMATION USING WELDING PROCESS

The welding technology has evolved into a sophisticated science not only to join metal parts together but also to re-inforce them with strength that could withstand tremendous operational stresses for application in industry, defence and space. The welding technology has been effectively adopted for repair/reclamation of critical and expensive metal parts, componenets and tools. The process could be used with equal success for rotating/non-rotating parts. The basic steps in the process include rebuilding of worn-out portion of the component and appropriate machining to required specifications using approved application procedures (AP) and consumables. The techniques have been developed to perfection to overcome the traditional limitations of welding process.

THERMAL SPRAY TECHNOLOGY

Thermal spary processes like wire metallising, metal powder sparying or plasma spraying are widely accepted techniques to rebuild worn-out machinery parts and to salvage mis-machined components. METCO (USA), DEGUSSA (Germany), FONTAGEN (Switzerland) with its R & D centres located through out the world are some of the leaders in development and practice of these techniques. These organisations have revolution alised the concept of maintenance management and are adequately represented within this country for production/marketing of their products and provide training. The techniques are compatible for jobs on almost all kinds of metal and their alloys under various trade marks and patents.

DIFFUSION SPARY

In this reclamation technique metal powder is sprayed over the component for rebuilding. This technique employs specially designed spary guns and welding consumables in the form of microfine powders, oxyacetylyne gas flame is used for preheating and fusion. The fusion can be be obtained using pre-spary or spray and fuse techniques. This technique provides strong bond due to atomic diffusion between parent metal and surfacing alloy. The technique is successfully used for repair/reclamation and provides life prolonging surface coatings. (LPF of 250% or even more obtainable). The process is simple, economic and precise (upto 0.2mm upwards coatings obtainable). The consumables used provide resistance to frictional and abrasive wear, tough overlay and high hardness at elevated temperatures.

COLD RECLAMATION

The essential difference from diffusion process is that virtually little or no preheating of job is required. The process uses subsequent coating and coating powder (surface coat) for specific applications. The bonding is achived through the exothermic reaction of bond coat on parent surface. The technique is suitable for applications like rebuilding of worn-out or part worn-out parts and providing protective surface coatings on new components for performance enhancement. The process enjoys an additional advantage that being a

Low temperature operation there is no danger of warpage, distortion or adverse metallurgical side-effects in the original parts.

NO HEAT MOLECULAR WELDING

Special repair and reclamation techniques are available using epoxy metal-ceramic materials for recycling of worn-out metallic/non metallic spare parts. The process usually consists of two components one being the hardening compound and other could be suitably selected to meet a particular application. The components are mixed and then applied over the wornout or corroded surface. The surface so obtained has required mechanical properties and could be machined suitably for appropriate shape/size.

APPLICATION IN THE ARMY BASE WORKSHOP

The Army Base workshop have the advantage of a professional management besides plant, machinery and special equipment and adequately trained technical manpower. Presently the Army Base workshop are involved in this key result area and large volume of components have been reclaimed by them using special equipment and trained technicians. However, there is a necessity of tasking the Base Workshops all the more by giving them specific targets for reclamation of components. This should be done in addition to the prime activity of Base Workshop to overhaul the weapon systems and equipment of Army.

MAJOR AREA OF APPLICATION

Major area of application of reclamation technique in the Base Workshop are 'B' vehicles, 'A' vehicles (including tracked vehicles of AD weapon systems), engineer equipment, instruments etc. Choice of appropriate technique could work wonders to overcome the serious problem of non-availability of spare parts. Specific areas which have been identified and tackled successfully in many Army Base Workshop are mainly pertaining to engineering, transmission system, brakes, body etc., of vehicles, armaments and other weapon system. The actuals could run in thousands, the will to work could be the only constraints.

Suggested application in the field of armament and small Arms are as follows :

- (a) 120mm Mortar — Firing pin hole of the worn out vent bush can be reclaimed.
- (b) Mounting of 40/70 Gun — Drilling of 3mm dia bypass hole in the housing of elevating gear
- (c) Machine Gun 7.62mm — Reclamation of cracked/broken feed tray hinges.
- (d) SA/Machine Gun — Reclamation of deformed/defected breech block.

CONCLUSION

The Corps of EME needs to be rendered more sensitive to equipment non-availablity with a quicker response. Repair and reclamation improve the technical performance of equipment. In case of imported weapon systems there are certain spare parts which are costly and in short supply. Reclamation technology provides an answer to these problems which not only caters for requirements of system reliability but also results in appreciable savings, besides adding to conservation of resources by recycling process. In the Army Base Workshops resonable work has already been done in this area using indigenous or imported techniques. Certainly much more could be done in this field by suitably harnessing the technological advancements in this specialised area.

RECLAMATION AND REBUILDING OF COMPONENTS

21

Col. R.K. Nambiar

CO 611 EME BN, C/O 56 APO

INTRODUCTION

From the stone age onward metals have been in the service of mankind. Man has over the ages extracted metals from its ores purified it, mixed and alloyed it and has shaped it to suit his needs. He has also learnt to repair and reuse metals that have cracked or worn out. Earliest methods were forging and soldering.

During the last two centuries, welding technology has evolved into a sophisticated science not only to join parts together but reinforce them with strength that could withstand tremendous operational stresses. This development in welding technology has been adapted to suit all kinds of needs, especially in the repair and reclamation of critical equipment parts, components and tools.

Thus reclamation is the process of restoring worn out damaged or distorted components which would otherwise be considered unserviceable to their original dimensions, configurations and mechanical properties in order to bestow on them a new lease of life and utility. Successful reclamation does away the need for replacing the defective component by a new one.

NEED FOR RECLAMATION

In a maintenance organisation, reclamation processes form an integral part of the totality of repair facilities. In the Army reclamation has lately been assuming a great deal of importance since a large range of equipment are of foreign origin and procurement of spares from the manufacturers involves the expenditure of foreign exchange. Even if foreign exchange were to be made available, it is not always possible to procure the spares from abroad because the equipment itself has usually gone out of service in the country of origin. Traditional sources of supply of spares for such equipment have thus either become inaccessible or have dried up altogether. Even in regard to equipment manufactured indigenously, an acute shortage of spares has peristed due to the fact that the manufacturers are busy in producing the main equipment and are not able to cope up with the demands for the entire range of maintenance spares over and above their own requirements for the main equipment. For various reasons, it has been decided to continue the older equipment in service for some more years. It has, therefore, become imperative to use existing components to the maximum advantage by reclaiming them as far as it is practical and economical to do so. Reclamation facilities impart a great deal of self reliance and flexiblility to a maintenance organisation.

RECLAMATION AND RE-BUILDING TECHNIQUES

Some of the techniques of reclamation and re-building, are:

(a) *Welding*: Arc welding was generally applied for large parts due to convenience speed of application. It is also suitable for repairing manganese steel castings, for which pre-heating is not desirable. One disadvantage of arc welding is the unavoidable dilution of the deposit with the melted surface. Gas welding is resorted to, for deposition of expensive non-ferrous hard faced alloys. This technique is specially used on high carbon steels which can be soft deposited and re-heated and quenched. It is excellent for building up and hard facing surfaces, edges, corners and recess on small parts. Another use of oxyacelytene is for hardening cast iron parts and high carbon deposits on steel which can be soft deposited and re-heated and quenched after machining. The argon-tungston arc process gives a very much smooth deposit with high rates of welding.

(b) *Metal Spraying*: In this process the metal is heated to a molten or semi-molten condition by passing through a high temperature heat source and depositing it in a finely divided form on a substrate. The molten or semi-molten particles flatten out on impacting the substrate and adhere to its surface. The structure of sprayed deposits is laminar. Before the sprayed coating is applied, the surface of the work piece must be cleaned and prepared so that sprayed metal particles adhere to it. Shrinkage of the metal being deposited must be taken into account because it affects the techniques of the deposit.

(c) *Hard Chromium Plating*: This is normally applied to the base metal for restoring mismachined or worn surface or to restore to original dimensions of the worn surface. The deposit significantly reduce fatigue strength. It is normally deposited to thickness ranging from few microns to few mms.

Reclamation on components of small arms and armaments that have been undertaken are at Appendix 'A'.

ECONOMICS OF RECLAMATION

Any methodology undertaken should be cost effective. Reclamation renders reduction in costs in the following:

(a) *Reduction in Cost of Replacement*: The replacement cost is sometimes more than hundred per cent at times. Hence it is more than necessary to reclaim them by various techniques. Moving parts in plant and equipment that come in contact with other parts or external loads result in friction, abrasion impact and erosion, thereby loosing effectiveness of their basic functions. Whatever be the type of wear, the cost of replacement can be saved by reclaiming the worn out parts for further service by correct choice of metal deposition and welding procedure. In some cases, the cost of re-building may equal or even exceed the cost of replacement. At times due to non-availability of that particular item from any other source, there may be no other alternative but to resort to reclaiming it by rebuilding to sustain the production line. In many cases the spares bottle-necks have to be met only by resorting to reclamation.

(b) *Reduction in Inventory Costs*: The reliance on spare parts as method of minimising serious breakdown requires a large inventory to eliminate any chance of higher lead time for delivery. Taking into account the hidden cost in carrying inventory like idle capital, storage space handling costs etc., the total inventory carrying cost per year adds np on an average 33% or 1/3rd of the purchase price of the spare parts. Thus not only the money is blocked in terms of "idle capital" but there is also a recurring expenditure in terms of inventory carrying cost. High inventory can be viewed as extra fat on a trim and efficient maintenance body. Quite simply, higher the spare part inventory, higher the inventory carrying costs. Reclamation processes eliminate the need for a large number of spares. Maintenance organisations relying on reclamation processes slash inventory by as much as 40% to 50% and free large amounts of capital tried up in spares. Inventory carrying costs are reduced by as much as 40%.

(c) *Reduction in Downtime*: Technological advancement in industry today tends to have counterveiling effects. Automation multiplies the problem of part and equipment failure by increasing the cost of downtime. With the advent of integrated process industries, consequences of part wear have become monumental. Programmed computers and inspection equipment now replace many worn tools automatically. Capital investment in machinery in industries like the petrochemical and automation is phenomenal. The value of the output per hour for machines in these industries is also enormous. But, by the same token, every hour of downtime takes a correspondingly high toll. Production managers today are infinitely more scared of "trouble". An hour of downtime in some industries can cost hundreds of thousands of rupees. Reclamation techniques have advanced to the stage where the service life of reclaimed components is extended many times. The advantages are obvious: downtime is reduced in frequency and duration by around 50%.

TECHNICAL ASPECTS OF RECLAMATION

To increase the life of the components,it is only logical to diagnose the wear problem which causes wear and tear of machine components. In brief 3 primary and 4 secondary causes of wear have been classified as under:

Primary Causes	*Secondary Causes*
Impact	Corrosion
Abrasion	Heat
Friction	Erosion
	Cavitation

(a) *Impact Wear*—It occurs due to sudden loading, jerk or thrust. Breakage of leaf springs of vehicles and suspension springs of guns during cross country run are examples of this wear.

(b) *Abrasive Wear*—This occurs due to the gauging and grinding action of the non-metallic particles on metallic surface. This wear is often encountered in conveyors, rock crusher rolls and Quarry Hammer heads etc.

(c) *Frictional Wear*—This occurs due to grinding action of one metallic surface on another. This is found on all types of bearing areas and shafts etc.

(d) *Corrosive Wear*—It occurs due to the chemical action of the fluids on the material of construction. The rate of corrosion increases when there is a flow of liquid, relative to the component. It obviously also depends on the corrosive nature of the fluid media handled. This occurs in pumps and components coming in contact with fluids.

(e) *Wear due to Heat*—This occurs due to action of heat (high temperature) on the component. Exhaust manifolds of vehicles become unserviceable due to this.

(f) *Erosion*—This occurs due to continuous striking of high velocity non-metallic abrasive particles on the surface of the metal. Wear of gas turbine blades is an example of this.

(g) *Caviation*—This occurs due to dynamic action of the liquid on the metallic surface. Pittings formed due to implosions of millions of bubbles formed inside the pumps are example of this.

After proper diagnosis of wear factors, the process of repair is to be chosen, which means incorporating wear resistance properties in machine components.

The parameters involved in different reclamation processes vary with each part and even with each type of equipment. The environment or type of materials in which the parts must work varies and has determining influence on the behaviour and resistance of the parts as well as on the efficiency.

Challenged by the differences in field welding conditions, engineers have developed coatings for stick electrodes and torch rods to overcome the problems posed by limitations of available welding equipment, skill levels, *in situ* welding, heat in-put, unknown base metals, contamination etc. Where required, additives, such as deoxidizers, degassifiers, nucleants etc, have been incorporated into the coating formulation to provide highest weldability, in terms of wash, fluidity, bead shape, liquidus and solidus.

INSPECTION AND SPECIFICATION

When critical spares are reclaimed stage inspection should be carried out. In the absence of suitable inspection we may not only lose the raw material and time but may also be faced with catastrophic failures of equipment alongwith the subsequent high cost. Aqeuate precision instruments and non destruction testing equipment are required to carry out stage and final inspection. Agencies like National Physical Laboratory and ISI which are equipped with such inspection facilities could be approached for assistance.

Specification and extensive inspection procedures should be laid down for the reclaimed components. The performance of the reclaimed components should be watched constantly to make sure that the reclaimed components give the required life time. The causes of unexpected failure of reclaimed components should be analysed and specialists should be consulted to improve the quality of spares.

In the absence of availability of working drawings, these should be prepared from the original spares. Analysis of relevant information such as specification of the raw material, physical properties and the characteristics of the product, are to be incorporated. The drawings should have clear indications of the dimensions including the tolerance limits and wherever the details of surface finishing are necessary they should be clearly mentioned. The information will help in selecting the reclamation process and in carrying out stage and final inspection of the reclaimed components.

CONCLUSION

There is no simple way or thumb rule available to ensure efficient reclamation of essential parts. Only study and step-by-step analysis based on experience and constant development could lead to efficient and certain results. To implement regular reclamation programme, the following steps are suggested :

(a) Senior management personnel in all maintenance organisations should be involved because of great cost saving potential in the adoption of reclamation processes. The encouragement and guidance from higher level of management is a MUST to sustain such a programme.

(b) In a specific section of the organisation, a study could be conducted with expert assistance, of critical equipment components which are frequently subjected to breakdown. The following aspects could be considered, and evaluated while recommending components of critical equipment for reclamation :

(i) Cost of the original items.
(ii) Saving in foreign exchange if the equipment is of foreign origin.
(iii) Economics of reclaiming the component.
(iv) Availability of the component.
(v) Criticality of the equipment/component.
(vi) Reliability expected and achieved from reclamation.
(vii) The complexity of the process of reclamation for each component in terms of special equipment, trained manpower etc.
(viii) Likely arisings of repairable components.
(ix) Availability of raw material.

(c) Selection of the best process among various alternatives will play a very important role. In this case we are handicapped because large number of cases of reclamation are unique. Actual case histories of reclamation of different components will be of great aid to the maintenance engineer rather than a text book approach only.

(d) Finally, training of not only workers and metal smiths but supervisors and management executors in the advanced Technology will be required to fully exploit the scope of Reclamation processes and establish its reliability.

REFERENCES

1. *Journal of the Indian Institute of Metals.*
2. *Metals in the Service of Man* - William Alexander.
3. *Hand Book on Welding Science and Technology* - Reynolds Metals Coy.

APPENDIX 'A'

IMPORTANT RECLAMATION UNDERTAKEN IN SMALL ARMS & ARMAMENTS

(a) *Body of Small Arms*—The housing hole of the barrel of body becomes oversize rendering the barrel loose. The oversize hole is built up by metal spraying and finished by lapping to the required dimension.

(b) *Breech Piece of Small Arms*—The pitted face and the hole of the breech piece is reclaimed by metal spray, and then lapping and file finishing.

(c) *Plate Base Mortar*—Rotating race of the base plate usually gets dented. Metal is sprayed on the dented surface as per eutalloy welding technique and is ground with a portable grinder and then polished with zero emery paper.

(d) *Arm Right/Left of a Gun*—The cracks found on the body surfaces were joined by welding, grinding and filing. Elongated locking way was built up by welding and filing to match with the lock.

(e) *Breech Block of a Gun*—Excessive cartridge head clearance is noticed in almost all the guns. This is due to the wear along the thurst surface of the guide ribs of Breech Block. The wornout surface of the guide ribs of Breech Block are built up by hard chromium deposition and brought to the required size by grinding.

(f) *Cradle of a Gun*—Due to normal use in service the cradle hook for equilibrator rope gets broken. This is a vital inability. The item is being reclaimed by MS Electrodes. The broken hook cradle is prepared by cutting from the end approximately 7.5 mm at specified angle. A separate steel piece is forged and prepared, then welded to the above. It is then machined to specified dimensions. Reclaimed cradle is subjected to a pull test of 3000 Kgs.

(g) *Assembly Worn Wheel of a Gun*—The spindle of worn wheel assembly gets wornout at working portion due to normal use. This results in excessive play in traverse. The wornout portion is built up by metal deposition and then machined to required size. This replacement of complete worn wheel assembly is avoided.

(h) *Conversion Cylinder of a Gun*—Scratches and pittings are found inside the conversion cylinder. This is reclaimed by depositing hard chromium inside the cylinder and then lapping it to achieve the specified dimensions. A device has been fabricated for clamping the conversion cylinder so that optimum distance between anode and cathode can be maintained inside the bath. This device is put in the hard chromium bath to hold the conversion cylinder in suitable position so as to achieve uniform thickness and desired adhesion.

IV

FLEXIBLE MANUFACTURING SYSTEMS AND THE FACTORIES OF THE FUTURE

IV

FLEXIBLE MANUFACTURING SYSTEMS AND THE FACTORIES OF THE FUTURE

DEVELOPMENT OF A GENERATIVE TYPE CAPP PACKAGE FOR HOLE MAKING PROCESS

22

V. Anurag,[1] V.M. Shamraj[2] and K.N. Srinivas[3]

Graduate Engineering Trainee[1]
Nagarjuna Steel Ltd., Patancheru, Hyderabad.

Professor, Mech. Engg. Dept.,[2]
Osmania University, Hyderabad.

Scientist 'C'[3]
DRDL, Kanchanbagh, Hyderabad.

ABSTRACT

This paper presents an academic exercise and describes the approach towards development of a generative type CAPP package for the hole making processes. The system has modular structure and all routines are interactive the package has been developed in C language on DOS platform which can be run on TC compatible PC.

1. INTRODUCTION

The integration of knowledge and decision logic is the major feature of a generative CAPP system. Generally the planning depends on the designer's knowledge and experience which can have some limitations but can be overcome by the decision methods of CAPP. Most of the CAPP systems developed both in India and abroad pertain to the rotational parts(1,2,3) and designed to serve a specific user. The approaches have been both feature based(4,5) and featureless(7,8). In addition they are limited to turning centres. In this context the present effort is directed towards the development of a CAPP package for hole making processes which can be integrated to similar CAPP systems of other machining processes[8] for the development of a comprehensive CAPP system.

2. THEORY

2.1 Selection of Machining Method

The recommended method of selecting a machining method involves two factors. One is the characteristic requirements of the part to be machined and the techno-economic ability of the machine tool. Thus the final selection is a suitable matching of these two factors. The requirements can be broadly placed in two groups. One is the desired accuracy of manufacture specified in terms of tolerance grades and the other is the surface finish which may be a default specification. There is no clear boundary between suitable and unsuitable process. It is only a question of a degree of match between the requirement and machining method. In actual practice the part requirement may exceed the capability of one method thus necessitating employment of two or three processes associated with hole manufacture. Therefore, a tree model need to be constructed to select the most suitable chain of processes (Fig. 1). For this purpose the processes associated with hole making have been classified in the following way.

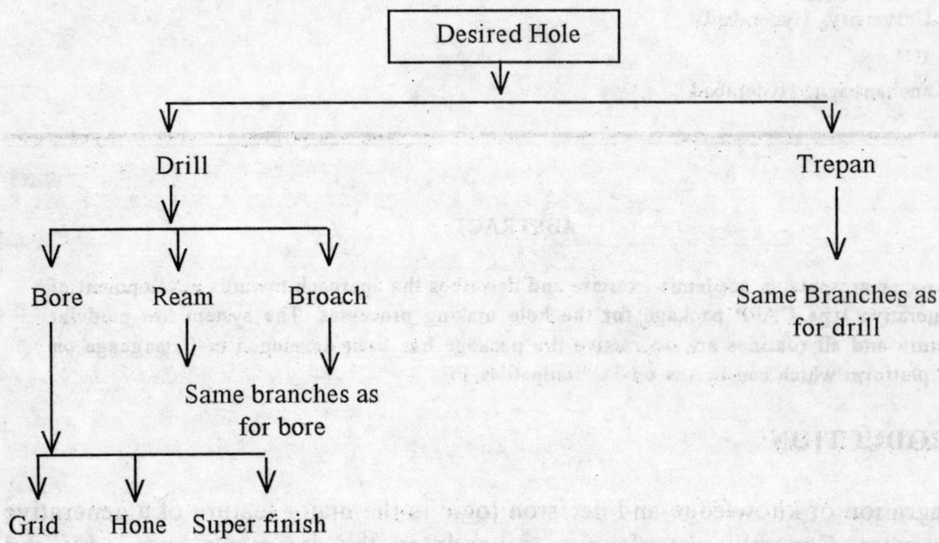

Figure. 1: Tree Model of probable chains of processes

A. Start up processes

Twist drill, Gun or Spade drills, trepanning

B. Improvement processes

1. For accuracy-Boring, reaming, broaching
2. For Surface finish-same as above plus internal grinding, honing and super finishing

The synthesis of suitability is obtained by adding the relative suitability of each link and selecting the most suitable chain. The relative suitability can be assigned numeric values between zero and 100 representing unsuitable and most suitable respectively.[9]

The flow chart of Fig. 2 illustrates the selection procedure for methods associated with hole production.

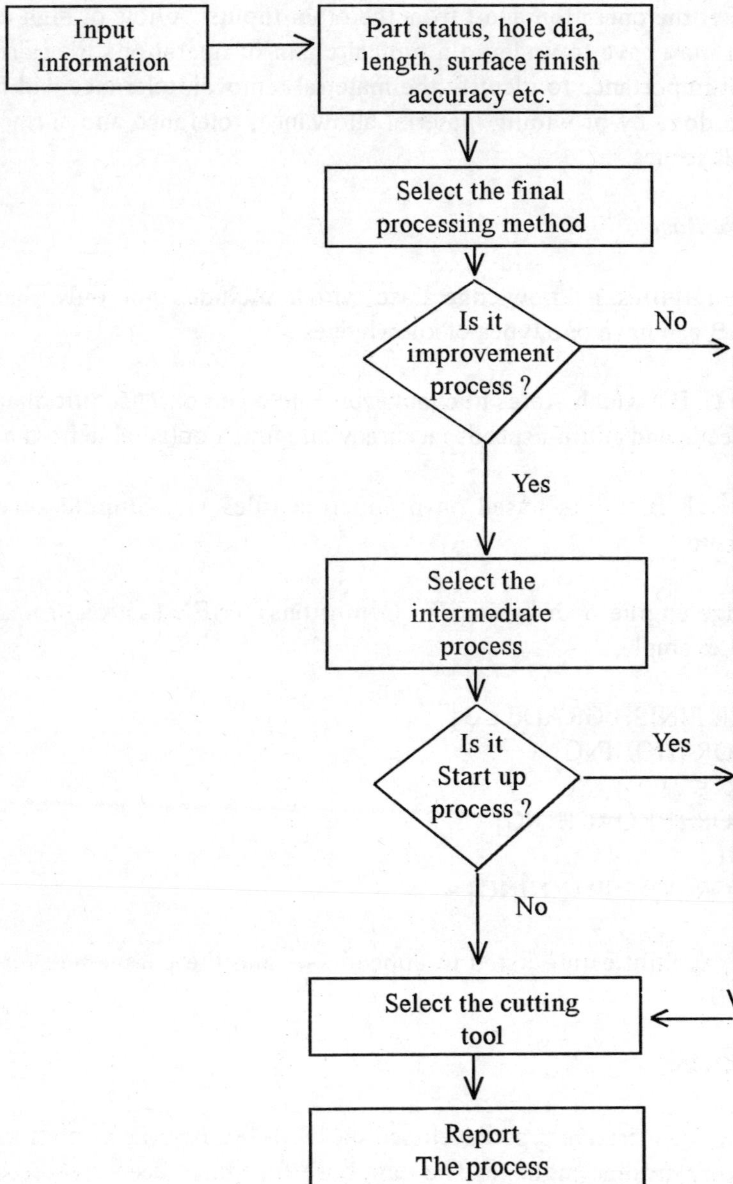

Figure. 2: Flow chart of selection of hole making process

2.2 Intermediate Part Data Generation

A backward planning method is used for solving the problem. The system begins with final part and proceeds towards the blank. Thus the part data before the first operation becomes same as raw material. To carry out the operation planning it requires the part data before and after the operation apart from the other inputs. A hole of high accuracy and surface finish may have to undergo a typical chain of operations like; drill-bore-hone. It is of great importance to identify the material removal, tolerance and finish in each steip. This is done by providing material allowance, tolerance and surface finish with certain default values.

2.3 The Knowledge Base

Process planning requires a knowledge base which includes not only theory but experience. The KB can have two types of knowledges

1. Facts base (F.B.) which stores unchangeable and commonsense information viz. Standard feeds and cutting speeds, accuracy and finish obtainable from a process etc.
2. Rules base (R.B.). It is based on production rules viz. Spindle speed, time estimation etc.

The knowledge engine operates on IF (Conditions) THEN (action) rules for the process plans. For example,

IF [SURFACE FINISH GRADE ≤ 3]
THEN GO FOR [HONING]
IF [IT CLASS ≤ 7]
THEN GO FOR [BROACHING]
IF [DIA ≥ 50]
THEN GO FOR [TRESPANNING]

The process capabilities are listed in appendix-A and the parameters for cutting tools in appendix B.

3. SYSTEM DESIGN

The CAPP system is generative type developed on IBM-486 on a DOS platform under TURBO C as implementing language. The data base files have been created from the commonly available manufacturing technology literature. The system has a modular structure with interactive routines. Basically it has fine modules.

Module 1	Input of part description
Module 2	Selection of machining process and tools
Module 3	Selection of cutting parameters
Module 4	Time estimation
Module 5	Reporting

The input information comprises the work material, its hardness, hole diameter and length, accuracy and surface finish desired. The cutting tool material is standardized as HSS. The selection of processes cutting tools and the cutting parameters such as spindle speed and feed rate are through the searches of relevant data files. This knowledge base has been categoriezed as FB (fact base). The time estimation and reporting module operate through the data base created from the production rules and this knowledge base hase been termed as RB (rules base). The contents of the out put report are intabular from listing the operation sequence, selection of process, tools, spindle speed in feed rate and time required for each process as well as cumulative time.

4. CONCLUDING REMARKS

This paper presents conceptual characteristics of a generative type CAPP system with some inherent limitations which can be improved by incorporation of additional algorithms and data files. The software developed has been tested with hypothetical inputs and the results were quite satisfactory.

REFERENCES

1. K. Mehta, P.C. Pandey and Lalit Mohan, *Development of Varient Computer Aided Process Planning System for Rotational Parts*, 14th AIMTDR conf., 1990, pp. 507-12.
2. N.H. Palsule and S.S. Pandey, *Computer Assited Generative Process Planning System for Turned Components*, 13th AIMTDR Conf. 1988, pp. G-01-G05.
3. S.R.K. Jasthi, P.N. Rao and N.K. Tiwari, *Process Plan Internal Representation in CAPP System for Rotational Parts*, 6th AIMTDR Conf. 1994, pp. 42-49.
4. S.R.K. Jasthi, P.N. Rao, N.K. Tiwari and S.N. Daga, *Macro Planning in GIFTS, a CAPP System for Rotational Parts*, 6th AIMTDR Conf. 1994 pp.15-21.
5. Tang Zhao-Lang, FBPMS—*A Feature Based Part Modelling System*, Proc. 11th Int. conf. prod. Res. 1991, pp. 1313-18.
6. Li Ming Zhang, Lie Hekun and Zhouji Yu Jun, *Feature Based Poduct Defintion*, Proc. 11th Int. Conf. on Prod. Res 1991 pp. 1335-38.
7. Tseng Pai-Chung and Lin Ken-Hsing, *Object-Oriented and Group Technology Coding Based Design of CAPP*, Proc. Int. Mfg. Engg. Conf. USA, 1996.
8. Naveen Babu, *CAPP for Rotational Parts with Multi Work Centre Processing*, M.E. thesis, Osmania University 1997.
9. Tang He Gao Dong, Zhu Mengzhou', *A Description and Decision Model for CAPP Systems*, Proc. 11th Int. Conf. on Prod. Res., 1991, pp. 1195.

APPENDIX-A

PROCESS CAPABILITIES

S.No.	Process	Accuracy	Surface finish
1.	Drilling	IT-10, 11	N-10, 11
2.	Boring	IT-7, 8, 9	N-7, 8, 9
3.	Reaming	IT-6, 7, 8	N-4, 5, 6
4.	Broaching	IT-6, 7, 8	N-4, 5, 6
5.	Honing	IT-5, 6	N-2, 3
6.	Super finishing	IT-4, 5	N-1, 2

APPENDIX-B

CUTTING TOOLS AND THEIR SELECTION PARAMETERS

1. Twist drills

Conventional drills	:	MS; C.1
High Helix drills	:	Soft and ductile materials
Low Helix drills	:	Hard and brittle materials

2. Gun drills	:	Deep holes
3. Micro drills	:	1-3 mm diameter, L/D = 40 to 60
4. Trepanning	:	D more than 50mm

PERFORMANCE OPTIMISATION OF FLEXIBLE MANUFACTURING SYSTEMS USING A SIMULATOR AND GENETIC ALGORITHM

23

R. Sridharan[1] and T.K. Manoj[2]

Assistant Professor[1]
Mechanical Engineering Department
Regional Engineering College, Calicut - 673 601

Graduate Student[2]
Mechanical Engineering Department
Regional Engineering College, Calicut - 673 601

ABSTRACT

This paper presents in detail, the salient features of certain simulation studies conducted for the optimisation of performance of Flexible Manufacturing Systems (FMSs). Initially, a data driven simulator has been developed for the analysis of design and scheduling problems of FMS. A multi-objective optimisation procedure based on genetic algorithm has been developed to optimise FMS performance. The optimisation procedure has been illustrated with two different FMS configurations with three different sets of processing requirements.

INTRODUCTION

A Flexible Manufacturing System (FMS) is a computer controlled manufacturing system consisting of numerically controlled or computer numerically controlled machines linked together by means of an automated material handling system. FMS has emerged as a potentially powerful manufacturing system with the objective of providing flexibility to produce a wide range of part types in smaller quantities and hence, bringing the economies of scale to batch production. However, due to the high investment involved, the installation of FMS should be preceded by effective modelling and thorough analysis of the factors that influence the system performance. Steckel identifies four hierarchical levels in which the decision problems of FMS are partitioned: design, planning, scheduling and control problems. Simulation modelling and analysis has been found to be a very effective approach to address the decision problems of FMS. Simulators are a class of simulation models that can be rapidly configured to model a wide variety of manufacturing systems. Montazeri and Van Wassenhove[2], and O'Keefe and Haddock[3] present the details of development and use of simulators for studies on FMS. This paper presents in detail, the salient features of certain studies conducted for the optimisation of performance of FMS using a simulator and genetic algorithm.

DEVELOPMENT OF THE SIMULATOR

A data-driven discrete event simulator has been developed in C for the analysis of design and scheduling problems of FMS. The entities in the simulator are parts, machines, pallets, work-in-process buffers and material handling devices (AGVs). The operation of FMS is conceptualised as a succession of events centering on the parts to be processed. The various aspects pertaining to the simulator are presented in the following subsection.

Operational Logic of FMS

In the simulator, the operation of FMS is modelled as follows. Orders for part types to be produced in the system are known at the beginning of the scheduling period. The parts are loaded onto the pallets based on *part loading rules* for subsequent launching into the system. The parts are then released to the machines according to *machine selection rules* as soon as AGVs are available. Otherwise, the parts shall wait until AGVs become available. If the input buffer of the machines are occupied, the parts will be unloaded at central buffer from which they will be picked up again based on suitable *buffer rules*. In the present study, it is considered that only a single space is available at the input and output buffer of each machine. A machine is loaded with the part that is waiting at its input buffer for processing. Since the input buffer is free at this time, the machine places a call for an AGV for inputting a part to the local buffer. After the machine completes processing the part, a check is made to find out whether the next operation of the part can be continued on the same machine. If so, the machine continues processing the same part. Otherwise, the machine releases the processed part on the output buffer and places an AGV call to remove the part. An AGV selected based on AGV selection rules (AGV rule) travels to the machine and picks up the part. If all the operations of the part are completed, the part will be unloaded at the load/unload station. Else, the machine for the next operation in the part route is identified. If the input buffer of that machine is empty, the AGV takes the part to the machine, otherwise, the AGV unloads the part at the central buffer. After an AGV unloads a part at the input buffer of a machine or at the central buffer, it tries to attend the pending calls. If there are no calls to be met, then an attempt is made to find whether a part loaded on pallet can be launched into the system. If this is so, then the AGV goes to the load/unload station. Otherwise, it remains idle. The system operates till all the parts are completed.

Based on the logic of operation presented above, appropriate events are generated for capturing the dynamics that are taking place in the system. Each event logic is coded as a C function. The various scheduling rules incorporated in the simulator are as follows.

(1) *Part Loading Rule*: Shortest Processing Time (SPT) and Smallest Proportion of

Jobs Launched (SPJL).

(2) *AGV Rule*: Least Utilised AGV (LUA) and Nearest AGV (NA).

(3) *Machine Selection Rule*: Least Utilised Machine (LUM) and Nearest Machine (NM).

(4) *Buffer Rule*: First Come First Serve (FCFS), Shortest Imminent Operation (SIO), Smallest ratio of Imminent Operation time and Total Processing Time (SIO/TPT), Smallest Product of Imminent Operation Time and Total Processing Time (SIO, TPT) and Smallest Remaining Processing Time (SRPT).

The input data for the simulator includes the following:

(1) *Machine Data*: Number of types of machines and the number of machines of each type, the distance matrix providing the distance between the various machines, load /unload station and central buffer and the machine rule.

(2) *Part Data*: The number of part types and the number of parts of each type to be produced, processing sequence and processing times for each part type and the part rule.

(3) *AGV Data*: number of AGVs, starting position of AGVs and speed of AGVs.

(4) *Pallet Data*: Number of pallet types and the number of pallets of each type.

(5) *Central Buffer Data*: Number of buffer spaces and the buffer rule.

The simulator provides the output values of the performance measures such as makespan, mean utilisation of machines, mean utilisation of AGVs, mean utilisation of buffer, throughput time, mean block time of machines and mean block time of AGVs.

The simulator has been subjected to a multi-level verification and validation exercise. This involves: (1) debugging the program, (2) tracing the program, and (3) running the simulator with different input data and checking the results for reasonableness.

DEVELOPMENT OF A GENETIC ALGORITHM FOR PERFORMANCE OPTIMISATION OF FMS

In the present study, an algorithm has been developed to optimise the system performance for a given set of part data and machine data by varying the input parameters within a specified range. This involves multi-objective optimisation of the objectives such as minimising makespan, maximising the mean utilisation of machines, maximising the mean utilisation of AGVs, maximising the mean utilisation of central buffer, minimising the throughput time of parts, minimising the mean block time of machines and minimising the mean block time of AGVs. The input parameters or the decision variables are number of pallets of each type, number of AGVs, number of central buffer spaces and the various scheduling rules namely, part loading rules, machine selection rules, buffer rules and AGV rules.

In the case of single criterion optimisation, the approach followed in genetic algorithm application is to transform this criterion to fitness function form and then proceed with the regular reproductive plans and the genetic operators. Golberg[4] presents a non-dominated sorting procedure that can be applied for multi-objective optimisation. This procedure has been adopted in the present study. This procedure is similar to single criterion ranking selection procedures except that the population is ranked on the basis of non-domination. All non-dominated individuals in the current population are identified and flagged. These are placed at the top of the list and assigned a rank of one. These points are then removed from contention and the next set of non-dominated individuals is identified and assigned a rank of two. This process continues until the entire population is ranked. Thereafter, reproduction count values or selection probabilities may be assigned according to the ranks. In the algorithm developed in the present study, the relative importance or the priority of the objectives is also considered.

RESULTS AND DISCUSSION

Using the optimisation program developed in the present study, a set of candidate solutions for design parameters and scheduling decisions are generated. This forms the input data for the simulator. The corresponding values of performance measures of the system are determined using the simulator. The performance measure values thus obtained, are used by the optimisation program to generate the next set of candidate solutions. The search procedure of genetic algorithm is terminated after a fixed number of generations, this number being experimentally determined as representing a reasonable compromise between the constraints of population convergence and computing time.

Two different FMS configurations (layouts) with three different sets of processing requirements are considered for analysis. For each layout, three sets of experiments are performed. For the purpose of illustration, the layout 2 is presented in Fig. 1. The corresponding processing requirements for this layout are shown in Table 1. In the first set of experiments, the decision variables other than the scheduling rules are optimised. The most promising values of design decision variables obtained is used in the second set of experiments, wherein the scheduling rules are optimised. In the third set of experiments, all the decision variables (design and scheduling decision variables) are optimised together. The results for this set of experiments for the layout 2 are shown in Table 2.

The results provided in Table 2 show the pareto-optimal results for the multi-objective optimisation of FMS performance. Among the solutions in the pareto-optimal set, some are not very promising. This is because of the effect of the mutation operator in genetic algorithm. Among the scheduling decision rules, the least utilised machine rule for machine selection provides better system performance. This is due to the high priority assignment for the objective of maximising the mean utilisation of machines. It is found that there is a choice among the scheduling rules for the decisions such as part loading, AGV selection and part selection from central buffer. This provides operational flexibility in scheduling.

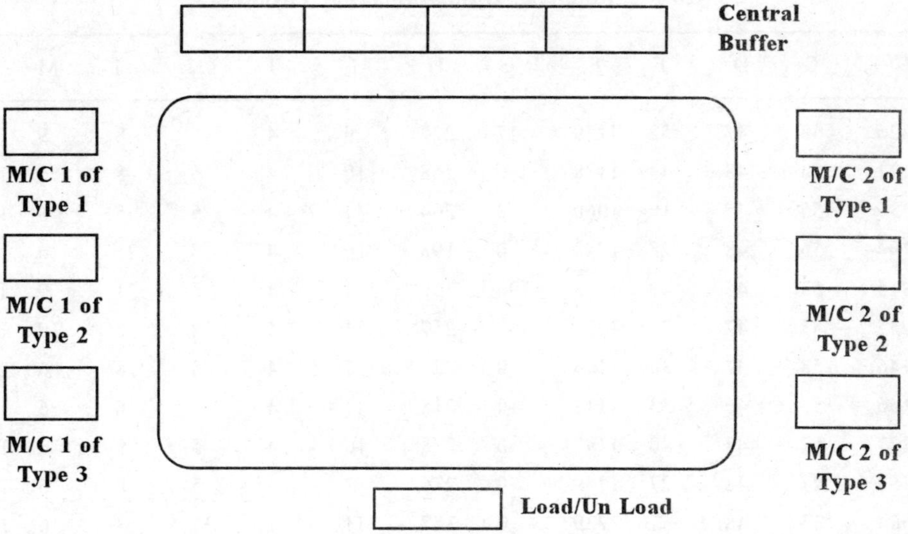

Fig. 1: Layout 2

TABLE 1: **Processing Requirements For Layout 2**

Part Type	Number of Operations	pallet Type	Production Quantity		Operation Number 1	2	3	4	5	6
1	3	1	20	A	1	2	3			
				B	5	25	10			
2	6	2	10	A	3	2	3	1	3	2
				B	3	10	5	25	5	15
3	4	3	5	A	1	2	3	1		
				B	10	20	30	5		
4	3	1	15	A	3	2	3			
				B	2	5	10			
5	3	2	25	A	2	3	2			
				B	5	15	5			
6	4	3	30	A	1	2	3	1		
				B	10	20	5	5		

A - Machine Type for Operation   B - Processing Time (Minutes)

CONCLUSION

This paper has demonstrated the multi-objective optimisation of the performance of FMS. A data-driven simulator has been developed for the analysis of design and

TABLE 2: **Results of Optimisation For Layout 2**

A*	B	C	D	E	F	G	H	I	J	K	L	M	N
1	2226	55	47	52	1159	17	277	9	4	5	8	9	1121
2	2121	58	48	43	1138	0	268	10	4	5	8	6	1142
3	2236	55	45	18	1060	0	204	11	4	5	5	6	1121
4	2194	56	48	28	1249	0	198	10	4	5	21	6	1142
5	2315	53	45	43	1268	94	206	11	4	5	21	9	1121
6	2255	55	47	25	1075	0	257	11	4	18	8	19	1121
7	2146	58	47	30	1106	0	224	11	4	5	8	6	2111
8	2166	57	46	33	1113	0	218	11	4	8	8	6	1121
9	2177	57	47	40	1192	0	278	10	4	5	9	6	1142
10	2554	48	48	27	1359	0	276	2	3	5	8	6	1121
11	3504	35	48	1	1739	0	357	11	2	11	8	6	1121
12	2143	58	47	39	1187	0	310	10	4	5	8	6	1122
13	2187	56	48	43	1142	0	262	11	4	5	8	9	1121
14	2236	55	45	18	1060	0	204	11	4	5	5	6	1121
15	2173	57	47	50	1206	0	320	10	4	6	8	6	1122
16	2749	45	47	13	1363	0	380	11	3	5	5	10	1121
17	2154	57	46	52	1134	6	243	11	4	5	8	11	1121
18	2154	57	46	52	1134	6	243	11	4	5	8	11	1121
19	2082	59	48	40	1105	0	203	10	4	5	8	6	1121
20	2187	56	48	43	1142	0	262	11	4	5	8	9	1121

* LEGEND

A Solution No.

B Makespan (Minutes)

C Mean Utilisation of Machines(%)

D Mean Utilisation of AGVs(%)

E Mean Utilisation of Central Buffer(%)

F Throughput Time (Minutes)

G Mean Block Time of AGVs (Minutes)

H Mean Block Time of Machines (Minutes)

I Number of Spaces in Central Buffer

J Number of AGVs

K Number of Pallets of Type 1

L Number of Pallets of Type 2

M Number of Pallets of Type 3

N Combination of Scheduling Rules

Machine Rule-AGV Rule-Buffer Rule-Part Rule

Priority Values Assigned to Performance Measures:

Makespan - 3 Mean Utilisation of Machines - 3 Mean Utilisation of AGVs - 1 Mean Utilisation of Central Buffer - 1 Throughput Time - 2 Mean Block Time of AGVs - 1 Mean Block Time of Machines - 1 scheduling problems of FMS. A Genetic algorithm based procedure has been presented for the optimisation. The optimisation procedure provides pareto-optimal set of solutions. Hence, there is a choice among the values of design variables and scheduling decision rules. This provides considerable flexibility to the decision maker in the design and operation of FMS. The capability of the simulator can be enhanced to address the other decision problems of FMS. Further, an appropriate method has to be developed for providing priority values for multi-objective optimisation. The authors currently working in these possible directions.

REFERENCES

1. K.E. Stecke, Design, Planning, Scheduling and Control Problems of Flexible Manufacturing Systems, *Annals of Operations Research*, No.3, 1985, p. 3.
2. M. Montazeri and L.N. Van wassenhove, Analysis of Scheduling Rules for an FMS, *International Journal of Production Research*, Vol. 28, No. 4, 1990, p. 785.
3. R.M. O'Keefe and J. Haddock, 'Data-Driven Generic Simulators for Flexible Manufacturing Systems', *International Journal of Production Research*, Vol. 29, No. 4, 1991, p. 1795.
4. D.E. Goldberg, *Genetic Algorithm in Search, Optimisation and Machine Learning*, 1988.

CO-OPERATIVE PRODUCTION.... NEED OF THE HOUR

24

Lt. Deepak Bansal[1] and Nidhi Bansal[2]

Staff Instructor, Naval Air Technical School,[1]
Naval Base, Kochi-682004

Scientist, Naval Physical and Oceanographic Laboratory,[2]
Kochi-682018

ABSTRACT

Indigenous production of military hardware began with Reverse Engineering. After a promising start, it petered out when more complex hardware was attempted to be re-engineered. Scant or poor knowledge of metallurgy was a major hurdle. After Reverse Engineering came the indigenisation drive. The Resource crunch and the sudden break up of the USSR compelled the services to set up their own indigenisation cells. Indigenisation provided freedom to the designer to choose material and alter designs of subsystems to the extent that overall weight and dimensions were adhered to. Though indigenisation helped in developing technology, many a project could not see the light of the day in the stipulated time frames, as a result obsolescence crept in very fast.

Concurrent engineering came to involve the production agencies at the conceptualisation stage of the design itself. This could be useful only if it did away with wastage which is a part and parcel of this philosophy.

The paper emphasises on the need of co-operative production in the wake of shrinking defence budgets. The present study explores the emerging technique of co-operative production, wherein, all the three agencies, viz. the user, the designer and the manufacturer are involved at the inception stage itself. The philosophy underlying this technique is pooling all resources of the agencies involved nation wide. The paper also discusses the benefits of automation, simulation, effective communication and technology development in the case of military hardware manufacture. These techniques make the process of design, devlopment and manufacture fast and effective. A few case studies illustrating the efficacy of the technique in the Indian context are also discussed.

1. INTRODUCTION

The perception of design and development has taken numerous twists and turns over the years. Design engineering as we know, began with the steam engine. Previously almost all manufactured items were the product of artisans. Earlier entrepreneurs normally worked closely with machinists who made parts from verbal descriptions or rough sketches provided by the boss. As the business grew, the founder could no longer attend to details, so he usually hired draftsmen, who, along with the machinists, defined the physical make-up of the product. The launching of Sputnik in 1957 brought a masive change in attitudes toward design engineers. Throughout the industry, analytical engineering has displaced yesterday's reliance on intuition and eyeball design. Rational design is pushing aside costly trial and error. Products are being designed and built with few, if any prototypes allowing companies to bring new products faster and at lower costs. Defence is one area where all these changes have had their first effect. In fact, till today, defence industry has been paving the path for other corporate houses in regard to new technology and methodology followed for product development.

Co-operative production will further the cause of defence production by following a *modus operandi* as follows.

- — Making efforts to maintain close liaison with the industry,
- — Periodic reviews,
- — Knowing the capacities and infrastructure available with the trade,
- — Taking steps to standardise equipment to help economies of scale,
- — Minimising the gap between induction of new equipment and conceptual design,
- — Identifying and associating production agencies and ensuring continuity in the orders to the extent possible,
- — Endeavouring to provide total quality assurance fron design development to the final product. The activity involved in indigenisaion of the systems is much more vast than it is thought to be. For example it involves carrying out technical evaluation of bids and offers by the industries, giving decisions on alternatives (materials, processes etc.) offered by these industries, preparing of Quality Assurance Instructions for the system and sub-systems, and providing guidance during development of pilot samples and monitoring quality of production. Faced with these challenges and keeping in the view the infrastructure available in the country in the private and public sector, a national body should be formed with whom would rest the responsibility of delivering the final product.

2. CO-OPERATIVE PRODUCTION : A NEED

What is co-operative priduction? well, it is that philosopy of engineering, where-in, all the three agencies, viz. the user, the designer and the manufacturer are involved at the ception stage itself. The philosophy underlying this technique is pooling all resources of the agencies involved nation wide.

As a result of predicting security developments, the ability of total defence system to adapt to changing and diverse threat is of fundamental importance for the safety and security of the nation and its people

To maintain a competitive edge it is mandatory that defence industry must have a technology edge. In the face of defence cuts and industry restructuring, it is the defence

R&D activity which has come under significant threat and therefore the evolution of a new "best cost" policy must be allowed to take place.

Concurrent Engineering has the peculiarity of early involvement of non-engineering functions in the design and development process. This involvement goes beyond merely including industry and users' representatives in meetings. It should be ensured that these departments have enough clout during planing to avoid maintenance, price or fielding problems. Also, important is collocation of development personnel wherever possible, combined with project leaders having enough authority to make decisions to keep the project moving. Inco-operative development, if the projects involve the talent of individuals which are geometrically dispersed, communication tools become important for keeping participants all on the same page of the playbook.

For efficient development process there is a need to have special divisions for technology transfer to the industries. These divisions should work colsely with the industry in establishing the correct methodology, quality parameters and cost controls. Another important area is pertaining to establishing links to broader research efforts at both national as well as international level. Efforts should be encouraged for co-operative production between industry, academia, R&D and defence personnel who are the ultimate users.

3. TOOLS FOR CO-OPERATIVE PRODUCTION

Collaborative engineering is a process, supported by a cadre of information and technical tools that interjects "immediacy" into the product development cycle. Through collaborative projects decisions can be made in real time, resulting in reduced product costs, better quality product and quicker time to field.

3.1 Co-operative Culture

One area that should be examined is how to overcome the cultural barriers and create an environment, which promotes co-operative production. Building effective communication channals and reqard structures, creating shared space, and introducing appropriate technology are among the important elements. Co-operative development means shared creation, i.e. two or more individuals interacting to create a shared understanding that none had previously possessed or would have come to of their own. Organisations are pouring vast amount of resources into the latest automation tools. To fully maximise the benefits of these tools, cultural changes must be made enterprise wide. Without this, automation may prove dysfunctional and one may arrive at faulty conclusions. To create such a culture several issues should be borne in mind.

— Language barriers should be handled as miscommunication can falter processes, inhibit relationships and lead to ambiguity and confusion.

— Another obstacle in effective communication is distinctly different functional areas.

— One main key in the co-operative development is to start with the tools people are already familiar with. Sometools which may be very effective may not have the desired effect if users feel uncomfortable using that tool. Video conferencing though enables users to have face to face meeting, still the quality plays a major part as it should make participants feel as if they were literally in the same room.

— Employees should not be rewarded for individual efforts but rather for their participation as a team.

3.2 Communication Skills

Another issue is information tools, on whichco-operative engineering is built and lets is happen easily and with organisation. Internet is one such option which has a common user interface. Intranet, which are private Web networks, provide a more secure way in which design teams can collaborate on project details safe from the public access of the Internet, and thus is a better option for defence projects. A project home page can be created and can act as an up to date bulletin board to manage and store all details of a particular project and provide interactive capabilities as well. Team members can reference back to this page either to post and retrieve information, follow hyper text links to additional resources, or monitor everything that individual team members have changed, commented on or completed during each step of the project. The page can also connect to databases of part information and the Web for research.

Besides understanding product histories and what might be faulty on a computer screen, successful product development will require broader communication skills. As it will require more interaction amont various groups, like engineers, manufacturing people, designers, users, environmental activists and so on. The world is in a period of heightened sensitivity about the impact of technology and design. Therefore, one has to be aware of *ethical* considerations in the coming century. Concurrent engineering requires more communication not only regarding other disciplines but also about final disposition of product.

A great obstacle to better project is the chasm between industry and academia. The culture of taking risk to cash in on brilliant research has still. to take roots firmly in our country. Effective communication can help in narrowing this gap.

3.3 Role of Automation

The role of automation, especially CAD/CAM in co-operative production can not be undermined. It is surprising to see as to how assembly modelling, visualisation, integration of CAD with Finite Element Analysis, and virtual reality, foster co-operative production and engineering. Along with other benefits, what this tool also encourages is, rather than putzing around, getting a detailed product specification letter perfected before making a formal presentation; one can make a pitch to management with an easily understood model. Three dimensional models eliminate what has been called as the drawings translation process: the time it takes to make sense of a 2D drawing. A few complex drawings could be so difficult that only their designers can understand them. In contrast, users only faintly familiar with a product modelled in solid, know exactly what it is, which is the main point here. Designing parts with an assembly on screen makes a good sense as it lets the users see the surrounding parts and find potentially harful interference with them and it lends quicker understanding to spatial position, function and a variety of other information.

Integration of CAD with finite element analsis saves the translation of an IGES file to such an analysis package. Doing so gives the designer an access to stress and deflection information while they mull over design modifications. The technology encourages testing many ideas without time and cost penalties that otherwise would be incurred.

Automation encourages co-operative production by helping manufacturer take the drawings off the critical path. The advantage is that the manufacturing engineers do not need a drawing to make critical decisions, such as, how to manufacture a part; assembly drawing, generally gives them the idea. It also helps creating spin off of the technology.

Transferring technology and swap of data is an area that warrants continuous improvements. Many software have come which hold different view of the same date for the benefit of various participants and thus eliminating the problem to a great extent. The virtual part technology may improve the them work substantially. For example, it can show the user as to how the final product may look like and function.

4. OTHER EFFECTIVE METHODS

Along with the co-operative production technique which could prove to be the back-bone of the defence development in future, there are a few other issues which can not be neglected. Time elapsed between scientific discovery and engineering development has come down drastically in the last one century, from ten years that was taken in the case of a nuclear reactor to a few months for a personal computer. So, to survive in this cut throat competition, delays should be avoided as plague and maximum efforts should be put in to develop the product in minimum time.

4.1 Simulation

Simulation can help cut the cost of future weapons through computer-based conceptualisation, development, test, evaluation, and training activities before construction and major spending. Such facilities can serve as a major hub for connecting researchers, users, developers, industry and academic scientists and engineers struggling with similar weapons integration issues. Many a time the project is delayed because of the user trials for which the availability of the required equipment may not be there.

Simulation of the environment in the analysis software can help deal with such problems to some extent, as one may look at the plot of same thing but it is more informative to be immersed in the fluid and watch things flow around oneself. Information like where the liquid cools, where it is last to cool, where impurities might collect, or where a void might form could guide manufacturing engineers in how to design expensive complex castings that would fill without potentially damaging flaws.

Simulation can also make the user have a feel about what they are opting for and let them suggest modifications in the beginning itself.

4.2 Standardisation

Another important tool that we have not exercised fully is the usefulness of standards and modular design, which can certainly speed up the development and deliver goods with a proven track record. It is generally seen that everytime a new project is taken up it is started from scratch or in other words, we start inventing the wheel all over again. Rather, a better way would be that the experience from the past be utilised to the full and shortcomings found in the earlier designs be improved upon. Modular design of some of the standard equipment would prove beneficial in this regard. Such modules are already tested for their reliability and functional aspects and thus would save the project team precious time. It also helps in reducing the maintenance time and enhancing the system's service life.

Defence equipment has to be proved for working in severe environment and for achieving such reliability, these are generally subjected to rigorous testing. In addition to this, even the maintenance procedures for every component used in military systems must mandatorily conform to specific standards. In many instances, it is found that there is complete ignorance in the industry about the standards followed by the defence services. As a result some components have to be rejected at the time of trials itself. Such delays can be avoided by indicating the test procedures clearly at the very outset. The standards one has to follows should be clearly defined to avoid any conflict later.

5. CASE STUDY

The time has come for progress to race with time and touch the needs of every Indian and for prosperity to be not just a dream nurtured by hope but reality earned by our sweat. To cite a few examples, the PSLV launch requires cryogenic engines and supercomputers. The US government had not only banned their sale to India but also prevented the Russians from selling them to us. What should be our answer when they refuse to sell? To accept it as a challenge and do it ourselves and for achieving this the whole nation had to come together and prove our mettle. Likewise, the US had banned the sale of Cray-XMP needed for the integrated Guided Missile Development Programme (IGMDP), here again we came together and produced a far superior alternative, the Pace Plus.

6. CONCLUSION

The feeling that the defence work is "classified", and therefore, must be carried out by government undertakings alone makes one question about why this criterion does not apply to many imported defence items where the suppliers belong to the private sector. Obviously, one cannot subscribe to the philosophy that Indian private sector is less trustworthy than any foreign supplier. It is also argued that the engineering industry is less quality conscious and cost efficient. This may be true to some extent but it cannot be overlooked that many of these units are already engaged in highly complex projects and thus have the required expertise in related areas. Also, it should be borne in mind that secrecy is relevant to a total system or to the overall plan and not to the individual components which could be separated and scattered over different companies. One stumbling block in defence development is that changing threat perceptions preclude the defence from projecting a long term profile of defence requirements. Moreover, these products are not as profitable a commercial proposition as goods for general consumption. Failure free operation of defence systems calls for high degree of quality and reliability of all the sustems which can not be compromised under any circumstances. Therefore, the sole criterion for deciding upon production of military hardware should be quality and reliability rather than the sector to which the manufacturer belongs.

Integrity of each part subjected to various and repeated stresses in use is vital for the ultimate performance and reliability of the end product. It is the basic responsibility of the manufacturers to ensure that the high levels of quality and reliability inbuilt into the design are not impaired. This is the challenge staring at our faces and this can only be met if all of us work together for the same goal.

REFERENCES

1. *Military Technology*, Vol. 21, 1997.
2. *Machine Design*, 24 July, 1997.
3. *Machine Design*, 22 May, 1997.
4. *Better Late Than Never*, Essay for USI Journal-Lt. D. Bansal.

COMPUTERISED MAINTENANCE MANAGEMENT SYSTEMS IN INTEGRATED IRON AND STEEL PLANTS

25

S.C. Bhatia, FIE

Dy. Chief Engr. (Design)/Elec, SAIL, Bokaro Steel Plant
Sector I-C/114, Bokaro Steel City-827 001, India

ABSTRACT

In a Large Integrated Iron & Steel Plant, the diversity and the magnitude of installed equipment calls for a well defined, procedure oriented and well documented system of maintenance. It is, therefore, of utmost importance to develop proper database and utilise the potential of computers to generate effective information system for decision making.
The implementation of CMMS has strengthened and improved the maintenance systems at the Integrated Iron & Steel Plants. The maintenance planning activities have been simplified with the information on critical pending jobs, ready availability of past data on maintenance, information on availability of spares at both stores and engineering units and updated status of all the on-going jobs.

INTRODUCTION

Maintenance is one of the very important key function in a process industry, especially in Integrated Iron and Steel Plant. The achievement of production targets with quality goods depends on the continued good health and reliability of equipment, which can be ensured by adopting a well conceived judicious system of maintenance. With the rapid advancement of production technology and use of high speed continuous equipment, the demand on maintenance organisation has become more and more stringent. In a large Integrated Iron & Steel Plant, the diversity and the magnitude of installed equipment calls for a well defined, procedure oriented and well documented system of maintenance. It is, therefore, of utmost importance to develop proper data base and utilise the potential of computers to generate effective information systems for decision making. CMMS aims at the above.

Development Philosophy for CMMS

1. Modular design : The whole system is divided into Modules.

2.	Menu Driven	:	The system is Menu driven for easy operation.
3.	Data Security	:	In built security at all levels prevents misuse.

DEVELOPMENT OF MODULES FOR CMMS

1. Equipment Classification Module

— Equipment classification.
— Plant Equipment Register.
— Explosion of equipment to assemblies.
— Explosion of equipment for spare parts.

2. Maintenance Planning Module

— Equipment inspection and Feedback record.
— Preventive Maintenance planning.
— Manpower requirement/Material requirement planning.
— Scheduled repairs/Capital repairs planning.
— Breakdown records/Delay records and analysis.

3. Materials Planning Module

— Spare parts Master Plan.
— Spares requirement plan.
— Spares Budget and Control.
— Spares procurement planning.
— Spares lifecycle monitoring.
— Spares consumption control.

4. Captive Engg. Shops Module

— Capacity planning for Engg. Shops.
— Make or Buy decision planning.
— Raw materials and Components planning.
— Planning, Scheduling and Monitoring.
— Documentation, preservation and retrieval.

COMPUTER HARDWARES FOR CMMS

1. Central Computer System

— Central Supermini Computer System (Super 32/70 of ECIL).

- — Dual CPU ND-500 and ND-100 at 3.3 MIP rating.
- — 16 MB Main Memory for ND-500.
- — 2 MB Local Memory for ND-100.
- — 1940 MB secondary disc storage memory.
- — 4 fixed and 2 removable disc drives.
- — 2 nos. Magnetic tape drives of 1600/6250 BPI.

2. Installation of PCs

- — 70 nos PCs in various locations.
- — Coverage for production/maintenance/Engg. shops.
- — Maintenance Planning Schedule/Material Planning Schedule.
- — Engg. shops Planning and scheduling.

3. Linkage of PCs & Central System

- — Provision of all PCs to link with Central system.
- — Installation of Telecommunication Networks.
- — Use of Modems at both ends for data reply.
- — Planning for maintenance of Computer systems.
- — Planning for maintenance of Networks.
- — Planning for effective data transmission.

DATABASE PREPARATION FOR CMMS

The Database preparation for CMMS is a voluminous task involving identification of each and every activity, area, equipment, mechanism, assembly, sub-assembly, spares, technical documentation, etc. Broadly the Database preparation is done in the following main catagories:

1. Equipment Classification & Codification

A 14 digit codification system is developed for identification of each and every part and component of various equipment, to be completed in a form of tree structure for all areas of maintenance to be covered by CMMS in relevant formats.

2. Job Catalogue Records

A total Job Catalogue records of about 25000 activities, both for Time based and Condition based maintenance jobs have been prepared and identification and stored in the Main Computer System:

— Area of maintenance.
— Equipment/Mechanism.
— Activity code.
— Job description.
— Repair code-Planned repair.
— Repair code-Breakdown.
— Frequency code for Time based job.
— Standard job duration.
— Manpower requirement.
— Job preparation details.
— Last execution code.
— Hostory code.

3. Inspection Checklist

Running inspection checklist for all the vital equipment for all departments have been prepared in the respective formats and stored in the Main computer system for easy retrieval and usage as and when required.

4. Development of Sub-Systems

Software packages have been prepared for the following activities:

— Inspection planning & Feedback record.
— Defect lists and Repair Plans.
— Breakdown jobs.
— Capital repairs.
— Procurement of spares.
— Cost and consumption control.

CRITICAL AREAS FOR CMMS

The following critical and vital maintenance areas have been selected for successful implementation of CMMS. The requirement of PCs and Terminals for CMMS for a 4.75 MT capacity Integrated Iron & Steel Plant have been identified as follows:

Department/Area	No. of PCs
— Raw Materials & Material Handling Plant	— 2
— Refractory Material Plant	— 1
— Coke Ovens & Bye Products Plant	— 4
— Sintering Plant	— 2

—	Blast furnaces	—	5
—	Steel Melting Shops	—	5
—	Slabbing Mill	—	2
—	Hot Rolling Mills Units	—	5
—	Cold Rolling Mills Units	—	5
—	Thermal Power Plant	—	2
—	Oxygen Plant	—	1
—	Compressed Air Plant	—	1
—	Engineering Shops	—	2
—	Electrical Repair Shops	—	2
—	Foundries & Forging Units	—	2
—	Structural Shop	—	1
—	Engg. Shops Inspection	—	2
—	Power Engineering Unit	—	1
—	Air Conditioning & Ventilation	—	1
—	Central Base Repair Shop	—	1
—	Operation garrages	—	1
—	Central Lubrication & Bearing shop	—	1
—	Central Civil Engg. Deptt.	—	1
—	Production Planning & Control deptt.	—	5
—	Spares Inventory & Consumption Control	—	5
—	CMMS Control Deptt.	—	5
—	Sr. Executives of Maintenance Deptts.	—	5
Total No. of PCs		—	70

CONCLUSION

The implementation of CMMS has strengthened and improved the maintenance systems at the Integrated Iron & Steel Plants. The maintenance planning activities have been simplified with the implementation of critical pending jobs, ready availability of past data, information on availability of spares and on line reporting on the status of various maintenance jobs. Unstinted support of the Top Management together with keen and active participation by end users holds the key for successful operation of CMMS in large process industries like the Integrated Iron & Steel Plants.

REFERENCES

1. V.P. Moudgil, Computerised Maintenance Mgt Systems.
2. B.N. Saha, Computerised Maintenance Mgt Systems.
3. K.K. Gupta, Computerised Maintenance Mgt Systems.
4. S.C. Bhatia, Computerised Maintenance Mgt Systems.
5. SAIL Documents, Computerised Maintenance Mgt Systems.

APPLICATION OF PROCESS CAPABILITY ANALYSIS IN THE MANUFACTURING INDUSTRY

26

A. Bhattacharyya[1] and N. K. Singh[2]

Mechanical Engineering Department[1]
Jadavpur University, Calcutta-700032

Senior Quality Assurance[2]
Establishment (General Stores), Hastings Calcutta-700022

ABSTRACT

Process capability analysis plays a very important role for control/improvement of quality characteristics of the products manufactured by the production process. Process capability indices are single dimensionless measures which are used to predict the future status of the quality characteristics of the product. Statistical methods e.g. Mean, Standard deviation, Skewness, Kurtosis and Analysis of Variance (ANOVA) as well as the process capability indices Cp, CPU, CPL, Cpk and K have been used for the analysis of process capability of Flat Heads Rivets produced, on three different machines and at five consecutive times, by an industry. Causes of variation and suggestion for the improvement of variation have been discussed.

Key Words : Process capability indices; Process variability; Analysis of variance; Shank diameter; Head diameter; End diameter; Head thickness.

1. INTRODUCTION

Process Capability Analysis plays a very important role for control/improvement of quality characteristics of the products manufactured by the production process. Besterfield (1989) defines "Process Capability Analysis is a statistical technique helpful throughout product cycle for quantification of process variability, analysis of variability relative to product requirements, specification development activities prior to manufacturing and assistance in development and manufacturing in eliminating variability". Process Capability indices are single dimensionless measures which are used to predict the future status of the quality characteristics of the product. Kane (1986) defines "Process Capability index measures relationship between the allowable process spread (natural tolerance) and the actual allowable process spread (specification range).

Kane (1986) introduced Process Capability index *Cp*, also called Process Potential index, which considers spread only

$Cp = (U - L)/6\sigma$, $Cp \geq 1$ for a capable process

Where U and L are Upper and Lower Specification Limites respectively and σ is standard deviation.

Kane (1986) introduced process capability indices (called Process Performance indices) as

$CPL = (\mu - L)/3\sigma$, $CPU = (U - \mu)/3\sigma$ and $Cpk = \text{Min}\ (CPL, CPU)$

CPL, CPU, $Cpk \geq 1$ for a capable process.

These indices take into account both spread as well as location.

Another index introduced by Kane (1986) is Process Off-centering index

$$K = \frac{m - \mu}{\left(\frac{U - L}{2}\right)}, \text{ where } m = \frac{U + L}{2} \text{ and } \mu = \text{mean of the characteristic.}$$

K varies between –1 and 1

If K is negative, the process is centered towards left and if K is positive, the process is centered towards right. At $K = 0$, the process is centered at the mid point of the specification limits.

Relationship between Cp and Cpk is

$$Cpk = (1 - |K|)\ Cp$$

The indices Cp, CPL, CPU and Cpk do not take into account of the the target value. Chan, Cheng and Spring (1988) suggested an index, which considers target value, as

$$Cpm = \frac{U - L}{6\tau} = \frac{Cp}{\sqrt{1 + \left(\frac{\mu - T}{\sigma}\right)^2}}, \text{ where } \tau^2 = \sigma^2 + (\mu - T)^2$$

It is obvious that Cpm is smaller than Cp.

The index Cpm is also called Taguchi Capability index. A lot of work on process capability indices has been done by Pearn, Kotz and Johnson (1992), Vannman (1993), Mukherjee (1995) and Mukherjee & Singh (1993, 1994, 1996). Monograph by Johnson & Kotz (1993) gives very detailed analysis of process capability indices. IS : 10645 - 1983 gives method for estimation of process capability indices.

Process capability measures are affected by measurement error (refer, Montgomery and Runger 1993-94 a,b).

Process capability indices follow certain theoretical probability distributions due to sampling error (refer Kane (1986), Gunter (1989), Bissell (1990) Kotz, Pearn and Johnson (1993) and Vannman and Kotz (1994, a,b).

Application of process capability measures is most important. Melloy and Chandra

(1992) discuss the effect of measurement error and the consequences of use of *Cpk* for the estimation of the proportion of non-conforming items with the help of industrial case study. Davis, Scott and Obray (1993) discuss the use of *Cp* and *Cpk* in the manufacturing process for continuous improvement programme. Taylor and English (1993-94) focus the attention on the Malcom Baldrige National Quality Award (MBNQA) criteria, a tool for measurement of quality improvement at strategic level, Six Sigma ($Cp = 2$) methodology as a means of measuring improvement at operational level and SQC at the tactical level. ISO : 3534-2 – 1993 mentions the use of *Cp, Cpk* and *K* in manufacturing process. ISO Technical Committee (ISO/TC 69) also advocates the use of process capability meausres (refer Mundel 1991 and 1996) and has, in preparation a Draft. Technical Report (DTR 12783) on Process Capability and performance measures.

Here the authors discuss the use of *Cp* , *CPU, CPL, Cpk* and *Cpm* alongwith statistical methods i.e. mean, standard deviation, skewness, kurtosis and analysis of variance (ANOVA) for the analysis of process capability of four quality characteristics of flat head rivets produced, on three different machines and at five consecutive times, by an industry. We also discuss the four charactristics of rivets taken from one machine during one minute production. Causes of variation and suggestion for the improvement of variation have been highlighted.

2. DESCRIPTION OF THE PRODUCT

Flat Head (cold forged) rivets are manufactured by an industry on various machines, as per specification supplied by the customers from the raw material purchased from approved sources. Figure 1 shows dimensions of the rivet.

Figure 1: Flat Head Rivet

d = Shank (Nominal) diameter = 6.0 ± 0.15 *mm*

d_s = End diameter = Min 5.82 *mm*

d_t = Head diameter = 11.3 – 12.0 *mm*

t = Head thickness = 1.5 + 0.40 *mm*
– 0.00 *mm*

r = Fillet radius = 0.3 *mm*

l = Normal length = 10 + 0.5 *mm*
– 0.0 *mm*

3. SAMPLE OBSERVATION/DATA

Five consecutive rivets are drawn from each three different machines at five specified times (time interval of two hours) during continuous production. Dimensions of four important quality characteristics e.g. Shank Diameter, Head Diameter, End Diameter and Head thickness are measured with Vernier Dial Callipers. Frequency distributions of the pooled observation for the four characteristics are discussed in figures 2 to 3. The variations among different machines and different machines and different times are discussed with help of Analysis of Variance.

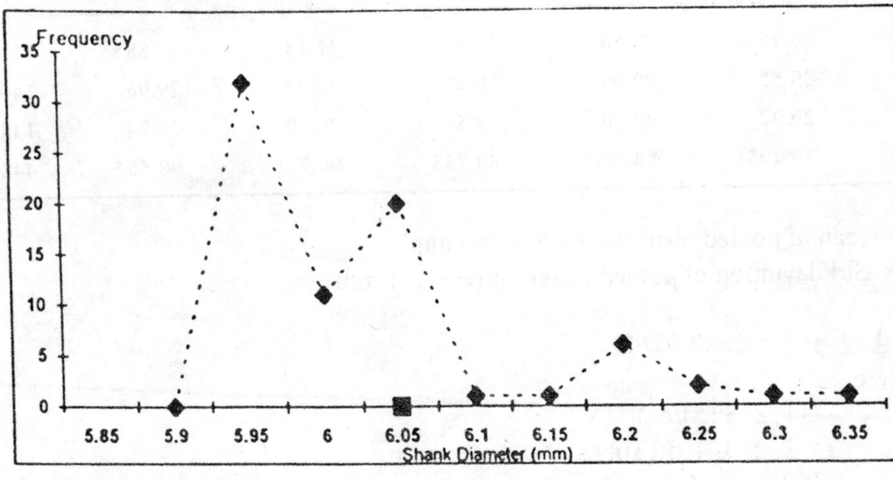

Figure 2: Distribution of Shank Diameter (mm)

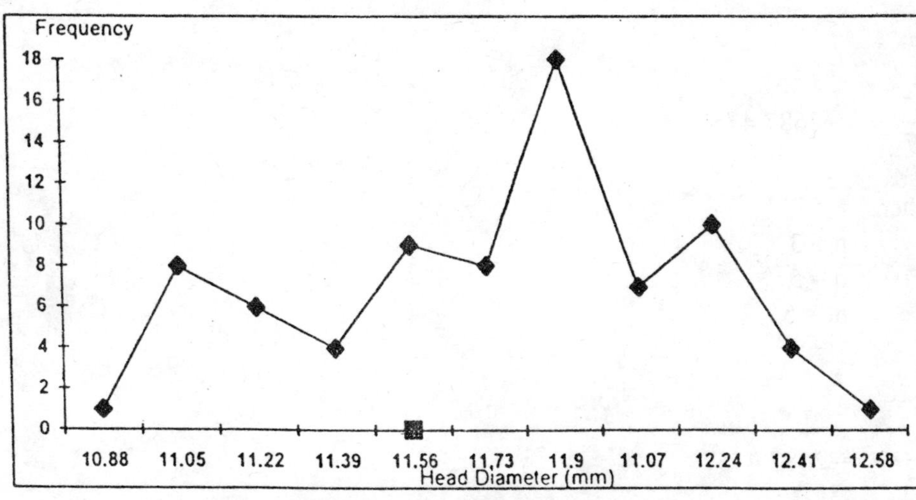

Figure 3: Distribution of Head Diameter (mm)

We also draw consecutive fifty rivets from a tringle machine during continuous production and analyse mean, dispersion skewness, kurtosis and process capability measures for the four characteristics.

4. ANALYSIS AND INTERPRETATION OF DATA

- **Shank Diameter (d) :**

TABLE 1: **Sum of observations**

Time → M/c ↓	T1 8:30 AM	T2 10:30 AM	T3 12:30 PM	T4 2.30 PM	T5 4.30 PM	Total
M_1	30.25	29.50	30.00	31.18	30.885	151.59
M_2	29.55	29.90	29.735	29.94	29.96	149.085
M_3	29.92	29.50	29.5	29.60	29.74	148.26
M_4	89.495	88.90	89.235	90.72	90.585	448.935

$\overline{x}$ = mean of pooled observation = 5.986 mm
$\hat{\sigma}$ = Std deviation of pooled observation = 0.1 mm

$\Sigma\,\Sigma\,\Sigma\, y^2_{ijk} = 2687.9768,$
where

i = 1, 2, 3 (M/cs)
j = 1, 2, 3, 4, 5 (Times)
k = 1, 2, 3, 4, 5
(No. of observation per cell)

$$\frac{\sum_i T^2_{i00}}{mq} = 2687.4757,$$

where

p = 3
q = 5
m = 5

$$\frac{\sum_i T^2_{0j0}}{mp} = 2687.4757$$

$$\frac{\sum_i \sum_j T^2_{ijo}}{m} = 2687.414$$

$$\frac{T^2_{000}}{mpq} = 2687.2351$$

TABLE 2: **ANOVA for shank diameter**

Source of variation	d.f.	SS	MS	F	F at level 1%	F at level 5%
Due to M/cs	2	0.2406	0.1203	107.41	4.98	3.15
Due to Times	4	0.1789	0.044725	107.41	3.65	2.53
Due to Interaction	8	0.255	0.031875	39.95	2.82	2.10
Error	60	0.0672	0.00112	28.46		
Total	74	0.7417				

It is observed from ANOVA table 5.3.2 that the variation due to M/c Time interaction is significant at both the levels.

We have

$$F = \frac{MS\ (M/_{cs})}{MS\ (Interaction)} = 3.774 < F_{0.01;2,8}(8.66)$$

$$< F_{0.05;2,8}(4.46)$$

$$F = \frac{MS\ (M/Times)}{MS\ (Interaction)} = 1.403 < F_{0.01;4,8}(7.01)$$

$$< F_{0.05;4,8}(3.84)$$

Hence, variations due to M/cs or Times w.r.t. interaction are not significant at any level.

Also

$$\hat{\sigma}^2_{\text{M/cs}} = 0.003537$$

$$\hat{\sigma}^2_{\text{Times}} = 0.000856 \approx 0$$

$$\hat{\sigma}^2_{\text{Interaction}} = 0.006151$$

It is seen that the variation of the characteristic due to times (among different time) is negligible. The variation due to m/c - time interaction is more than the variation due to m/cs.

It may concluded that there is the variation of the characteristic among machines and the variation changes with respect to time in different machines.

Actually the Shank diameter is not manufactured on these machines. It is manufactured on cold drawing machine where there may variation of the characteristic with respect to time due to different settings of dies during processing.

- **Head diameter (d_t)**

TABLE 3: **Sum of Observations**

Time → M/c ↓	T_1	T_2	T_3	T_4	T_5	Total
M_1	56.645	58.9	59.925	58.59	58.445	292.505
M_2	60.275	59.065	60.15	59.805	59.53	298.825
M_3	61.675	57.025	55.931	61.765	60.69	297.086
Total	178.595	174.99	176.16	180.16	178.665	888.416

$\overline{x} = 11.84, \hat{\sigma} = 0.41$

$$\Sigma \Sigma \Sigma \quad y^2ijk = 10536.253, \qquad \frac{\sum_i T^2_{i00}}{mp} = 10524.625$$

$$\frac{\sum T^2_{0j0}}{mp} = 10524.972, \qquad \frac{\sum_i \sum_j T^2_{ij0}}{m} = 10531.966$$

$$\frac{T^2_{000}}{mpq} = 10523.773$$

TABLE 4: **ANOVA for Head Diameter**

Sources of Variation	df	SS	MS	F	F at level 1%	F at level 5%
Due to M/cs	2	0.852	0.426	5.96	4.98	3.15
Due to Times	4	1.199	0.29975	4.19	3.65	2.53
Due to Interaction	8	6.142	0.76775	10.74	2.82	2.10
Error	60	4.287	0.07145			
Total	74	12.48				

It is observed from ANOVA table 5.3.4 that the variation due to m/c - time intraction is significant at both the levels.

We have

$$F = \frac{MS\ (M_{/CS})}{MS\ (Interaction)} = 0.56 < F_{0.01;\,2,8}\ (8.65)$$

$$< F_{0.05;\,2,8}\ (4.46)$$

$$F = \frac{MS\ (Times)}{MS\ (Interaction)} = 0.39 < F_{0.05;\,4,8}\ (3.84)$$

$$< F_{0.05;\,4,8}\ (3.884)$$

Hence, variations due to m/cs or times w.r.t interaction are not significant at any level.

$\hat{\sigma}^2$ M/c ≈ 0, $\hat{\sigma}^2$ Time ≈ 0 and $\hat{\sigma}^2$ Interaction ≈ 0.1393

It is seen that the variations due to m/cs or times is negligible. The variation of the characteristic among different machines changes with time.

- **End diameter (d_s)**

TABLE 5: **Sum of Observations**

Time→ M/c ↓	T_1	T_2	T_3	T_4	T_5	Total
M_1	29.544	29.50	29.865	29.91	29.92	148.74
M_2	29.50	29.515	29.39	29.52	29.49	147.415
M_3	29.59	29.453	29.165	29.267	29.18	146.655
Total	88.635	88.468	88.42	88.697	88.59	442.81

$\bar{x} = 5.9,\qquad \hat{\sigma} = 0.053$

$$\Sigma\Sigma\Sigma\, y^2ijk = 2614.6178, \qquad \frac{\sum_i T^2_{i00}}{mq} = 2614.4983$$

$$\frac{\sum_j T^2_{0j0}}{mp} = 2614.4128, \qquad \frac{\sum^i \sum j T^2_{ij0}}{m} = 2614.5623$$

$$\frac{T^2_{000}}{mpq} = 2614.4092$$

TABLE 6: ANOVA for End Diameter

Sources of Variation	d.f.	SS	MS	F	F at level 1 %	F at level 5 %
Due to M/cs	2	0.0891	0.04455	48.16	4.98	3.15
Due to Times	4	0.0036	0.0009	0.97	3.65	2.53
Due to Interaction	8	0.0604	0.00755	8.16	2.82	2.10
Error	60	0.0555	0.000925			
Total	74	0.2086				

It is observed from ANOVA table 5.3.6 that the variation due to times is not significant at any level but the variation due to m/c time interaction significant at both the levels.

We have

$$F = \frac{MS\ (M_{/CS})}{MS\ (Interaction)} = 5.9 < F_{0.01;\,2,8}\ (8.65)$$

$$< F_{0.05;\,2,8}\ (4.46)$$

$$F = \frac{MS\ (Times)}{MS\ (Interaction)} \quad 0.1192 < F_{0.01;\,4,8}\ (7.01)$$

$$< F_{0.05;\,4,8}\ (3.84)$$

It is seen that the variation due to machines w.r.t. interaction is significant 5% level.

Also,

$\hat{\sigma}^2$ M/c = 0.00148 $\quad\hat{\sigma}^2$ Time = 0 and $\hat{\sigma}^2$ Interaction = 0.001325

It is observed that the variation among machines is more than the variation among machine w.r.t. time.

• Head Thickness (t):

TABLE 7: **Sum of Observations**

Time → M/c ↓	T_1	T_2	T_3	T_4	T_5	Total
M_1	12.1	10.575	10.48	10.615	10.49	54.26
M_2	11.275	10.415	12.37	12.42	11.657	58.137
M_3	12.88	13.7	14.595	11.85	10.645	63.67
Total	36.255	34.69	37.445	34.885	32.792	176.067

$\overline{x} = 2.35, \quad \hat{\sigma} = 0.27$

$$\Sigma\,\Sigma\,\Sigma\, y^2_{ijk} = 418.65867$$

$$\frac{\sum_i T^2_{i00}}{mq} = 415.11709, \qquad \frac{\sum_i T^2_{0j0}}{mp} = 414.1485$$

$$\frac{\sum^i \sum^j T^2_{ij0}}{m} = 417.97662, \qquad \frac{T^2_{000}}{mpq} = 413.32784$$

TABLE 8: **ANOVA for End Diameter**

Sources of Variation	d.f.	SS	MS	F	F at level 1 %	F at level 5 %
Due to M/cs	2	1.78925	0.894625	78.65	4.98	3.15
Due to Times	4	0.82066	0.205165	18.04	3.65	2.53
Due to Interaction	8	2.03845	0.5096125	44.80	2.82	2.10
Error	60	0.68247	0.0113745			
Total	74	5.33083				

It is observed from ANOVA table 5.3.8 that the variation due to times is not significant at any level but the variation due to m/c time interaction significant at both the levels.

We have

$$F = \frac{MS\ (M_{/C})}{MS\ (Interaction)} = 1.75 < F_{0.01;\,2,8}\ (8.65) < F_{0.05;\,2,8}\ (4.46)$$

$$F = \frac{MS\ (Times)}{MS\ (Interaction)} \quad 0.0.41 < F_{0.01;\,4,8}\ (7.01) < F_{0.05;\,4,8}\ (3.84)$$

Hence the variations due to m/cs or times with the interaction are not significant any level.

Also,

$\hat{\sigma}^2$ M/cs = 0.0154 $\quad \hat{\sigma}^2$ Time = 0 $\quad \hat{\sigma}^2$ **Interaction** = 0.0996

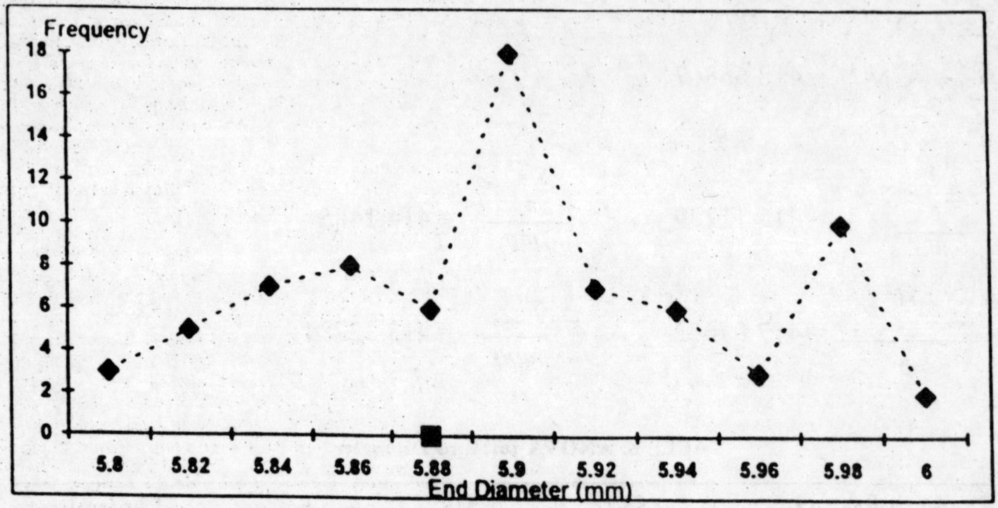

Figure 4: Distribution of End Diameter (mm)

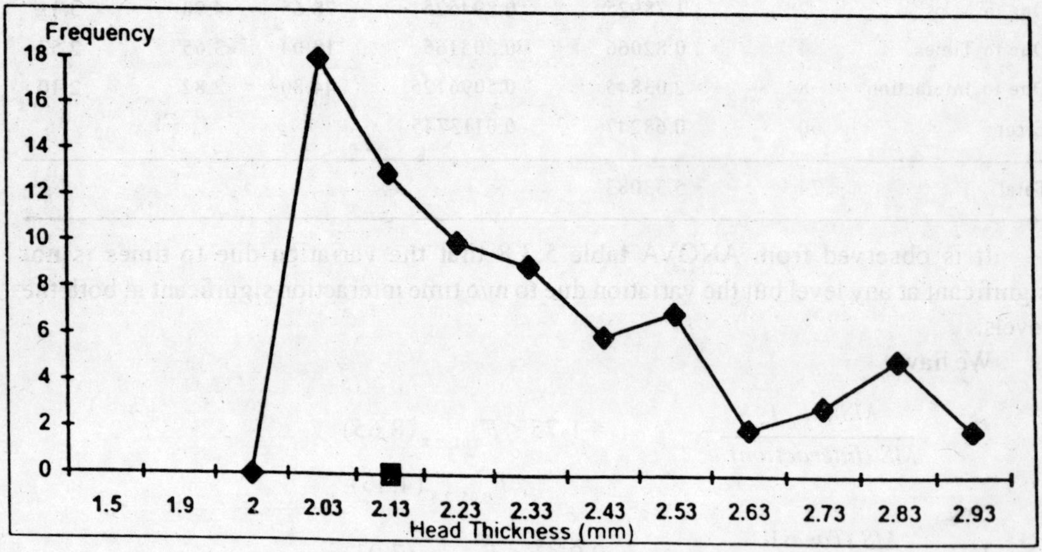

Figure 5: Distribution of Head Thickness (mm)

The variation due to machine time interaction is much more than the variation due to machines.

It is observed from the analysis of variances of the four quality characteristics that the variation due to the different time is not significant and negligible. The variations occur among machines and the variations chang among machines with respect to time.

Frequency distribution curves (see figures 2 to 5) for four quality characteristics show trimodal distribution. This is possible because the data constitute a mixture of

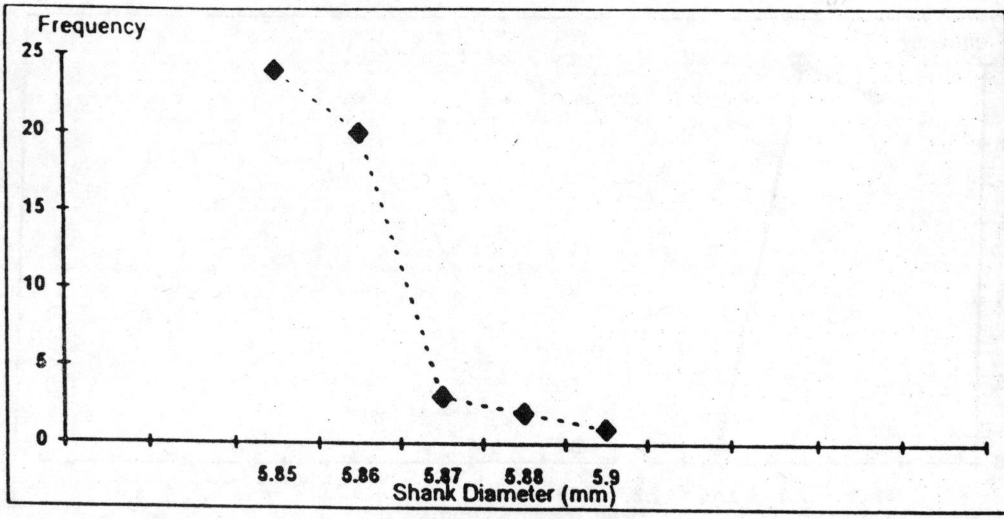

Figure 6: Distribution of Shank Diameter (mm)

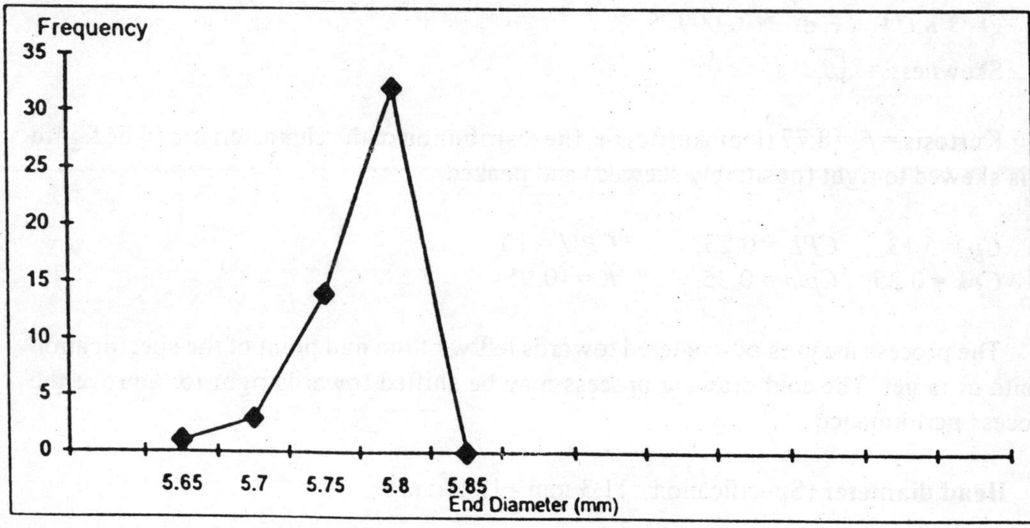

Figure 7: Distribution of End Diameter (mm)

outputs from three different machines whose performances in terms of means of the characteristics studied are different. Let us study the four characteristics of the rivels taken from one machine during one minute continuous production.

- **Shank diameter** (Specification: 6 ± 0.15 mm)

On numerical computation, we get

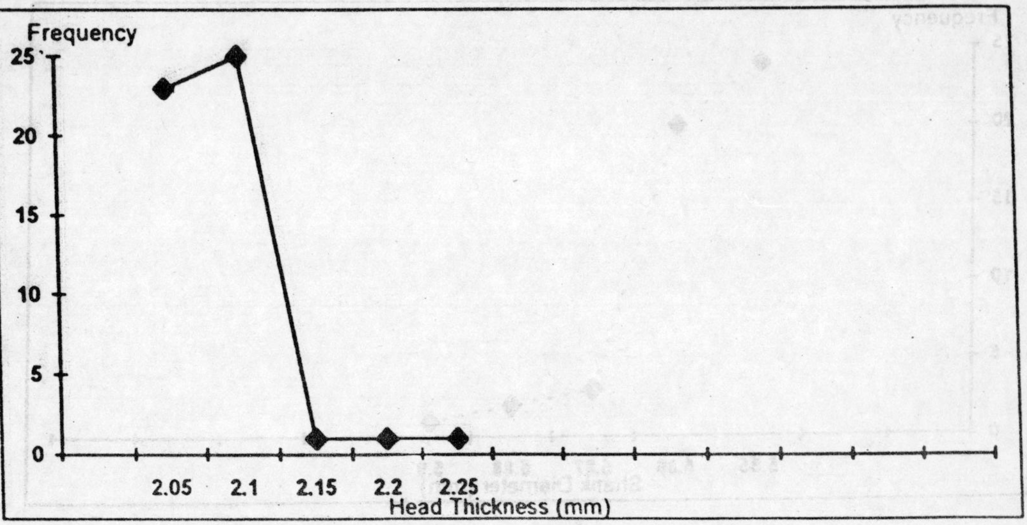

Figure 8: Distribution of Head Thickness (mm)

$\bar{x} = 5.8574$ $\hat{\sigma}$ d $= 0.00975$

Skewness $= \sqrt{\beta_1} = 2.09$

Kurtosis $= \beta_2 = 8.77$ (leptokurtic) i.e. the distribution of the characteristic (vide figure 6) is skewed to right (positively skewed) and peaked.

$Cp = 5.13$ $CPL = 0.25$, $CPU = 10$
$Cpk = 0.25$, $Cpm = 0.35$, $K = -0.95$

The process mean is off-centered towards left w.r.t the mid point of the specification limits or target. The cold drawing process may be shifted towards right to improve the process performance.

- **Head diameter** (Specification : 11.3 mm - 12.0 mm)

On numerical computation, we get

$\overline{X} = 11.4158$, $\hat{\sigma}_{dt} = 0.038$

Skewness $= \sqrt{\beta_1} = -0.42$ (skewed towards left)
Kurtosis $= \beta_2 = 3.15$ (almost mesokurtic)
$Cp = 3.07$, $CPL = 1.02$, $CPU = 5.13$, $Cpk = 1.02$
$K = -0.67$

The process is off centered towards left. The process needs to be shifted towards the mid point of specification limits to improve process performance.

- **End diameter** (Specification : Min 5.82 mm)

On numerical computation, we get

$\overline{X} = 5.79 \qquad \hat{\sigma}_{ds} = 0.03$

Skewness = $\sqrt{\beta_1} = -1.5$ (skewed towards left)
Kurtosis = $\beta_2 = 5.54$ (leptokurtic) (vide figure 7)

Even $\overline{X} + \hat{\sigma}_{ds}$ does not exceed the lower specification limits. Thus more than 60% of the items are off specification. $Cpk = 0$

Significant process improvement is needed to improve process performance and the shifting of the process beyond LSL.

- **Head thickness** (Specification : 1.5 + 0.4 mm)
  − 0.0 mm

On numerical computation, we get

$\overline{X} = 2.1 \quad \hat{\sigma}_t = 0.034$

Skewness = $\sqrt{\beta_1} = 2.85$ (skewed towards right)
Kurtosis = $\beta_2 = 15.7$ (highly leptokurtic) (vide figure 8) i.e. less dispersion and greater concentration around mean.

All observations lie outside the upper specification limits but

$6\,\hat{\sigma}_t (0.2) < U - L\,(0.4)$
$Cp = 1.95, K_T = 3, K_m = 2$

where m = mid point of the specification limits.

The process is highly off centered towards right (i.e. beyond USL). The process may be shifted towards left i.e. towards target to improve process performance.

5. CAUSES OF VARIATION

- **Shank Diameter** : Cold drawing process is shifted towards the lower specification limit due to setting of dies of low dimensions at different times and also due to wearing of the dies.
- **Head Diameter** :The process shifted towards the lower specification limits due to low impact pressure applied on the rivet.

- **End Diameter** :High shear pressure is applied at the end of the rivet resulting in low dimension.
- **Head Thickness** :Low impact pressure is applied on the rivet resulting in high thickness. The variation may be due to the high carbon content of the raw material, no heat treatment after cold drawing, skill of operator, different machines, different methods of operations.

6. SUGGESTION FOR THE REDUCTION OF VARIATION

— There should be control on the raw material composition and on cold drawing process for the achievement of the target.
— The material may be next treated after cold drawing.
— There must be control on operators, machines and method of operation.
— SQC method must be used to control the quality and the productivity.

7. ACKNOWLEDGEMENT

The authors are thankful to Prof. S. P. Mukherjee, Centenary Professor of Statistics, Calcutta University and eminent quality expert for his invaluable guidance and suggestions for the preparation of the paper.

REFERENCES

1. A. B. Mundel : Standard Column, *Quality Engineering* 3(4), 551-60 (559), 1991.
2. A. B. Mundel : Standard Column, *Quality Engineering* 8(4) 699-704, 1996.
3. A. F. Bissell : How Reliable is your capability Index, *Applied Statistics* 39, 331-40, 1990.
4. B. Gunter : The Use and Abuse of *Cpk Quality Progress* 1(72-73), 2 (108-109), 3 (79-88) and 4 (86-87),1989. Also see The Use and Abuse of Revisited January 1991, 90-94.
5. B. J. Melloy, and M. J. Chandra : *International Journal of Production Research* 30 (10), 2253-2263, 1992.
6. D. H. Besterfield : *Quality Control,* 2nd ed. Prentice Hall, New Jersey, N.J., 1986.
7. D. C. Montgomery and G. C. Runger : Gauge Capability analysis and Designed Experionents Part-II; Experimental Design models and variance components estimation. *Quality Engineering* 6(2), 289-305, 1993-94b.
8. D. C. Montgomery and G. C. Runger : Gauge Capability and Designed Experiments, Part-I; Basic Methods, *Quality Engineering 6(1),* 115-135 (1993-94), 1993-94a.
9. E. J. Davis, G. F. Scott and C. D. Obray : Process Capability for Manufacturing Processes, *Quality Forum* (*Journal of Institute of Quality Assurance*, England) 19(3), 147-154, 1993.
10. G. D. Taylor and J. R. English : A Bench marking frame work for quality improvement, *Quality Engineering* 6(1), 57-69, 1993-94.
11. IS : 10645 — 1983. *Method for Estimation of Process Capability*, Bureau of Indian Standards, New Delhi.
12. K. Vannman : A unified approach to capability indices, *Research Report*, Division of Quality Technology and Statistics, Luleo University, *Statistica Sinica* 3 (2), 1993.

13. K. Vannman and S. Kotz : A superstructure of capability indices—Distributional properties and Implications, *Research Report 2*, Division of Quality Technology and Statistics, Luleo University, 1994a.
14. K. Vannman and S. Kotz : A superstructure of capability Indices Asymptotics and its application, *Research Report 5*, Division of Quality Technology and Statistics, Luleo University, Sweden, 1994b.
15. L. K. Chan, S. W. Cheng and F. A. Spiring : A New Measuse of Process Capability, *Journal of Quality Technology*, 30, 162 -75, 1988.
16. N. L. Johnson and S. Kotz. : *Process Capability Indices*, Chapman and Hall, London, 1993.
17. S. Kotz, W. L. Pearn and N. L. Johnson : Some Process Capability Indices are More Reliable than One Might Think, *Applied Statistics*, 42 (1) 55 - 62, 1993.
18. S. P. Mukherjee and N. K. Singh : A Process Capability Index for Two Corrected Quality Characteristics, *IARQR Transactions 18* (2), 49-55, 1993.
19. S. P. Mukherjee and N. K. Singh : Sampling Properties of an Estimater of the Bivariate Process Capability Index, *Economic Quality Control* 9(2), 73-78, 1994.
20. S. P. Mukherjee : Process Capability Indices and Associated Inference Problems, *Proceedings of the International Conference on Statistical Methods and Statistical Computing for Quality and Reliability Improvement* (ICSQP'95), 1995.
21. S. P. Mukherjee and N. K. Singh : Sampling Properties of an Estimater of a New Process Capability Index for Weibull Distributed Quality Characteristics, (To appear in *Quality Engineering, 10 (2), 191-194, 1997)*, 1996.
22. V. E. Kane : Process Capability indices, *Journal of Quality Technology 18*, 41-52. Corrigenda 265, 1986.
23. W. L. Pearn, S. Kotz and N. L. Johnson : Distributional and Inferential Properties of Process Capability Indices, *Journal of Quality Teachnology 24*, 216-23, 1992.

AN FMS CONCEPTION FOR GAS METAL ARC WELDING WITH KNOWLEDGE BASED OBJECT ORIENTED PROCESS PLANNING

27

R.K. Sahoo, L.N. Panda

Readers, College of Engineering and Technology,
OUAT, Bhubaneswar.

ABSTRACT

In Today's world of competitive manufacturing there is demand for quality products of several designs. GMAW with flexibility in design combined with Knowledge Based Object Oriented Process Planning is a step forward in achieving this. Ultrasonic testing stationed in the system helps in isolating quality products and keeps defectives to the minimum. The knowledge Based Process planning technique ensures not only quality but also cost. All these aspects have been enumerated in the present paper.

INTRODUCTION

In the present age of globalisation, liberalisation and privatisation the competitiveness without flexibility and cost effectiveness of the manufacturing firms can not be sustained. They require the flexibility to produce varieties of products of quality at the price to cater to the changing needs of the customers in a market oriented society. To achieve this the firms are expected to adopt new strategies by meeting the challenges of changing technologies such as superior and cheaper products, shorter delivery time, quicker sales quotation, faster drawing and production rates, lower cost of production, labour and development. The current emphasis now-a-days sway towards Flexible Manufacturing Systems, since it integrates the various functions of a manufacturing enterprise which also simplifies many problems effectively by increasing the level of intelligence within the manufacturing system. Significant contributions in the development of intelligent-knowledge-based object oriented process planning system (IKOOPPS) for knowledge intensive activities and decision-making are necessary to achieve the required level of integration and benefits. Nevertheless much research effort has been expended in the development of new manufacturing processes, methodologies and computer-integration technologies to support the shorter product development cycles. Manufacturing organisations including the fabrication units incorporating arc welding processes can take advantages of the new technologies to improve their competitive edge.

PROCESS PLANNING

High precision arc welding methods in fabrication industries use process planning function to establish methodology, modes of metal transfer, current and voltage values, shielding gas requirements to make the operation cost effective for the final assembled product. It involves the determination of the following items to convert raw materials to finished product.

(i) A suitable size of raw material.
(ii) A set of compatible welding operations to form the mode of metal transfer.
(iii) A set of compatible welding power sources for voltage and current combination.
(iv) The required welding parameters such as welding speed, stickout values.
(v) A sequence of setups and setup configurations.
(vi) A sequence of welding operations within each setup.
(vii) Estimates of welding/setup time for costing and scheduling.

Within the arena of fabrication by arc welding method, the process planning is generally the domain of experienced welder as the required skills and knowledge are highly specialised. It follows that the effectiveness of a process plan depends heavily on the knowledge, experience and consistency of the welder. Any company willing to introduce flexibility and facilities, the skills needed to operate such capital intensive equipment require to be installed in the equipment in absence of skilled expertise.

OVERVIEW OF IKOOPP SYSTEM

An Intelligent Knowledge Based Object Oriented Process Planning (IKOOPP) removes the inconsistencies and other problems associated with manual process plan. That is why a model is developed to automate and standardise the process planning for arc welding operations for the tube joining. The IKOOPP system automatically plans the setup sequences, selects the mode of metal transfer, selects and controls gas flow rates for shielding, ultrasonic testing, heat treatment requirement and sequence operations to minimise cost.

AUTOMATED PROCESS PLANNING

There are two approaches for automated process planning, viz. (a) Variant and (b) Generative approaches. The latest trend may also be added which involves use of expert system or Knowledge based process planning as explained below.

IKBS techniques offer some recent trend in research for automated process planning. It provides a means for capturing the knowledge and interaction of experienced process planners for automatic generation of process plans. Thus consistency and standardization of process plans can effectively be achieved. The techniques incorporating knowledge and characteristics of a component include :

(i) Node and links in associative and semantic networks.
(ii) Condition action pairs in rule based of fabrication system.
(iii) Slots, facets and values in frame or object systems.

The automation of process planning function is a difficult task because the required knowledge is highly complex and ill structured. While conventional algorithmic programmes have been successfully implemented in CAD, CAE and CAM systems these are individual productivity tools which need to be analysed in a sequential manner. Automated process planning system requires simultaneous process of working knowledge, geometry and data.

AUTOMATIC FEATURE RECOGNITION

The main function of a CAPP system is to transform geometrical and topological information of a product model held in a CAD system into relevant manufacturing instructions for a CAM system. It is initiated by the desire to enable interpretation of a part design so that process plans, fixture design, GT codes and NC programs can be automatically generated. An integrated CAD/CAPP/CAM system requires a subsystem which can directly utilize part definition data from CAD system and Arc welding information from the welding databases to facilitate the automation.

Feature Extraction

It involves to develop suitable algorithms to identify and extract form features from CAD geometry models. The attributes of the extracted features together with their geometrical relationships serve as input to a CAPP system for the generation of process plans. Further the following considerations are essential to follow up the object oriented programme in general.

(i) Procedures and object classes form a table.
(ii) Objects may supply their own procedures.
(iii) FUNCALL and APPLY enable procedure norms or description to be computed.
(iv) Object centered programme is becoming popular.
(v) Messages facility in object centered programmes and Flavour enable procedure to be constructed from inherrent parts.

Feature Extractor of the IKOOPP System

The automated process planning for the metal arc welding is designed for producing large quantity of accurately fabricated component having interchangeable feasibility. It performs sequence of operations on tube assembly. The component requires heat treatment to relieve the thermal stresses from the heat affected zone, which can be studied by ultrasonic test indicating sources of enhanced responces from the Heat Affected Zone.

IKOOPP System

The attributes of an object representing a welding feature can be retrieved from the knowledge base through an inference engine. The geometrical relationships within the features can be represented using attributes and methods. Each instance can also communicate with other instances by message passing techniques. All knowledge bases are built around the IKOOPP system to ensure data integrity and consistency of feature interpretations. Four different techniques were used in the representation of welding features, planning knowledge and manufacturing resources within the IKOOPP system. These techniques include the object oriented schema, production rules, database and dedicated procedures.

Production Rules

The overall planning strategy together with the specific process planning knowledge within the IKOOPP system are represented as forward-chaining production rules of the form:

IF [condition] THEN [action]

The rules for controlling the overall planning strategy are also known as meta-rules. When the IKOOPP system is executed, its inference engine selects a production rule whose condition is true, and fires it. Firing a rule is effectively executing its action part. The firing of a rule may modify the contents of the working memory so that other rules may become applicable. This process of selecting and firing applicable production rules continues until all the process planning information has been inferred. A priorty number can also be specified for each rule. If several rules are applicable at the same time, the inference engine will select a rule with the highest priority. The priority of each rule can be dynamically modified so as to influence the planning strategy used in the IKOOPP system. Production rules are organised into several knowledge base modules according to their functionalities. Each set of rules can be individually or collectively loaded into or unloaded from the working memory as requred in the planning process. When a rule is loaded into the memory, the inference engine then checks its condition for applicability. This allows the inference engine to focus specifically on a small set of rules at any time, thus improving the speed of the inference process.

COST CONSIDERATION

A comprehensive formula in a simplified form is incorporated to indicate the cost effectiveness of fabrication.

$$F = t \times c + L \times m + C/48n\,(K + 0.05)$$

where

F = the cost of welding a particular fabrication
t = the hours booked to the job (Standard Data)
c = the hourly cost rate which will include overheads
L = the cost of consumables
m = consumable cost rate
C = capital cost of plant
n = output in number per week
K = a depreciation factor

CONCLUSION

A feature extractor is in the process of development to allow the automatic extraction of welding features for the metal gas arc welding system. The extracted attributes are used by the IKOOPP system to effectively develop the fabrication. The ultrasonic testing helps in deciding post weld heat treatment for the HAZ. Further cost estimates helps in deciding the cost effective process plan to be utilised. Successful demonstration of laboratory model will open up new avenues for its practical application.

REFERENCES

Allen, D.K., 1979, *Generative Process Planning Using the DCLASS Information System.* Monograph N. 14, Brigham Young University, Utah, USA.

Allen, D.K., 1987, *An Introduction to Computer Aided Process Planning, CIM Review*, 4(1), 7-23.

Bhaskaran, K., 1990, Process plan selection, *International Journal of Production Research*, 28 (8), 1527-39.

Midge, P.J., *Size Measurement and Characterisation of Weld Defects by Ultrasonic Testing*, The Welding Institute, Abington, Cambridge.

Houldcroft, P.T., *Welding Process Technology*.

Hawkes, Barry, *The CAD/CAM Process*, Pitman Publication.

V

ARTIFICIAL INTELLIGENCE AND ROBOTICS IN PRODUCTION

SIMULATION OF MOBILE ROBOT MOTION PATH PLANNING FOR ROBOT OF DIFFERENT 2D CONFIGURATIONS USING DIJKSTRA ALGORITHM

28

Viswanath D.S,[1] B.M. Rajaprakash,[1] Dr. B.K. Muralidhara[1] and Dr. V.K. Basalalli[1]
Department of Mechanical Engineering, Bangalore University,[1]
University Visveswaraya College of Engineering, K.R. Circle, Bangalore - 560 001

ABSTRACT

The autonomous mobile robots which need very little human intervention for their operation find widespread applications in space exploration, undersea work, automated guiding systems, automated manufacturing systems, etc. These autonomous mobile robots for effective functioning have to develop the path planning intelligence on their own for obstacle avoidance. The robot is treated as a two dimensional object in an appropriate space called configuration space and the obstacles are mapped in this space taking into consideration the robot size. By accomplishing this, the obstacle dimensions are apparently increased and consequently the free work space area is apparently reduced. By adopting this, the problem of planning the path/motion of a three dimensional object simplifies into a problem of planning the path/motion of a centre point of the two dimesional robot.

In this short term investigation, attempts have been made to simulate the path planning of the mobile robot having circular and rectangular configuration. The problem of path planning has been transformed to one of the graph searching . This has been done by considering the mapped obstacle end points, initial centre position of the robot (source) and final centre position of the robot (destination) as nodes. Later, a connectivity graph has been constructed by joining each of the nodes to each of the other approachable nodes. Thus constructed non-directed graph has been searched for the shortest path using Dijkstra algorithm which is more popularly known as A* algorithm as applied to motion path planning. By incorporating above mentioned steps, an optimal path has been generated and the robot motion is simulated from source to destination in the vicinity of planar obstacles such as polygons, circle, ellipse etc.

1. INTRODUCTION

In the field of robotics, it is ultimately desirable to create autonomous mobile robots which need very little human intervention. The user of these types of robots has to specify only "what is to be done" and it is not required to specify "how it is to be done". While developing these types of autonomous robots, it is necessary that a path planning intelligence is in built in the robots such that the shortest path is explored by the robot. These types of autonomous mobile robots find wide spread applications in space exploration, automated guiding systems, construction, undersea work, automated manufacturing system, etc.

There are two different approaches of developing path planning intelligence viz., local approach and global approach. In case of local approach, the obstracles have to be identified first and then avoided while robot is in motion. Invariably, this approach necessitates the use of sensors and associated feed back system. Where as in case of global approach, before proceeding with the analysis of the connectivity of the free space, the obstacles are well defined both in terms of geometry and location. Some examples of global approach are Road Map Method and Cell Decomposition Method.[1-5]

The authors in their earlier investigation[6] have simulated the planning of the path/ motion of a three dimensional robot by treating the robot as a point in an appropriate space and by mapping the obstacles in this space.

2. SCOPE OF THE PAPER

In this paper, results of the attempts made to simulate the path planning of a mobile robot by treating it as a two dimensional reactangular or circular object for obstacle avaoidance using global approach have been presented.

For the problem of path planning dijkstra algorithm, more popularly known as A* algorithm as applied to motion planning has been used. The details are presented in the forthcoming paragraphs.

3. THE PRESENT WORK

For the purpose of understanding, a simple illustration has been considered and the same has been presented in figure 1 schematicallty in Fig. 1 where P_1 to P_6 are obstacle vertices co-ordinates, P_0 is the source co-ordinate and P_7 is the destination co-ordinate of the robot. Two typical obstacles (Obs-1 and Obs-2) each having three vertices in the robot space have been considered. Further, the robot in this illustration has been considered as a Circular object in two dimensions.

The problem of path planning for the robot has been approached in two phases as follows:

In the first phase, the obstacle dimensions are mapped to the robot dimensions (radius of the circle). By accomplishing this the obstacle dimensions are apparently increased and consequently the free work space area is apparently reduced.

In the second phase, the co-ordinates of the mapped obstacles, the centre of the circular robot in initial position (source) and in final position (destination) are considered as nodes. Later a connectivity graph has been constructed using these nodes and has been searched for the shortest path using Dijkstra algorithm.

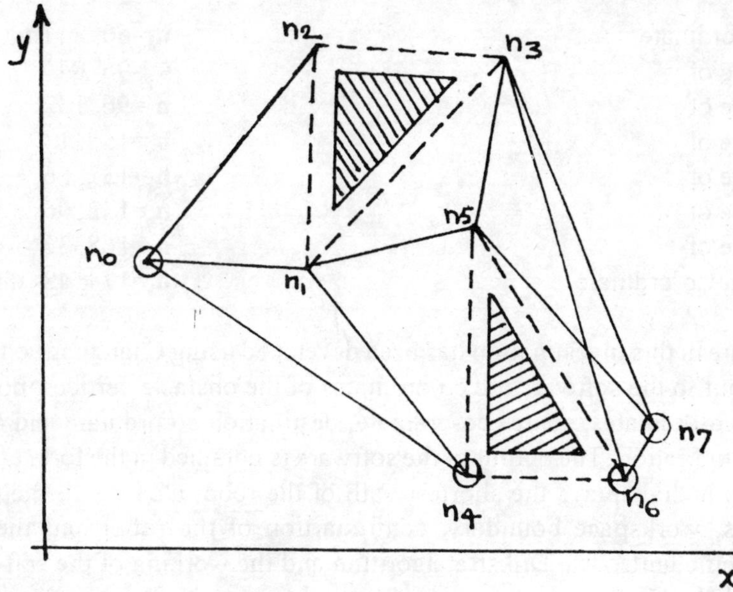

—— before mapping

------ after mapping

Figure 1: Schematic representation of the obstacles, source and destination considered in the illustration.

The assumed x and y co-ordinates of the obstacle vertices in specific units before mapping are given below:

Source co-ordinate	P_0=60, 84
Co-ordinate of vertex	P_1=102,100
Co-ordinate of vertex	P_2=102,126
Co-ordinate of vertex	P_3=124,126
Co-ordinate of vertex	P_4=138,42
Co-ordinate of vertex	P_5=138,74
Co-ordinate of vertex	P_6= 157,42
Destination co-ordinate	P_7=174,48

Radius of the circular configuration robot has been assumed as 6 specific units.

Mapping is basically pushing each and every point of all the obstacles through a distance equal to the radius of the circle in a direction determined according to the configuration of the obstacles. This is done by using established mathematical equations used in computer graphics.

Now the computed co-ordinates of the obstacle vertices in specific units obtained after mapping are as follows:

Source co-ordinate	$\mathbf{n}_0$=60, 84 (unchanged)
Co-ordinate of	$\mathbf{n}_1$=96, 84
Co-ordinate of	$\mathbf{n}_2$=96, 132
Co-ordinate of	$\mathbf{n}_3$=138, 132
Co-ordinate of	$\mathbf{n}_4$=132, 36
Co-ordinate of	$\mathbf{n}_5$=132, 96
Co-ordinate of	$\mathbf{n}_6$=168, 36
Destination Co-ordinate	$\mathbf{n}_7$=174, 48 (unchanged)

The software in this investigation has been developed using C language on a PC-386 system. The input to the software are co-ordinates of the obstacle vertices, boundary of the workspace co-ordinates, source co-ordinate, destination co-ordinate and dimension of the robot configuration. The output of the software is obtained in the form of graphical representation which displays the shortest path of the robot along with the display of obstacle shapes, workspace boundary, configuartion of the robot and the distance travelled in specific units. The Dijkstra algorithm and the working of the software have been explained below for the illustration under consideration.

The vertices of the obstacles, the vertices of the workspace boundary, the source co-ordinate of the robot, the destination co-ordinate of the robot and the dimensions of the robot configuration are accepted by the computer. By using established mathematical equations used in computer graphics the obstacles are mapped according to the robot dimensions. Ther vertices of the mapped obstacles are then considered as the nodes and are numbered as $\mathbf{n}_1$, $\mathbf{n}_2$, $\mathbf{n}_3$, $\mathbf{n}_4$, $\mathbf{n}_5$ and $\mathbf{n}_6$. The centre of the robot configuration is made to coincide with the source co-ordinate and this co-ordinate is numbered as n_0. Similarly n_7 is the destination co-ordinate of the robot.

Now a Link[][] matrix is created (Size of Link[][] = Number of nodes X Number of nodes). Link[][] is a 2D matrix representing the distance between any two nodes as formed above. If the straight line segment joining any two nodes (say node i and node j) does not pass through any of the obstacles' interior, then these two nodes (i and j) are said to be approchable and the geometric distance between them is assigned to the Link[i][j]. But if the straight line segment joining these nodes (i and j) lies in any of the obstacles' interior even partly, then it is said that the two nodes are not approachable and the value of infinity is assigned to Link [i][j]. The Link Table pertaining to the illustration under consideration has been presented as Table 1. The distances between the nodes are shown in this Table. The blank elements in the Table 1 indicate that the two nodes are not approachable and the value of infinity is assigned to these elements.

Thus, after the creation of the link table the next step is to find the shortest path using A* algorithm. For this purpose a single dimensioned array called dist [] has been used (The size of dist [] = Number of nodes). The dist [i] represents the distance of any node i from the source.

Intially the first row of the link table is assigned to the dist [] array. All the nodes (n_0,..,n_7) are structures which contain x and y co-ordinates, index to identify the vertex

TABLE 1 : **Link Table Indicating the Distances**

→ Nodes

Nodes	0	1	2	3	4	5	6	7
0	0	36	60		86			
1	36	0	48	64	60	38		
2	60	48	0	42				
3		64	42	0		36	101	91
4	86	60			0	60	36	
5		38		36	60	0	70	62
6				101	36	70	0	13
7				91		62	13	0

and the link pointer. The link pointer helps in tracing back the shortest distance path after all iterations are completed. The Dist Table pertaining to the illustration under consideration obtained after all iterations as explained below are over has been presented as Table 2.

TABLE 2: **Dist Table Indicating the Values of Dist[ ] at Each Iteration**

Iter No.	Node selected	Nodes visited earlier	dist[1]	dist[2]	dist[3]	dist[4]	dist[5]	dist[6]	dist[7]
—	0	—	36	60		86			
1	1	0	36	60	100	86	74		
2	2	0,1	36	60	100	86	74		
3	5	0,1,2	36	60	100	86	74	144	138
4	4	0,1,2,5	36	60	100	86	74	122	138
5	3	0,1,2,5,4	36	60	100	86	74	122	138
6	6	0.1.2.5. 3,4,	36	60	100	86	74	122	136

Now, the source node has been considered as root node and the link pointer of this node has been initialised to NULL. All other nodes have been considered as child nodes. A one dimensional bit array S[ ] has been created (size of the S[ ] = Number of nodes).

For node i, S[i] = 0 means that the shortest path has not yet been found (the node i is unvisited).

S[i] = 1 means that the shortest path has been found (the node is visited).

Initially all S[i] have been made equal to 0 except S [0] which has been made equal to 1 (S[0] pertains to source node) and then the following steps have been carried out.

Step 1. Select node u (among 0 to 7) which has minimum dist [u] value in the dist [ ] array of Table 2 among the nodes with S [u] = 0 (unvisited nodes) (Refer coloumn 2 of Table 2).

Step 2. If dist [v] > {(dist [u] + Link [u] [v]} for v ranging from 0 to 7, then store the value of right hand side of the above inequality in the dist[v]. At the same time redirect the link pointer to node v to point it to the index of node u (ie, the node number). In other words, redirection of the link pointer is only for those nodes whose dist[ ] values are updated. This is to facilitate the identification of the shortest path at the end of all iterations.

Step 3. Repeat through Step1 and Step2 until S [Destination Node] i.e., S[7] become equal to 1. This results in visiting the destination and end of iterations.

Step 4. Now using the link pointer of the destination node we can know the index of the previous node say node 'A'. From this node 'A' we can now know the index of its previous node say node 'B'. Similarly from node 'B' we can now know the index of its previous node say node 'C'. Consequently by continuing this search we get the source node. Thus the path is found backwards as:

Dest Node → Node A → Node B → ... → Source Node

This path is suitably modified to get the path from source node to destination node.

By refering to Table 2 the Step 4 has been explained with reference to the illustration under consideration as follows.

Once the shortest distance has been found for the destination i.e, when the condition S[7] = 1, the next step is to trace back the path so as to get the intermediate nodes from source to destination.

Select node 7 and starting from the last itertion check where the dist [7] column value has changed and the node selected at this iteration gives the preceeding via point. In this step it is node 6. Hence the node 6 is selected as first via point. Next repeat the above procedure for the dist[6] column. In this column the change has taken place in the 4th iteration and the node selected at this iteration is node 4. Hence node 4 is selected as second via point. Repeat the same procedure for dist [4] column values which results in selection node 0 as the third via point which itself is the source point. Hence the path is found backwards as shown below.

7 → 6 → 4 → 0

The final path corresponding to shortest distance thus has been found as

$$0 \rightarrow 4 \rightarrow 6 \rightarrow 7$$

and the shortest distance is 136 specific units as obtained from dist [7] of Table 2.

One can check the correctness of shortest path between the source and the destination by refering to Figure1. It can be observed clearly from Figure 1 that the shortest path between source (node n_0) to destination (node n_7) is through node 4 and through node 6. However the shortest distance between the source and the destination has to be read from the Table 2.

In this investigation, various obstacle shapes and various work space boundaries have been considered and the above program was run. The typical outputs obtained have been presented in Figure 2(a) and Figure 2(b). It can be observed that these outputs are graphical representations which display the shortest path of the robot along with the display of obstacle shapes, robot configuration, work space boundary, distance travelled in specific units, source and destination.

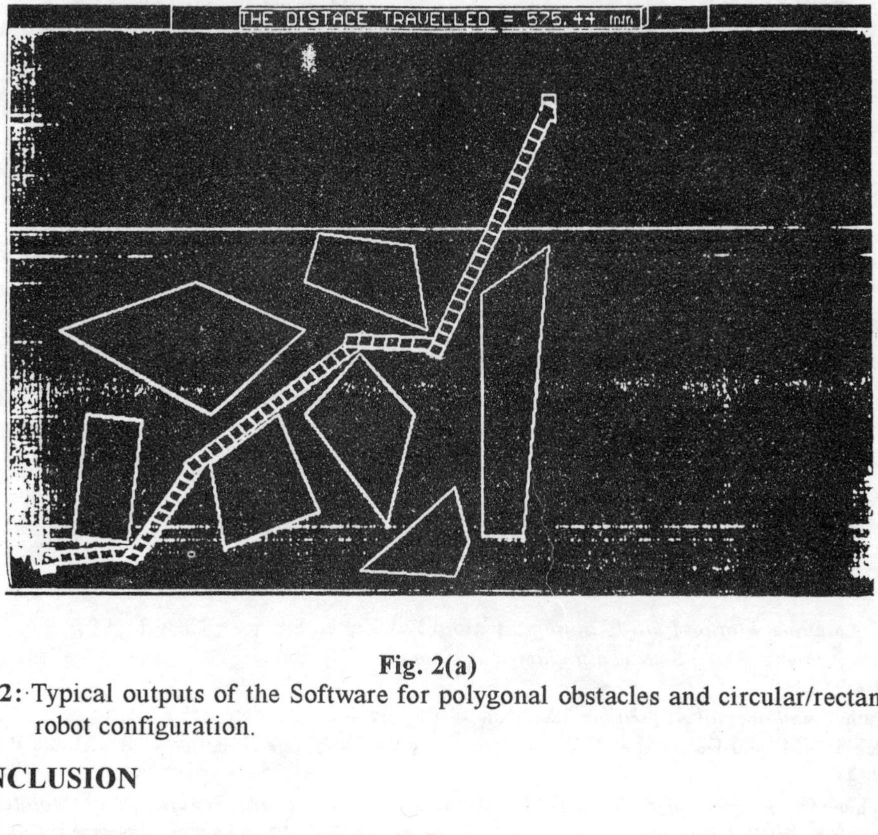

Fig. 2(a)

Figure 2: Typical outputs of the Software for polygonal obstacles and circular/rectangular robot configuration.

4. CONCLUSION

In this short-term investigation, attempts have been made to simulate the path planning of the mobile robot having circular and rectangular configuration for obstacle avoidance using global approach. The problem of path planning has been transformed to one of graph searching. This has been done by considering the vertices of the mapped obstacles,

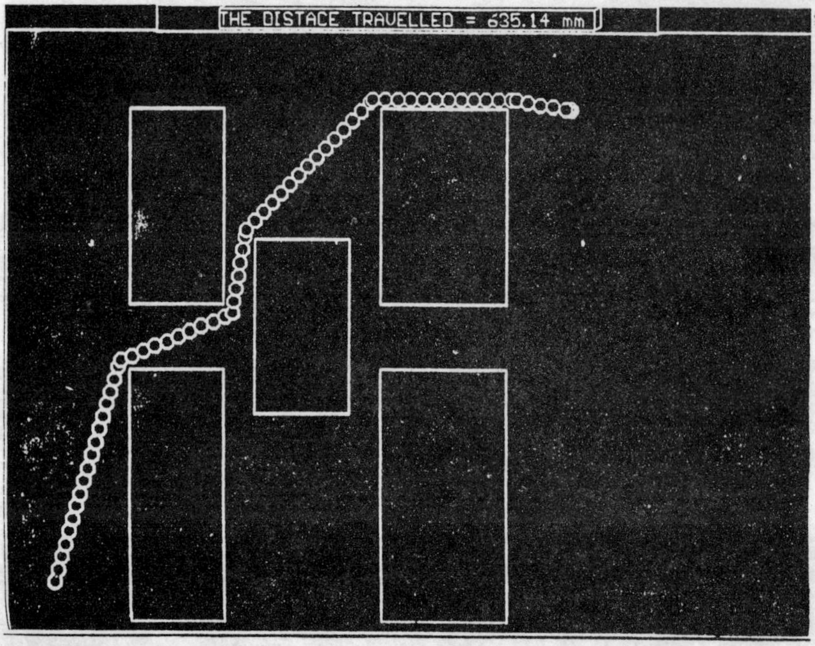

Fig. 2(b)

Figure 2: Typical outputs of the Software for polygonal obstacles and circular/rectangular robot configurations.

initial centre position of the robot (source), final centre position of the robot (destination) as nodes. Later, a connectivity graph has been constructed by joining each of the nodes to each of the other approachable nodes. Thus constructed non-directed graph has been searched for the shortest path using Dijkstra alogirthm which is known as A* algorithm as applied to motion path planning. By adopting the above described steps, an optimal path has been generated and the robot motion is simulated from source to destination in the vicinity of planar obstacles such as polygons, circle , ellipse, etc.

REFERENCES

1. J.C. Latumbe, *Motion Path Planning*, Stanford Publication Services, USA, (1992).
2. Ellis-Horowitz, Sartaj Sahani, *Fundamental Computer Algorithms*, Galgotia Publications (P) Ltd, India, (1996).
3. Knuth, *Fundamental Algorithms*, Addison Weslay Publishing Company, USA, (1989).
4. Ritchie D.M. and Kernighan, B.W., *C Programming Language*, Prentice Hall of India Pvt. Ltd., (1994).
5. Sudheendra Adiga, Rajaprakash B.M., Muralidhara, B.K. *et.al.*, *Simulation of Mobile Robot Motion Path Planning using Modified Dijkstra Algorithm (A* Algorithm)*, National Seminar on Manufacturing Automation, The Institution of Engineers (India), Jabalpur, Oct. 1997.
6. Omkar H.N. Viswanath, D.S. *et al*, Group Project report titled *Simulation of Mobile Robot Motion Path Planning for Obstacle Avoidance*, submitted for award of BE Degree by Bangalore University, (1997).

ROBOTICS IN INDIA

29

Subir Kumar Saha

Dept. of Mech. Eng., I.I.T., Hauz Khas, New Delhi

ABSTRACT

Starting in late 1970s, the robotic research in India has come to a state that may be worth mentioning. However, the robot utilization in Indian industries is almost nil. It is estimated that only about 60 robots are working in various industries. This is mainly due to the fear of unemployment amongst the workers. Recent reports by private and governmental organizations, e.g., by the Science Advisory Council to the Prime Minister on "Induction of Robotics in Manufacturing Automation in India" (DST Proceedings, 1988), reveal that the fear of unemployment is untrue if the technology is adopted suitably. This paper looks into the present status of the robotic technology in India and analyzes various issues related to the development and adoption of robotics in Indian industries.

INTRODUCTION

It has been almost twenty years that robotics research has started in India. However, it had very little or no impact on Indian industries. This is evident from the fact that only about 20% of the estimated total of 250 robots in India are in the industries (Bhattacharya, 1996). The poor industrial acceptance can be attributed mainly to:

1. lack of proper perspective to the robot technology;
2. fear of unemployment amongst the workers;
3. non-availability of locally available robots and its sub-assemblies;
4. high cost of imported robots.

A serious thinking on the above causes will reveal that the second one is the direct consequence of the first. One should not evaluate the technology based on its usage in developed countries, where robots were introduced mainly for higher productivity and, hence, more profitability. Following the same trend in India will obviously create a havoc. Indian robots should be doing inhumane, monotonous jobs, sparing human workers for more interesting and challenging jobs like teaching a robot, path planning, etc. The last two reasons, however, can work to our advantage. The proof is India's achievement in the defense and space activities, where in many instances foreign technologies were denied. For example, the denial of CRAY super-computer to the

Defense Research and Development Organization (DRDO) has led to the development of PARAM by the Centre for the Development of Advanced Computing (C-DAC), Pune.

The paper is organized as follows: A brief historical background of robots and their impact is given in Section 2; Section 3 describes the present status of robotics in India, followed by its adoption strategy in Section 4. Finally, the conclusions are given in Section 5.

2. ROBOT AND ITS IMPACT

The term "Robot"derived its name from the Czech word *robota*, which means "forced labour" or "compulsory service" (Poole, 1989). The word was first used in 1923 in two plays written by the Czech author Karel Capek. The more popular one is *Rossum's Universal Robots* (RUR).

The first industrial robot, however, appeared in 1961 when Unimation Inc., owned by Joseph F. Engelberger (known as the *the Father of Industrial Robots*), has installed its first of the three prototype machines in the General Motors Turnstedt plant in New Jersy, USA (Saveriano, 1988). Even though the technology has started in the USA it grew faster in Japan. The Japanese were quick to use robots due to a labor shortage, a good relationship between the workers and management, and, most importantly, the managers' long-term view on market share and industrial competitiveness based on manufacturing productivity. A comparison of the growth pattern of robots in Japan, along with some other countries are shown in Table 1 (DSIR Report, 1992).

TABLE 1: **Growth of Industrial Robots (DSIR Report, 1992)**

Country	1981	1989
Japan	14 246	1 80 000
USA	4 700	42 000
Germany	1 420	22 395
UK	713	5 889
Sweden	700	2 500
France	620	7 063
World Population		2 30 000

Today it is estimated that Japan and USA produce 50 000 and 30 000 robots in a year, respectively (Bhattacharya, 1996). The major population of robots works in Automobile and Manufacturing industries to do jobs like, welding, painting, loading and unloading, etc., which were primarily done by human workers. Thus, the fear of unemployment is justified. However, with respect to an economy as a whole, precisely the reverse relationship is seen to hold: nations which make the greatest use of robotics and automation technologies tend to have low levels of unemployment. For example, Japan with some 3 50 000 industrial robots has an unemployment rate of less than 3% (Gascoigne, 1996). Whatever interpretation is placed on these figures, they can hardly be dismissed as statistical abnormalities.

3. STATUS OF ROBOTICS IN INDIA

The reports on the studies of the robot technology and its implication in India conducted by the Department of Science and Technology (DST Proceedings, 1988) and the Department of Scientific and Industrial Research (DSIR Report, 1992) in 1987 and 1992, respectively, provide a very good overview of the robotics status in the country. While the former reports the robot developmental activities in India, the latter gives more critical analysis of the technology in India and abroad. Few highlights from the DSIR Report (1992) are as follows:

- In India, Research and Development (R&D) thrust is mainly provided by three government departments, namely,

1. Department of Science and Technology;
2. Department of Electronics; and
3. Department of Ocean Development.

They all provide funding to different academic institutes and R&D organization, e.g., Indian Institutes of Technology (IITs), Indian Institute of Science (IISc), University of Roorkie, Regional Engineering Colleges, and Central Manufacturing Technology Institute (CMTI), Centre for Artificial Intelligence and Robotics (CAIR), etc.

- The industries involved in the robot developmental activities include:

1. *Alpine Hi-Tech Instruments & Robotics Pvt. Ltd.*, New Delhi: It markets educational robots.
2. *Bhabha Atomic Research Centre* (BARC), Mumbai: It is actively engaged in robotics research. In fact, BARC has an exclusive division for Remote Handling and Robotics for taking up R&D activities for nuclear applications.
3. *Bharat Earth Movers Ltd.* (BEML), Bangalore: The company has designed and developed pick-and-place and arc-welding robots mainly for their captive consumption.
4. *Bharat Electronics Ltd.* (BEL), Bangalore: BEL has developed robot for TV tube handling.
5. *Bharat Heavy Electricals Ltd.* (BHEL), Hyderabad: They have major programme in robot design and manufacture. With IIT, Delhi BHEL has developed a Gantry robot.
6. *Central Manufacturing Technology Institute* (CMTI), Bangalore: The company has already developed few robots for machine tending, parts transfer,

and assembly.

7. *Electro Pneumatics and Hydraulics*, Mumbai: The company has developed heavy duty industrial robots.
8. *Hindustan Machine Tools Ltd.* (HMT), Bangalore: They designed and developed robots for their captive and as well as their CNC market needs. Recently, HMT together with BARC has developed the Bilateral Master-Slave Servo Manipulators (HMT Today, 1997) for the handling of radio active waste materials in the nuclear radiation environment at Trombay and Kalpakkam.
9. *Hyderabad Science Society*, Hyderabad: Since 1980 the society has been involved in remote controlled automated robots.
10. *Pravak Cybernetics*, New Delhi: It has indigenously developed educational robots.
11. *Sieflex Automation and Robotics Co.*, Chennai, which produces pick-and-place robots.
12. *Systemantics India Pvt. Ltd.*, Bangalore: The company takes up jobs for the customized robot design and development.

Besides, a few foreign companies, like Asea Brown Boveri (ABB), and Fanuc, have set up their units in Bangalore, mainly, to market their product in India. ABB, however, opened a training institute in Bangalore.

- R&D activities in places other than mentioned above are:

1. Centre for Artificial Intelligence and Robotics (CAIR), Bangalore;
2. Central Mechanical Engineering Research Institute (CMERI), Durgapur;
3. Central Scientific Instrument Organization, Chandigarh;
4. Crompton Greaves Ltd. (Switch Gear Division), Nasik;
5. Departments of Mechanical Eng., Electrical Eng., and Computer Sc. & Eng., at IIT-Bombay, Delhi, Kanpur, Kharagpur, Madras; and IISc.
6. Department of Production Eng., Jadavpur University, Calcutta;
7. Larson and Tubro, Mumbai;
8. Mechanical Engineering Research and Development Organization, Chennai;
9. Widia (I) Ltd., Bangalore.

- Some of the problems related to the technology gaps, as cited in the DSIR Report (1992), are as follows:

1. Lack of testing equipment;
2. Reliable and quality components;
3. Non-availability of trained man-power;
4. Reluctant of end-user industry because of agitation from worker unions.

- A few key recommendations by DSIR (DSIR Report, 1992) are:

1. Inexpensive and cheaper applications having widely spread market should be attempted by the industrial robot manufacturers;
2. Indigenous development of simple robots requiring fixed sequence motion control;
3. Non-users should be exposed to production processes of industrial robot users;
4. Government sponsored testing labs to evaluate the performance of the robots;
5. Centralized data bank to be used by anybody interested in robotics;
6. Training to industry workers, supervisors, engineers, managers, and top management personnel to appreciate the benefits.

ADOPTION OF ROBOTICS IN INDIA

It is a well-known even to Indian managers and workers both that the use of robots can provide *quality* product with higher *productivity*. Then, the question is why not robots are used widely by Indian companies. The answer is simple: fear of unemployment, which is already in a bad shape, and consequent agitation by the workers. Thus, there is hesitation regarding the adoption of robotics in India. To settle the issue let us first answer the following questions associated to the unemployment:

1. Are we concern about our safety and health while working in a hostile environment, for example, in front of a furnace at 300°C or handling toxic materials?
2. Do we want monotonous job like welding two parts for the whole shift of eight hours or for that matter year after year?

If one replies "yes" to the first question and "no" to the second one, then, in the author's opinion, no second thought will be given about the usage of robots in those environments. Then, what is the fear? If other machines like lathe, milling, motor vehicle, etc. can be used for the betterment of human lifestyles what is so wrong with *just* another machine, which is called *robot*? The mistrust of robots in India may be perpetuated from their utilization in industries abroad that was mainly driven by high productivity and profitability. Later, however, strict industrial laws enforced the robot utilization in hazardous environments. The workers safety and health hazard components were not adequately emphasized, even in abroad, in the well publicized advantages of robot technology. It is said that the invention of *wheel* also created the fear of unemployment. The introduction of computers in India about a decade ago was opposed. But today are we really unhappy with the induction of computers, for example, in banking transactions, railway booking, etc.?

Assuming now that the Indian managers and workers agree to use robots in their industry, where do they look forward? As reported in the DSIR Report (1992), which are also mentioned in Section 3, there are problems related to the robot technology in India, particularly, with the availability of quality robot and its components. Thus, one attempts to import robots. In many instances, however, these companies are discouraged by the exorbitant import prices and inherent drawbacks, like non-availability of the spare parts, services, and customization demanded by the user company. In this situation, the solution is the indigenization of the technology. In line with the recommendations of the DSIR (DSIR Report, 1992), the following measures can be taken for further development, adoption, and popularization of the technology in India:

— Form consortia with representatives from user and supplier companies, experts from different R&D institutions, and government officials to study the requirement of the companies and come up with a few robot configurations that may then be produced in bigger scale for industry consumption.
— Built simple robotic systems requiring 2 to 3 degrees of freedom (DOF) motion for which India has fairly high level of confidence. In case of complex motion requirement more than one simple robots can be used. One such case is reported by Systemantics India Pvt. Ltd., Bangalore (Jagannath Raju, 1996), where to coat a paint to the top surface of a 200 mm disc placed on a rotating table two 2-DOF robots costing a total of Rs. 5.0 lakhs were used instead of a general 6-DOF robot priced about Rs. 10.0 lakhs.
— For customized robots, user industries themselves can participate and sponsor for the development of the system. That will help them to get enough expertise to service the system themselves and, if required, they can develop similar systems later.
— For the popularization and awareness of the technology and its availability, organize meetings, conferences, open houses, video and movie shows; publish magazines, etc. One such attempt by the author was the Technology Appreciation Seminar (TAS) on *Industrial Robotics* at IIT, Delhi in April, 1997 (TAS Proceedings, 1997), where many industry participant confessed that they were not aware of the availability of the expertise at IIT, Delhi. It generated a little enthusiasm, as one industry participant wants to develop a cement bag handling arm for their cement filling machines. The negotiation is underway with IIT, Delhi. It encouraged the author also to organize a open house in future where demonstration will be given with real robots and animated software.

CONCLUSIONS

The present status of robotics in India is discussed. The aversion of the technology by the Indian industries are analysed. It is suggested that the issue of safety and health should not be compromised and human workers must be relieved from hazardous environment. In other situations, like in monotonous jobs, workers can work with robots where human intelligence will be used for robot path-planning, programming, etc., for the effective utilization of the robot, leaving the inhumane work to the machine. Finally, some outlines are provided for further development, adoption, and popularization of the robot technology in India.

REFERENCES

Bhattacharya, P., 1996, Those Man-like Machines, *Dataquest*, (Computer magazine, Jan. 16-31), V.XIV, No. 2, pp. 122-24.

DSIR Report, 1992, Technology Status Study on Industrial Robots, *A Report for the Dept. of Sc. & Ind. Res.*, (Min. of Sc. & Tech.), Divas Communications, New Delhi.

DST Proceedings, 1988, Robotics, *Proceedings of National Workshop*, April 1987, Oxford & IBH Publishing Co. Pvt. Ltd., New Delhi.

Gascoigne, A.E., 1996, Technology and Ethics, *IEEE The Asia Pacific Channel*, Issue 1, Feb., pp. 2-3.

HMT Today, 1997, HMT supplies bilateral master-slave servo manipulators to BARC, *Bulletin of the Machine Tool Marketing Division*, 25:1, Jan-Mar.

Jaggannath Raju, G., "Robotics on the Indian Industrial Landscape", *Proceeding of the Technology Appreciation Programme on Robotics: Its Appreciation and Adoption in India*, IIT, Madras, July 9, pp. 21-24.

Poole, H.H., 1989, *Fundamentals of Robotics Engineering*, Van Nostrand Reinhold, New York.

Saveriano, J.W., 1988, Pioneers of Robotics. *International Encyclopedia of Robotics*, John Wiley and Sons, New York, Vol. 2, pp. 1078-92.

TAS Proceedings, 1997, *Proceedings of the Technology Appreciation Seminar on Industrial Robotics*, IIT, Delhi, April 19.

ARTIFICIAL INTELLIGENCE AND ROBOTICS IN PRODUCTION

30

Wg. Cdr. B.R. Dhingra
DTE of Maint Plans & QA.
Air HQ. (VB), New Delhi

INTRODUCTION

1. Once, simply pictured as mechanical beings, robots have emerged on the factory floor where they relieve human workers of many onerous tasks. Could we ever imagine an umanned factory, a few years ago? Well, today, it is surprisingly, a reality. One of the most famous automated factories, is the Yamazaki machine tool plant in Japan. The plant consists of a flexible machine centre that can perform a wide range of metal-shaping/ cutting operations and a variety of other production activities. The entire operation of the factory, including accounts, preparation of financial statements, and production control, is performed automatically. The factory runs three shifts—the first shift employs seven people, the second five and night shift runs without anybody being present. There is a vast difference between a highly automated plant staffed by a group of supervisors (machine-minders) and factory with no one on the shop floor. Perhaps, the reality in the foreseeable future will lie somewhere in between these two. Such factories will still need people, but not many. These industries employ flexible manufacturing systems (FMS) and can turn out a variety of products by re-programming the Computer. However, the product is limited to within the same family of items. Factories of future employing flexible manufacturing systems (FMS) would require three levels of highly trained engineers: planners at the overall programme level, computer operators at computer production level and technicians at the workshop level. Most importantly, the labour content of the production process will be drastically reduced. The ability of the robot to work in hazardous places such as outer space and under the sea, makes them the obvious choice. Technical advances in robotics are further enhancing their likeness to human.

ROBOTS IN PRODUCTION

2. A robots in classical sense is a computer controlled mechanical machine that looks like men & women (androids) and performs actions that replicate those of their human

counterparts. The present generation Robots generally speaking are mechanical arms controlled by computers, which can be programmed to undertake a huge range of handling activities, normally done by people. Much of the manufacturing industry is concerned with production of goods, not in large runs in which the items seldom vary but in small borken up streams during which factory manager frequency change the type of products being turned out to suit the demands of consumers. The new manufacturing systems often built around robots offer a flexibility that can match the variation in demand. A visit to a modern engineering factory (robotized) is a fascinating experience. A few years ago, such establishments featured collection of manually operated tools. Each operator tended the machine, acting on instruction passed down a factory hierarchy from supervisors. Today, the picture is changing. Many of the machining operations are left to computerized tools that for most of the time can operate untended. These machines obtain commands not from the blue-collar supervisors, but from data sent along transmission grids from computers in another part of the factory.

3. Industrial robots play an important part in the computerization process that is increasingly making itself felt on factory floors around the world. The obvious reason for this is the discrete advantages offered by the industrial robots such as availability of "off the shelf" automation robots, reduction in the debugging of the manufacturing hardware and their re-use after completion of their initial application. The specific industrial tasks that robots currently undertake can be split in to three distinct areas. These are material handling (Loading/unloading, Lifting between work stations, Packing and Heavy-duty palletizing), tool operation (Welding, Drilling, Cutting, Surface treatment, Deburring, Testing and Inspection) and assembly (Insertion of specific components of standard shape in to Printed circuit board (PCB), Putting together PCB's and production of computer related products). These are only a few examples of robot applications on the factory floor. The list is endless as far as the applications in the fields of medicine, education, entertainment and space etc.

ROBOTICS AND ARTIFICIAL INTELLIGENCE

4. Let me explain here few concepts of artificial intelligence and the dependence of robots on AI... Many of today's Robots possess a sense of touch and can "See" with at least moderate ability. Furthermore, researches are hard at work at perfecting the design of robots that walk like human being, and think for themselves using the computers that operate according to the principles of artificial intelligence. Machines with this extra power obtain information about events in the outside world in the form of feed back and hardware reacts according to the changes in circumstances, instead of repeating a fixed routine of instructions. The gamut of reaching to change in circumstances or the reasoning power is based on the field of "artificial intelligence" which is well established and is contributing to the design of real life Robot, the intelligent machines.

5. The challenge facing those involved in A1 to find what sorts of programmes are required in order for a computer to become an intelligent? And what is intelligence?

Intelligence, in my views undisputedly involves some kind of intelligent thinking. If we term the capability to remember long sequences of activities and perform the computerization to check that they are being performed correctly would be an unintelligent thinking. However, if the thinking is associated with their ability to perceive and understand their surroundings and some sort of "skill" called common sense, which would enable them to react to events and make decisions, would be an intelligent thinking.

6. What are the areas of development, which can give computers the common sense or a moderate kind of intelligence which they will need to, take decisions? The areas of developments which aim at giving robots, the common sense, centre upon three traditional areas of A1 research, namely, game playing, problems solving and use of natural i.e., every day language and one comparatively new area i.e., specialized types of computer programmes that are known as expert system. The traditional areas of game playing and problem solving are closely related and allow the robots to work out for themselves how to tackle tasks that are described in general terms rather than leading them through jobs step by step. The ability to understand and communicate in natural language will be essential if Robot are to make use of sense of hearing (and perhaps the power of speech) in order to collaborate with human workers who are not versed in computer language. Finally, the use of expert systems allows the computers to master the specialized kind of intelligence used by human beings—the sort of combination of knowledge and reasoning based on experience which allows a doctor to diagnose a disease or an engineer to see how to tackle a design problem.

GAME PLAYING

Game playing had attracted the attention of computer programmers even before the term A1 came into being. The example of chess playing by machine is well known. All that a computer needs is a set of instructions i.e. an algorithm to play a game. In other words a clear method of thinking or working. In A1, as in all other branches of computer programming, an algorithm is a basic requirement. The programmer must visualize the way of tackling the problem before he can formulize it as a programme. The key to success is clearly the ability to look ahead to calculate the consequences of a move at the present stage of the game for future play. The reasoning processes are based on what is known as decision free i.e., a node branching in to further nodes, each representing a state that would result, if one particular move were made. Such a decision free is constructed at each state to explore only a limited area of the chessboard. If the search of a particular are quickly reveals that all possible moves lead to disaster, then that search is dropped and other areas are examined. However to decide whether the move is good or bad, certain thumb rules have to be employed. These rules are called heuristics, i.e., based on data or experience as in case of human being. The obvious question haere is how to equip a computer with such rules. Some rules could be straigthforward and be programmed. But a programme solely relying on such pre-packed judgements will never play a game of great subtlety and it will take very little time for an experienced human opponent to see through its reasoning. The most interesting aspects of the game playing programme is the method used to allow a machine to refine or even invent completely new one for itself. The essential point is that the programme must be given experience. Over the period of time, the machines heuristics are developed to a point which perhaps, could be said to be a product of its experience than of the basic one it started with. The algorithms generally employed for searching/evaluating the decision tree are mini-maxing or alfa-betaying. The fact that a machine capable of playing chess at tournament standard can now be bought off the shelf, is some measure of how for this branch of A1 has developed. However there would always exist a difference between the mysterious way the human being take decision and the way the robots are programmed to take decisions.

PROBLEM SOLVING

Problems, as every human problem solver knows, come in all shape and sizes. There are the formal problems of the crossword puzzle type, there are practical problems involved in making things work, the organizational problems of getting people work together and human problems of living together. The sort of problems A1 is concerned with, tend to be very elementary/primitive. One approach to problem solving is decision tree method in game playing. The other way is to break the problem in to its sub-problems, each of which when solved, bring the overall solution one step nearer. These approach takes advantages of the fact that unlike chess problems, many practical problems of the type that robot might have to tackle have a clearly defined finishing state and a starting state. Hence it is easier to construct a decision tree. Although this method has achieved some success, there are numerous kind of problems, many of them quite trivial in human being terms, unsolvable by robots employing this technique.

USE OF NATURAL LANGUAGE

Any one who has tried their hands at computer programming would have realized, the high level programming languages in which most of the communication between computers and people is conducted are "languages" by courtesy only. In truth, the words that make up a language such as BASIC, COBOL or PASCAL are more like the labels on a set of push buttens than the words we use in everyday speech. However, to computer they are logical intructions, which it can transform in to machine codes of 1's and 0's and act upon. Natural language is a far more complicated affair. How to teach such language to a computer? To answer it let us consider how a child with a vocabulary of say 100 words leans to combine and form legitimate grammatical sentences where there are innumerous way to combine the words. The argument normally offered to such cases is that the traditional grammer (which defines the legitimate structure of the language) deals only with the "surface structures" of the languages. Beneath the separate set of structure, one for each language, there lay a "deep structure" shared by all languages. From the viewpoint of A1, the important thing is the set of logical rules "production rules" which are innate to human brain which allow us to transform and generate sentences that have meaning and are grammatically legitimate. For example we can re-arrange the words used to ask the question, "was Ashoka at the party when the clock struck mid night"? In order to form the statements, "Ashoka was at party when clock struck mid night" or "the clock struck mid night when Ashoka was at party". But we can not transform the question into the statement, "the party struck midnight where Ashoka was at the clock". This sentence is illegitimate, not merely because it is nonsensical, but because the way in which the relationships between the elements of original question have been transformed violate the grammatical rules. Attempts were made in the developmental stages to design language using programmes, which operated, at the level of deep structure. However, the formulation of grammar rules alone, thinking language as a matter of manipulating abstract symbols, could not solve the problem. The language of human communication, is a matter of semantics; words have meaning to people because they are about or related to reality. One solution to this kind of problem was if programmes were provided with "Scripts" each appropriate to a particular situation. But still how can a computer ever "know what it is talking about" in the same sense as a human being does? This could be solved only if in some primitive fashion, computers could experience reality in same way as people. However, once they have senses, they will be able to see and feel things and to learn the words, which describe what they see or feel. They may ultimately build up a picture of the world and the ability to talk about it in ways, which make sense. Such a state of robotics will largely depend on the development of advanced sensory equipment.

EXPERT SYSTEMS

The areas of A1 defined till now cannot match the skill of human beings unless some new approach is developed. This approach is expert systems. Most of the work in last one-two decades has gone is this field. We may not still understand the sort of rules and algorithms we use to cope with the trivial problems of every day life, but there are many areas of human knowledge where information and experience have been carefully organized and codified into systematic, regular, algorithmic structures. Expert systems are computer programmes, which incorporate and provide access to, bodies of human expertise, e.g., medicine, physics, chemistry, law, geology etc. Their novelty lies in the fact that they attempt not merely to store knowledge employed by a human expert, but also to reproduce the structure of that knowledge, the process of reasoning, judgement and even institutions which an expert employs when he brings his knowledge to bear on a particular problem. Using an expert system is thus more like actually consulting a real expert than simply looking up the relevant facts is a database. The actual working of expert systems are complex, so much so that a whole new discipline, knowledge engineering is coming in to being in order to cope with the task of reformulating human expertise into a shape in which it can be incorporated into programmes. The crucial point is that an expert does not follow simple rules of the "If A then B". Weighing up a whole range of dactors arrives at his judgements, each of which may have varying significance according to circumstances, and many of these factors can only be evaluated in the light of experience. Two points are perhaps more fundamental than any others in construction of the expert systems. First, the information provided by the human experts, the material that makes up the programme's knowledge base, must be provided in a form which allows the statements to be related to each other in terms of the implications which each holds for the other. The second important feature of the expert system is that, unlike the most computer programmes, the knowledge base, the part of programme which contains data, is separate from the part which contains the manipulation of that data. This latter bit of programme, the "knowledge interpreters" as it is called, is in turn sub divided in to an "inference machine" which directs the step by step tactics involved in the solution of the problem and a "control section" oversees the strategy. The expert systems have already achieved a considerable success. They seem to offer even greater potential in the fields of medicine, where knowledge and experience is already accumulated at a rate which far exceeds the capacity of individual human experts to absorb and make use of it, is largely responsible for the resurgence of interest in A1 over the past few years. Robots, being machines whose whole need is to understand and act upon the real world, are unlikely to be able to make use of the formalized systems of expertise until they have achieved a much greater understanding of the nuts and bolts of reality.

CONCLUSION

7. We must remember that a super computer would be required to reproduce the functioning of only one brain cell, out of millions, a human brain has. Then how could a robot, a computer, could perform the assigned task in diverse fields, as performed by human beings. This seems to be a distant reality for the time being. However, it would not be out of place to emphasize that the dramatic advances in robotic technology that have taken place in the recent years have clearly brought out that in times to come, the division of labor and the content of jobs will change dramatically as robots became more sophisticated. There will be greater distance between workstations and less contact between workers. The conditions of work will probable be safe with the worker more separated from work process. It is likely that the workers will have a responsibility for a larger span of production because there will be a greater system integration and fewer workers manning the production equipment. Many workers will merely carry out a monitoring role patrolling and inspecting a system when all appears to be functioning properly. However he will be expected to react sharply to an incipient crisis and take corrective action when anything goes wrong. This may involve knowledge and competence of a depth essential to handle a highly integrated system of machines. There is also a possibility that as the robots become more and more sophisticated and complex, many workers will find their jobs less demanding and devoid of satisfaction. Advanced robotized plants are also likely to demand different kind of supervisory skills. The traditional human skills of the supervisor will become less and less important as a premium is placed on technical competence. There will be fewer levels of supervision and

fewer workers. The need to ensure the maximum utilization of costly equipment and imperative of avoiding shut downs will lead to much closer supervision. Production schedules are likely to be more demanding. Supervisors will also find that, as their traditional human skills are not important, they will become increasingly dependent on skills and knowledge of individual skills.

VI

MICRO MACHINING PROCESSES

PERFORMANCE STUDY OF SINTERED SILICON NITRIDE CUTTING TOOL

31

Dr. B.J. Ranganath[1] and B.N. Shanthapriya[2]

Dean, Prof., Indl. & Prod. Engg.,[1]
National Institute of Engg., Mysore

Sr. Lecturer, Dept. of Mechanical Engg.[2]
Manipal Institute of Technology, Manipal

ABSTRACT

This paper deals with the performance study of Sintered Silicon Nitride Cutting tool and compared with popular Tungsten Carbide Cutting tool. Finite element analysis is used to study the stress and temperature distribution at the cutting edge. Tool life curves are discussed for the performance studies. The results indicates that Sintered Silicon Nitride Cutting tool is a better performing tool due to its favourable properties to resist higher stresses and temperature. It is observed that this tool performs better over Tungsten Carbide tool by 2-3 times in meeting the machining requirements.

INTRODUCTION

Metal machining is a large deformation process and the work material undergoes deformation in the cutting zone. In the cutting edge region of a tool, high range of temperature and stresses are developed. The distribution of stress and temperature on the cutting edge of a tool during machining has significant effect on the properties of tool material and the performance of the cutting tool. Selection of proper cutting tool material is an important factor in the design of cutting tool. To meet the present demand of machining toughter, harder and stronger work materials and to produce a better surface finish, better dimensional tolerance with a greater tool life, newer tool materials are developed. Sintered Silicon Nitride is a new tool material developed to meet such challenges.

SILICON NITRIDE

Silicon Nitride is a primary material in the family of Nitride Ceramics. Nitride ceramics have a major advantages over metals in their high temperature capability. These ceramics have higher strength at temperature above 1000°C and better oxidation and corrosion resistance in addition to higher thermal shock resistance. Further Sintered Silicon Nitride

Cutting Tool consistently show a greater strength and fracture toughness than the traditional tungsten carbide cutting tool.[1]

Silicon Nitride Cutting Tools are produced by power metallurgy technique.

The requirements of Si_3N_4 powders are :

(a) Low oxygen content leads to good sintering behaviour and good mechanical properties. High oxygen content results in poor sintering behaviour and mechanical properties of Si_3N_4.
(b) Carbon impurity must be low to exclude CO and SiC volaties which discrupt the forming process.
(c) The alpha-Si_3N_4 contest must be as high as possible.
(d) Equiaxed notrodlike powder leads to greater density and strength.
(e) The particle size must be as small as possible. With small grains there is no variation in strength while strength decreases at larger grain size.[1,2]

SINTERING

Sintering of pure Si_3N_4 powder is not possible. In Si_3N_4 the volume diffusivity is not large enough to offset the densification retardation effects of surface diffusion and volatilization phenomena; as a result sintering is difficult. The covalent bond is believed to be the reasons for such low-volume diffusivity. Therefore dense Silicon Nitride material can be obtained only by alloying Silicon Nitride with additives that promote sintering. The various oxides and nitrides have been found to be effective sintering aids. The most commonly used solid solution additives to Si_3N_4 are MgO, CeO_2, Y_2O_3, AI_2O_3, ZrO_2, AlN and SiO_2. The additive combines, at the sintering temperature, with the SiO_2 oxidation layer on the Si_3N_4 power raw material to form a liquid which wets the Si_3N_4. This liquid penetrates between the Si_3N_4 grains providing a high diffusivity path for mass transport. Material transport and reprecipitation on the Si_3N_4 surfaces adjacent to the pores cause the grain reshaping necessary for sintering. These are two hexagonal polymorphs of Silicon Nitride, the α-and β-phases, with the latter stable at higher temperatures. By this mechanism, c-based ceramics are sintered to a minimum 98% of theoretical density.[1,2,3]

During cooling the sintering liquid is retained in the grain boundary areas as a thin glassy layer. Pressureless sintered Si_3N_4 mechanical properties because of accelerated grain boundary crack growth and pore formation in the low viscous grain boundary phase. Reaction sintering with a transient liquid phase, which will be incorporated in the Si_3N_4 lattice by the formation of high-temperature solid solution phase Si-AI-O-N, or crystallization of high symmetric oxides, silicates and oxynitrides from the glassy phase on cooling have been successfully demonstrated to improve the high-temperature mechanical properties of pressureless sintered material.[3] The different properties of Silicon Nitride as compared with & WC is shown in Table 1.

TABLE 1: **Properties of Silicon Nitride and Tungsten Carbide**

	Si_3N_4	WC
Hardness HV30	1400+30	1450
TRSN/mm^2	1000	2200
Comp Strength N/mm^2	5000	4600
Young's Modules KN/mm^2	280	550
Thermal Conductivity W/m/K	29	45
Co-efficient of thermal expansion K	3.5×10^{-6}	6.7×10^{-6}
Poisson's Ratio	.27	0.22

CUTTING TESTS

Metal cutting test were conducted by machining Mild steel with Sintered Silicon Nitride Tools. Tests were conducted at different cutting speeds keeping the feed and depth of cut the same. The results were compared with tungsten carbide tools. Flankwear Criterion was considered for the evaluation of the performance of the tool.

ANALYSIS

Finite Element method and with the advances in computer technology and CAD system it is possible to accurately idealize analyse and evaluate the thermal and stress conditions in the cutting tool material. The physical shape and geometry of the cutting tool can also be effectively designed by CAD technique.[4] In the analysis finite element package ANSYS is used to create tool model and for stress and thermal analysis of Sintered Silicon Nitride and Tungsten Carbide tool.

RESULTS

The equivalent stress distribution in finite element model of Si_3N_4 tool at the cutting edge is shown in Fig. 1. It is observed that the maximum stress is developed in the principle cutting region. The distribution of induced stress in Rake and Flank surface of Silicon Nitrode tool as compared with tungsten carbide are shown in the graph in Fig. 2. From the graph, it is observed that Si_3N_4 tool exhibits greater resistance for static cutting forces compared to conventional tungsten carbide.[5]

The cutting edge deformation when machining with Si_3N_4 tools from the FEM analysis is illustrated in Fig. 3.[6] It is observed that Si_3N_4 possess a better resistance for edge deformation compared to WC tools. The temperature distribution at the cutting edge for the tool is shown in Fig. 4. The Temperature distribution curve is illustrated in Fig. 5. It is observed that thermal properties to resist of heat absorption and material expansion

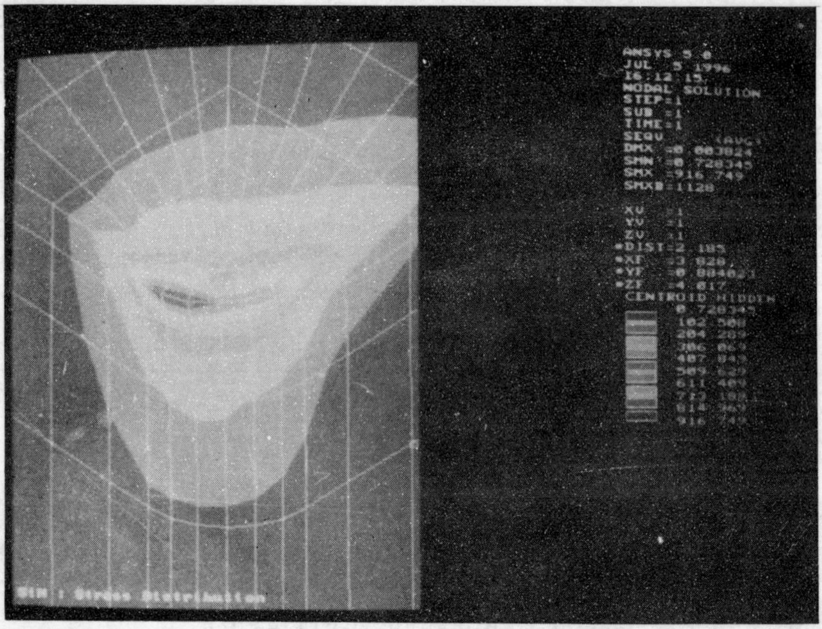

Figure 1: Stress Distribution in Finite Element Model of Si_3N_4 tool.

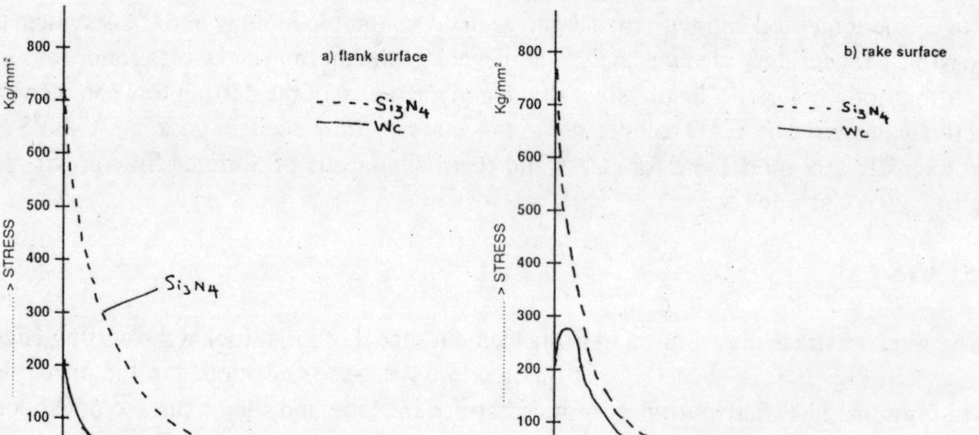

Figure 2: Stress distribution at the cutting edge in silicon nitride cutting tool

of Si_3N_4 is better than that of WC tools.

The tool life curve of Si_3N_4 is shown in Fig.6 and is compared with WC cutting tool. It is found that the Si_3N_4 tools. Performs as 2-3 times better than WC tools. These tools are observed to be performing extremely well at higher cutting speeds.

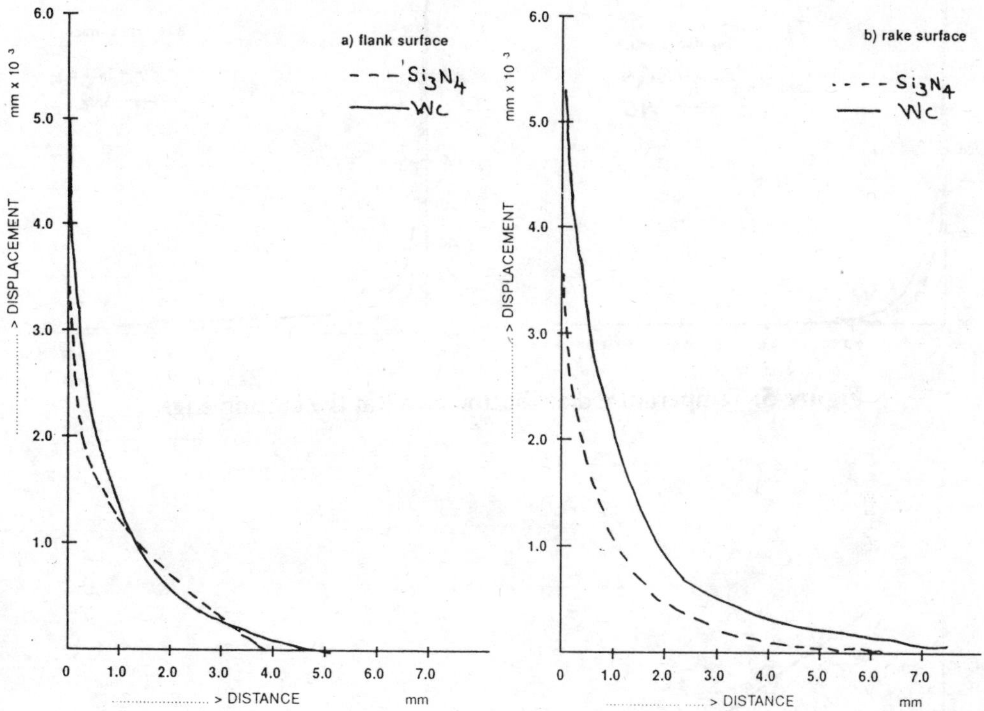

Figure 3: Edge deformation in Si_3N_4 tools

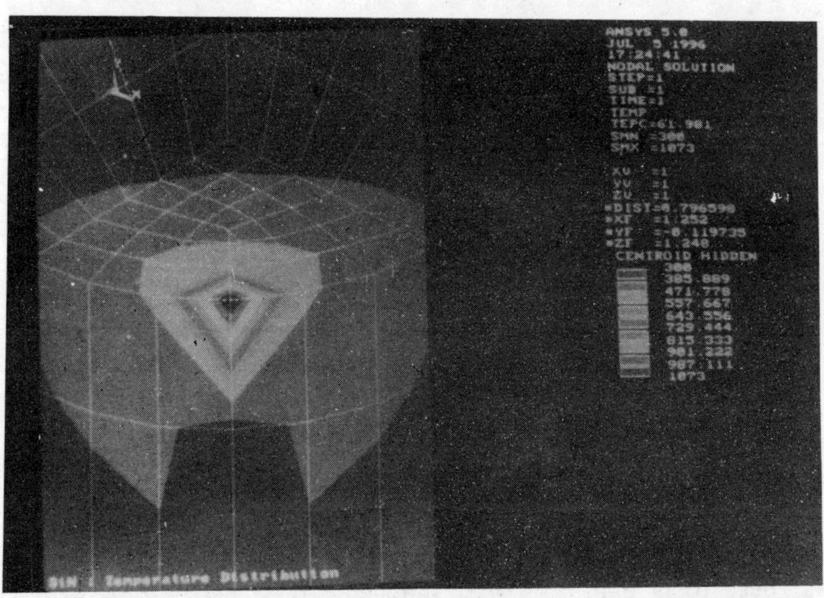

Figure 4: Temperature distribution at the cutting edge

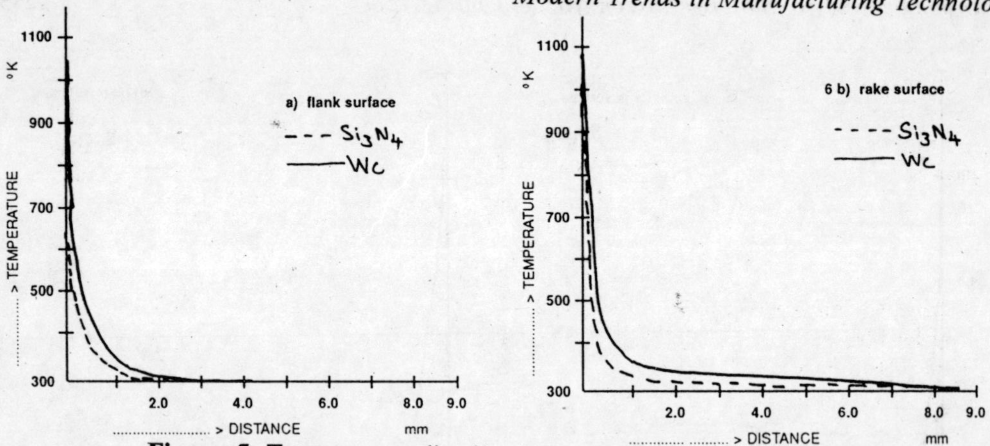

Figure 5: Temperature distribution curve at the cutting edge

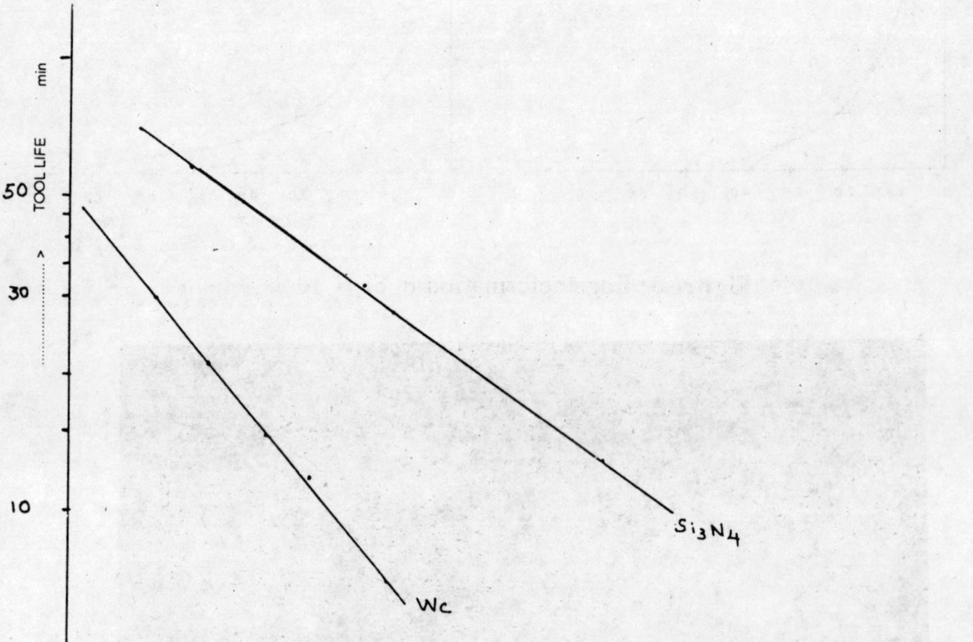

Figure 6: Tool life curve of Si_3N_4 tool

CONCLUSION

Silicon Nitride Cutting Tools posses good properties required for better performing cutting tools.These tools exhibits better induced stress distribution with smaller deformation at the cutting edge. Silicon Nitride Cutting tools possess greater resistance for heat absorption and thermal expansion. The tool runs cooler with reduced thermal stress at the cutting edge. The tool life of Silicon Nitride Cutting tool is found to be about 2 to 3 times more than Tungsten Carbide Cutting tools, producing better surface finish. Silicon Nitride tools should find a place in the modern metal cutting industries in the near future.

REFERENCES

1. Petzow, G. and Grgeil, P. (1980). *Dense Silicon Nitride Processing Properties and Applications.* Powder Metallurgy & Related High Temperature Material.
2. James H. Admas, bod Anschuetz, Gene White Field (1989). *Ceramic Cutting Tool-ASME Materials Hand Book.*
3. Ranganath, B.J. (1993). *Metal Cutting and Tool Design.* Vikas Publication.
4. Ranganath, B.J & Venkatesh, V.C. (1980). A Study on Wear of Cemented Titanium Carbide Tools. *4th Int.Conf. of Production Engg.*, Tokyo Japan.
5. Ranganath, B.J. and Shanthapriya, B.N. (1997). *Sintered Silicon Nitride-A Prospective Cutting Tool Material.* 17th AMTDR, Warangal.
6. Ranganath, B.J. & Shanthapriya, B.N. (1977). Stress Analysis of Cutting Tool Insters by FEM Technique. *Int. Conf. on Recent Advances in Mechanical Engg.* Roorkee.
7. Ranganath, B.J. and Shanthapriya, B.N. (1977). Stress Analysis in Sintered Aluminium Oxide and Sinitered Silicon Nitride Cutting Tool Material. National Seminar on *Emerging Tredns in Design Engineering*, Allahabad.

MICROSCOPIC ANALYSIS OF EDM PROCESSES

32

V.S.R. MURTI[1] and S.A. HASAN[2]
Professor, Mech. Engg. Dept.,[1]
Osmania University, Hyderabad
Research Scholar, Mech. Engg. Dept.,[2]
J.N.T.U., Hyderabad

ABSTRACT

The morphology and topography of surfaces obtained from EDM process have been analysed for a better understanding of the basic mechanism of surface generation as well as the surface texture characteristics. Metallurgical and scanning electron microscope were employed for analysing the individual and successive spark craters, erosion debris and spark eroded surfaces. EDXA and EPMA studies reveal significant incorporation of tool material into the machined surface. The results show the dominant mode of erosion as volatilisation rather than atomisation of molten metal of the spark craters.

1. INTRODUCTION

In electro discharge machining (EDM) process the erosion occurs from high frequency electrical sparks between the workpiece (generally anode) and the tool (cathode) which are immersed in a dielectric and separated by a small gap, generally less than 100 microns. The small gap and high frequency renders the observation of sparking process extremely difficult. As a result the theories put forth for the erosion mechanism are speculative in nature. Commonly believed theory stresses melting and suggests possibility of evaporation of metal from the spot of spark impingement leaving behind a crater with some residual metal.[1] But the sizes of erosion particles are not compatible with the theory of erosion by atomisation from molten state.[2]

In this set of experimental studies the morphological characteristics of WEDM surfaces have been analysed and compared with similar studies on SEDM surface to investigate the surface generation when a wire is used as electrode vis-à-vis a solid electrode. This also can help in a better understanding of spark erosion phenomena and surface generation in the EDM process.

2. METHODOLOGY

The studies include both SEDM (shaped electrode) and WEDM (wire electrode) surface and their transverse sections. Isolated spark craters from individual and successive sparks were obtained on polished specimens. Erosion debris were collected and studied under SEM. Hollowness was tested by crushing them before SEM observation. Tool material incorporation was tested by EDXA (energy despersive X-ray analysis) and EPMA (electron probe micro analyser) studies of the machined surface. The specimens were ultrasonically cleaned and suitably mounted on bakelite moulds before macroscopic analysis.

3. RESULTS AND DISCUSSION

3.1 Morphology of Spark Craters

The spark craters produced by individual and successive sparks in WEDM process are shown in Fig.1. Sparks are discrete and occur one at a time. Their location depends on the nature of surfaces of the two electrodes and the impurities present in the dielectric. Spark occurs due to dielectric breakdown when the voltage gradient between the two electrodes reaches the breakdown strength of the dielectric. The first spark occurs where the

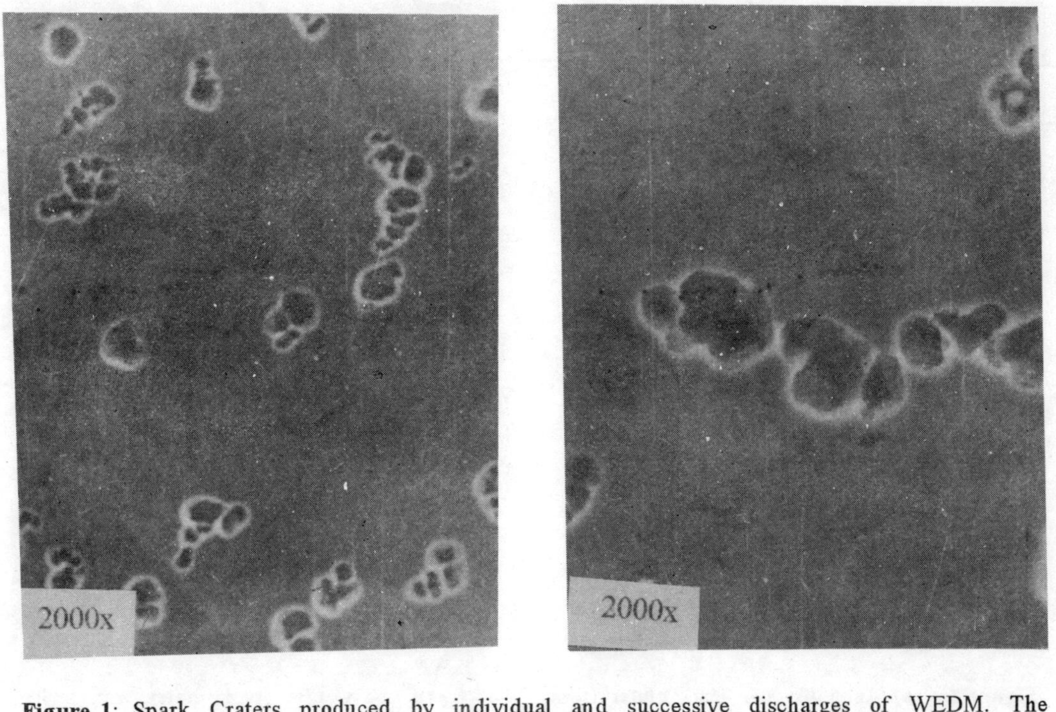

Figure 1: Spark Craters produced by individual and successive discharges of WEDM. The characteristic spherical shape and chain form overlapping craters can be observed.

interelectrode gap is shortest as a result of surface irregularities and the presence of impurity particles or debris. The spark produces two craters, one large one at the anode (work piece) and the other at cathode, a much smaller one, both of which have raised rims. The most likely spot for the second spark (and subsequent ones) would be a point on the rim of the crater and nearest to the electrode producing an overlapped crater. This process would continue until the whole length of the wire-work interface is subjected to sparking. The whole process is repeated as the table is fed and wire traverses the programmed path.

The electrode being a wire, a single dimension-linear entity the successive sparks also occur in the same fashion and manifest in a chain form of clusters of craters (Fig. 1). Fig. 2 shows similarly obtained spark craters on SEDM surface. The difference in the morphology of spark craters from the two process is striking. Two distinct types of craters are identified. Fig. 2(a) shows a normal crater with raised rim whereas in Fig. 2(b) is a crater with spilled poll of molten metal from which the explosion of metal was not effective. Both these pictures clearly indicate the thermal nature of erosion from molten state. On the contrary the neat craters of WEDM suggest the erosion to have occurred in vapor state with very small residual metal, a transition state of liquid phase sticking to crater rim due to surface tension forces. This leads to the inference that the dominant mode of erosion in SEDM is in liquid form as believed popularly to be the erosion mechanism in EDM[3,4] but in WEDM the dominant mode of erosion appears to be in vapour form. The reason for this disparity is not difficult to seek. The spark discharges in WEDM are of very

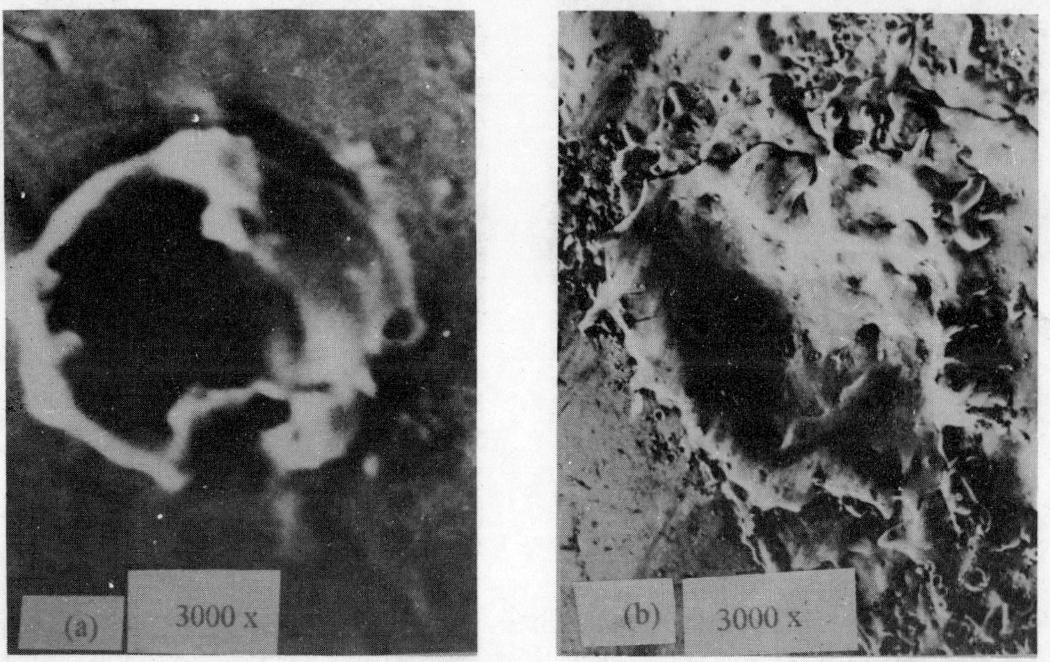

Figure 2. (a) An individual spark crater from SEDM. A significant residual metal at the crater rim can be observed. (b) A similar spark crater with spilled pool of liquid metal from which the explosion of metal was comperfect.

small duration due to the associated relaxation generator which produces in extremely rapid discharge of high energy density causing evaporation of crater metal. But in SEDM the pluse duration are much longer with low energy density and larger spark craters resulting in melting and evacuation by atomisation of crater metal by the spark force with considerable residual metal spilled and retained at the crater rim.

Another difference is the highly randomly varying sizes and locations of successive spark craters in SEDM. Fig. (3) shows such a network of spark craters. Since the tool work interface is two dimensional, the sparks occur all over the interface area randomly. The stochastic nature of the craters is derived from the surface irregularities, varying gap dimensions and debris density distribution which affects both the location of spark discharges as well as the crater size. The latter depends on the spark energy which in turn is effected by ignition delay and resistance of the spark channel.[5] In WEDM also there is random variation of locations of spark discharges due to spark gap variations caused by departure from straightness in the wire. Fig. 1 shows such a network a craters but the craters occur in linear groups before location change. However the crater size is significantly uniform in WEDM. The reason for this is fairly uniform pulse energies in WEDM where successive machining zones involve fresh bright drawn wire and work interface with feed motion to both as the machining progresses. Whereas in SEDM both the tool and work electrodes have rough and worn surfaces as the machining progresses.

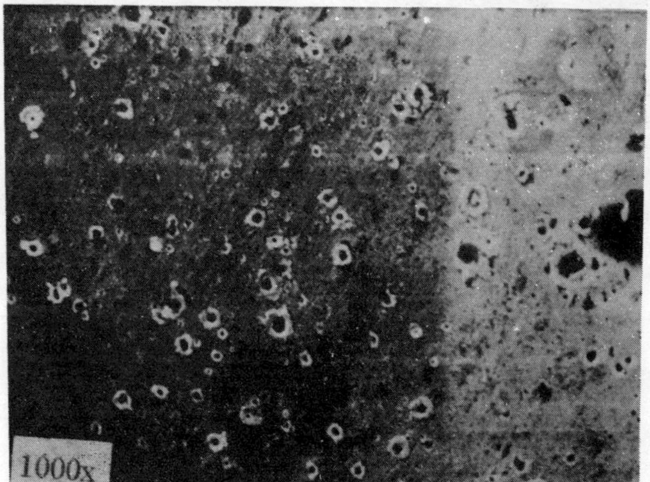

Figure 3: A network of randomly located spark crater all over the surface in SEDM.

3.2 Transverse Sections

Metallographic examination of the transverse section of SEDM surfaces revealed the presence of a resolidified layer of metal which is traditionally termed as white layer owing to its such appearance. It is extremely hard and inetcheable.[6] Significantly it sometimes even accentuates the spherical nature of spark craters (Fig. 4a). Significantly the WEDM surfaces do not exhibit any such resolidified layer (Fig. 4b) which further lends credence to the suggestion that the erosion mechanism in WEDM being in vapour form. The main reason for the occurrence of the white layer is the kerosene dielectric which dissociates into carbon and hydrogen in the spark heat. The carbon diffuses into the residual metal in the spark crater and on getting quenched by the surrounding dielectric forms hard carbides. By contrast in WEDM the dielectric is deionised water so carbide formation does not occur. Also the residual metal being negligible, the white layer does not form.

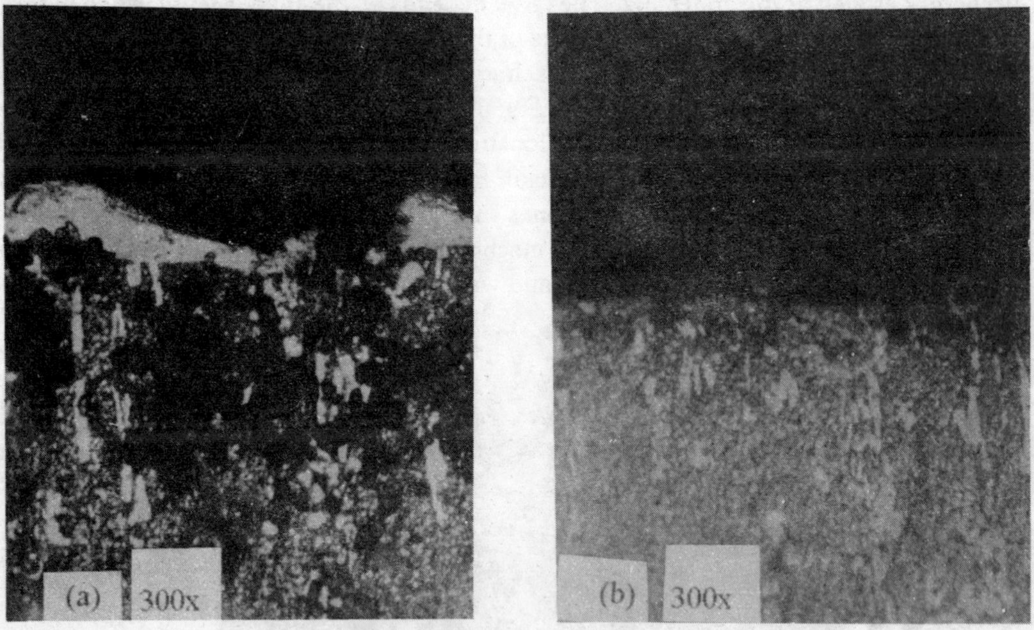

Figure 4: The transverse sections of machined surfaces
(a) The white layer on SEDM surface.
(b) Absence of white layer on WEDM surface

3.3 Tool Material Diffusion into the Machine Surface

The EPMA examination of machined surface from WEDM show significant incorporation of wire material into the cutaneous layer of machined surface. This was observed sometimes even on a visual examination of the machined surface.

Further corroborative tests were taken up on EDXA and the results were confirmed when the spectra indicated the presence of both copper and zinc on the machined surface. But when the tests were repeated on SEDM specimen this phenomenon of tool material incorporation was not witnessed. Some reports of SEDM have shown it to occur but there the machining conditions were suitably modified to promote the tool material diffusion into the machined surface deliberately by employing reverse polarity and PM electrodes.[7] This is yet another result which corroborates the suggested theory that the predominant mechanism of erosion in WEDM is in the vapour form and in SEDM in liquid form. Diffusion of wire material into the machined surface can have an interesting application whereby surface modification can be incorporated simultaneous to the machining process.

3.4 Debris Analysis

The size of the erosion debris ranged between 3 to 65 microns whereas the size of spark craters varied between 5 to 200 microns. This size distribution is highly incompatible with the theory of erosion by atomisation from molten pool of metal in the spark craters. A more credible mode of erosion appears to be by vaporisation. The spark energies generate temperatures in the range of several thousand degrees celsius.[8] This also indicates the higher probability of evaporation of metal in the spark craters. The spherical shape and hollow structure of several of the eroded chips strongly support this theory (Figs. 5 & 6).

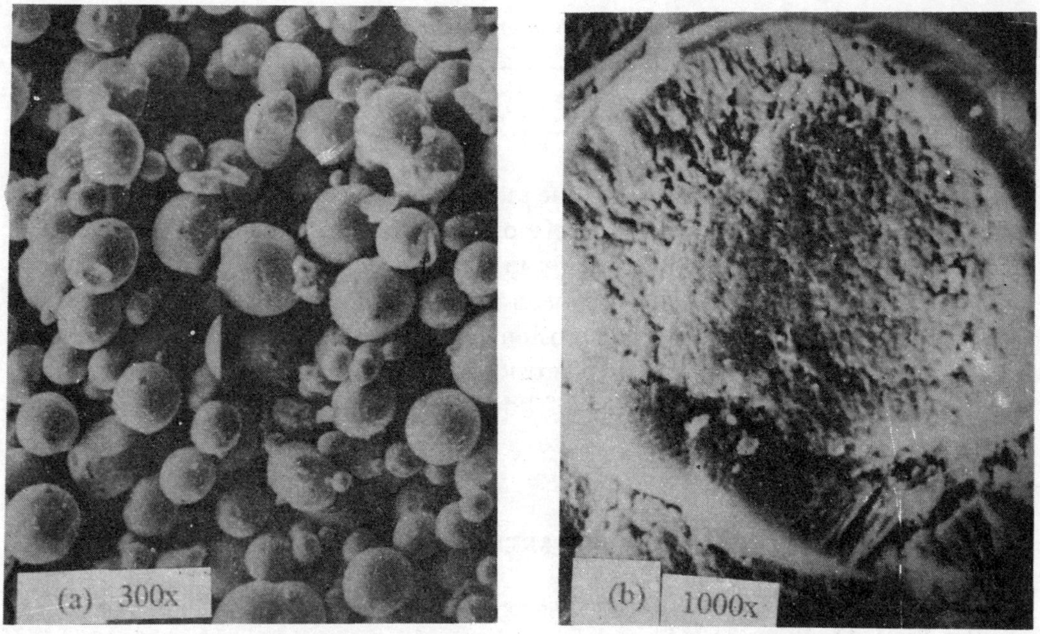

Figure 5:(a) The erosion debris with spherical shape (b) Solid particle

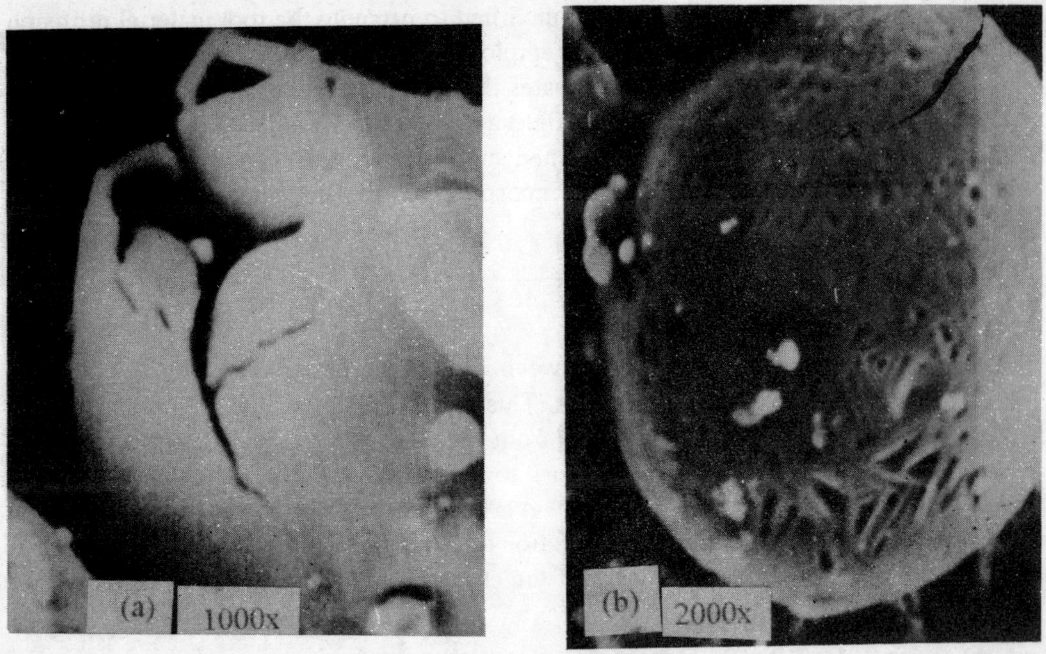

Figure 6: (a) and (b) Hollow particles. At high magnification, the dendritic mode of solidification can be observed.

4. CONCLUSIONS

The EDM surfaces have matty texture due to overlapping craters formed at the spots of spark impingement. The dominant mode of erosion appears to be volatilisation rather than atomisation from liquid state particularly in the case of WEDM. In SEDM there is a considerable uneroded and resolidified metal from the transitive liquid phase. However, the relative sizes of spark craters and erosion debris and their follow structure strongly support the volatilisation mechanism of erosion to be dominant. But, however, limited it may be, the erosion by atomisation of liquid metal from spark craters cannot be discounted.

REFERENCES

1. Crookall, J.R. and Khore, B.C., *Electrodischarge Machined Surfaces Proc.* 15th Int. Mach. Tool. Des. Res. Conf., 1974, 373-383.
2. Murti, V.S.R. and Philip, P.K., Analysis of debris in ultrasonic assisted EDM, *Int. Jl of Wear* (UK) V. 119 (1987) 241-50.
3. Bucklow I.A. and Cole, M. Spark, *Machining, Metallurgical Reviews,* No. 155, 1969, 103-18.
4. Van Dijck, F. And Snoeys, R. '*Metal Removal and Surface Layer in EDM*', Proc. Int. Conf. Prod.

Engg., Tokyo, 1974, p. 46-50.

5. Murti V.S.R., Philp, P.K. '*Textural Characteristics of EDM Surfaces*', Proc 13th All India Machine Tool Design and Research Conf. 1988, p. F01-05.
6. Crookall, J.R. and Khore, B.C., '*Residual Stresses and Surfaces Effects in EDM*', 13th IMTDR Conf. 1972, pp. 331-38.
7. Gangadhar, A. *et al.*, 'Surface modification in EDM with a powder compact tool electrode' *Int. Jl. of Wear,* V. 143, 1991, pp. 45-55.
8. Trezise K.E., '*A Physicist's View of Wire EDM*' Proc. IMTDR, 1985, pp. 413-19.

RELATIVE EVALUATION OF BURNISHING PROCESS WITH CONVENTIONAL AND COUNTER SPEED AND FEED DIRECTIONS

33

V.S.R. MURTI[1], A. M.K. Prasad[1] and S. Mastan[1]
Mechanical Engineering Department,[1]
Osmania University, Hyderabad- 500 007, A.P., India

ABSTRACT

Turning and subsequent burnishing are normally performed with counter clock-wise rotation and right to left feed direction. In the present work, the effect of counter feed and speed directions on the surface finish in burnishing is studied. The results exhibit highly significant improvement in the surface finish in both the cases of counter speed and feed directions individually as well as collectively.

1. INTRODUCTION

Burnishing is a finishing process whereby a superior finish is obtained by plastic deformation of roughness asperities by the application of pressure through a ball or roller. The plastic deformation also eliminates surface defects thus improving the fatigue strength. Considerable research work has been reported[1,2,3] on burnishing elucidating the basic principles and the process parameters. For improved characteristics vibratory, oscillatory, ultrasonic and impact burnishing processes have been developed.[4,5] The present studies suggest employing speed and feed directions opposite to those employed in the basic machining process so that a more effective metal flow is obtained to obliterate feed and lay marks.

2. THEORY

2.1 Mechanism of Roughness Generation in Metal Cutting

Figure 1 illustrates a schematic model of generation of roughness asperities in the basic machining process employing a sharp tool without nose radius. For simplicity consider the tool up machining a groove in one pass for a particular depth of cut, the generated groove is illustrated in Fig. 1(a). With a given feed rate the subsequent grooves suffer mutual interference and the resultant roughness asperities are shown schematically in Fig. 1(b). One can easily observe that there is no effect of depth of cut on the roughness

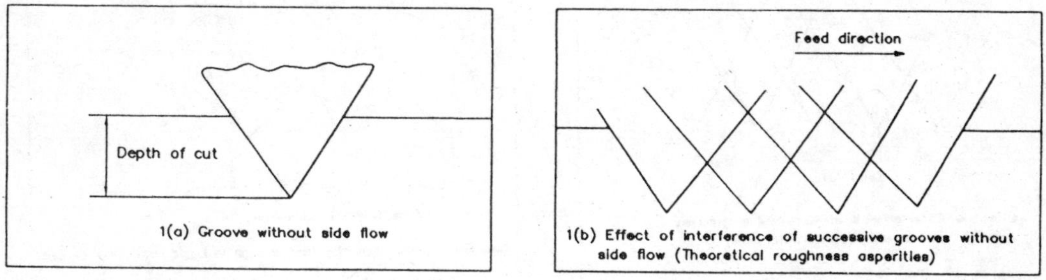

Figure 1: Schematic representation of generation of roughness asperities without side flow.

asperities. The tool geometry and feed rate are only the influencing factors. The material in groove is removed in the form of chips by shear mechanism. But the compressive force exerted by the tool also produces a plastic deformation causing flow of metal along both the flanks of the tool[6,7] and the resultant groove will exhibit a 'pile up' or 'side flow' on both flanks. This is shown in Fig 2. The interference of two such grooves shall have an interesting result whereby the pile up or side flow on the left flank shall have an inclination or shift towards the preceeding groove and the pile up on the right flank is eliminated during the generation of subsequent groove. The final roughness asperities from interference of subsequent grooves formed by the feed motion of the cutting tool is

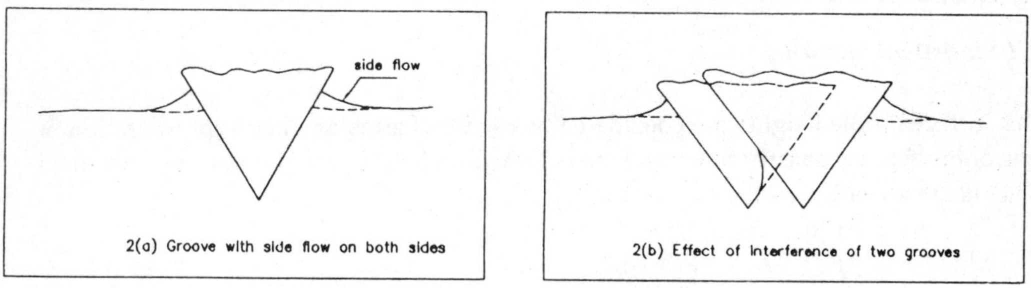

Figure 2: Effect of plastic flow on the geometry of machined groove.

illustrated in fig. 3. The plastic flow or side flow caused by the compressive force exerted by the cutting tool occurs on the flank opposite to the feed direction. Consequently it can be envisaged that if the burnishing feed is given opposite to the feed direction of the basic machining process it can increase the metal flow by the combined action of the burnishing force in the form of direct compression and bending of the surface asperities. Fig. 4 schematically illustrates it.

2.2 Analysis of Surface Roughness

The conventional parameters presently used in describing surface roughness viz. Ra. Rq.

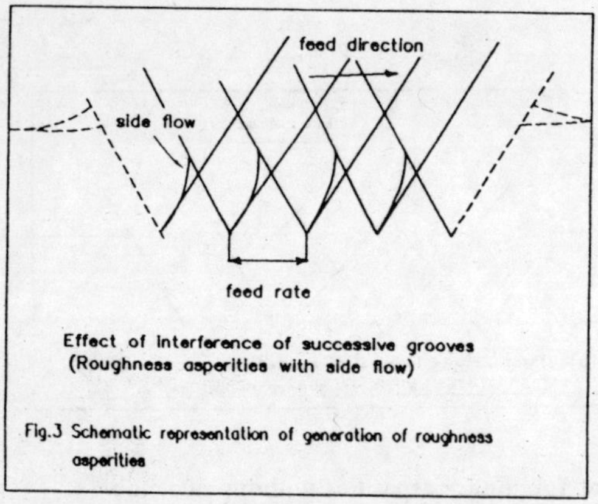

Figure 3: Schematic representation of generation of roughness asperities.

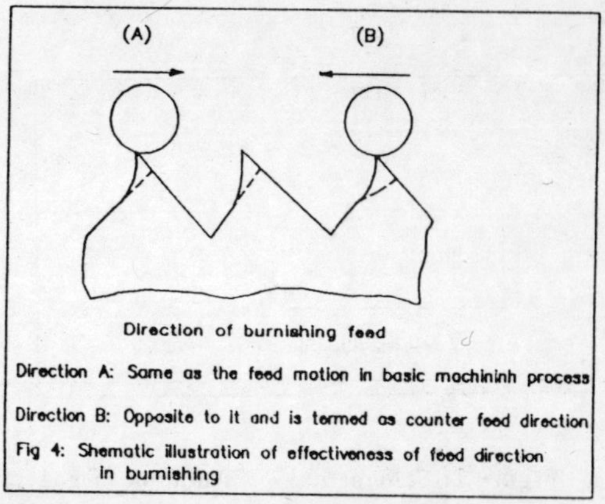

Figure 4: Schematic illustration of effectiveness of feed direction in burnishing.

Rz etc. are discrete and convenient for a fast appraisal of surface finish. Even the roughness height average (Ra. Rq) is supplemented with Rt, Rmax to further describe the roughness. However, their utility is very limited in specifying exact nature of the surface. Statistical description of the surface profile is more useful than isolated measurements of particular parameters. Such a description remains valid for all functional applications. One attractive approach to a general description of the height distribution is to use its central moments. The RMS value (Rq) defines the scale of the distribution whilst the moment coefficients of skewness and kurtosis define its shape sufficiently.

2.2.1 Statistical Moments

If the surface profile heights are considered as random variables, their representation in terms of probability density function P(z) is known as height distribution, the statistical moments are governed by the expression (I).

$$M_n = \frac{1}{\sigma^n} \int_{-\alpha}^{+\alpha} Z^n \, P(z)\, dz \qquad \ldots\ldots \quad (1)$$

Where Z = Profile ordinate value

n_2 = The moment number

σ = Variance

The first moment is mean of d.c. level which is generally removed before data processing and is therefore zero.[9] The second moment is variance and is a measure of the spread of data. The third moment is skewness and indicates the fullness of the profile. A Gaussian profile is symmetric and has zero skewness whereas positive skewness denotes an empty profile and negative skewness, a full profile. The fourth moment is kurtosis and is a measure of peakedness. A Gaussian profile has kurtosis equal to 3. A 'Platy-kurtic' surface has kurtosis less than 3 whereas a 'Leptokurtic' surface has kurtosis more than 3., the latter having higher peakedness. Skewness and kurtosis therefore thus define the SHAPE of the roughness profile and in combination with Ra and Rq can suitably classify the final taxture of the machined surface.[10]

The discrete value expressions for RMS roughness (Rq), Skewness (Rs) and kurtosis (Rk) are given below:

$$Rq = \left[\frac{1}{N} \sum_{i=1}^{N} Zi^2 \right]$$

$$Rs = 1/\sigma\ 3 \left[\frac{1}{N} \sum_{i=1}^{N} Zi^3 \right]$$

$$Rk = 1/\sigma\ 4 \left[\frac{1}{N} \sum_{i=1}^{N} Zi^4 \right]$$

Where Zi is the deviation measured from least square line fitted for the roughness profile and N is the number of data points.

3. Experimental Plan

Aluminium and mild steel specimens were turned and subsequently burnished on a precision lathe. High carbon-high chromium steel was the ball material for each specimen. Only one pass was employed and a new ball was used. Ball diameter was 40 mm. The feed rate was 0.1 mm/rev with a depth of penetration of 0.2 mm. Burnishing speed was kept at 30 m/min in both the cases. The initial roughness on aluminium was higher than in the case of MS. The roughness was measured on a stylus type instrument called perthometer. The sample length of 4.8 mm with a cut off length of 0.8 mm was selected. The roughness indices Ra, Rmax Rz were noted in each case.

The digitised values of roughness profile ordinates were further analysed statiscally for skewness and kurtosis. A second set of specimens were prepared from aluminium with higher initial roughness. The roughness profiles were digitised and their statistical parameters were computed.

4. RESULTS AND DISCUSSION

4.1 Conventional Indices of Roughness

The roughness indices of the basic machined surface and the burnished surfaces under different conditions are tabulated and shown in table 1. Since only one pass was employed, the improvement in surface finish is not high but significant differences in each case could be detected. As anticipated the surface finish is superior in burnishing with counter feed and counter speed directions in both the cases of aluminium and MS specimens. Interestingly counter speed direction has better results than counter feed direction. This can be attributed to superior obliteration of lay marks. In a similar way the best results occurred when both counter speed and feed directions were employed. The contributing causes have been already discussed in the preceeding section on the theoretical back ground. In most of the reports the basic mechanism of burnishing action is defined as plactic flow of metal from the 'peaks' into the 'Valleys' of the roughness asperities and is associated with the compressive force of the burnishing ball or roller. But the effect of direction of rotation and feed on the effective direction of this compressive force has not been considered. This should be studied in conjunction with the feed and speed directions of the basic machining processes. As a logical consequence it is expected to result in lower residual stresses and surface imperfections. It will not be out of place to emphasize that the burnishing process is not so simple as it is made out to be if one goes by a survey of the available literature. Apart from the process parameters which have been mentioned earlier, the compliances of the machine tool, work and tool holders and the machine vibrations are vital factors in the production of final surface texture and must be considered in the ultimate analysis.

TABLE 1: **Surface Finish Obtained on Aluminium and Mild Steel Specimen in Burnishing (Depth of Penetration 0.2mm, Feed Rate 0.1 mm/rev.)**

Sl. No.	Specimen Specification	Aluminium Roughness parameters (μm)			Mild Steel Roughness parameters (μm)		
		Ra	Rmax	Rz	Ra	Rmax	Rz
1.	Basic turned surface	4.06	17.53	15.38	1.69	7.4	6.3
2.	Burnished surface						
2.1	Conventional	3.32	15.72	13.06	0.98	7.1	5.8
2.2	Contrafeed direction	2.71	15.31	12.92	0.98	6.4	5.3
2.3	Contraspeed direction	2.06	14.49	10.07	0.84	5.9	5.0
2.4	Contra feed & speed direction	1.95	8.58	7.83	0.55	5.19	3.19

4.2 Statistical Parameters

The second set of results are listed in table 2 for the statistical parameters computed from the digitised values of the roughness ordinates. The CLA values of roughness (Ra) once again has considerable reduction when counter speed and feed directions were employed. The skewness and kurtosis in all the cases donot conform to the normal Gaussian

TABLE 2: **Statistical Parameters of the Roughness Profiles**

Sl. No.	Specimen specification	Roughnss parameters (μm)				
		Ra	Rpavg	Rvavg	Rs	Rk
1.0	Basic turned surface	8.0	17.5	–16.3	1.42	2.2
2.0	Burnished surface					
2.1	Conventional	6.6	11.9	–11.4	2.7	8.7
2.2	Counter feed direction	2.6	5.3	–5.8	1.5	2.6
2.3	Counter speed direction	4.2	7.3	–8.7	1.6	3.0
2.4	Counter speed & feed direction	3.8	7.4	–7.4	1.4	2.3

distribution. The positive skewness indicates nonsymmetric or empty surface with open texture. The other moment kurtosis which is a measure of peakedness, is generally equal to 3.0 for normal distribution. For the surface from the basic turning the kurtosis has a near normal value whereas the burnishing causes a high increase in the kurtosis significantly the kurtosis reduces to near Gaussian value when counter speed and feed direction were employed for burnishing. The high peakedness of conventionally burnished surface can again be observed in the average Rp and Rv values. In all the cases the Rp and Rv values have nearly same magnitude though they are significantly reduced when counter feed and speed directions were employed in burnishing. This indicates the effect of plastic flow from burnishing originating from peaks but transimitted to the valleys also. The consequent shift of mean line or center line is such that Rp and Rv are equally affected from the plastic flow during burnishing.

5. CONCLUSIONS

A theoretical analysis of the basic mechanism of generation of surface roughness asperities indicates the pile up or plastic flow of metal in a direction opposite to the feed direction in the basic machining process. The experimental analysis of the burnished surfaces show significant improvement of surface finish when the burnishing speed and feed are employed in opposite directions to those of the basic machining process. This has been attributed to a better obliteration of feed and lay marks which are the characteristic features of roughness asperities generated in a machining process.

The burnished surfaces have positive skewness indicative of empty or open texture. However, the skew as well as kurtosis was more for the surface with conventional feed and speed direction in burnishing. The peakedness was significantly low when counter speed and feed directions were employed during burnishing. The effect of plastic flow during burnishing was similar for peaks as well as valleys of the roughness profile.

REFERENCES

1. Murty, R.L. and Kotiveerachari, B., *Burnishing of Metallic Surfaces—A Review*, Precision Engg., 1981, pp. 172-79.
2. Loh, N.H., Tam, S.C. and Miyazawa, S., Application of Experimental Design in Ball Burnishing, *Int. J. Mach. Tools*, Manufact., 1993, pp. 841-52.
3. Pande, S.S. and Patel, S.M., Investigation of Vibratory Burnishing Process, *Int. J. Mach. Tools*, Manufact., 1984, pp. 195-206.
4. Loh, N.H. and Tam, S.C., *Effect of Ball Burnishing Parameters on Surface Finish, A Literature Survey and Discussion*, Precision Engg., 1988, pp. 215-20.
5. Maracov, A.I. (*et.al.*), Ultrasonic Diamond Burnishing, *Russian Engg. Journal*, 1973, pp. 58-62.
6. Tsukizoe, T., *et al.*, On the Generating Mechanism of Surface Roughness, *Bulletin of the JSME*, 1974, pp. 363-69.
7. Hasegawa, M. *et al.*, On the Generating Mechanism of Surface Roughness, *Bulletin of the JSME*, 1974, pp. 367-75.
8. Sayles, R.S., The Profile as Random Process, *Rough Surfaces*, ed. J.R. Thomas, Longman, London, 1982.
9. Nayak, P.R., Random Process Model of Rough Surfaces, *ASME Jl. of Lub. Tech.*, 1971, pp. 398-407.
10. King, T.C. and Spedding, T.A., *On the Relationship Between Surface Profile Height Parameters*, Preprints. Int. Conf. Metro. Prop. of Engg. Surfaces, 1982, pp. 1-16.

INVESTIGATIONS ON THE SURFACE ROUGHNESS PRODUCED BY BALL BURNISHING ON CNC MACHINE

34

M. Manzoor Hussain[1] and T. Yadesh[2]

Lecturer, Mech. Engg. Dept., J.N.T.U. College of Engineering[1]
Kukatpally, HYDERABAD 500 072

M.Tech (Prod) Student, J.N.T.U. P.G. School,[2]
HYDERABAD 500 028

ABSTRACT

Burnishing is a post machining, a plastic deformation, surface finishing process. In this plastic redistribution of surface material is seen in which gives good surface finish with improved surface hardness. Experimental were conducted on CNC training machine to establish the various ball burnishing parameters, diameter of ball burnishing speed, depth of burnishing ball penetration and feed rate. Materials selected are Aluminium and En19 steel. The surface roughness parameters first decreases and then increases with increasing the size of ball diameter. The effect of depth of burnishing ball penetration, speed of burnishing and feed rate also showed similar trend. The initial surface roughness of 1.98 μm obtained in turning of Aluminium reduced to 0.21 μm with parameters infeed 0.2 mm, feed rate 0.05 mm/rev, ball diameter 20 mm and spindle speed of 35 m/min. Similarly the initial roughness of EN19 steel of 2.39 μm reduced to 0.39 μm at the parameters of speed of 35 m/min, feed rate is 0.05 mm/rev, infeed 0.2 mm and the ball diameter of size 12 mm. The use of CNC machine enables the pre-machining and burnishing operations to accomplished automatically in sequential order.

1. INTRODUCTION

More than ninety-five percent of total machining work is done by metal process like turning, milling, drilling etc. These metal machining operations give the required shape and size to the components and to improve the surface characteristics of the components. The components are subjected to a metal finishing process. The finishing process apart from improving the functional performance of the components also improves the life of the component and gives a better appearance. One of such process is burnishing. Burnishing is a post machining process, it cold works the metal surfaces by applying forces that exceed yield strength of the metal through hardened ball. This can also be termed as an un-conventional finishing operation. In this process as the roller or ball comes in contact with a machined surface, the ridges or peaks are compressed into the surface and valleys tend to rise as the material flows on the microscopic level (fig.A). As the burnishing ball moves on to the second zone, the yield strength of the metal is exceeded, producing cold flow. After the workpiece has been subjected to the maximum compressive strain under the bottom of the wall, it is relieved elastically in the third zone. The workpiece leaves the roller or ball with a smooth, hard surface and with residual compressive and tensile stresses. As the applied loads are compressive and the plastic deformation is localised, virtually any metal can be burnished. This includes brittle materials, which although weak in tension can sustain compressive loads and have sufficient plastic flow to produce an acceptable surface. Thus the type of materials which can be burnished are almost unlimited. Burnishing can be performed on any machine which is capable of rotating the burnishing tool, or the part to be burnished. There can be any standard spindle driven machines, single or multipurpose, hand or machine feed, automatic or NC controlled.

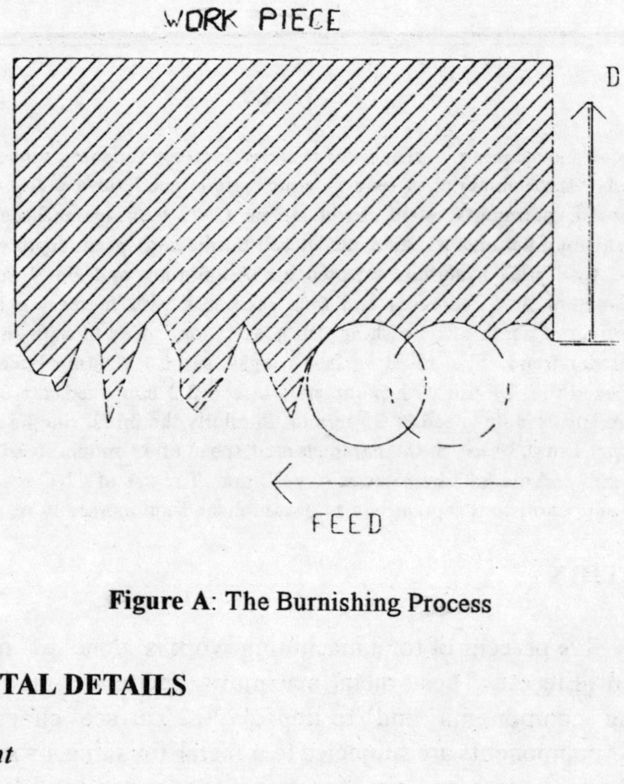

Figure A: The Burnishing Process

2. EXPERIMENTAL DETAILS

2.1 Test Equipment

A single tool was designed and constructed to carry out the experimental work. Carbon Chromium steel balls were used. The balls, having Rockwell hardness HRC63 and surface roughness average (Ra) of 0.012um, are commercially available on market usually used in ball bearings. Different ball diameters 8mm, 9mm, 9.5mm, 12mm and 20mm.

The tool was designed to permit the use of balls with different diameters by changing the collars. Also the collar was designed in such a way that it could be removed from the tool and clean the ball and in the ball cavity in the tool when it was necessary. The use of CNC machines enables the pre-machining and burnishing operations to be accomplished automatically in sequential order.

2.2 Test Materials

The work-pieces were selected as cylindrical bars of 38mm & 25mm diameter of Aluminium (99.6% pure), 30mm diameter of mild steel, 35mm diameter of EN19. The bars were cut to appropriate lengths (225mm to 250mm) and each work-piece was divided into 6 to 11 regions (segments) according to the parameters of the studies.

As an example, the work-piece prepared to study the cutting tool direction for different ball diameters had 11 regions. The left of the work-place is divided into 6 regions.

Each region was taken a length of 30 mm by making 5mm × 2mm groves. Each region was intended for exposing to different set of conditions during the experimentation.

The chemical compositions of EN19 was

Carbon	0.35 to 0.45
Manganese	0.50 to 0.80
Nickel	Nil
Chromium	0.90 to 1.50
Molybdenum	0.20 to 0.40
Sulphur & Phosphorus	0.50

2.3 Test Parameters

Table 1 shows the values of the burnishing parameters used in the present investigations. The effect of these parameters on the surface micro roughness and micro hardness of the test materials was studies.

TABLE 1

Ball Diameter in mm	8, 9, 9.5, 12 and 20
Infeed in mm	0.1, 0.2, 0.3, 0.4 and 0.5
Speeds in rpm	48, 76, 116, 270 and 421
Feed rate in mm/rev	0.028, 0.039, 0.049, 0.069 and 0.099
Cutting tool motion	Left to Right and Right to Left
Burnishing conditions	No Lubricant

2.4 Burnishing Parameters

Roughness and Hardness Measurements

The surface roughness (Ra) was measured by using a SORTRONIC-3, a portable equipment for measuring the surface roughness and surface hardness was measured by using a Vickers micro hardness testing, machine model - BV120(S) under a load of 5 Kgf for Aluminium and 30 kgf for mild steel and En19.

3. RESULTS

3.1 Effect of Ball Diameter on Surface Roughness and Hardness

Fig.1 illustrates the effect of burnishing on surface roughness for different ball diameters on Aluminium, Mild Steel and EN19. It can be seen that a ball diameter ranging from 10 to 15mm gives the minimum surface roughness under the working conditions of infeed = 02mm, speed = 421 rpm and feed rate = 0.049 mm/rev.

Fig. 5 shows the effect of ball diameter on micro hardness for the materials Aluminium, mild steel and EN19. At the ball diameter 12mm gives the greatest hardness. The general trend of the curves shows that the increase in feed causes a decrease in hardness.

3.2 Effect of Infeed on Surface Roughness and Micro Hardness

Fig. 2 shows the effect of infeed on surface roughness for the materials Aluminium, mild steel and EN19. The infeed of 0.2mm gives the good results of minimum surface roughness. Under the working conditions of ball diameter = 12mm, speed 421 rpm and feed rate = 0.049mm/rev.

Fig. 6 shows the effect of infeed on micro hardness for the above three materials. The infeed of 0.2mm gives the greatest hardness at ball diameter = 12mm, speed = 421mm and feed rate = 0.049 mm/rev.

3.3 Effect of Speeds on Surface Roughness and Micro Hardness

The speeds of the samples are mainly depend on the diameter of the work-piece. The good results are found at (speed 35 m/min) speed is 421 rpm at infeed is 0.2 mm, ball diameter = 12 mm and feed rate = 0.049 mm/rev as shown in Fig. 3. Similarly, as shown in Fig. 7 the greatest hardness achieved at the same parameters as discussed above.

3.4 Effect of Feed Rate on Surface Roughness and Micro Hardness

The surface roughness was gradually decreasing by increasing feed rate and at 0.05 mm/

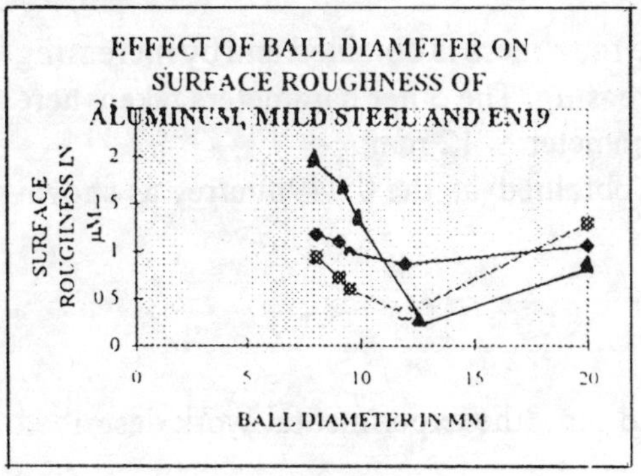

INFEED = 0.2 MM
SPEED = 421RPM
FEED RATE = 0.049 MM/REV

◇ ALUMINUM
□ MILD STEEL
△ EN19

Figure 1

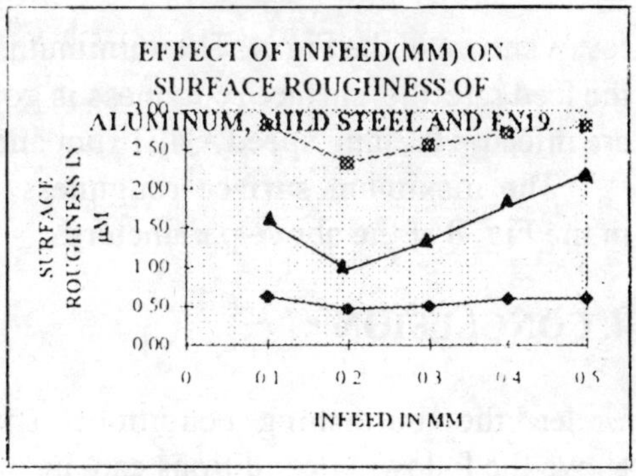

INFEED = 12 MM
SPEED = 421 RPM
FEED RATE = 0.049 MM/REV

◇ ALUMINUM
□ MILD STEEL
△ EN19

Figure 2

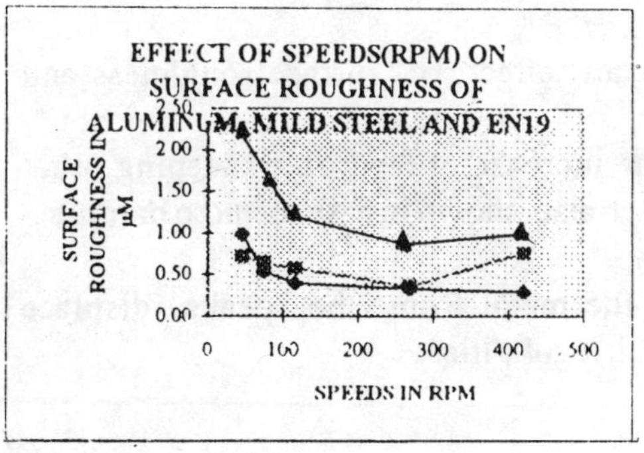

INFEED = 0.2 MM
BALL DIA = 12 MM
FEED RATE = 0.049 MM/REV

◇ ALUMINUM
□ MILD STEEL
△ EN19

Figure 3

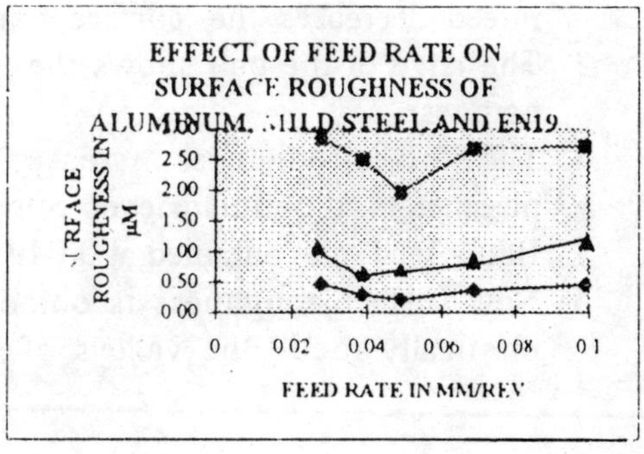

INFEED = 0.2 MM
SPEED = 421 RPM
BALL DIA = 12 MM

◇ ALUMINUM
MILD STEEL
EN19

Figure 4

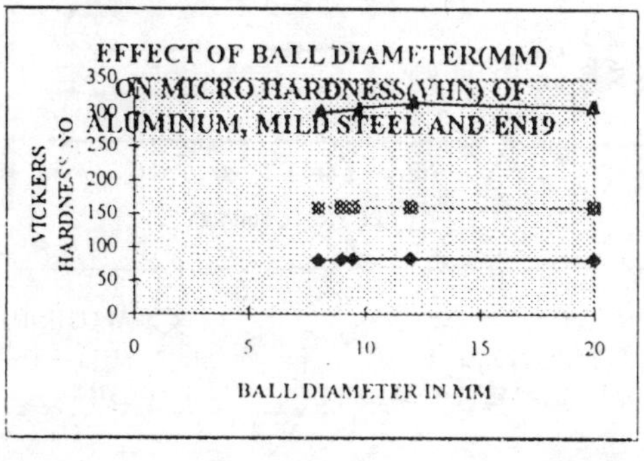

INFEED = 0.2 MM
SPEED = 421 RPM
FEED RATE = 0.049 MM/REV

◇ ALUMINUM
□ MILD STEEL
△ EN19

Figure 5

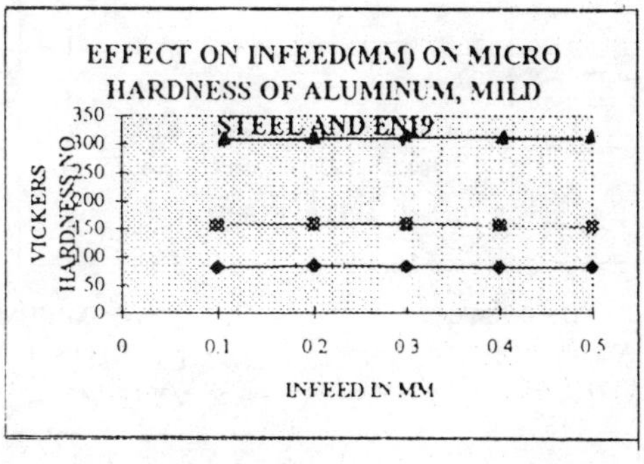

BALL DIAMETER = 12 MM
SPEED = 421 RPM
FEED RATE = 0.049 MM/REV

◇ ALUMINUM
□ MILD STEEL
△ EN19

Figure 6

rev as shown in the Fig. 4. The minimum surface roughness is obtained and by increasing the feed rate the surface roughness is go on increasing. The other parameters taken here are infeed = 0.2mm, speed = 421 rpm and ball diameter = 12 mm.

The maximum surface roughness is also obtained at the 0.049mm/rev as shown in the Fig. 8 at the above parameters.

4. CONCLUSION

Under the burnishing conditions considered in the experimental work described above the following conditions can be made.

1. There is an optimum speed of 30 m/min to 40 m/min at which better results could be obtained. High speeds are not required in grinding.
2. The effective infeed of ball burnishing is obtained at 0.2 mm. Further increase of infeed decreases the surface roughness.
3. The size of the ball shows the significant effect of surface roughness and hardness.
4. The surface roughness increases with the increase of feed rate keeping other parameters at optimum level. Similar effect also shown in case of micro hardness. Better feed rate obtained at 0.049 mm/rev.
5. New surface roughness is obtained as the metal from the peaks displace plastically to fill the valleys of surface irregularities.

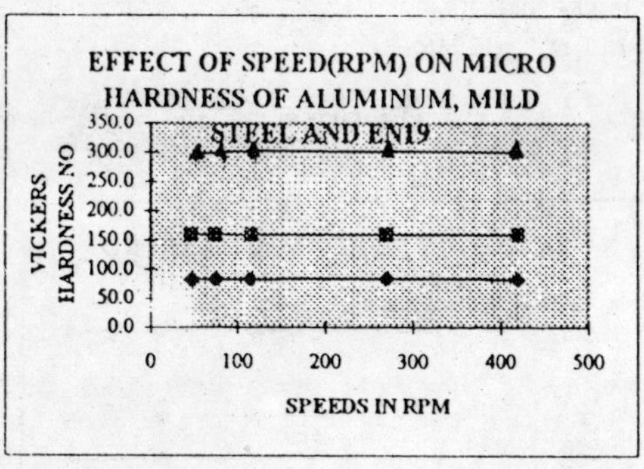

INFEED = 0.2 MM
BALL DIAMETER = 12 MM
FEED RATE = 0.049 MM/REV

◇ ALUMINUM
□ MILD STEEL
△ EN19

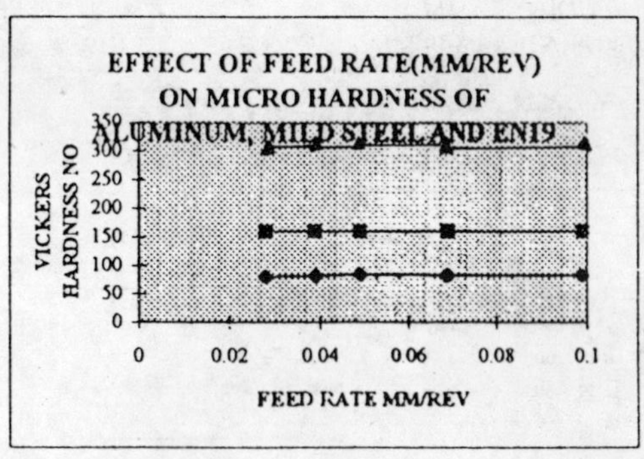

INFEED = 0.2 MM
SPEED = 270 RPM
BALL DIAMETER = 12 MM

◇ ALUMINUM
□ MILD STEEL
△ EN19

Figure 7

Figure 8

REFERENCES

1. N.H. Loh, S.C. Tam and S. Miyazawa "*Ball Burnishing of Tool Steel*" Precision Engineering, April 1993, Vol. 15.
2. K.E. Prasad, Dr. M. Komaraiah, Dr. Chakravarthi and R. Markandeya, "Surface Characteristics of Roller Burnished Components, "All India Seminar on Emerging Trends in Metal Machining organised by *The Institute of Engineers (India)*, 25 and 26th of December, 1993.
3. N.H. Loh, S.C. Tam and S. Miyazawa, "Surface Hardening by Ball Burnishing", *Tribology International*, December 90, Vol. 23, No. 6.
4. Abdul Mahamood Hassan, Aiman Sharef Al-bsharat, "Influence of Burnishing Process on Surface Roughness, Hardness and Microstructure of Some Non-Ferrous Metals" EAR 199 (1996), 1-8.
5. Kotiveera Chari. B. and Murthy. R.L., "Study of Some Aspects of Burnishing, *International Journal of Production Research,* 23(13), 1985.
6. Dr. Komaraiah. M and Niranjan Rao P., *Some Experimental Studies on Oscillatory Burnishing*, 13th AIMTDR Conference, Jadavapur University.

MANUFACTURING PROCESSES: MODERN TRENDS—An Overview

35

Col. V.P. Munjal
Armoured Troops Workshop, Western theatre.

ABSTRACT

Manufacturing processes, as we know them today, owe their classification to basically volume and variety of production. On one extreme we have the project form of manufacturing process as compared to the process industries on the other extreme, with intermittent and continuous flow processes falling inbetween. The project form which is characterised by a definite beginning and ending and has a limited life, is ideally suited when complex tasks involving many different functional specialisations have to be performed against strict deadlines. While intermittent or the batch production provides maximum variety at low cost, it is the continuous flow process which gives the maximum volume of production at the least cost. With the invasion of computers in almost all fields, many modern techniques like CAD/CAM/CAE; Group Technology; MRP II; Flexible Manufacturing; Robotics, etc., are available with us to really optimise the volume variety mix of the output. The author, in the paper, has ventured to give an overview of the various manufacturing processes, their inherent characteristics, advantages, disadvantages and the latest modern trends available to make these processes more effective and efficient.

INTRODUCTION

What is a manufacturing process ? In good old days when the emphasis was only on goods and not on services, one could define the manufacturing process as the process of converting inputs into products. But with the advent of information technology, the service sector has come into the limelight thereby necessitating the broadening of the scope of manufaturing process to encompass 'Services'. Therefore, the term 'Operation' covers the functions of 'manufacture' also and thus we can say that operations is the process of converting inputs into outputs thereby adding value to some entity. In this paper an attempt has been made to classify various manufacturing processes, based on their determinants. Description of these processes includes their advantages and disadvantages and how the disadvantages, to an extent, can be overcome by various modern techinques.

DETERMINANTS OF MANUFACTURING PROCESS

The transformation process that converts inputs into outputs with added value is the core element in the operations function. It is, therefore, a strategic decision for most organisations. The process selected will, to a very large extent, determine both the quality and quantity of men and women to be employed as well as the amount of capital required for the production of goods and services. In fact, many organisations are slowly coming round to the view that operations has been the missing link in the traditional approach of formulating a corporate strategy wherein the production or operations function is expected to play a supportive role to marketing.

The transformation process, therefore, has to be such that it can provide the desired product attributes and at the same time remains cost-effective. This can be best achieved by taking a strategic view of the production/operations function and by integrating the operations function including process selection while formulating the corporate strategy of the firm.

The manufacturing or transformation process largely depends upon the following :

(a) Volume and the variety.
(b) Produce to stock or produce to order.

Effect of Output Characteristics

As stated Earlier the form of the transformation process depends to a large extent on output characteristics like volume/variety and whether produced-to-stock or produced-to-order. Figure 1 illustrates these comments by showing the relationship in a diagrammatic form.

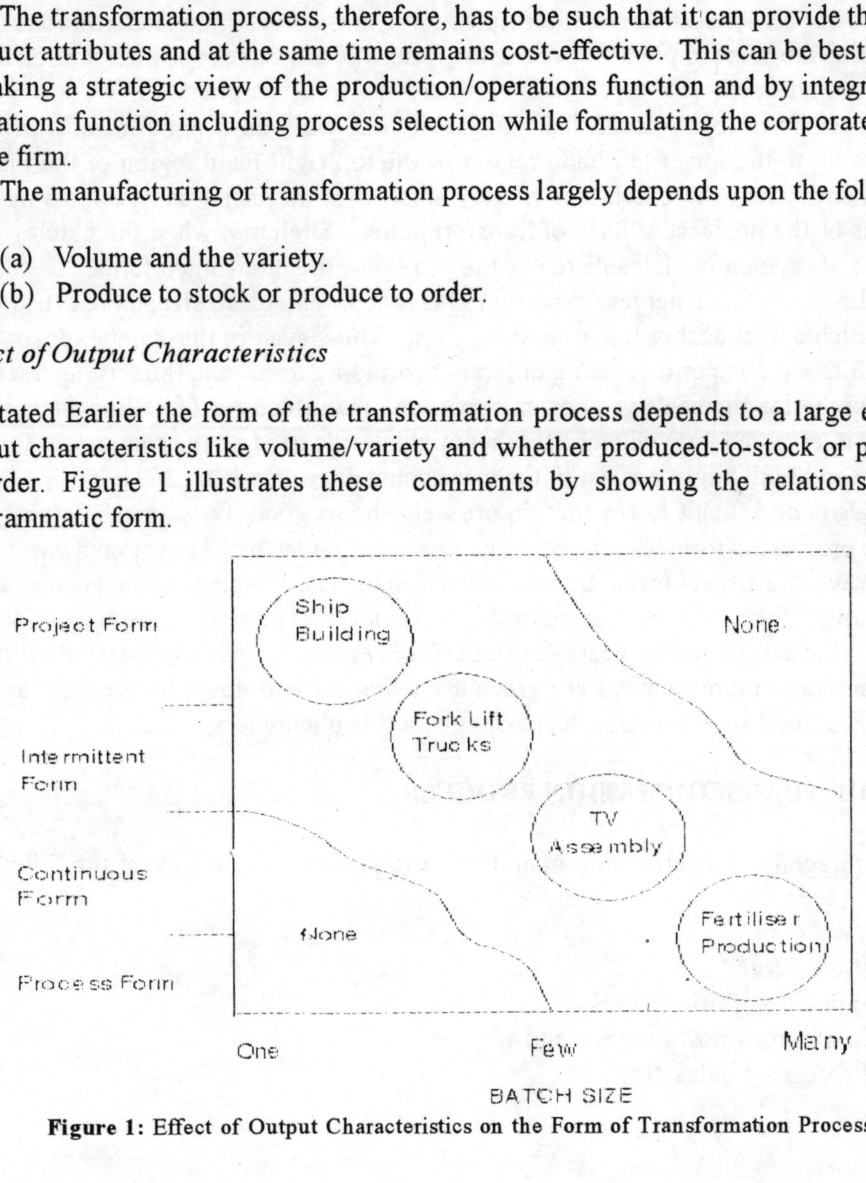

Figure 1: Effect of Output Characteristics on the Form of Transformation Process

In figure 1 the horizontal axis which shows the output chracteristics is represented in terms of the batch size. On one extreme we have products produced in batches of size one, i.e. each product is different from the other. On the other extreme we have products produced in infinitely large batch sizes. Thses are products with no variety and have the characteristics of a commodity like fertiliser, sugar, cement etc.

The form of transformation process is similarly represented on the vertical axis. The top end represents the project form where each project is followed by another project. No two projects are exactly alike and detailed planning, scheduling and monitoring has to be performed to keep the project costs and durations under control. As we go down the vertical axis the flow of materials becomes more smooth and uniform. These can be categorised as batch production or interrupted form, mass production or continuous form, and finally, as the name implies the processing form wherein there is no interruption in the flow of materials at all, as in a petroleum refinery or a fertiliser plant.

However, it is to be noted from Figure I that we would not find any process corresponding to the lower left hand region or the top right hand region of the Figure. That is to say, when the batch size is very small it is not at all advisable to use the continuous or the processing form of transformation. Similarly, when the batch size is really large, it is again inadvisable to use the project or the interrupted form.

Another point that emerges from Figure I is that for any batch size, there is usually a choice available in choosing the processing form. Thus, even in the same industry one may find different competitors using different processing forms and thus trying to create a special niche for themselves. For example, one manufacturer of ceiling fans might choose the interrupted form whereas another might decide to adopt the continuous form of production and both might coexist in the same competitive market.

It is also not difficult to see that Figure I also holds good for services (except that there is no processing from for service). The service provided by a lawyer on a law-suit is almost always of a project form. Services provided by a government agency is usually of the interrupted form whereas for some high volume services the continuous form is employed. In fact, in recent years, as the service sector is growing faster than other sectors, more and more services are gradually being pushed down the vertical axis of Figure I. Fast food service is a typical example of this phenomenon.

FORMS OF TRANSFORMATION PROCESS

From the foregoing it is clear that manufacturing process can be any of the following forms :

(a) Project form,
(b) Intermittent flow process,
(c) Continuous flow process, and
(d) Processing industries.

Rest of the paper is devoted to describing each of the above mentioned process forms highlighting their characterstics, advantages, disadvantages and the modern trends.

THE PROJECT FORM

Project operations are characterised by complex sets of time-bound activities that must be performed in a particular order. Distinctly different from all other forms of transformation process each project has a definite beginning and a definite completion, the project form of transformation is very useful when complex tasks involving many different functional specialisations have to be performed against deadlines.

If the output of the transformation process is a product, such products are generally characterised by immobility during the transformation. Such operations are referred to as Fixed Position assembly and can be seen in the production of ships, aircrafts, and construction of buildings, roads, etc. As projects have limited lives, a project team is usually setup to manage a project. Resources such as men, materials and equipment are brought together for the duration of the project. Some materials are consumed in the transformation process, while others like equipment and personnel are redeployed for other uses at the end of the project.

The fast pace of technological developments is forcing many companies to adopt to the new technologies. Such developments are taking place not only in the manufacturing technologies but also in packaging technology, material handling technology, computer technology and so on. Implimenting a change is usually carried out through a project operation. Increased competition, similarly, is forcing companies to launch projects on cost reduction, higher productivity, better methods and so on.

Characteristics of Project form

Project operations are different from other forms of transformation process in the way resources are organised and deployed as also in the planning and control of various activities that constitute the project. Some of the characterstics of project operation are as under :

(a) Short life cycle,
(b) Consequent personnel problem,
(c) Matrix organisation, and
(d) Importance of scheduling and control.

INTERMITTENT FLOW PROCESSES

Referring to Figure I, the intermittent process form is generally suitable when the variety is large and consequently the volumes are low. The transformation process should be able to take care of this large variety and also in a manner that the cost of the processing is not excessive.

Characterstics of the intermittent form

Some important characterstics of the intermittent form are as given below :

(a) Flexibility,
(b) Organised around standard operations,
(c) Excessive Material handling and in-process inventery, and
(d) Difficulty in management of resources.

Advantages of the Intermittent Form

In transformation processes, there is always a trade-off between flexibility of operations and the efficiency of use of resources. Intermittent transformation processes are chosen whenever flexibility is considered more important than mere efficiency. Other advantages of this process from are:

(a) Variety at Low Cost,
(b) High Capacity Utilisation, and
(c) Staff Advantages.

Disadvantages of the Intermittent Form

The intermittent form will not remain the best form of processing if the volumes for some outputs become high. The in-process inventories could become excessively high and the operations planning and control could get out of hand necessitating the use of expediters. A few other disadvantages are:

(a) More Costly for High Volume,
(b) Complex Operations Planning and Control, and
(c) Large In-process Inventory.

Modern Trends in the Technology for Intermittent Flow Operations

There have been quite a few developments towards increasing the efficiency of intermittent flow operations. Many of these developments are based on using the computer for many planning and control activities and some, like group technology, are based on using continuous flow principles for outputs which have a large variety.

Computerised Production and Inventory Control Systems—Many different types of computer packages are available which can link the input and output requirements, check with the inventory at hand and automatically raise purchase orders and also prepare different types of statements for planning and control purposes. Given a schedule of output requirements, the computer can work out the requirement of raw material and other bought out items and can plan the procurement and production of these so that there is no hold up of production due to non-availability of material.

Integrated Computer—Aided Manufacturing- These computer packages tie up the previous systems with mechanical systems that control machinery and material handling equipment. These packages do not carry out manufacturing of parts alone but also process planning, costing, tool design, production planning, material ordering etc. The rate of development in this area is extremely rapid and is also accelerating. Computers are used for both planning as well as execution of the plans.

Manufacturing Resource Planning (MRP II)—If the computerised production and inventory control systems could be linked with other planning and accounting systems of organisation, it would result in comprehensive computer packages on manufacturing resource planning. Such a system would integrate marketing, finance, personnel, payroll and other systems and can prepare statements on funds requirement, promotional need, capacity planning and so on.

Group Technology—Group technology has developed over the years to become a complete philosophy rather than a single technique .The common thread running through all these techniques is the attempt to find groups which can be used in organising the transformation process. The purpose of grouping is to overcome some of the disadvantages of intermittent flow processing as outlined above and the grouping can be of component parts, machines, equipment and people.

In general, component parts are grouped into families so that the processing required for members of a family is similar. The machines and equipment are also grouped into cells so that the volumes through a cell are higher and the variety smaller. Therefore, the principles used in continuous flow processing can be used for each of these groups.

The benefits expected from group technology are really fourfold :

(a) Reduced amounts of time and costs because the nature of operations and their sequence is similar for a family of component parts.
(b) Reduced material handling as the machines and equipment in a cell are physically close to each other.
(c) Shorter throughput times as the waiting period between operations is minimal.
(d) Reduced in-process inventories, again because of minimal waiting between operations.

CONTINUOUS FORM

As distinct from intermittent flow processes, all outputs are treated alike in this form of processing and the workflow is thus relatively continuous. The production process is therefore geared to produce one output, perhaps with some options added on. The variety is small and volumes are high thus making it worthwhile to focus the transformation process on the output. This would mean arranging the facilities in the sequence in which they are required for the output, using high speed special purpose machines, laying out the facilities to minimise the movement of materials and designing the production system so that there are no bottlenecks as well as no idle time for any of the resources.

Characteristics of Continuous Flow Processes

The continuous process form is characterised by relatively standardised outputs and consequent fixed inputs, fixed sequence of operations and also fixed processing time. As the variation from one output to another is very samll, the transformation process is selected and designed to maximise the efficiency of the resources and in the process flexibility of operations is sacrificed. In other words, it is characterised by the following:

(a) High Volumes,
(b) Easier Planning and Control, and
(c) Linear Workflow.

Advantages of the Continuous Form

The continuous form of processing requires a great deal of effort while designing. But once implemented, it offers many simplicities in its operation. Some of its advantages are:

(a) Low Unit Cost,
(b) Lower Operator Skills, and
(c) Simpler Managerial Control.

Disadvantages of the Continuous Form

Although the continuous form of processing offers a low cost alternative when volume of production is high and the variety low, there are some disadvantages in organising the production in this form which are listed as under.

(a) Difficult to Adapt,
(b) Possibilities of Stoppage of Line,
(c) Balancing the Line,
(d) Low Worker Morale, and
(e) High Initial Cost.

Continuous Form Versus Process Form

The processing industries e.g. fertiliser, petrochemicals, petroleum, milk, drugs, etc. also use continuous processing. However, they deserve a special mention as they differ from organisations producing either discrete products or services. In general , the operations in these organisations are highly automated with very sophisticated controls, often electronic or computerised. The labour requirements are generally low and the role of the production workers is limited to monitoring and taking some corrective action if necessary. However , maintenance of equipment is very critical and the skills required in maintenance are of high order.

A Single Input—In processing industries, there is usually a single principle input material which is processed into one or more different products. In discrete manufacturing, on the other hand, there are many different materials which are processed and assembled to form the product.

Analytic and Synthetic Processes—In an analytic process, a single input is processed into many separate outputs. A typical example would be a petroleum refinery, where the single input, viz. petroleum is processed into petrol, diesel naphtha, furnace oil and a host of other intermediates. In a synthetic process, on the other hand, many different inputs are synthesised into one output. Processing industries generally use analytic processes where as continuous flow processing in discrete manufacturing generally use synthetic processes.

Continouous Processing—In spite of the differences mentioned above, there is a basic similarity in the concept as well as the approach followed in both flow shops and the processing industries—only variety in outputs is nil so far as processing industries are concerned. Because of this, automation could be carried out to its physical limits and the process is designed for a specific mix of outputs. The result is that initial set up of equipment and procedures is even more complex and critical than for continuous flow processing.

Modern Trends in the Technology for Continuous Flow Process

Recent developments in computer applications have had their effect on continuous flow operations as well. The attempt in all this is to increase the flexibility of production and assembly lines.

CNC/DNC—Machines and processes which have been automated using some form of electronic system are said to use numerical control or NC. In the early machines, instructions for machine control were coded on punched paper tapes to be read by tape readers. In CNC (Computer Numerical Control) machines, relatively simple programmes can be stored in the umemory of the computer and so it is not necessary to read the control tape for every item manufactured. This is an advantage since the control tapes and the associated tapes readers are among the most unreliable components of an NC machine.

In DNC (Direct Numerical Control) machines, programmes for a number of NC machines are stored in a single computer of large capacity than the type used in CNC. Also, the integration of a number of machines and processes by one computer enables a set of machines to work as a manufacturing system, with scheduling and process monitoring. Automation by numerical control can be thought of as soft automation as this allows fast changeovers form one component part to another.

Robotics—According to the Robot Institute of America," A robot is a reprogrammable multi-functional manipulator designed to move material, parts, tools or specialised devices through variable programmed motions for the performance of a variety of tasks." Robots have come in a big way in the task of moving, transferring and manipulating materials in between operations as well as during some specialised operations. An industrial Robot has three principal components:

(a) One or more arms, usually situated in a fixed base, that can move in several directions.
(b) A manipulator, being the "hand" that holds the tool or the part to be worked.
(c) A controller that gives detailed movement instructions.

Robotics is helping continuous flow processes to changeover from one output to another since the material handling equipment which was earlier designed as part of a production or assembly line, can now be independently programmed.

CAD/CAM/CAE—This trilogy of terms stands for Computer Aided Design(CAD), Computer Aided Manufacturing (CAM) and Computer Aided Engineering(CAE), In these systems, the computer aids in the design process by providing different images of the designed product from different views—the computer screen acting as the designer's drawing board. The CAM ties the NC machines with the material handling equipment so the manufacturing operations are working together. In CAE, the computer is used to aid in analysing engineering problems, particularly structured analysis where the structure has previously been designed using CAD. In its widest sense, these imply the automation using computer control of all activities necessary to take a product from concept to its completed manufacture.

Flexible Manufacturing—Current usage of the term flexible manufacturing relates to automated manufacture. Traditionally, automation in manufacturing has been possible only for high volume low variety products where the production process adopted had been of the continuous flow process form. Such process had suffered from inflexibility—not only in terms of output characteristics but also of output. In flexible manufacturing an attempt is made to introduce flexibility not only in terms of component design but also operation sequence, batch sizes and overall production capacity. Flexible, manufacturing tries to combine the advantages of conventional automation with the strategic advantages attached to intermittent processing viz , increased variety, improved response to customer orders, updated product designs etc.

CONCLUSION

An attempt has been made in the paper to describe various process forms which every manufacturing industry can adopt. Their characterstics alongwith relevant advantages/ disadvantages too have been highlighted. Never-the-less the four forms of manufacturing processes that have been referred to in this paper are really four simplified extremes of what is likely to be observed in practice. We will find very few organisations using only one of these processing forms in its pure sense. Infact most organisations combine two or more of these process forms to produce defferent components and the final product.

However the modern trends in the manufacturing technology, like group technology, flexible manufacturing, use of CAD/CAM/CAE and roboticsare paving the way for use of the process forms in their somewhat pure form as they tend to eliminate the inherent disadvantages and incorporate the advantages of the other process form.

VII

ENVIRONMENT CONCERNS IN MANUFACTURING

EFFECT OF SHIELDING GASES ON THE PERFORMANCE OF WELD BEAD IN MIG WELDING

36

A. Chenna Kesava Reddy,[1] K. Gokul,[2] P. Mahesh,[2] G. Sudharshan Reddy[2] and C.R. Suresh[2]

Dept. of Mechanical Engg., M.J.C.E.T.,[1]
Road No. 3, Banjarahills, Hederabad - 500 034

Students, Dept. of Mechanical Engineering,[2]
M.J.C.E.T, Road No 3, Banjara Hills, Hyderabad -500034.

ABSTRACT

The function of a shielding gas is to protect the molten metal and the electrode end against atmospheric contamination. The major shielding gases used for metal inert gas (MIG) welding are argon, helium and carbon dioxide. In order to study the effects of these three shielding gases and which gas combination provides the best overall performance and economic advantages, a series of experimental welds were performed employing various gas mixtures and straight uses of argon, helium and carbon dioxide. Only when no shielding gas was used, the evidence of atmospheric contamination has been found. It appears that the amount of spatter is directly proportional to the amount of carbon dioxide used in the shielding gas. Straight carbon dioxide produced the deepest penetration, but also the worst weld surface appearance. Weld bead profile and finish were significantly enhanced by the addition of either helium or argon.

INTRODUCTION

Shielding gas serves to keep harmful atmospheric gases, such as oxygen, hydrogen and nitrogen away from the weld as the molten metal solidifies. These elements, when not effectively kept away from the liquid metal as it solidifies, produce in ferrous metals the majority of weld defects, such as porosity, blowholes and weld brittleness. Therefore, the type of shielding gas used can have a profound effect upon many of the weld and base metal properties as well as the finished weld bead appearance.

Effect of Oxygen

Oxygen is a major element in gas contamination of the weld metal as it is present in significant quantities in the electrode wire. Oxygen is also present in the atmosphere, in the parent metal as oxide or scale. Oxygen may be absorbed into the weld, forming iron oxide. Iron oxide may react with carbon in the steel to form carbon monoxide resulting in blowholes. If iron oxide is present, oxidation of the weld will occur and this will produce a great increase in the grain size. Absorption of oxygen by weld reduces its tensile strength and ductility and decreases its corrosive resistance.

Effect of Hydrogen

The main source of hydrogen is the atmosphere. Hydrogen begins to diffuse out of the weld metal immediately after the welding process and continues to do so over a long period. The presence of hydrogen reduces the tensile strength of the weld, makes the arc erratic and contributes to the formation of micro cracks or larger cracks.

Effect of Nitrogen

Nitrogen is present in the parent metal, the electrode wire and in the atmosphere. Because of its solubility in iron at the elevated temperature, nitrogen precipitates out of the iron as it cools, forming iron nitride. Nitrogen tends to increase tensile strength and hardness, decrease ductility and impact resistance and also lowers the corrosion resistance.

EXPERIMENTAL SET UP

In the metal inert gas (MIG) welding process, a consumable wire was fed at a preset speed through a welding torch where in it was provided the electrical connection and the shielding gas. The arc, which was struck by direct contact between the wire electrodes and the work piece, was maintained at a constant length by the interaction of electrical parameters. The system was made sensitive by the use of constant voltage power source and thin welding wire. The welding parameters are given in Table-1. The chemical composition of electrode wire is given in Table-2. The base metal is mild steel. The welding set up is shown in Fig 1.

SHIELDING GASES

The major shielding gases used for MIG welding are argon, helium and carbondioxide.

Argon

It is a non-consumable, non-expensive gas obtained from air by deep refrigeration and fractionation, wherein it is present to the extent of 0.93%. It is about 23% heavier than air. Argon is non-toxic but can cause as phyxiation in confined spaces by replacing the air. In a standard cylinder, the gas is kept under a pressure of 15 N/mm^2.

TABLE 1 : **Welding Parameters**

Parameters	Units	Quantity
Welding current	amp	280
Wire diameter	mm	1.2
Wire-feed speed	mm/sec	146.7
Melting rate	kg/hour	4.66
Air travel speed	mm/sec	6.17
Electrode extension	mm	21.6
Gas feed rate	litre/min	15
Pre heat and inter pass temperature	ºC	120-150
Position	—	FLAT

TABLE 2 : **Composition of Wire Electrode**

Particular	% By Weight
Carbon	0.11
Manganese	1.49
Silicon	0.82
Phosphorous	0.02
Sulphur	0.015
Oxygen	0.0095
Iron	97.53 (Remainder)

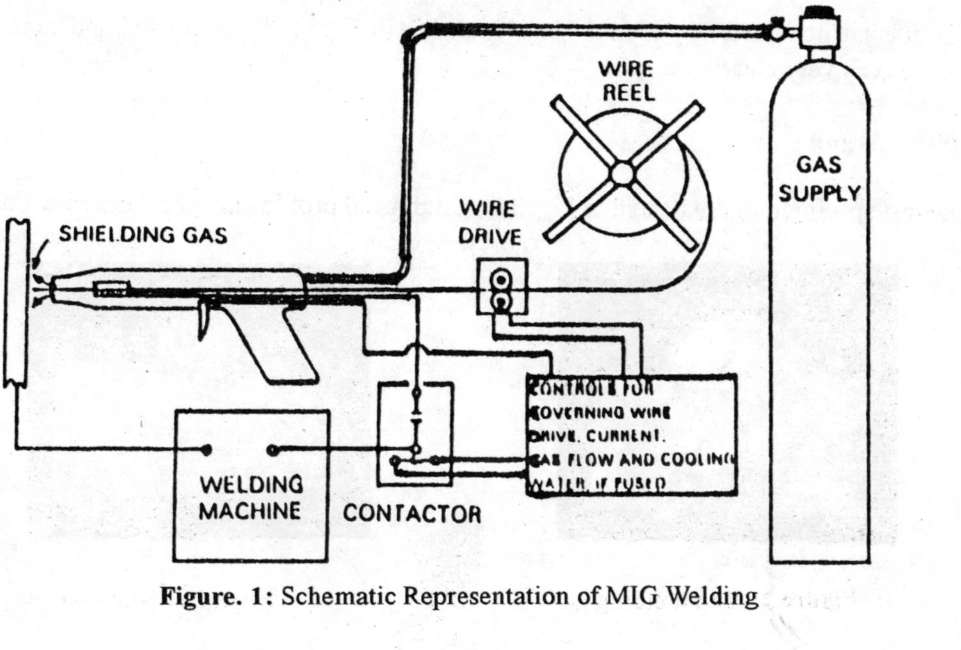

Figure. 1: Schematic Representation of MIG Welding

Helium

It is a rare gas. It is present in atmosphere to the extent of only 0.52×10^{-3} %. It is a light gas weighing only 1/7th that of air. This complicates the weld pool protection and results in increased gas consumption on account of its high cost, helium is comparatively less used inert gas. It is stored in standard gas cylinder under a pressure of 15N/mm.^{2}

Carbondioxide

It is a colourless gas with a slightly perceptible odour. When dissolved in water it gives a acidic taste. It is about 1.5 times heavier than air. Industrially, carbondioxide is prepared by calcination of coke or anthracite in specially designed boiler fire boxes. A standard 40 litre cylinder holds 25 kg of liquid which produces about 15 m^3 of gas on evaporating. The pressure of the gas in the cylinder depends on the temperature which goes down as more gas is tapped from the cylinder.

A series of experimental welds were performed employing various gas mixtures and straight uses of argon, helium and carbondioxide.

RESULTS AND DISCUSSIONS

Weld beads were made on flat test plates and the test results are discussed.

EFFECT ON BEAD CHARACTERISTICS

No Shielding gas

The effect of no shielding gas on the bead is shown in Fig. 2. Weld porosity and inclusions can be seen very clearly.

100% Argon

The test specimen as illustrated in Fig. 3 has high bead profile and poor penetration. The

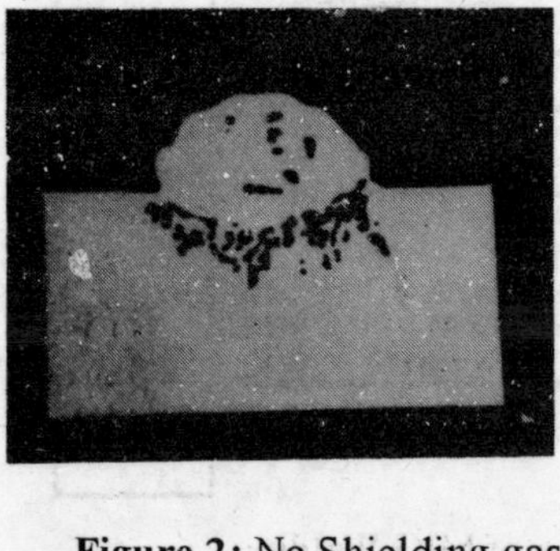

Figure 2: No Shielding gas

Figure 3: 100% Ar

surface appearance was rough with a number of high and low spots. 100% Argon as a shielding gas is not recommendable because of its high cost and poor penetration.

100% Carbondioxide

The specimen shown in Fig. 4 exhibits a medium rough and irregular surface having a slightly inconsistent bead height and width. It also reveals small glassy scales along the edges. The bead ripples were not uniform. The use of only carbon dioxide produced on aggressive, violent arc and large amounts of spatter around the plate surface. There is deep weld penetration. Formation of large spatter would be most undesirable, considering operator safety and comfort and also be a nuisance to remove from welded products requiring clean surface.

80% Carbondioxide, 20% Argon

This mixture doesn't produce either a good bead appearance or profile, and it was narrow and irregular in shape with a high bead profile. Fig. 5 reveals a narrow finger of penetration with evidence of unfused metal along the outer edges, as well as an apparent increase in the amount of weld spatter.

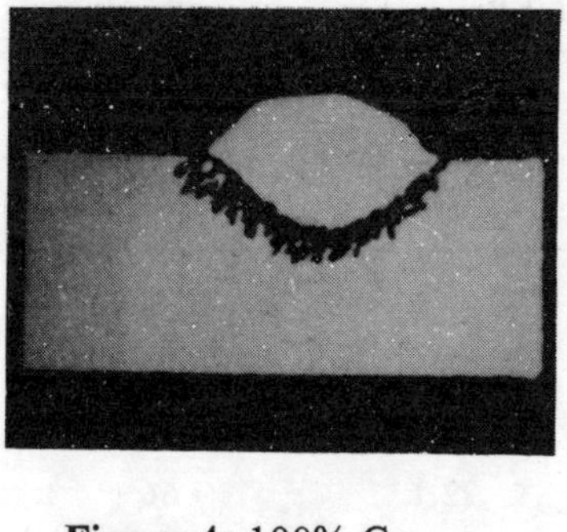

Figure 4: 100% Co_2

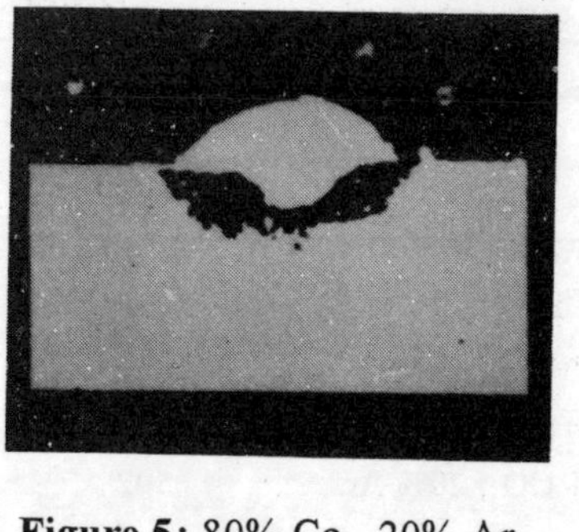

Figure 5: 80% Co_2, 20% Ar

80% Carbondioxide, 20% Helium

This mixture proved to produce good results. The weld bead profile and surface finish of the specimen were excellent as shown Fig. 6. The penetration is deeper and more uniform.

60% Carbondioxide, 20% Argon, 20% Helium

The base surface appearance was nearly the same as that of 80% carbon dioxide and 20% Helium, with a little less regularity in the bead rippling. The penetration is uniform and broader (Fig. 7).

Figure 6: 80% Co_2, 20% He

Figure 7: 60% Co_2, 20% Ar, 20% He

EFFECT ON ALL -WELD PROPERTIES

The mechanical properties of weld beads performed with different gas mixtures are given in Table 3. The mechanical properties are improved using gas mixture of 80% carbondioxide and 20% Helium. This gas mixture exhibits high tensile strength and low impact strength. This might be due to deeper and uniform penetration and reduced loss of alloying elements in the form of spatter.

TABLE 3 : **All Weld Metal Properties**

Gas Mixtures	Tensile strength N/mm2	Yield strength N/mm2	Elongation %	Reduction of Area %	Impact strength J
100%CO_2	538	422	26.9	68	67
80% CO_2, 20% Ar	562	435	25.6	68	64
80% CO_2, 20% He	609	490	24.9	66	35
60% CO_2, 20% Ar, 20% He	592	485	22.1	66	63

CO_2 : Carbon dioxide

#Ar : Argon

#He : Helium

CONCLUSION

There was an evidence of atmospheric contamination of weld bead when the shielding gas was not employed. It appears that the amount of spatter is directly proportional to the amount of carbon dioxide used in the shielding gas. The use of carbon dioxide only produced the deepest penetration, but also the worst surface appearance. Weld bead profile and finish were significantly improved by the addition of argon or helium.

Helium had a greater effect in controlling the amount of spatter than did argon when added with the higher percent mixtures of carbon dioxide. The best over all performance including cost advantages for a given shielding gas used in MIG welding of mild steel was achieved by using a gas mixture of 80% carbon dioxide and 20% Helium. This mixture produced good weld bead profile appearance, uniform and deep penetration with improved all-weld metal properties.

REFERENCES

1. Allum, C.J., *MIG Welding—Time for Assessment*, Metal Construction, Vol. 15, No. 6, pp. 347-53, June 1983.
2. Aroin, M., *Synergic Pulse MIG Welding*, Metal Construction, Vol. 13, No. 6, pp. 349-53, June 1981.
3. Cooksey, C.J. and MIlner, D.R., *Metal Transfer in Gas Shielded Welding, Physics of Welding Arc —A Symposium*, IIW, London, pp. 123-32, 1966.
4. Ma, Jilong and APPS, R.L., *MIG Transfer Discovery of Importanc to Industry, Welding and Metal Fabrication*, Vol. 52, No. 7, pp. 307-16, 1982.
5. Ma, Jilong and APPS, R.L., *Analyzing Metal Transfer during MIG Welding*, Welding and Metal Fabrication, Vol. 51, No. 3, pp. 119-28, 1983.
6. Ma, Jilong and APPS, R.L., *New MIG Process Results From Metal Transfer Mode Control*, *Ibid*, Vol. 51, No. 4, pp. 168-75, 1983.
7. Parmer, R.S., *Development of Consumable for Gas Metal Arc Welding Processes*, Paper 7, Seminar on Welding Equipment's & Process Trends, The Indian Institute of Welding (Delhi), New Delhi, Feb 11 - 12, 1983.

AIR POLLUTION IN FOUNDRIES
A Comparative Study

37

Prof. J.M. Gadgil, Prof. M.R. Gidde and Prof. S.K. Gajendragadkar
Bharati Vidyapeeth's College of Engineering,
Dhanakawali, Pune

INTRODUCTION

The foundry industry which dates back to Harapan period has witnessed an impressive growth in the post independence period on account of progressive policies adopted by the Government. However, rapid industrial development has led to several miseries and one of them is pollution.

The foundry industry has been accused as one of the culprits of air pollution and solid waste generation. The numerous manufacturing process of casting involve a great number of operation. All the processes are accompanied by the evolution of dust and gas in large quantities. The metallic fumes, silica dust and various gases are the main pollutants. The metallic fumes consist of oxides of metals, dust and gases.

Study conducted by Mujumdar in the South India Foundry indicate that the dust levels are much above the allowable standard prescribed. When exposed to the dusty atmosphere, particles less than 5 microns are found to escape the nasal track and are deposited into the lung air sack (alveoli). This causes natural reduction of elasticity of fabrous tissues in the lung resulting in shortness in breath. A general term used for dust disease is pnenoconiosis. In foundry atmosphere the free silica content of the moulding sand result in silicosis.

Iron oxide emanated during the melting and pouring operation, may cause siderosis or pigmentation of lung. These dust disease can be controlled by regulating the dust in the environment. When the molten metal is poured into the mould the sand nearer to it, is burnt.

The chemical emitted into atmosphere is addition to those allocayed with the traditional moulding and core making material such as clay bonded and oil bonded sand are placing an increasing load on the foundry working environment and that of the immediate neighbourhood of the foundry.

Faced with such an array of potential problems the foundry men needs to have as much up to date information as possible about the working environment and the effects.

MATERIALS AND METHODS

Monitoring of foundry environment was carried out in the following types of foundries and furnaces:

— Cast Iron A, C, E, F
— Steel B, D
— Cupola A, F
— Electric arc B,
— Electric Induction D, E
— Channel type C,

In the foundry itself, considering the various processes, the various locations were selected.

The instrument used was HVS. The Whatman make glass fibre filter was used for SPM determination. The instrument was kept as near as possible to the foundry process.

Also the ambient air quality outside the foundry was determined.

RESULTS

The data collected from six foundries with different types of furnaces and capacity had revealed some partinent facts about SPM concentration levels inside the factory and outside ambient air. The SPM levels varied with:

1. Location of different units vis a vis each other
2. The quality of scrap used
3. The method pouring the molten mass

TABLE 1: **SPM Concentration at Various Locations**

Sr. No.	Location/Foundries	A	B	C	D	E	F
1	Sand Mixing	—	—	—	1166	1228	3489
2	Core making	—	—	—	—	—	1667
3	Moulding	1284	—	1591	—	—	1663
4	Near furnace	2492	3680	2700	857	3680	856
5	Metal pouring	—	2988	3032	—	—	928
6	Knock out	2512	7636	4875	1983	2685	—
7	Finishing	—	1032	—	1032	1030	4442
8	Exit door	—	1904	—	1904	—	—
9	Outside the foundry	1290	555	2634	855	1250	430

All conc. in micrograms/m^3

TABLE 2: **SPM Conc According to Type of Furnace**

Sr. No.	Type of Furnace	Dist in M	SPM conc in ug/m^3
1	Cupola	3	2492
2	Electric Arc	5	3680
3	Electric induction	3	857
4	Channel type	3	2700

TABLE 3: **Chemical Composition of Dust Evolved in Cupola**

	Contents of components % (by mass)				
Blast	SiO_2	Fe_2O_3	CaO	Al_2O_3	MnO_2
Hot	30.35	24.45	4.28	2.78	1.90
Cold	28.00	22.18	3.66	3.04	1.52

4. Type of furnace

Based on the monitoring results the typical, distribution of SPM concentration levels in various section of the foundry can be discussed based on the above specific factors.

1. SPM concentration is maximum where the electric arc furnace is used because of open dipping of electrodes into furnace. Higher the capacity of furnace it was found that higher the SPM concentration. In a particular foundry (C) the borings are used for charging the furnace. This foundry showed three times more concentration of SPM than the foundry (D) using cleaned and pure scrap. Whereever (C) the burnt sand is used for moulding the conc. of SPM observed was 66% more than the places where clean sand is used. As compared to the other foundry processes the knock out operation showed 2-3 times more concentration. At the sand mixing places the wet method showed 36% less concentration than dry method. It is also found that the dust clouds are emitted into atmosphere during pouring of sand into mullers. At the steel foundry where the electric induction furnace is used the SPM concentration is found to be least. This is because of controlled melting process and use of pure scrap.

2. In most of the cases the pollutants emitted from different processes in the foundry are naturally dispersed out of the foundry. The results showed ambient SPM conc. higher than Ambient Air Quality standards within range of 20 to 30% higher. In a foundry where resin bonded sand especially formaldehyde based resin there is every possibility that the emissions from burning sand may contain hydrocarbons. However, in the present study the analysis of these gases was not done due to non-availability of appropriate facilities. Therefore, as far as possible use of chemical bonded sand should be avoided to prevent emissions of hazardous gases.

3. In a foundry where the measures are taken to disperse pollutants by installing the fans at various locations the conc. of SPM observed was less as compared to other foundries. This shows the necessity of adopting proper ventilation system to disperse the pollutants. Generally the cooling area is neglected from environmental point of view. When castings are cooled, burning of sand is still continuously going on resulting in emissions of smoke. Proper control measures should be taken to prevent this pollution. The cooling area should be isolated and provided with proper ventilation units in such a way that these emission will be driven out easily and may not create environmental problems to indoor air. After cleaning the castings these are sent for finishing. At these places the grinders are used. This process is found to create noise pollution as level reaches to 90-100 dB. By using ear plugs the effect of noise pollution can be reduced.

4. The air temp. near the furnace is found to be about 44 deg. C. This increase in temp. results in reducing efficiency of workers. Proper air cooling system will provide better working environment. The workers in the foundry are not using the protective equipments. Even some of the workers work bare footed. This due to lack of knowledge of pollutional problems. This indicates strong need of creating awareness among the workers about the environmental hazards associated with the different processes inside the foundry. In general it is found that the pollutional level inside and outside the foundry is at higher level. Proper control measures should be adopted to protect the health of workers.

CONCLUSIONS

1. The SPM concentration inside the foundry is from 1500 mic. gm/Nm3 at finishing operation to 4500 mic.gm/Nm3 at fettling operation. The ambient air concentration of SPM at various foundries is from 500 mic.gm/Nm3 to 1200 mic.gm/Nm3. This is 2.5 times more than the ambient air quality standards.
2. In iron foundries, harmful substances like NO_2, SPM, SO_2 are evolved in cupola furnaces. It is necessary to take all possible measures for improving the manufacturing processes, perfecting the equipment used, introducing effective system to remove the waste gases from the foundry to minimise the level of pollution.
3. The castings should be extracted from moulds and cleaned in isolated places with respect to other processes.
4. Human handling should be minimised at processes where excessive dust emissions takes place.
5. All the equipments viz. Mullers, Ovens, Shot Blasting Machine should be air tight to prevent leakages of SPM.
6. Processing equipments mainly furnace should be provided with fume extraction system to take out the emissions from the places where they are generated.
7. The shot blasting unit is a source of high dust concentrations. Problems usually arise due to leaking seals, insufficient extraction as a result of blocked in the

ducts or binding of fabric filters. These should be avoided as far as possible by proper and regular maintenance.

8. The monthly examination and testing of extraction system is necessary.
9. At the pedestal grinding the wheel should be enclosed and SPM should be extracted.
10. Proper casting design and production practices shall be followed by removal of protruding parts.
11. The workers should be provided with protective equipments like Gas Masks, Goggles, Aprons, shoes, helmet, ear plugs, etc.
12. The ways and means should be devised to educate the workers to make use of these personal protective equipments.
13. At the sand preparation plant the sand should be made slightly wet to avoid evolution of dust cloud.
14. Mixing and preparation of sand should be done in closed equipment.
15. The pure and cleaned scrap should be used for charging of furnace.
16. Baking of cores is done in ovens. These should be provided with proper extraction system.
17. To control emissions from cupola modification of conventional furnace to blast fuel efficient furnace should be done. And also coke to metal ratio of 1:4—1:5 should be improved to 1:8—1:10. Cupola should be provided with air blast control. Air pollution control equipment (fabric filter) should be installed to reduce the emissions.
18. Fans should be provided near furnace, mullers, grinders.
19. Clean and new sand should be used for moulding.

BIBLIOGRAPHY

1. J.G. Morley, "The Environmental Effects of Moulding and Coremaking Processes", *Indian Foundry Journal*, Oct. 1992.
2. S. Andonyev, O. Filipyev, '*Dust and Fume Generation in the Iron and Steel Industry*', MIR Publishers.
3. M. Lakshmanan and O.V. Krishnaiah Chetty, 'Evaluation of dust hazard index in ferrous foundries', *Indian Foundry Journal*, January 1990.
4. Terry Blackman, "*Dust and Fume Control in the Fettling and Dressing Shop*", The Foundryman, March 1993.
5. R.P. Sharma, "Environmental Management in Foundry Industries", *IFJ*, May 1990.
6. 'Industrial Ventilation' 18th edition, American Conference of Governmental Industrial Hygienists.

VIII

POSTDATED PAPERS

RECLAMATION AND REBUILDING OF COMPONENTS

38

Maj. Rajiv Joshi

636, EME BN HQ, Central Command, Lucknow.

INTRODUCTION

1. Equipment management in today's mechanised Army is one of the most important Command function. The mordernisation of the armed forces, trying to keep pace with the fast changing environment, has led to introduction of a variety of sophisticated equipment both indegenous and imported. The variety of small population equipment has complicated the inventory management process so much that it has become virtually impossible for all echelons of repair to have an inventory which can solve the downtime problem. The deployment of the equipment in the far flung areas along the vast border of the nation has further complicated the issue.

2. The financial crunch has forced us to retain the equipment in service for double or even more than double of its life planned at the time of inception. This has led to extinction of a well planned spares back up of such equipment. The disintegration of USSR worsened the situation for the back up of the imported equipment as a bulk of our equipment is of east Europian origin. All such factors put together has forced the managers of equipment to find a way out of this crisis.

THE PROCESS OF WEAR AND BREAKAGE

3. The continous usage of vehicles and equipment leads to wear and breakage of components. The phenomenon of wear and breakage is accelerated due to the extreme cliamatic condition in which the army equipment is deployed and stored The training of soldiers, the deployment in operations and the difficult terrain conditions lead to unusual wear and breakage of components which would have otherwise given a more prolonged life.

4. *Wear:* Wear is a relentless loss of material or material integrity caused by enviornment or enviornment innovatives. It is a surface phenomenon. The various parameters that promote wear are : Abrasion, erosion, corrosion, heat and frition.

5. Breakage on the other hand leads to a sudden failure of a component. It is caused due to cyclic fatigue, sudden loading of a part, irregularities in the composition of the parent metal or mishandling during transit, operation or storing.

RAPAIR

6. The wear or breakage of a component or an assembly renders an equipment or a vehicle out of action/off road. To restore the serviceability of the equipment or vehicle the broken/worn outcomponent has to be replaced and adjusted. The process of repair can thus be definend as a process to rectify defects and restore the equipment to a serviceable state by replacement/adjustment of defective components and or by simple basic process like carpentry, welding brazing or insulating wires etc. However this process will lead to certain minimum downtime which will depend upon the work involved and also to a great extent on the availability of the spares/components.

INVENTORY MANAGEMENT

7. To reduce downtime and increase availability, equipment management has gained significant importance in recent years. To eliminate failure which may result in unacceptable downtime or high non availability the stress is on building up of costly inventories or huge inventories of costly spares.

8. The problem of downtime or MTTR is solved to a great extent by this but this type of superfluous solution to solve this problem leads to financial strain because of :

(a) Huge capital block in building up of inventory of Spares.
(b) Spare parts and assemblies are very expensive and every year Crores of rupees are spend for purchase of new spare parts.
(c) The inventory carrying cost is also 50% of the value of inventory.

9. In army though cost is not an overriding factor however handling of a huge inventory at various levels is definatly a cause for concern. The variety of equipment being handled by each echelon of repair is so vast that it leads to building up of huge inventory at all levels. Though the permissive repair schedule check building up of unwanted inventories at all levels but this also increases the downtime. A simple example is overhaul of jeep engines which is carried out as base repaires. The downtime in this case is two to three years which is almost half of the total life of the equipment which is seven years. The cost of spares and also the inventory cost can be reduced by :

(a) Minimizing wear—Protective methods
(b) Recycling the scrap—Curative methods
(c) Retrival-Process of removel for reuse of assemblies/components from the equipment declared fully unserviceable or unwanted surplus.

RECLAMATION AND REBUILDING

10. One of the methods to reduce cost of inventory is to rebuild and reclaim spares/ components by advance welding, metal depositing and machining techniques. This can considarably reduce the downtime at the same time keeping a ckeck on inventory built up.

11. *Reclamation*—It is a process by which a wornout part or component is restored its original condition i.e. original shape size and metallurgical properties and a useful life compatible with the expenditure incurred is obtained. Reclamation can also be defined as recycling of worn, damaged or degraded parts so as to bring their dimensions and strength to original or near original value, with the intention of using them again for a period close to the original life of the part.

12. *Rebuilding* —In this process surfacing is employed to restore the original dimensions of a worn part by adding metal of same or similar composition as the base metal. This can be considered as the first stage of reclamation. This process can be gainfully utilised to treat and recycle worn out/damaged components thereby accuring a considerable reduction the cost.

13. The factors that would be involved in the process are correct analysis of the wear, selection of the right components, choosing a correct procedure, taking proper precautions, using proper jigs and fixtures and finally data collection. A careful assesment of the above factors is extremely essential for a successful and economical reclamation programme. A successful reclamation programme would accomplish a number of advantages such as :

(a) increased service life of components.
(b) reduced maintenance costs.
(d) increased capacity utilisation of base workshops.
(e) reduced inventory of spares.
(f) reduced work load on all EME tradesmen.
(g) maximum availability of equipment to the user.

PROCESSES USED IN RECLAMATION

14. *Roto-Tec*—A revolutionary metal spraying technique enables us to restore worn out bearing surfaces of mechanical parts like shafts and journals etc. back to original or desiered dimensions. Because of the unique exothermic reaction of the bond coat powder (XUPER BOND) all roto-tec coatings are metallurgically bonded. It acquires the following :

(a) Temperature of the work piece never exceeds 250°C.
(b) Such coatings can withstand metal to metal frictional wear conditions excellently hence reclaimed parts can be expected to far out last the original

parts.

15. Roto-Tec torch can be mounted on tool parts or hand held. Spray pack modules lock in place on the gun, powder is gravity fed into the flame and propelled to the work piece. Oxygen and methane gas are used as fuel. The main advantages of this process are:

(a) The equipment is simple to understand and operate therefore no special skills are required and reclamation can be carried out quickly and easily.
(b) All undesirable effects of overheating are avoided.
(c) Can withstand metal to metal friction.
(d) The components reclaimed may out last original components due to controlled permeability.

16. *Eutalloy*—A metal joining process which combines the advantaes of the low heat input of brazing with greater strength and homogeneous joints obtained by fusion welding of the parent metal. The base metal is not brought to the fusion temp. The heat input is considerably diminished when compared with conventional fusion welding. The surface alloying is the result of diffusion of atoms from the eutactic alloy into the base metal. This diffusion process results in the formation of surface alloying between the base metal and the filler metal.

17. *Principle of Eutalloy*—"A block of salt melts if heated to 1400oF. If the same is combined with solvent it can be melted at 33°F." The advantages of this process are :

(a) Low heat input therefore minimum disturbance to the base metal.
(b) Prolonged life span of parts.
(c) Simple and easy to apply even on contaminated metal less time required for rebuildings and joining.

18. *Metallizing*—The basic difference in this process is that a wire is used instead of powder. With the help of an oxy-acetylene flame the wire being fed is melted and sprayed.

19. Once the metal deposition on rebuilding of the worn or damaged components is done with the help of one of the above methods the next step is to bring them to the original or desired dimensions by machining. Other than conventional the machining processes used are :

(a) Abrasive jet machining.
(b) Ultrasonic machining.
(c) Electro-chemical machining.
(d) Thermo-electrical machining:

  (i) Iorn beam machining,
  (ii) Plasma arc machining, and

(iii) Laser beam machining.

EXCLUSIVE RECLAMATON CELL

20. In case the reclamation is to be undertaken at a large scale as in the army base workshop in our case than a seperate organisation/section will have to be dedicated for this. The exclusive reclamation cell concept aims at running such a section/department which includes laboratary method of analysing wear, monitoring performance, intoroducing advance methods of reclamation and finally documenting the data on life and savings accrued.

21. *Preliminary Survey*—It includes firstly a complete survey of equipment and determining the fast moving components that are being scraped and secondly a through examination of spare part inventory, service life of component, downtime cost, cost in menhours, dismentalling and reassembling costs.

22. *Proposal for Treatment*—Once the scrap components have been identified and index diagnosis of the causes of breakage and wear is conducted the most effective product and process are recommened to comb the wear.

23. *Proposal for Savings*—The information provided in the initial survey and proposal for treatment provides a sound basis for an estimate of savings. These savings comprise of reduced cost in new part replacement, decrease in inventory carrying cost and downtime. The balance sheets drawn upto show cost and savings of each item. This gives an exact picture of how the programme would benifit the organisation.

24 *Applying Anti Wear Coatings*—Once the schedule is drawn up the parts are delivered regularly to the receipt section of exlusive reclamation cell. Work schedules are drawn up and reclaimation work is carried out as per process sheet. In certain cases jigs and fixtures are made for ease of welding prevention of distortion etc. The reclaimed components are stores scientifically for future use/issue.

25. *Management Information System*—The performance of components treated in the exclusive reclaimation cell is monitored and whose necessary changes are incorporated. This MIS includes documentation and monitoring of parts life treated in the cell.

26. RECLAMATION PROCESS OF AUTOMOTIVE ENGINE PARTS

Cylinder block and head

(a) Composition (in per cent) — Si — 6 — 10

Mg — .2 — .4

Al — balance

(b) Defect — Cracked

(c) Process —(i) Thoroughly clean the area of crack

(ii) Cut a 90 Vee grove along the lay of the crack

(iii) Drill a 1/8" hole on the start and end of the crack to avoid its further development.

(iv) Pre heat the block sufficiently but avoid over heating and also ensure it is protected from draught.

(v) Support the block on the table evenly to avoid warpage.

(vi) Weld by low temperature welding.

(vii) Allow the block to cool slowly at room temperature.

27. CRANK SHAFT

(a) Composition (in per cent)

C	—	0.14	—	0.21
Mn	—	0.25	—	0.55
Si	—	0.17	—	0.30
Cr	—	0.35	—	1.65
Ni	—	4.0	—	4.5
Fe	—	balance with traces of impurities		

(b) Defect — Worn out.

(c) Process — (i) Thoroughly clean the crank shaft.

(ii) Undercut the pins and journals keeping in view the minimum essential diameter required for bearing loads.

(iii) The building up operation is preceded by preparation of surface by roughning it.

(iv) Metal spray (Rototec, Eutalloy) and finish.

28. GUDGEON PIN

(a) Composition (in per cent)

C	—	1		
Ni	—	3	—	5
Cr	—	1		
Fe	—	balance		

(b) Defect — Worn out

(c) Process — This can be reclaimed by two processes.

(i) By plastic deformation where the pin is heated in an electric furnace upto austentic range and then a die of diameter little more than the internal dia of the pin is pressed through increasing dimensions of the pin. It is than quenched to the correct size.

(ii) The pin is ground on a very delicate ginder and then polishing is done. Then the component is chromeplated.

29. GEARS

The process of reclamation of gears is as under :

(a) Place the gear to be reclamed on a one CM thick pure copper sheet placed on steel sheet. Connect one terminal to the steel plate.
(b) Place the template conforming to the profile of gear around the gear.
(c) Build up worn teeth with a suitable electrode. The building up can be done in stages for thick gears.
(d) Finishing the built up profile by filling or machining.

30. Other components which can be gainfully reclamed in the base Workshops are:

(a) Body of small arms.
(b) Breech piece of small arms.
(c) Breech block of gun when guide ribs are worn out.
(d) Cradle of a gun.
(e) Pressure plates of vehicles.
(f) Shafts of all types.
(g) Gear of all types.

CONCLUSION

31. The circumstances in the country today demand that the expenditure on the Armed Forces be kept to the bearest minimum at the same time the mechanised army today needs more and more resources to keep the wheel moving. In such environment techniques like reclamation gain an great importance. As a maintenance engineer if we exploit the potential of this technique we can not only accrue gainful savings but also reduce the non-availabilty to great extent.

ENHANCING COMPONENT DESIGNS FOR MANUFACTURE THROUGH EXPERT SYSTEMS

39

Prahlada Rao K.,[1] Syam Sunder, V.,[2] and Venu Madhav, D.[3]

Lecturer in Mech. Engg., J.N.T.U. College of Engg.[1]
Anantapur - 515 002

Student of Final Mech. Engg.,[2]

Student of Pre Final Mech. Engg.[3]

ABSTRACT

The paper describes expert systems approach for integrating the various aspects of design, material selection, manufacture and trouble shooting of bearings. The paper also presents a methodology suitable for bearings design to incorporate all these aspects and implement these in an expert system.

1. INTRODUCTION

The design of power transmission elements/components requires the diverse sources of knowledge such as material selection, manufacture and trouble shooting analysis. In addition design of each component requires additional knowledge other considerations. For, example, the design of bearings requires the diverse knowledge sources, such as bearing type/class, alloy selection, manufacture, and lubricants which serve to minimize the friction and wear during service. However the design, materials engineering and manufacture are functionally separate fields. The successfull design always require the simultaneous success of all the engineers who are involved in the design, materials engg., and manufacture.

Because of the traditional separation of design and manufacture fields, it is extremely difficult to integrate various aspects of manufacture with design.

Expert systems which is a subject of Artificial Intelligence offer great help for integrating the various aspects of design and manufacture. Expert systems approach is applicable for the design of specialized group of products such as bearings. Bearings design is a specialized and diverse field which requires simultaneous inputs of human expertise in diverse fields. The paper outlines the methodology and architecture of expert systems for the design, material selection, manufacture and trouble shooting of bearing failures.

2. EXPERT SYSTEM

The Principal components of an expert system are[1] a knowledge base, an inference engine and a user interface (Fig. 1). The knowledge base contains domain expertise which is both declarative knowledge (facts about objects or events) and procedural knowledge (information about courses of action). The system will contain two types of knowledge either separate or integrated. The most prevalent form of knowledge representation is rule based production system or frame based systems. The knowledge will be in the form of "IF-THEN" production rules in a rule based system. However, all the rules do not pertain to the system's domain. Some rules called 'meta-rules' pertain to themselves. A meta-rule (rule about a rule) specify the condition under which certain rules should be followed instead of others.

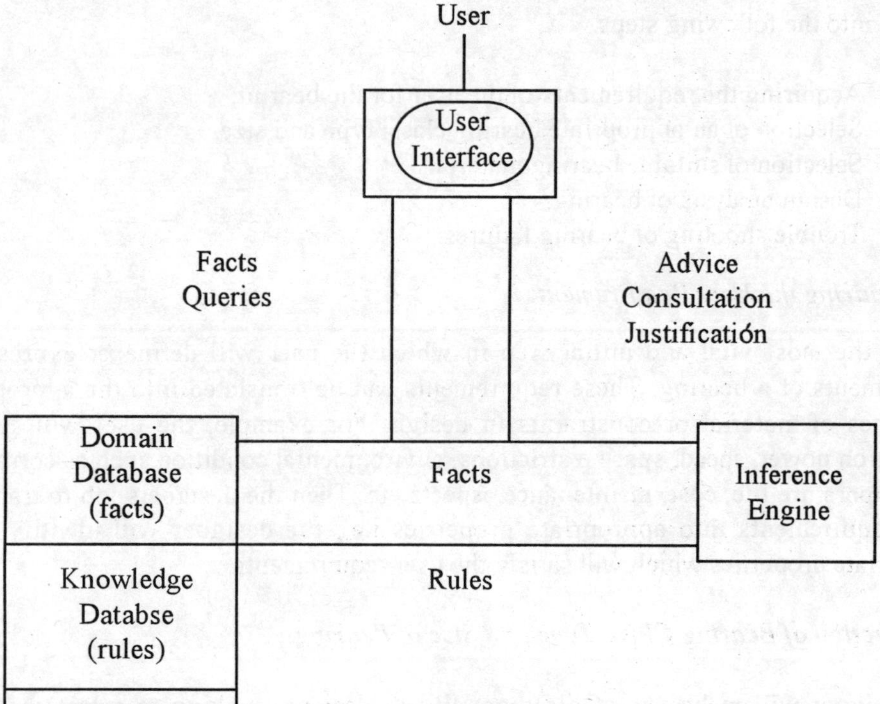

The inference engine is that component of the expert system that controls its operation by selecting the rules to use, accessing and executing these rules and determining when a solution has been found. In simple words, the inference engine decides which heuristic search techniques are used to determine how the rules of the knowledge base are to be applied to the problem.

The user interface allows the user to communicate with the systems. The communication performed will be bidirectional. The user will describe the problem to the system and the system will respond with its recommendations.

3. FORMALIZATION OF BEARINGS DESIGN

The two important stages in the development of an expert system for bearings design are evaluation of a methodology for bearings design i.e., formalization and finally the stage two; i.e. implementation of the methodology of design in a suitable programming language.

Stage one: evolution of a methodology for the bearings design. The methodology incorporates the selection of type, geometry, configuration of bearing; material selection, for manufacture of bearings and finally the lubricant selection which serves to minimize the friction and wear during bearing service. The methodology of bearings design falls broadly into the following steps.

1. Acquiring the requirements of the user for the bearing.
2. Selection of an appropriate bearing class, type and size.
3. Selection of suitable bearing material.
4. Design analysis of bearing.
5. Trouble shooting of bearing failures.

3.1 Acquiring the User Requirements

This is the most vital and initial step in which the user will define or express his requirements of a bearing. These requirements can be translated into the appropriate properties of material or constraints in design. For example, the user will specify application power, speed, space restrictions, environmental condition such as corrosion, low temperature life, cost, maintenance aspects etc. Then the designers job to tranform these requirements into appropriate properties i.e., the designer will identify most appropriate properties which will satisfy the user requirements.

3.2 Selection of Bearing Class, Type and Size of Bearings

The designer will make use of his ingenuity in decision making to select the most suitable class i.e., Rolling or sliding bearing then appropriate type and size depending upon space, load, power noise, cost of life requirements.

3.3. Selection of Suitable Bearing Material

This choice of material is critical factor which decides the life economics, manufacture of bearings. This is also vital stage for integrating various design and manufacture properties of bearing materials. The most important properties of bearings are: (1) Compatibility, (2) Embeddability and conformability, (3) Corrosion resistance,

(4) Compressive and fatigue strength, (5) Cost and availability. The manufacturing properties include bondability, machinability, hardenability. All these factors are to be critically examined before making the final decision on the choice of an alloy.

3.4. Design Analysis of Bearing

During this stage the various dimensions of the bearing are calculated from the stand point of user requirements. In general, one pre-engineered model of the design is selected and the values are obtained by routine design calculations.

3.5 Trouble Shooting of Bearing Failures

The designs are always acceptable only after a few modifications are made to it in order to eliminate bearing trouble during service. Therefore rapid accumulation of experience with past troubles and means of diagnosing and rectifying the trouble will help the designer a lot during design stage.

4. IMPLEMENTATION OF BEARING DESIGN METHODOLOGY IN EXPERT SYSTEMS

The implementation involves selection of appropriate programming language to incorporate the design methdology. It also involves structuring the knowledge of entire design process into various discrete steps or modules for ease of implementation. It also involves generating an exact architecture of the expert system for implementation of the design process. The suitable architecture evolved fcr the design is shown in figure. The various steps of design process of bearings implemented in expert systems approach are as follows.

4.1 Acquiring the User Requirements

During this stage the programme interacts with the user in an intelligent way and acquires the requirements of the user related to the bearing type. Later, the programme identifies an appropriate set of material properties relevant to the bearing.

4.2 Selection of Bearing Class, Type and Size of Bearing

Depending upon the user requirements such as space, power, load and cost requirements the programme refers to a knowledge base, which contains a set of rules for identifying and selecting an appropriate bearing. Here the selection of bearing is limited to identify the broad category of bearing such as rolling contract or sliding contact bearings and then select suitable type and size of the bearing. The knowledge base contains various facts and rules that will specify the current choice.

4.3 Selection of Bearing Material

This forms the vital step, in which both the mechanical and manufacturing properties are considered during the alloy selection. Therefore, a database of the properties (mechanical, technological and cost factors) is desirable to make a judiwise selection of an alloy.

4.4. Design Analysis of Bearing

During this stage the programme selects a pre-engineered model of the design from the algorithm base and determines the various demensions of bearing. The programme gives an output of various dimensions requirement of artificial cooling and appropriate choice a lubricant for minimizing the wear and tear.

4.5 Trouble Shooting of Bearing Failures

This is an independent module of the system, which is mainly ment for analysing or diagnosing the causes of failures. The system also suggest suitable remedies for future designs. The system has also the capability of modifying, deleting or adding a new sources or causes of troubles. This is mainly a diagnostic type of expert system module.

5. THE SCOPE AND STATUS OF WORK

An expert system is being developed for the design of bearings. The architecture of the system is also presented in the previous section. The modules are programmed in Turbo 'C'. The last module for trouble shooting of bearing failures is being programmed in Turbo Prolog. At present the system discapable of designing journal bearings only. The system is further to other classes of bearings. The same methodology can also be extended for the design of gears, connecting rods etc.

REFERENCES

1. Andrew Kusaik, *Intelligent Manufacturing Systems*, Prentice Hall, Englewood Cliffs, 1990, pp. 77-80.
2. Henry, C. Mishokoff, *Understanding Artificial Intelligence*, B.P.B. Publication, 1986, pp. 53-78.
3. Wilcock & Booker, *Bearing Design and its Application*, McGrow Hill, 1988.
4. James, Martin, Steven Oxman, *Building Expert Systems*, Prentice Hall Englewood Cliffs, New Jersey, 1990.

ARTIFICIAL INTELLIGENCE AND ROBOTICS IN PRODUCTION

40

Capt. Subramanian R.
614, EME Bn. C/O 56 APO

INTRODUCTION

1. Robotics is a new field of Science which deals with the study, research and development of Robots. In science fiction a Robot is depicted as an artificial mechanical man capable of doing wonders. But in reality, none of such men exist. However, some of the R&D laboratories in USA and Japan have made such Robots which could move from room to room and recognize some of the objects with their vision. These Robots could also sense as electric socket and use this to charge their batteries in case their battery voltages go below certain threshold values. Research on such mechanical men i.e., Robot is still continuing and it may take years before these could be thought fit for commercialization.

2. The growing interest in Robots has been largely motivated by the needs of automated production, industrial safety and the newer technologies such as nuclear, space, underwater and bio-technology. Robots are extremely useful for work in hazardous environments, the recovery of underground and undersea resources and in space exploration.

3. In Army, Robots would find their use in mine field breaching, bomb disposal activities, in Army Base Workshops and Ordnance-oriented factories and for simulating the manual actions in a battle field scenario.

HISTORICAL BACKGROUND

4. Robots were depicted as mechanical anthropoid devices capable of clumsy imitation of human actions. Robots were often endowed with super human strength and powers, sub-human intelligence and sinister intentions.

DEFINITION OF ROBOT

5. A large number of definitions for the word Robot have been put forward by various

authors, institutes and dictionaries as few of these are as under :

(a) *As per Webster's Dictionary*—"A Robot is an automatic device that performs functions ordinarily ascribed to human being".

(b) *According to Japanese Industrial Standard*—"A Robot is defined as a mechanical system which has flexible motion functions analogous to the motion functions of the living organisms or combines such motion functions with intelligence functions".

(c) *As per the Robot Institute of America*—"A Robot is programmable multifunctional manipulator designed to move materials, parts and tools or specialise devices through variable programmed motions for performance of variety of tasks".

GENERAL APPLICATION CHARACTERISTICS OF ROBOTS

6. *Hazardous or Uncomfortable Working Conditions*. In job situations where there are potential dangers or health hazards due to heat, radiation, or toxicity, or where the workplace is uncomfortable and unpleasant, a Robot should be considered as a substitute for the human worker. This sort of application has a high probability for worker acceptance of the Robot. Examples of these job situations include hot forging, die casting, spray painting and foundry operations.

7. *Repetitive Tasks*. If the work cycle consists of a sequence of elements which do not vary from cycle to cycle, it is possible that a Robot could be programmed to perform the task. This is especially likely if the task is accomplished within a limited workspace. Pick-and-place operations and machine loading are obvious examples of repetitive tasks.

8. *Difficult Handling*. If the workpart or tool involved in the operation is awkward or heavy, it might be possible for a Robot to perform the task. Operations involving the handling of heavy workparts are a good example of this case. A human worker would need some form of mechanical assistance to lift the part, which would add to the production cycle time. Some industrial Robots are capable of lifting payloads weighing several hundred (or even more than a thousand) pounds.

9. *Multishift Operation*. If the initial investment cost of the Robot can be spread over two or three shifts, the labour savings will result in a quicker payback. This could mean the difference between whether or not the investment can be justified. Plastic injection molding and other processes which must be operated continuously are examples of multishift Robot applications.

APPLICATION AREAS FOR INDUSTRIAL ROBOTS

Material Handling

10. This involves moving parts from one place to another. Even several parts are moved

at one time. Application include packaging of materials, arranging them for further processing. Robots have special advantages when the environmental conditions are hostile to people such as, in very cold or hot environments or in handling heavy loads and in moving parts which would require overhead reaching, current applications material handling in masonry, glassware, fabric, plastic and rubber industries. In a big departmental store in Japan Robots start working after it is closed for customers at night. They lift the items from stores an fill up the bins which are depleted during day.

Mechanical Loading

11. Machine-tool loading and unloading generally requires more support engineering than material handling. With proper placing, a Robot can increase the utilisation factor of the machine they load or unload. In many cases, machine tool cycles are much longer than manipulator cycles. This allows the same Robot to be used to load and unload several machines without, in any, extending the time of the machining cycles. In these application, the machines are grouped around a Robot or the Robot is put on a moving base. In such systems a single end-effector will usually have to be aligned to execute two or more functions.

Die Casting and Plastic Moulding

12. The unloading of die casting machines and the subsequent handling of the casting and scrap is the most important application areas for manipulations. For this reason die casting process deserves special discussion, although the unloading of die casting machines is simply one example of machine unloading. Manipulators have been applied to all arts of the die casting cycle. They have been used to load insert into the die cavity, spray die lubricant into the machine, remove the casting from the open die, dip the casting into quench bath, load the casting into a trim press. A typical application involves several of these operations. In addition, it is rather common to have a single manipulator servicing two die casting machines. Manipulators play a similar role in various plastic moulding operations.

Foundry and Treatment

13. In these applications, tremendous amound of heat makes the job hazardous and also the persons working in these environments are quite futigued because of which a fair amount of inaccuracies creep in. In heat treatment operations where loading and unloading of parts from furnaces and quenching in various baths is quite frequent, there the end effector with extra long fingers are used to keep the power units away from the heat. Robots in all these applications have found a great use.

Welding Machining, Inspection and Spray Painting

14. In these operations, Robots hold and move a tool rather than part being worked. It provide a good deal of uniformity while working in rather unconventional and polluted environments. In spot welding and are welding, Robots are extensively being used. In machining, the most common operations are grinding, polishing and debarring. The hand tools in such cases are either pneumatic or electric. In spray painting the end effect of the manipulator carries the spray gun. These manipulators are generally high priced, hydraulically driven and continuous path controlled six or seven degrees of freedom devices. Robots performing the job of spray painting find their extensive use in automative industry, appliance industry, furniture and computer industries. They can accomplish their tasks with good deal of uniformity while working in rather unventilated and pollute environments.

Assembly

15. Assembly is an application area that every one talks about and very few manipulators do. Virtually no assembly work is carried out with general purpose six degree of freedom manipulators. Although some successful commercial assembly operations do exist, most of the work in this area is still experimental and is in the development stages. The most successful assembly operations have involved rather simple (three or four degrees of freedom) modular, or special purpose, manipulator systems. These systems relay heavily on parts and feeders, passive-compliance devices and special end effectors as well as sensors.

Non-manufacturing Applications

16. Robots can be ideal for working in environments which are hostile to humans. Prime examples are the handling of radio active materials, and working under seas, under ground and in outer space. In such applications the Robots are usually remotely controlled by human operators using job stick or master slave type of control inputs. The operator requires a visual link to the end effector and environment, this is accomplished with video or other image processing when direct view through shielded glass is not possible.

Examples of Some Robotics Systems

17. (a) *Arc Welding*. The system controls six degrees of freedom of the manipulator with 0.5mm repeatability or better and with axis transformation and path contouring ability. It supervises control or two degrees of freedom workpiece positioner which could be point to point controlled. While operating it supervises and controls current, voltage and other parameters as required for a particular weld. Vision system could also be included for seam welding.

(b) *Paint Spray*. The system can spray paint on the moving pieces with the help of five degrees of freedom manipulator having 3mm repeatability or better and with path countering ability. It supervises control of the paint spraying mechanism i.e., ON, OFF, wipe spraying gun and so on. It compensates for change in line speed. The paint flow rate can be controlled via an analogue or output from the Robot controller to save paint.

(c) *Belt Picking with Vision System*. In this the Robot has the ability to move to each part as required by moving around its various axes by amounts as decided after getting feed back from its vision system. It also compensates for change in conveyor speed if there is significant distance between the Camera and the Robot system.

APPLICATION IN ARMY

18. Robots would find tremendous use in Army where most of the jobs are hazardous Research on Robotics for Defence purposes in advanced countries is still on and countries like the United States of America are spending billions of dollars in this field. A few of the probable areas, where these Robots could be applied are given in the following paragraphs.

19. *Mine Field Breaching*. Presently mine-field breaching is done either manually or by mechanical means. In all those situations where manual breaching is warranted, Robots can effectively be employed. A single mobile Robot or a group of such Robots with Mine Detector or prods in their grippers can move in side the mine field, detect mines by sensing the pressures or the metal in the ground and, if required, can remove them. The vital part of this type of Robot will be the sensors. To sense any metallic mine we can have the electronic arrangement as is presently being used in the metallic mine detectors. To detect non-metallic mines, simple micro-switch can be used as a sensor. Even force sensor can perform the function of sensing a non-metallic min. Once a few of the mines (may be 10 or 15) are detected, then the print out of the complete mine field can be provided by the output device and controller of the Robot because most of the mine fields are generally laid in some standard pattern.

20. *Disarming Undesirable Explosives*. Robots are very useful in disarming undesirable explosives. Presently some of the countries are employing Robots for this application in Defence as well as mining industries. If details about the explosive in term of the type of explosive material, type of fuse used, number of turns required to be moved to make to the fuse ineffective are known then the Robot can be programmed to do the required function. A Video Camera can also be fitted on the Robot and Robot can be directed remotely in case of any picture will come in the Video screen of the man controlling the Robot. Angle of Camera can also be changed remotely alongwith zoom-in and zoom-out facilities.

21. Use in the Battle Field

(a) *Throwing Smoke Bombs*. In the offensive operations, throwing of smoke bombs becomes necessary in certain situations. But this has the disadvantage of giving out your own position. In these cases, a mobile or stationery Robot with Gun in its gripper can fit the smoke bomb and fire it when desired. Also location of Robot will act as a deception plan for the enemy and doesn't give our own position.

(b) *To Provoke Firing*. A few Robots can be sent on different directions to provoke fire. Once these Robots get fired at the "Intelligence System" of central Robot i.e., Computer will calculate the direction of fire thus giving hint about enemy probable locations.

22. *Use in Army Base Workshops and Defence Oriented Factories*. Army is holding a variety of mechanical, electrical, electronic and optical equipments. Minor repairs to these equipments are done at the field workshop levels whereas overhauling and stripping an equipment down to the component levels is done in Army base Workshops. These are like big factories and manufacture some of the components also. Robots, being highly accurate and fast machines, with the capability of operating in the hazardous environments, can efficiently be used in these workshops as well as other defence oriented factories. Also as Robots are reprogrammable, these can be switched from production of one item to another. This fact is very useful during war times, when demand for certain components like Shells, Bullets etc. increase tremendously. Robots can thus be diverted from non-essential items to production of high demand items. Most of the applications described above for the industries are also applicable to the Base Workshops and Defence Oriented Factories.

CONCLUSION

23. Robotics is a new field of science and would lead the way into areas of technology where man has not entered so far. Besides, when applied to carefully chosen manufacturing and other processes, Robot technology can ensure high quality and competitive profits. This may make Indian products acceptable to the International market thus boosted our economy. Advanced countries have already shown interest in this field and are now trying to exploit its use for industrial as well as military purposes. US Air Force is working on one project ICAM since 1978 with one of its aims as the extensive use of Robots in a Computer Controlled Factory. They are spending millions of Dollars per year on this project. Japan is also flowing ample amount of money in this field and has produced some of the good Robots.

24. It is obvious that Robots are going to be one of our kith and kin in the broader sense of them. It is in our own interest that we know them today so that we can use them to our advantage tomorrow.

REFERENCES

1. CAD/CAM by Mikell P. Groover & Emory W. Zimmers, J.R.
2. Robotics by Faculty of Electronics, MC EME, Secundrabad.

FMS—THE PRACTICALITIES SYSTEM DESIGN, ANALYSIS AND OPERATION

41

Col. P.S. Uppal

Chief Maintainability Engineer, MAG No. 1,
C/o Bharat Electronics, Jalahalli, Bangalore - 560 013

ABSTRACT

This paper discusses analysis and design tools used in the FMS/CIM system development lifecycle. The development lifecycle consists of eight primary technical tasks: Problem Analysis, Requirements Defintion, Preliminary Design, Detail Design, Construct & Verify, Integrate & Validate, Implementation & User Acceptance, and Maintenance & Support.

INTRODUCTION

1. Any weak concept team tasked to start a FMS right from beginning who want the factory to be very flexible will buckle. But if they stick to the point all through the different stages without giving way to Easy options (flexibility lessen when difficulties arises e.g., detailed studies, heart breaking reconsiderations etc.), they will surely succeed to get the desired results.

PROBLEMS FACED IN IMPLEMENTING FMS

2. Today in the field of manufacturing, flexible manufacturing systems (FMS) have fast growing importance because of their clearly defined advantages (e.g., increased productivity and product-quality, decreased production costs, etc.).

3. These flexible and adaptive systems are too complex to design and to control economically without the most advanced methods and tools (SW, HW, equipment). As the tools and equipment of design and control are developing very fast, the strategies, the methods and techniques also have to be changed frequently.

WHAT IS CIM? (BOUNDING CIM)

All work can be analyzed into at least three basic components: intellectual, motoric and sensoric. As direct labour cost have been reduced batch manufacturing has seen commensurate increases in indirect labour costs. The intellectual work previously performed by direct labour is now performed by indirect labour.

5. CIM does not necessarily imply total process automation, although a part of an FMS/CIM system may be automated. CIM essentially deals with how you do business and is primarily focussed on how to manufacture the manufacturing system and not on how to manufacture the product. This is an important distinction because a total-automation-viewpoint ensures a narrow use of the computer as a tool for solving manufacturing problems.

CIM AND INDUSTRIAL ENGINEERING

6. Industrial Engineering deals with general engineering tools for ensuring an individual company's competitiveness. The objective using these tools is to achieve the best selection/development and combination/organization of tasks, people and machines (tools) in a specific company. The methods and techniques for doing this are in themselves tools. In this way the term "tool" is used in the most general sense, denoting a means for doing a work or handling a situation.

7. We can thus describe a tool hierarchy. An example of the hierarchy from process planning would be :

(a) *Level 1*. Process planning using traditional tools and techniques specifying processes to be used in producing a part including design of special cutting tools and fixtures.

(b) *Level 2*. A system designer using computer techniques to design a CAPP system to help the process planner.

(c) *Level 3*. A theory of process planning to guide system designers in designing CAPP system.

8. To stay competitive using the potentialities of a new technology not only means solving existing tasks with the new technology, but also means adjusting/modifying existing tasks to achieve the most effective use of the new technology. This is why managers must understand that CIM implies a new business/management philosophy. Since no single tool can adequately represent all relevant perspectives of the industrial enterprises, the challenge is to select existing tools, define and develop new tools needed, and organize them in a suitable framework. General tools/methods for developing unique CIM solutions must consist of an organised set of tools, covering both the technical, the organisational and the personal aspects of a company.

THE CHALLENGE

9. Trying to address this challenge raises many questions some of which are :

(a) How do we describe the intellectual work to be done?

(b) How do we describe the correspondence question to find the right tool-task combination?

(c) How do we rationally organize the development process?

THE FMS/CIM DEVELOPMENT LIFECYCLE

10. A major tool in FMS/CIM projects is the recognition and use of the FMS/CIM development lifecycle model. The FMS/CIM development lifecycle has eight primary technical tasks grouped as follows under four phases:

(a) *Phase 1 — Analyse Problem*

(i) Problem Analysis.

(ii) Requirements Definition.

(b) *Phase 2 — Formulate and Justify Solution*

(iii) Preliminary Design.

(iv) Detail Design.

(c) *Phase 3 — Construct and Integrate Solution*

(v) Construct and Verify.

(vi) Integrate and Validate.

(d) *Phase 4 — Formulate and Maintain Solution*

(vii) Implement and User Acceptance.

(viii) Maintenance and Support.

PHASE 1 — ANALYSE PROBLEM

Phase Description

11. In the "Problem Analysis" task the manual operation is analyzed to determine the way it currently exists. The analysis consists of building function models, information models and behaviour models (simulation models) of the current manufacturing system. The act of constructing these models forces the CIM project team to bound the problem domain and understand the system within the bounds.

12. Within the "Problem Analysis" Task the "System Environment Specifications" (SES) defines the current system. This specification consists of the following :

(a) System functional relationship model.
(b) System information structure model.
(c) Dynamic behaviour model (simulation model).
(d) Physical layout.
(e) System document library.

13. In creating the "System Environment Specification" the CIM team moves through a discovery process that ensures all project personnel thoroughly understand the system and its problems. The SES is a consensus definition of the existing manufacturing system and its problems.

14. In the "Requirements Definition" task the Problem Analysis task results are evolved to produce models of what the CIM system should be. This includes the process and material handling flow, and computer hardware and software data flow.

15. Through these models a system is defined that corrects the problems identified in the Problem Analysis task. They form the basis for a set of requirements specifying the structure and behaviour of the CIM system and are incorporated into the simulation model. The product of this task are formal CIM system requirements specification documents against which the system is designed, formal testing requirements specifications documents specifying how the system testing is performed, and models of the CIM system.

Applicable Tools

16. The various models are as follows :

(a) *IDEF-0 Function Modeling*, which captures those activities in the system that transform inputs under constraints into outputs, and shows the information flow between these activities.
(b) *IDEF-1 Information Modeling*, which captures the rules, conventions, and laws that govern the structure and operation of information in a manufacturing system.
(c) *IDEF-2 Behaviour Modeling*, which captures the time-varying behaviour of the system, which is commonly done in and known as computer simulation.
(d) *SDM System Development Methodology*, which plans, system development efforts so that appropriate administrative and technical tools and methodologies can be chosen.
(e) *Documentation System*. It is rarely viewed as a powerful administrative and technical tool. It is particularly important for a CIM project because it represents the interim results and may be the only visible project output until the implementation phase.

PHASE 2 — FORMULATE AND JUSTIFY SOLUTION

Phase Description

17. This phase consists of the Preliminary Design and Detailed Design tasks. In the Preliminary Design task alternative approachs to meet the requirements specifications are conceptualized and models constructed. The models are used to select a specific alternative. The selected alternative determines the basic design approach to be taken in developing a solution and the model's detail is increased for use in the Detail Design Task.

18. In the Detail Design task the structure and components of the alternative selected from the Preliminary Design task for designed in detail. In addition, component testing procedures that are consistent with the system testing procedures are designed. This phase results in the detailed system design used to implement the CIM system and procedures to test the system components.

Applicable Tools

19. This phase has been the focus of activity in software engineering during the past decade and has the best developed support tools.

PHASE 3 — CONSTRUCT AND INTEGRATE SOLUTION

Phase Decription

20. The Construct and Integrate Solution phase consists of the Construct and Verify task and the Integrate and Validate task. In the Construct and Verify task the detailed logic associated with the detailed design is specified and used to build the system components. These components are verified and assembled into subsystems that are also verified. Verification is the process of ensuring that the software programme logic matches the specified logic.

21. In the Integrate and Validate task the interfaces between components and subsystems are tested and integrated together to form the CIM system. This sytem is tested to validate that it meets the system requirements specifications. The results of this task will be an operating CIM system that has been shown to meet the requirement specification.

Applicable Tools

22. The primary tools here are code development environments that support converting detailed logical designs into programme code. Unfortunately, this is an emerging technology with few commercially available tools. Most work is performed manually

with wome support from windowing systems, interactive debuggers and incremental compilers.

PHASE 4 — IMPLEMENT AND MAINT SOLUTION

Phase Description

23. In the Implementation and User Acceptance task the CIM system is installed in a production environment and users are trained to operate the system. The system operation is monitored and evaluated to determine if the requirements specifications are met under production conditions.

24. In the Maintenance and Support Task System problems that arose while operating the CIM system are analyzed, and engineering changes to the hardware and software are specified to solve them. The changes are implemented and the system operations evaluated for correct performance. The result is an operational CIM System.

Applicable Tools

25. This area has been almost completely neglected in terms of support tools. The primary tool used is a system emulator that is designed and developed by the project group for the specific FMS/CIM system.

TECHNICAL REVIEWS

26. Technical reviews are tools taht support both the administrative tasks and the technical tasks through out the entire development cycle. They allow management to track activities and correct problems while corrective action is still possible. They provide management with a better appreciation for staff competence, both individually and collectively.

ACKNOWLEDGEMENT

27. The author's acknowledgement openly goes to the authorities who detailed me to volunteer to submit a paper on the subject under my name.

ERGONOMIC CONSIDERATION IN INTELLIGENT MANUFACTURING

42

Z.A. Khan, Z. Mallick and S.A.H. Rizvi

Department of Mechanical Engineering, Faculty of Engineering and Technology
Jamia Milia Islamia, New Delhi

1. INTRODUCTION

Today's era of Advanced Manufacturing Technology (AMT) has led all of us to very conclusively and firmly believe in the fact that the ultimate engine of the world's economy is manufacturing. On the other hand, the execution of manufacturing activities needs an enterprise. A manufacturing enterprise encompasses a variety of activities: extraction of customers' needs, design, engineering of a new product, devising and optimization of the process, the manufacturing itself, quality control, inventorying and shipping, packaging, sales and marketing etc. All these activities get further shadowed by the impact of computerization, thereby, channelising the manufacturing technology on the track of automation. One of the most challenging problems being encountered by Concurrent Engineering (CE), Computer Aided Acquisition and Logistic Support (CALS) lies in how to integrate the enterprise. In this process of integration of a manufacturing enterprise one of most ignored dimensions has come to be covered under the banner of the ergonomic considerations in intelligent manufacturing. Present paper made an attempt to put forth the state-of-art pertaining to the role of human factors engineering/ergonomics in the design, development, function and growth of the advance manufacturing technology. The review of literature on the theme revealed some basic facts of the interaction that the end-users have with AMT systems. With the advent of computerization in general, and with the wide spread utility of computers in manufacturing like flexible manufacturing systems (FMS), and Robotics, role of ergonomics has become very critical.

2. CONCEPT OF INTELLIGENCE AND ARTIFICIAL INTELLIGENCE

Research on human brain, its fundamental mechanism, and its molecular structure is probably the most challenging scientific field of today. This research is expected to culminate in reasonable brain control and in using the laws of its functioning to design various machinery. Which would accelerate the technological revolution. Applications of the findings of basic research in brain activities to control engineering encounters formidable difficulties for lack of fairly complete models of artificial intelligence which would be consistent with state-of-art knowledge of brain activity in natural conditions. Natural versus artificial intelligence is also a field of research where various philosophical questions have to be answered. To put it differently, natural intelligence (in primitive form, animal intelligence, and in higher form, human intelligence) is operated by objectively cognizable processes and mechanism. In designing artificial intelligence the researchers found it necessary to define the intelligence and its features so as to make cooperation between neurophysiologists, physchologists, and engineers enabling them to embody these features in models and hardware. Mason(1987) was probably the first control engineer to come to a conclusion that intelligence cannot be understood and an intelligent machine cannot be developed if that machine is in cabaple of prediction. The predicting ability is what makes all the differences between the human brain and most sophisticated hardware. The value of the goal and prediction has been most throughly discussed by Fogel, Owens and Walsh (1966). In defining the "artificial intelligence" they try to find the characteristic common for both natural and artificial intelligence. They are perfectly right when they concentrate on the logic of the mechanism which add up to the intelligence rather than on the accuracy and speed of performing specific activities. The foremost among these mechanisms are the decision making and prediction a goal formulation, mechanism. The major weakness of research in basic specific characteristics of the natural and artificial intelligence at this stage can be identified as lack of a model which would incorporate all the stages in the generation of intellectual acts. Such a model should obviously also represent the neurophysiological mechanism of every step of intellectual processes. Fogel et al. (1966) tried to develop an evolutionary model of artificial intelligence which was to improve its main properties via the sophistication of primitive mechanism through a chain of generations. Note, through, that in modeling the experience is generalized in a somewhat different way than in evolution. Before answering these questions, one basic finding of many years of research has to be formulated. None of the above properties of brain activities which are regarded as characteristic feature of intelligence emerged abruptly, upon crossing some evolutionary frontier before which it did not exit. This may seem strange because intelligence has for ever been described as an out-standing feature of living matter inherent atleast the most sophisticated representatives of the animal kingdom. This problem is resolved when we imagine the way in which intelligence came into being. Let us take up for illustration the prediction of events or results of an activity performed by a specific functional system. Under what external and internal conditions is prediction possible? Prediction is made possible, first of all, because the sequence of events about which a prediction is made has occured many times in the past. Our intelligence predicts that an evening will follow just because this sequence has been occuring for millions of years. The basic properties of natural and artificial intelligence will never be understood unless neurophysiological rearms itself with new ideology and develops new tools and methodologies. The first and foremost need is to use the systems approach which would make it possible to study the highest forms of brain activity such as decision making, goal pursuance and prediction. The concept of a functional system will bring science closer to resolving some mysteries of intelligence.

3. ERGONOMICS IN MANUFACTURING

The word Ergonomics literally means the measurement of work and is concerned with the study of those aspects which fit a machine or a process to its operator or user. It aims at enabling man/woman to work with optimum physical and metal comfort and to use his/her senses with the best effects (Ray, 1993). A number of disciplines and profession have contributed to the building up of the pool of knowledge that ergonomics offers today. The anatomy and anthropometry made available the data pertaining to the anatomy of human to help supplying information on the energy requirements of the work and the functioning of the body. Psychologist on the other hand provided an insight into the effects of varieties of parameters on industrial life and behaviour of man. Ergonomics plays a vital role in the design of man and his working environment. It was reported by researchers that injury to humans in a user-product-environment system may occur through three general processes, (i) Due to sudden over stress of any part of the body or over stress for a prolonged period, (ii) Exposure of air contaminates, physical agents like noise and vibration, electromagnetics, ionizing radiation exposure for over a period of time, (iii) Through physical impact with some of the objects which result in physical injury (Venkatesan, 1993). The recent technological developments in the field of manufacturing systems have led to the design and use of a number of sophisticated equipments in solving varieties of manufacturing related problems. The aim of using these equipments is to achieve complete automation. In automated systems of production the number of workers get considerable reduced but the role played by humans in the production environment gets very critical. Even a very small amount of error on the part of end-user due to incompatibility between his/her and the system of production might cause a total failure of the system. Therefore, the whole system needs to be ergonomically redesigned to an optimum level from both the user and machine points of view. This suggested that the Ergonomists have to contribute in a big way in the design evaluation and implementation of highly sophisticated automated system of production. In ergonomic design of such system of production in general, and the CIM system in particular would focus upon the optimisation of the HCI.

4. HCI AND MANUFACTURING AUTOMATION

Wherever automation is there in any manufacturing system very little involvement of human is visualized. In the form of forecast, Burrows had rightly maintained that an automated system of production completely supervised by Computer hierarchy would become Operational in 1990 (Burrows, 1990). Under such a system of manufacturing, the production system would have to seek the help of humans in terms of initial orientation of parts, control of quality and maintenance of the manufacturing system. It is here that ergonomists would come to the rescue of the system designers in the execution of their decision-making process. In terms of the operational aspects of manufacturing systems, humans would be shouldering the responsibilities of developing an appropriate query-system in specific language to understand the problem and difficulties encountered by the manufacturing system. It has been reported in literature that injury to humans in a user-product environment system may occur through three general processes: (a) due to sudden over-stressing for a prolonged period, (b) exposure of air contaminants, physical agents like vibration and noise, electro-magnetic, ionizing radiation exposure for over a period of time, (c) through physical impact with some of the objects which result in physical injury (Venkatesan, 1993). Keeping the above in view there is a basic necessity of designing the modern Human-Computer Interaction System (HCI) and the associate automated manufacturing systems such that these incorporate the ergonomic considerations too in the design and operational aspects of computer-based automated systems of manufacturing. The emergence of the newer field of research, the HCI, is due to the advent of computer which has revolutionized the whole world of activity and laid down the foundation for an efficient and intelligent manufacturing world of tomorrow.

5. CIM VIS-A-VIS HCI

Computer technology has had a dramatic effect on the growth and development of automation. Virtually all production system installed today use computer system. The term CIM denotes the use of computers in design of the products, plan of the production, control of the operations and accomplishment of many of the business related functions in the concerned manufacturing by means of computer systems. It is the data processing and information flow within a firm that this integration primarily occurs (Groover, 1994). CIM makes use of the ful range of the capabilities the digital computers holds for manufacturing. Computer not only have the capability to perform various production related functions in bits and pieces of manufacturing activity but these also help in the entire system of automated manufacturing. Since computers have the tremendous potential to integrate the entire system we have the title of computer integrated manufacturing (CIM). Basic model of a CIM system would be based on CIM technology tying together all the manufacturing and related functions in a company by means of a computer system (Radhakrishnan, 1995). These function include product design, planning, purchasing, manufacturing, automated work centres, warehousing, finance, information management and working. This suggested that computers are at the central position in a CIM system. The successful implementation of CIM system to derive best results, in terms of increased productivity, quality products at much lower cost and reduced labour efforts etc., require an adequate design of CIM system with major emphasis on the effective design of the Human Computer Interaction (HCI) system taking all the relevant factor including the ergonomic ones into consideration.

6. FMS AS VIEWED BY ERGONOMISTS

Flexible manufacturing systems are under the direct control of a computer network. If an FMS has to be operated for a long period of time the system can't be made to run without exercising a prespecified degree of supervision on the computerization process of the FMS. It is here that human component becomes a part of the FMS. Humans have to interact with the computers in order to control the flexible manufacturing system. Ergonomists, in this context, play a very important role. They design the man-computer interaction system so that the production continues uninterrupted on an optimum scale. Human characteristics pertaining to the skill and judgment are considered to be the basic ingredients in the optimum design of the FMS. In an automated system of manufacturing like FMS the quanta of work that was otherwise being carried out by humans has enormously decreased, but at the same time the demand for a exceedingly high quality of decision-making and information processing has increased on the part of humans. So far as the human supervisory control (HSC) is concerned in the word of Sharit and Salvendy (1985), 'very little is known about HSC capabilities in the batch manufacturing environment.' Recently some of the ergonomists have been actively involved in the design and evaluation of future FMSs (   ).

The FMSs are presently in the early stages of the development. Future trends in the FMS developments indicate a vast potential of the ergonomics applications. Bessent (1985) has indicated the following dimensions along which FMS in future has to be evolved.

(a) Provision for handling rotational as well as prismatic component.
(b) Provision for sheet metal working FMS.
(c) Provision of FMS for assembly work.
(d) Provision of FMS for non-metal working activities.
(e) Handling and transportation system.
(f) Robot setting and tool adjustment along with the in-process tool-weat monitoring and computer aided replacement programme.

In almost all of these provisions the human component would be at play in one form or the other. In this respect all the futre FMSs will have to based on ergonomic principles.

7. VARIABLES IN ERGONOMIC DESIGN OF INTELLIGENT MANUFACTURING

Human component remains an essential component of all the Intelligent Manufacturing System that have been developed or that are likely to be evolved in future. As a result, organisational, behavioral, social and all the organismic variables are needed to be given due consideration in the design and development all automated manufacturing systems.

The performance level of an automated system can be evaluated on the basis of the individual performances of the two functionaries of such systems the man and computer. The role of the system-designer, in this context, eould be to allocate responsibilities in an optimum manner between these two functionaries. A very well celebrated approach for evaluation of human performance in any working environment, from the ergonomics point of view, has emerged in the form of studies pertaining to the degree or level of arousal in humans. The same approach may be employed to design ergonomically the Manufacturing Systems also. So far as the joint responsibility of man and computer are concerned an ergonomists task would be to determine the degree of decision-making allocated to man and computer. In this respect, the study conducted by Hwang et al. (1984) provides a guide-line that can be successfully implemented for the efficient operation and control of Intelligent Manufacturing System. According to Hwang et al. three major functions in the operation of Intelligent Manufacturing System can be demonstrated: the control of the system, the monitoring of the system and physical operation of the system. Human involvement in these major functions may be visualized in such tasks as maintenance, loading and unloading stations and interventions of operators. The nature of work Intelligent Manufacturing System is such that humans involved in the production task are not at high level of motivation. Moreover, as observed by Blumberg and Alber (1984), work on such systems is not very satisfy is stressful too.

8. CONCLUSION AND FUTURE DIRECTION OF RESEARCH

Looking at the nature of the activities associated with the performance of human component in Automated Systems of productions it is concluded that in the design, development, operation and finally maintenance of all kinds of Automated System of production ergonomic principles must be taken into consideration. According to Falster et al. (1983) 'not much research has yet been done on the management information functions in cellular manufacturing environment', while requirements for job extension and work satisfaction are bound to bring in a change in the human-machine interaction procedure in the over-all trame work of the management and technological planning systems. As a result, the future Intelligent Systems of Production would have to be evolved such that these systems of manufacturing provide as working environment fully compatible to the human capabilities and their limitations.

There are two very distinct visions of future. The one extremes of AMT would exhibit an almost unmanned FMS, controlled fully by CAD/CAM software systems. The other side of the extreme would present a large number of small specialised systems being run by micros and sophisticated kinds of tooling systems to which the operator or the system-designer would add his/her own level of skills and experience. Keeping the above in view, it may be recommended that future studies related to the design and evaluation of Automated Systems of Production from ergonomics point of view should take into account variable associated with the decision-making of humans, their supervisor control characteristics, maintenance and repair skills and, finally, manual control of tooling systems. In terms of of the allocation between humans and computers it may be pointed out that cognitive and information processing capabilities of humans would have to be studied. So far as our country, India, is concerned the operators associated with our future manufacturing scenario are going to be certainly different from their counterparts responsible for operation, control and maintenance of such systems in countries like Japan, U.S.A., Germany, France and U.K. As a result, a lot of responsibilities goes to the shoulders of the future designers in India. They must incorporate the ergonomic principles in the evolution of these systems. To assist the Indian manufacturers, ergonomists would have to generate relevant ergonomic data (may be in the form of a data base system) to meet the basic objective of evolving a better and more efficient intelligent manufacturing system, particularly, from the viewpoint of ergonomics.

REFERENCES

Burrows, L.D., 1984, "The Design to Product Aley Demonstrator", *Proc. Int. Conf. Dev. Flexible Assembly Systems*, London: IEEE Publication.

Blumberg, M. and Gerwin, D., 1984, "Coping with Advanced Manufacturing Technology", *Journal of Occupational Behaviour.*

Fogel *et. al.*, 1966, *Artificial Intelligence through Simulated Evolution*, John Wiley & Sons, Inc., New York.

Falster, P., 1983, *The Integration of Production Management and Flexible Manufacturing in Advances in CAD/CAM*, Edited by Ellis & Semenkov, Netherlands: North Holland.

Groover, M.P., 1994, *Automation, Handbook of Design Manufacturing and Automation*, John Wiley and Sons, Inc., USA.

Hwang, S. *et al.*, 1984, "Integration of Humans and Computers in the Operation and Control and Flexible Manufacturing Systems", *Int. J. Prod. Res.*

Makarov, I.M., 1987, *Cybernetics of Living Matter*, Mir Publishers, Moscow.

Radhakrishnan, P., and Subramanaym, S., 1995, *CAD, CAM, CIM*, New Age International Publishers, New Delhi.

Ray, G.G., 1993, "Application of Ergonomics in Equipment and Production Design", *National Workshop on Ergonomics*, Visakhapatanam, India.

Sharit, J. and Salvendy, G., 1985, "Supervisory Control and Flexible Manufacturing System, An Exploratory Investigation", *Ergonomics International*, U.K.

Venkatesan, R., 1993, "Ergonomics Introduction", *National Workshop on Ergonomics*, Visakhapatnam, India.

MANUFACTURING CONSIDERATIONS IN PRODUCT DESIGN

43

Nikhil Shyam Gurjar[1] and Sharatchandra D. Jog[2]

Engineer, Training Centre, Indian Oil Corporation Limited,[1]
Gujarat Refinery, Vadodara - 391 320
Assistant Professor, Department of Mechanical Engineering,[2]
Indian Institute of Technology, Mumbai - 400 076

ABSTRACT

The design of a new product needs a thorough understanding not only of the market requirements but also of the operational constraints of the manufacturing unit. The productivity based approach is useful in reducing the overall costs and time of manufacture. The present work is based on a study which dealt with the generation of synthetic time standards at a factory which was using batch production technique. The work helps us to understand the impact of technological choice on the manufacturing process. An algorithm was developed on how to link the operational aspects of manufacture with the product design. The economic aspects have been considered in order to evaluate the design and analyze the work in a wider perspective. The cases emphasize on using appropriate technology for the given technological software rather than technological developments in the area.

Keywords: M.O.S.T., Appropriate technology, Productivity.

INTRODUCTION

Product design involves the use of engineering knowledge, sciences and techniques to develop on existing resources in such a way so as to satisfy the needs of the society by providing with an enhancement in productivity. The understanding of product design in the modern industrial environment needs a thorough understanding of technology and it's implications. Technology as understood today is defined as 'skills, knowledge and procedures for making, using and doing things.' Appropriate technology is a concept, a set of ideas or a framework within which to think and act for the society.[1,2,3] The concept aims at providing a basis and a method for the choice of technology. It's a normative concept and thus, it's necessary to review notions about technology and product design in order to fully understand it.

The term technology is often identified with the hardware of production and distribution, be it in the form of machines, factories, roads, storage facilities, communication, etc. Technology however, also includes software aspects such as knowledge, know-how, experience, education, organizational forms and management techniques. In this work, the various considerations of technological software and hardware have been elucidated by means of certain case studies which give us a better perspective in terms of technological appropriateness and product design.

METHODOLOGY USED

The methodology involved the generation of synthetic time standards based on Maynard Operation Sequence Technique.[13] The technique is reported to be *a clever mapping of surrogate measures to achieve results that sacrifice minimal accuracy while greatly reducing the observer time necessary to establish standards*. The general procedure followed was:

- Studying the existing systems and practices in the given setup.
- Studying the existing performance levels at the workplaces selected.
- Establishing MOST time standards at the work places.
- Calculation of allowances involved at the selected workplaces.
- Calculation of standard time at the workplaces.
- Establishing the maximum production capacity based on the standard time obtained.
- Suggesting improvisations at these workplaces, understanding the technological alternatives, supplemented by appropriate MOST analysis and feasibility studies.[15]
- The existing setups were assumed as already to have been recovered in terms of the finances involved in the balance sheets. (The book value of the existing setups is zero).
- The procedure has to be repeated for different designs and technological alternatives chosen to get the exact nature of the tradeoffs.

Case 1: Fixture Design Problem of the Vertical Boring CNC Machine

The Machine and the Jobs

This is a two pallet machine which performs the machining operation at the top, bottom and the internal bore of a motor housing.... The machine has the following features:

A self-centering three jaw pneumatic chuck which align the job with the pallet. During the machining operations, the pallet of the machine turns while the tool remains stationery. The input to the machine is a motor housing casting. The fixtures presently in use at the workplace are modular fixtures. The machine has a flood coolant and a coolant

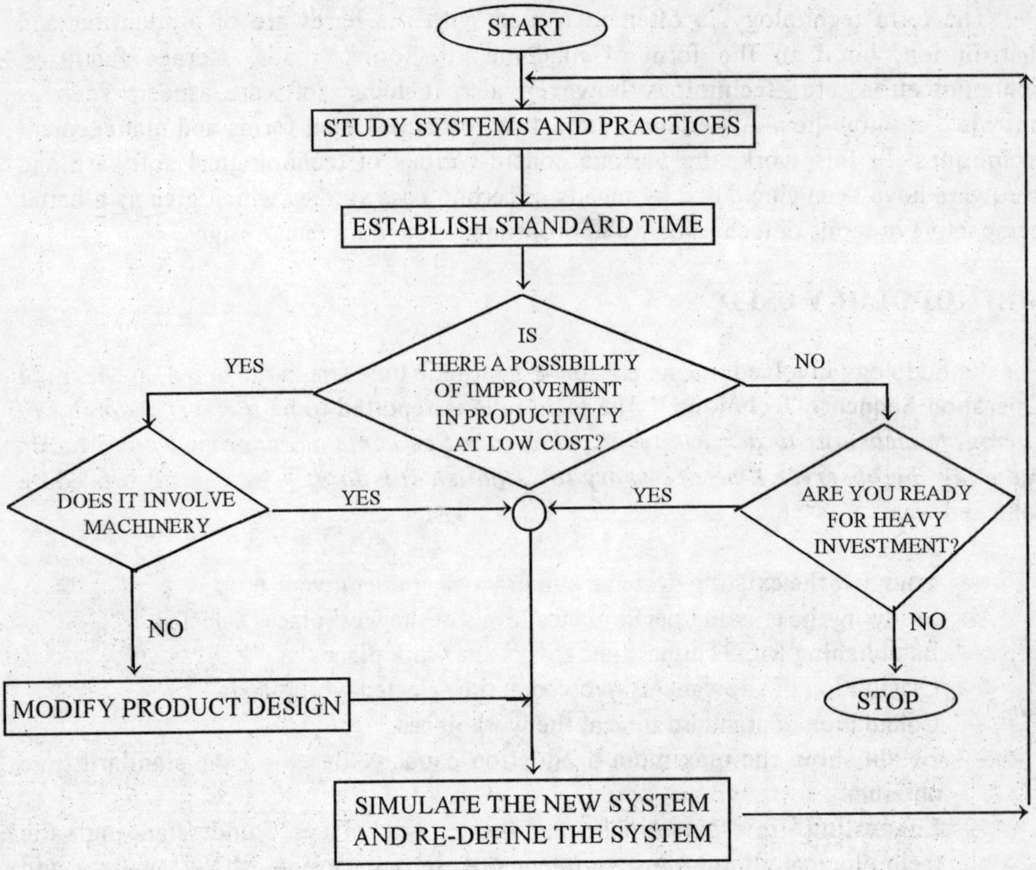

Fig. 1: Algorithm for incorporating productivity in the manufacturing environment

gun for the machining operations. It also has a pneumatic gun for cleaning the pallet after the job is done. The normal handling operations involve the loading of the job using a jib crane and then, truing the top surface with a reference gage.

The average job specifications are as follows:

Weight: 450kg, Length : 850, Bore size : 600mm, Machining time : 120 minutes.

The Setup Operations

The main operation where the idle time was involved was the setup operation of the modular fixture. The modular fixture can be understood as a combination of a main block, an adapter plate, additional triangular pads and a wedge assembly. The setup operations include the replacement of fixtures for the corresponding motor housing series and the replacement of the jaws of the centering device. This involves the removal and tightening of around 124 bolts and around 8 transport moves using the jib crane.

Further, the fixture assemblage was fairly complex. This required the setup time of 4 hours and 20 minutes as given by MOST. It amounted to loss of Rs. 3000 per hour. Hence, it was essential to reduce the time.

The problem was attacked using the algorithm shown. Initially, the changes in machinery were tried out and the results were studied. Thereafter, the changes in the product design were studied and the results were compared.

The use of block assembly models in place of modular fixtures proved to be effective in reducing the setup time because the block assembly model required removal or tightening of only 52 bolts and a reduction of the jib crane operations to 4 transport moves. Though the inventory cost in this case would be higher, the recovery and overall profits made it more lucrative unlike as technologically expected in[4,5,6] a long-term perspective. Table 1 given below compares the proposed block assembly fixture model with the existing fixture design.

TABLE 1. **Comparing Fixture Designs on the Vertical Boring CNC Machines**

Parameters	Existing	Proposed 1
Setup time for one pallet	4 hours 20 minutes	2 hours 14 minutes
Requirements of inventory	12 present	44 more required
Advantages	Modular fixture, adaptable design, less requirement of space	Reduction in the setup time by 48.5 %, lesser operator fatigue, simpler design, no change elements, lighter.
Disadvantages	Many change elements, high setting time, higher operator fatigue, more complex, heavier.	Not an adaptable design, more requirement of space
Recovery time	—	270 setups

Another proposed operational modification was the use of a pneumatic torque wrench for the existing fixture design. The comparison of the alternatives with the existing is shown in Table 2.

TABLE 2. **Comparing Fixture Design with the Second Alternative Proposed on the Vertical boring CNC Machine**

Parameters	Existing	Proposed 2
Setup time for one pallet	4 hours 20 minutes	1 hour 57 minutes
Requirements of inventory	12 present	No extra inventory
Advantages	—	Reduction in setup time by 55%
Disadvantages	—	Higher operator fatigue continues in this case.
Recovery time	—	7 setups

A Case for Product Innovation

The productivity can further be increased by changing the design of the product to cater to the manufacturing constraints. This can also help in reducing the fixture inventories required for the particular workstation. The existing motor housing is mounted on a machine using the features of ribs and strength reinforcing external pads. In the existing design of the motor housing, the heights of these features differ and their differential height also differs with the motor series. Further, some of the motor housings didn't have feet. Seeing the wide variety of combinations, it was suggested that the following design modifications should be made for the products. The feet and the rest pads should be at the same height. It could be so adjusted that 4 similar fixtures have to be mounted for all the cases. Further, the design should ensure that the same fixture could be used for all the series. This yields a reduction in fixture requirements to 4 fixtures per pallet or 8 fixtures overall in place of existing 12 fixtures. The setup operations can further be simplified using some guided movements of the fixture on the pallet in order to quickly change the radius with respect to the desired series to be loaded. This case compares itself with the existing as shown in Table 3.

TABLE 3: **Comparison of Existing Fixture Design with Product Innovation Proposed**

Parameters	Existing	Proposed 3
Setup time for one pallet	4 hours 20 minutes	15 minutes
Requirements of inventory	12 present	12-4 required
Advantages	Modular fixture, can accommodate all the designs of the motors	Virtually no setup time, Easy to maintain and operate, No change elements, no operator fatigue, no storage spaces required.
Disadvantages	Many change elements, high setup time, higher operator fatigue, more complex, heavier, require storage space.	Constraints imposed on the housing design
Recovery time	—	3 setups

Case 2: Die Casting Machine Cooling Characteristic

About the Machine and the Jobs

The die casting machine performs the die casting operation to give us Aluminium die cast rotors of a motor. The input to the machine are turned shafts and rotor laminations. The machine has four workplaces, which are the furnace, pressing machine, die-casting machine and the shrink fitting machine of which the die casting machine creates the bottleneck in the nromal operations. At this workplace, the pressed and stacked rotor laminations are die-cast. The Aluminium enters the cavities due to the notches in the laminations. The molten Aluminium is prepared in the main furnace. It is then transferred to the slug ejector through the dosing furnace, which pushes the molten Aluminium into the lamination cavities. The average size of the rotor jobs is 1200 length and a diameter of 600.

About the Normal Operations

The die casting machine has a cooling problem which has to be solved. The processing time for the machine is 3 minutes. However, the die cooling time is of the order of 7 minutes. The cooling time is responsible for creating the bottleneck.

This problem was again attacked using the algorithm. In this case, however, it was seen that changes in the product design were not required. A change in the machinery was considered to be the best solution. The change in the manufacturing process was also considered but has been reported here.

The cooling time is due to the principle of operation of the machine. There is a slug ejector in the machine which is shown in figure 2.

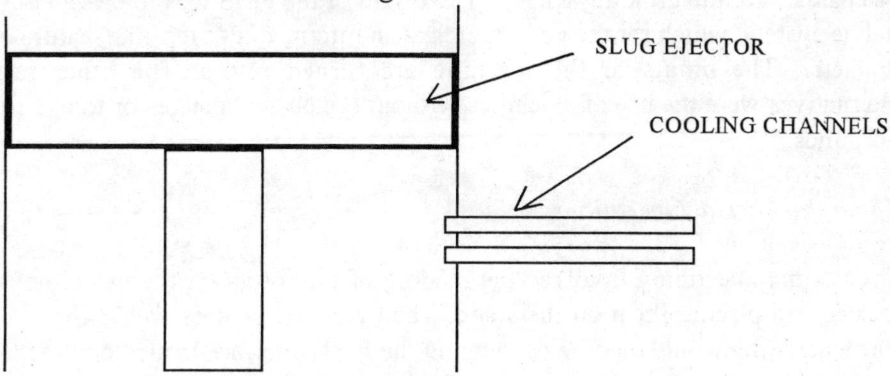

Fig. 1: Slug Ejector of the Die Casting Machine

The thick lines in the figure show the boundaries that are heated due to the molten Aluminium. The piston moves in the cylinder using the following mechanism. The assembly initially is having an interference fit. When liquid Aluminium comes into the chamber, the cylinder walls get heated to a higher temperature than the piston, as the piston is air-cooled. This converts the interference fit to a clearance fit. This ensures wear free motion of the piston in the cylinder. Under the shop floor conditions, this mechanism was reported to be giving maintenance problems.

An effective solution to this problem was to give a ceramic coating on the piston. This would ensure the clearance fit when required by maintaining a temperature differential. The other solution was to allow the minimal possible wear to occur by tribologically attacking the problem. The two solutions have been compared as shown below in table 4.

TABLE 4: **Comparative Study of the Alternatives for the Die-casting Machine**

Parameters	Existing	Proposed 1	Proposed 2
Cycle time	10 minutes	3 minutes	3 minutes
Risk	Low	Moderate	High
Recovery time	—	30 rotors	—

Case 3: On Line Gauging for the Shaft-grinding Machine

About the Machine and the Jobs

The CNC machine performed the grinding operation on the shaft at various locations. The machine had the following features: It had hydraulic centers for mounting the jobs. It had an on-line gauging system for the machining operations. It had a self-dressing mechanism for the grinding wheels. The origin of the FMS was to be redefined using an online system, which set the coordinates at an intermediate step-like feature on the shaft diameter. The inputs to the machine are turned rotors. The other technological alternatives were the use of machines without the on-line gauges or to use conventional machines.

About the Normal Operations

The normal machining involved the loading of the rotors on the machine using lifting tackles and placing them on the stand. The hydraulic centers would then be activated. The machining would then be done using the FMS interface loaded on the machine. The feasibility of the existing technology had to be looked into as the cost of the on-line gauge setup was around Rs. 800 per hour.

The algorithm is used here to compare the difference in productivity that was expected in the various cases. Here, there requirement of heavy investments has been re-considered in view of the productivity difference expected in the entire manufacturing operation.

The use of manual systems for the grinding operations had to be compared with the on-line technique in order to quantify the tangible improvement in productivity as would be expected. The improvement in terms of the normal operations is 12 minutes when compared to the use of conventional machines for the same purpose. However, the features of setup operations take a longer time in the case of the CNC grinding machine. This feature, however, is compensated for by the ease of operations involved in the CNC machine with on-line features. This is a case when heavy financial expenditures can improve the productivity and also the operational procedure.

DISCUSSIONS

The above cases show that operational constraints are important in the considerations for the product design. The improvisations in the product design are to be considered only on the basis of the recovery time expected and the ease of operations. These facts are emphasized in the algorithm used for the work. The focus of the work being on the productivity based approach, the concept of appropriate technology has been understood. It is important to understand technology not just as modern development but as a conjunction of the hardware and the software.

ACKNOWLEDGEMENTS

We would like to take this opportunity to thank Mr. Nitin Aptikar, Mr. Anil Singh Shikarwar and Ms. Preeti Shyam Gurjar for the valuable discussions and exchange of ideas we had with them. We would also like to thank Mr. A.B. Mehta, Mr. J.N. Buch, Mr. Ramamurti, Mr. D.P. Shah, Ms. Shailly Garg, Mr. Vinod Kumar Yadav, Mr. Parag Kothari and the MIS staff for the valuable help, support and encouragement they have given us during the course of this work.

REFERENCES

1. Anil W. Date, *Understanding Appropriate Technology*, Methods for development planning: scenario, models, micro-studies, The UNESCO Press, Paris 1981, Edit: S. Cole, L. Acero and H. Rush, pp. 201-17.
2. Anil W. Date, *Technology Design as if Development Mattered*, Proc. of Int. Conf. on Management of Technical Education, Dec. 14-16, 1995, Tata McGraw Hill, Edit: A. Subash Babu, S.C. Sahastrabudhe, B.B.D. Chopane, pp. 12-38.
3. U. Subha Raju, N. Rangaraj, A.W. Date, *The Influence of Development Perspectives on the Choice of Technology*, Technological Forecasting and Social Change 48, pp. 27-43, 1995.
4. S.K. Hargrove and A. Kusiak, Computer Aided Fixture Design: A Review, Int. J. Prod. Res., 1994, Vol. 32, No. 4, pp. 733-53.
5. B.K.A. Ngoi and G.L. Leow, *Modular Fixture Design: A Designer Assistance*, Int. J. on Prod. Res., 1992, Vol. 32, No. 9, pp. 2083-2104.
6. Lim Beng Siong, T. Imao, H. Yoshida, K. Goto, S.L. Koh, D. Lim, L. Chin and S.C. Gan, *Integrated Modular Fixture Design, Pricing and Inventory Control Expert System*, Int. J. Prod. Res., 1992, Vol. 30, No. 9, pp. 2019-44.
7. Chowdiah, M.P., *Agile Manufacturing for Global Competition*, Proc. ICAM, 1996.
8. Goroshkin, *Jigs and Fixture Handbook*, Mir Publications.
9. International Labour Office, *Introduction to Workstudy*, Oxford and IBH.
10. Nagesh, S.V.S., *Project Report on Improving Machine Output Using MOST Time Standards*, NITIE, 1996.
11. Shigeo Shingo, *A Revolution in Manufacturing: The SMED System*, Productivity Press, 1985.
12. Venkatesh, V.C. and Chandrashekharan, H., *Expreimental Techniques in Metal Cutting*, Prentice Hall of India, 1987.
13. Zandin Kjell B., *MOST Work Measurement Systems*, Marcel Decker Inc., New York, 1990.
14. Nikhil Shyam Gurjar, *Fixed Asset Productivity*, Project Report, IITB, 1996.
15. Nikhil Shyam Gurjar, *Tools Used in Feasibility Studies and Prediction of Product Life Cycles*, Project Report, IITB, 1996.

INDIGENISATION OF HIGH PRESSURE RUBBER SEALS/PACKING RINGS

44

U.S. Nerwal

HQ 12 Corps, EME Branch, C/O 56 APO

INTRODUCTION

1. The process of development of automative systems with power assisted brakes, power operated clutches and automatic transmission system has led to introduction of high pressure rubber seals/packing rings, connecting pipes and hoses for these systems. The importance of high pressure rubber seals, hoses and connecting pipes in hydraulic system needs no extra emphasis. All the Russian equipments including AFVs/ICVs have a large No of high pressure lines operating between various hydraulically operated components. Failure of high pressure rubber seals and packing rings in these equipments have been a perpetual problem since the imports are very costly. The problem has been compounded by breaking up of Soviet Union. Hence the indigenisation of these rubber seals and packing rings is of great importance for better equipment availability and maintainability.

CLASSIFICATION OF RUBBER

2. Natural and synthetic rubber constitute the most important raw material of the rubber industry. The natural rubber is tapped from nature through the rubber tree called Haves, but the synthetic rubbers are chemically made broadly known as general purpose and special purpose rubber. Rubber can be broadly classified into three types:

(a) Natural Rubber
(b) Synthetic Rubber
(c) Reclaimed Rubber.

Natural Rubber

3. It is extracted from sap of Hevea Braziliensis—a latex which contains 35% rubber. By adding 5% Barium chloride (Bacl) or acetic acid to the latex, coagulant of rubber is

obtained. When the rubber coagulant is dried at 50°C in closed furnace, it gives crepe sheet of rubber. And when the coagulant is dried at 50°C in smoke houses, smoked sheet of rubber is obtained. Processing of latex to obtain natural rubber involves various steps viz mastication, compounding, moulding and vulcanising.

Synthetic Rubber

4. Synthetic Rubber is of the following two types:

(a) Butadiene based synthetic rubber.
(b) Non-Butadiene based synthetic rubber.

5. *Butadiene Based Synthetic Rubber*—There are large number of Butadiene based synthetic rubbers. Their properties and applications vary depending upon the chemical composition of compounding materials. Some of the important one's are:

(a) *Buna-S*—It is also known as government styrene rubber (GSR) or Styrene Butadiene rubber (SBR). It has 75% butadiene and 25% styrene. Once it is filled with carbon black and vulcanised, it has strength of (UTS) 3800 PSI. It is used as substitute for natural rubber in heavy duty tyres.
(b) *Nitrile Rubber*— It is poly (butadiene-Co-Acrylonitrile) having 75 parts of butadiene and 25 parts of acrylonitrile. It is basically oil resistant and is used for making oil seals or rubber pipes/hoses used for passage of lubricants through system/joints. It does not get deformed or softened under high pressure of oil/lubricant.
(c) *Neoprene Rubber*—It is poly of chlorobutadiene. It is basically sea-water resistant. It does not get corroded or worn out by sea-water or hard water. This type of synthetic rubber has wide use in ships and submarines.
(d) *Butyl Rubber*—Chemically it is also poly having 98% isobutylene and 2% butadiene. It is impervious to air. It is widely used for connecting rubber pipes or hoses of pneumatic system in tanks/ICVs and in aircrafts, helicopters and aerospace.

6. *Non on Butadiene Based Synthetic Rubber*—Some of the synthetic rubbers have no base of butadiene in its chemical composition while compounding. They are primarily ethylene based with more molecular bonding of carbon thus giving greater strength and making it less flexible and non-deformable. Some of the important non-butadiene based synthetic rubbers are:

(a) *EPR (Ethylene Propylene Rubber)*—It is acid resistant. It is used for chemical purposes in the laboratories.
(b) *Viton Poly (Tetra Fluora Ethylene-Co-hexafluora Propylene)*—It is a high

temp resistant rubber. It is used for oil seals, rubber hoses, connecting pipes in the tanks and aircrafts.

(c) *Silicone Rubber*—It is compatible with human flash, basically used for artificial heart components like valves.

(d) *Polyurethe*—It is a high impact resistance rubber. It has very high density. It is generally used for automobile parts like bumpers etc.

(e) *Plasticized Polyvenyl Chloride*—It is used for domestic purposes and garments like foot wear, rain wear, pvc tiles and flexible rubber coating.

Reclaimed Rubber

7. There is one more type of rubber known as reclaimed rubber. It is made from many rubber articles which have lives their useful lives. They are subjected to action of chemicals, steaming at high temperature and after addition of oils re-plasticised by mechanical working.

HIGH PRESSURE RUBBER SEALS/PACKING RINGS

8. High pressure Rubber Seals/Packing rings form a vital part of various war like Military equipments like AFVs, Guns and numerous other equipments. They are used to keep the lubricants/hydraulic fluid in position and avoid leakage. Since the lubricants/hydraulic fluids are subjected to very high temp and pressures, the seals and packing rings should be able to withstand these. Also some of the components like seals come into contact with water and dust on the exterior side, they should not be easily affected by moisture and should be able to give a prolonged life. Whatever be the quality of rubber seals/packing rings, they have to deteriorate after continuous usage and have to be replaced both as a break down repair and maintenance. The replacements for the rubber seals for the East-European equipments have been a problem during the last few years due to various reasons like cost of imports and breaking up of Soviet Union. In order to provide effective engineering support to these equipments in future, the requirement of indigenisation of these items needs no emphasis.

Manufacturing Process

9. The high pressure rubber components can not be directly manufactured from the raw rubber materials. There are various steps of processing these raw rubber materials so that they can be used further for moulding into desired size and shapes of high pressure rubber components like oil seals and packing rings. The various steps of processing are as follows:

(a) Compounding,
(b) Mixing, and
(c) Vulcanising.

Compounding

10. The commercial value of the raw rubber is not much, and its use for manufacturing of rubber products is also hardly any. The raw rubber materials have to be compounded for its use into manufacturing of rubber components. For this it has to be modified by mixing with it a variety of substances called compounding materials. These compounding materials are so chosen as to produce rubber products with a wide range of properties to suit the application of the products.

11. There is a great similarity between the art of rubber compounding and that of the baking of a pastery or the job of a baker. The term recipe, often used for cooking or baking is also very familiar terminology in the dictionary of rubber technologists while referring to the formula which gives the type and amounts of the materials comprising a rubber mix. The term compounding can be well defined as the process of mixing of raw rubber with different catalytic agents which will effectively help the developed rubber mixes to withstand the conditions under which the products made from them are to be used and at the same time the compounded rubber so developed must be capable of being processed without undue difficulty in the factory. Although chemically the rubber mix so prepared is not a compound in true sense as it does not loose its basic characteristic, the processed rubber so obtained after being mixed together with the compounding ingredients and which is ready for another step of processing, known as vulcanising, is usually described by the rubber technologists as a "Compound".

12. The process of developing a rubber compound involves mixing of various ingredients in the form of a 'recipe'. Every recipe prepared for the process of compounding contains a number of compounding ingredients. Each ingredient has a particular characteristic which leads to development of a specific property either in the processing of volcanisation or in the functioning at the end use of the product.

13. The compounding of raw rubber means to convert the fluid dispersion into tractable form. The compounding ingredients are mostly powders. Special grades of these ingredients are often used to prepare the 'recipe' for use in compounding of rubber. Some of the important compounding ingredients which are generally used for forming the different "recipes" are:

(a) Sulphur,
(b) Zinc oxide,
(c) Red iron oxide, and
(d) China clay, etc.

Mixing

14. While preparing rubber compound, mixing is another important phase. Once the mixing of rubber is carried out, the compound so prepared is ready for moulding into desired shapes and sizes. Depending upon the end use of the rubber product and its application, the following ingredients in the desired proportion are added:

(a) Polymers,
(b) Fillers,
(c) Processing aids,
(d) Vulcanising ingredients, and
(e) Other additives to give specific properties.

15. All the above ingredients alongwith the additives which the compounder has decided on, have to be mixed together. Before mixing, the compounding materials are masticated between two roller mills to make them easily processible. Once the mastication is done, the compounding ingredients are mixed step by step to produce a master batch of the compound. After mixing, a homogeneous compound is ready for manufacturing of rubber items through the moulds. The rubber thus prepared is also known as vulcanisate.

Vulcanisation/Moulding

16. Volcanisation or curing of the compounded rubber mix or the formed product is the final stage of the manufacturing process in a rubber industry. The process basically involves applying of heat at a desired temperature for the desired time. The application of desired temperature and time differs form product to product depending upon the end use or also size of a component. When a product is being manufactured for the first time, the trial and error method has to be used for moulding of rubber compound for a small size of batch. For regular production, the compression or transfer moulding by means of electricity or steam heated fly press or hydraulic presses are used. Injection moulding can also be used but it is costiler for basic machining, but can prove cheap when large No of components are to be manufactured. When a metal part is to be impregnated in a rubber component e.g. metal impregnated oil seals, packing rings etc., the metal should be thoroughly cleaned to be free from any rust or oil-grease.

Selection of Rubber and Process

17. Selection of rubber and process is the most essential aspect to get the required properties of the end product. This has been a challenging task for the technologists and continues to be so. Due to problems of imports and in order to indigenise, so many firms both public and private have been trying to manufacture rubber components like seals and packing rings required in various AFVs with varying degrees of success. There have also been trials to blend different types of rubber in various proportions alongwith compounding agents to get the required properties of these high pressure seals and packing rings. Nitrile rubber and Polyurethane rubber have been found most suitable so far for these components. Nitrile rubber which is a poly of butadiene and acrylonitrile in the ratio of 75:25 is oil resistant and retains its sealing characteristics when in contact with oils and lubricants. Polyurthane-80 or polyurethane-90 rubber can also be used for these applications.

18. For use in contact with acid, the best suited rubber is ethylene proplylene rubber (EPR). It is a non butadiene based synthetic rubber and has the acid resistance properties. For use in Tks and ICVs the rubber should have the following properties:

(a) High temperature resistant,
(b) Oil resistant, and
(c) Non deformation (should retain shape while in storage).

19. Best suited rubber for the above properies is "VITON". It is a poly of tetra fluora ethylene and hexa fluora propylene. It has application in air crafts also.

Testing of Products

20. Testing of products both in laboratory as well as underfield conditions is very important before a particular seal or packing ring is introduced as a indigenous substitute for an imported one. A mere shape, size and visual similarity is not sufficient. The fact that a large number of seals/packing rings manufactured by commercial firms have not proved very successful indicates lack of testing/trial before introduction. Retention of shape and other properties for a long time during shelf life are also important. In order to achieve best results, the aspect of testing and trial can not thus be ignored.

Chemical Testing

21. The Synthetic rubbers which are generally in use are actually procured from trade. The adding of processing aids like vulcanising agents, activators and re-inforcing agents etc. in recommended proportions must be done under a careful supervision. Even the individual characteristics of the additives must be maintained since any deviation is bound to affect the end product. All these ingredients must be tested in a laboratory. Similarly, chemical tests must be carried out on the mix during various intermediate stages of production. End product should also be tested for its chemical properties as a sample check.

Mechanical/Physical Test

22. Before acual production takes place, it is equally important to test the physical properties like hardness, tensile strength or elongation.

User Trials

23. High pressure rubber seals/packing rings are vary important components in AFVs and other war like equipments. Since our aim is to reduce reliance on imports to the minimum, it is very important that the indigenous components should be able to give the same performance as imported ones. There is lot of difference in testing under laboratory

and field conditions. Our equipments operate from sub zero high altitudes to high humidity East and high temp dry deserts of Rajasthan. Unless a product is tried under all the weathers/terrains where we are to operate before its final introduction, we are bound to face problems. There is no dearth of expertise and infrastructure in our country. There is a requirement of undertaking the job in the right earnestness and given the priority it deserves.

Quality Control

24. Although all the ingredients in a compound are specified, a strict and continous quality control is necessary for each step i.e. compounding, mixing as well as moulding/ vulcanising. There are various fctors like when the agents are to be added in mixing, time taken for moulding or temperature given which must be followed strictly. These are only attained by long experience by a rubber technologist. Hence these operations should be carried out in the presence of an experienced rubber technologist when a product is required to be made for the first time.

Involvement of Public Sector and DRDO

25. It has been seen tht there is no clear out policy for indigenisation of these packing rings and rubbe seals. So many firms in private sector come out with these products which have not come any where near the original ones. It is obvious that any commercial private firm looks for profits and keeping in view quantum of our requirements, there is not much scope for the same. Therefore, it is worth considering that DRDO and public sector is actively involved. Since quality components require elaborate laboratory and R&D facilities, all private firms can not afford these. Keeping in view the vitality of these components, DRDO and public sector must be involved for developing and producing the indigenous equivalents for at least vital components. Fitment of any sub-standard equivalents would definitely result in poor reliability and can be thus disastrous in war.

CONCLUSION

26. Indigenisation of high pressure rubber seals and packing rings is a milestone towards selfreliants and technical know-how. The quality of products supplied so far as substitutes needs to be improved. Presently, the shelf life of a rubber product is spelled out to be two years, which is much less compared to the rubber products being originally fitted in East European equipments. The indigenous rubber components supplied so far, invariably loose size and shape in storage very soon. Even in respect of other physical characteristics, the indigenous components are no match to the originals so far. There is a need to improve the rubber technology much beyond the present level which will boost the life of the hydraulic and pneumatic system and increase the reliability and availability of war like equipments. There is an earnest need to involve DRDO and public sector for this purpose.